A Programming Language

KENNETH E. IVERSON

A Programming Language

JOHN WILEY AND SONS, INC. NEW YORK • LONDON • SYDNEY

7 8 9 10 11 12 13 14 15 16

Library of Congress Catalog Card Number: 62-15180
Printed in the United States of America

To My Many Teachers

PREFACE

Applied mathematics is largely concerned with the design and analysis of explicit procedures for calculating the exact or approximate values of various functions. Such explicit procedures are called algorithms or *programs*. Because an effective notation for the description of programs exhibits considerable syntactic structure, it is called a *programming language*.

Much of applied mathematics, particularly the more recent computer-related areas which cut across the older disciplines, suffers from the lack of an adequate programming language. It is the central thesis of this book that the descriptive and analytic power of an adequate programming language amply repays the considerable effort required for its mastery. This thesis is developed by first presenting the entire language and then applying it in later chapters to several major topics.

The areas of application are chosen primarily for their intrinsic interest and lack of previous treatment, but they are also designed to illustrate the universality and other facets of the language. For example, the micro-programming of Chapter 2 illustrates the divisibility of the language, i.e., the ability to treat a restricted area using only a small portion of the complete language. Chapter 6 (Sorting) shows its capacity to compass a relatively complex and detailed topic in a short space. Chapter 7 (The Logical Calculus) emphasizes the formal manipulability of the language and its utility in theoretical work.

The material was developed largely in a graduate course given for several years at Harvard and in a later course presented repeatedly at the IBM Systems Research Institute in New York. It should prove suitable for a two-semester course at the senior or graduate level. Although for certain audiences an initial presentation of the entire language may be appropriate, I have found it helpful to motivate the development by presenting the minimum notation required for a given topic, proceeding to its treatment (e.g., microprogramming), and then returning to further notation. The 130-odd problems not only provide the necessary finger exercises but also develop results of general interest.

Chapter 1 or some part of it is prerequisite to each of the remaining "applications" chapters, but the applications chapters are virtually independent of one another. A complete appreciation of search techniques (Chapter 4) does, however, require a knowledge of methods of representation (Chapter 3). The cross references which do occur in the applications chapters are either nonessential or are specific to a given figure, table, or program. The entire language presented in Chapter 1 is summarized for reference at the end of the book.

In any work spanning several years it is impossible to acknowledge adequately the many contributions made by others. Two major acknowledgments are in order: the first to Professor Howard Aiken, Director Emeritus of the Harvard Computation Laboratory, and the second to Dr. F. P. Brooks, Jr. now of IBM.

It was Professor Aiken who first guided me into this work and who provided support and encouragement in the early years when it mattered. The unusually large contribution by Dr. Brooks arose as follows. Several chapters of the present work were originally prepared for inclusion in a joint work which eventually passed the bounds of a single book and evolved into our joint *Automatic Data Processing* and the present volume. Before the split, several drafts of these chapters had received careful review at the hands of Dr. Brooks, reviews which contributed many valuable ideas on organization, presentation, and direction of investigation, as well as numerous specific suggestions.

The contributions of the 200-odd students who suffered through the development of the material must perforce be acknowledged collectively, as must the contributions of many of my colleagues at the Harvard Computation Laboratory. To Professor G. A. Salton and Dr. W. L. Eastman, I am indebted for careful reading of drafts of various sections and for comments arising from their use of some of the material in courses. Dr. Eastman, in particular, exorcised many subtle errors from the sorting programs of Chapter 6. To Professor A. G. Oettinger and his students I am indebted for many helpful discussions arising out of his early use of the notation. My debt to Professor R. L. Ashenhurst, now of the University of Chicago, is apparent from the references to his early (and unfortunately unpublished) work in sorting.

Of my colleagues at the IBM Research Center, Messrs. L. R. Johnson and A. D. Falkoff, and Dr. H. Hellerman have, through their own use of the notation, contributed many helpful suggestions. I am particularly indebted to L. R. Johnson for many fruitful discussions on the applications of trees, and for his unfailing support.

On the technical side, I have enjoyed the assistance of unusually competent typists and draughtsmen, chief among them being Mrs. Arthur

Aulenback, Mrs. Philip J. Seaward, Jr., Mrs. Paul Bushek, Miss J. L. Hegeman, and Messrs. William Minty and Robert Burns. Miss Jacquelin Sanborn provided much early and continuing guidance in matters of style, format, and typography. I am indebted to my wife for assistance in preparing the final draft.

KENNETH E. IVERSON

May, 1962
Mount Kisco, New York

CONTENTS

ILLUSTRATIONS

chapter 1

THE LANGUAGE

1.1 INTRODUCTION

Applied mathematics is concerned with the design and analysis of algorithms or *programs.* The systematic treatment of complex algorithms requires a suitable *programming language* for their description, and such a programming language should be concise, precise, consistent over a wide area of application, mnemonic, and economical of symbols; it should exhibit clearly the constraints on the sequence in which operations are performed; and it should permit the description of a process to be independent of the particular representation chosen for the data.

Existing languages prove unsuitable for a variety of reasons. Computer coding specifies sequence constraints adequately and is also comprehensive, since the logical functions provided by the branch instructions can, in principle, be employed to synthesize any finite algorithm. However, the set of basic operations provided is not, in general, directly suited to the execution of commonly needed processes, and the numeric symbols used for variables have little mnemonic value. Moreover, the description provided by computer coding depends directly on the particular representation chosen for the data, and it therefore cannot serve as a description of the algorithm per se.

Ordinary English lacks both precision and conciseness. The widely used Goldstine-von Neumann (1947) flowcharting provides the conciseness necessary to an over-all view of the process, only at the cost of suppressing essential detail. The so-called pseudo-English used as a basis for certian automatic programming systems suffers from the same defect. Moreover, the potential mnemonic advantage in substituting familiar English words and phrases for less familiar but more compact mathematical symbols fails to materialize because of the obvious but unwonted precision required in their use.

Most of the concepts and operations needed in a programming language have already been defined and developed in one or another branch of mathematics. Therefore, much use can and will be made of existing notations. However, since most notations are specialized to a narrow field of discourse, a consistent unification must be provided. For example, separate and conflicting notations have been developed for the treatment of sets, logical variables, vectors, matrices, and trees, all of which may, in the broad universe of discourse of data processing, occur in a single algorithm.

1.2 PROGRAMS

A *program statement* is the specification of some quantity or quantities in terms of some finite operation upon specified operands. Specification is symbolized by an arrow directed toward the specified quantity. Thus "y is specified by $\sin x$" is a statement denoted by

$$y \leftarrow \sin x.$$

A set of statements together with a specified order of execution constitutes a *program*. The program is *finite* if the number of executions is finite. The *results* of the program are some subset of the quantities specified by the program. The *sequence* or order of execution will be defined by the order of listing and otherwise by arrows connecting any statement to its successor. A cyclic sequence of statements is called a *loop*.

1	$v \leftarrow x \times 3.1416$
2	$v \leftarrow v \times x$

Program 1.1 Finite program

1	$z \leftarrow 1$
2	$z \leftarrow y \times z$
3	$z \leftarrow 2 \times z$ (→ 2)

Program 1.2 Infinite program

Thus Program 1.1 is a program of two statements defining the result v as the (approximate) area of a circle of radius x, whereas Program 1.2 is an infinite program in which the quantity z is specified as $(2y)^n$ on the nth execution of the two-statement loop. Statements will be numbered on the left for reference.

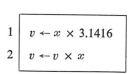

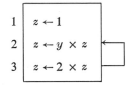

A number of similar programs may be subsumed under a single more general program as follows. At certain *branch points* in the program a finite number of alternative statements are specified as possible successors. One of these successors is chosen according to criteria determined in the statement or statements preceding the branch point. These criteria are usually stated as a *comparison* or test of a specified relation between a specified pair of quantities. A branch is denoted by a set of arrows leading to each of the alternative successors, with each arrow labeled by the comparison condition under which the corresponding successor is chosen. The quantities compared are separated by a colon in the statement at the branch point, and a labeled branch is followed if and only if the relation indicated by the label holds when substituted for the colon. The conditions on the branches of a properly defined program must be disjoint and exhaustive.

Program 1.3 illustrates the use of a branch point. Statement $\alpha 5$ is a comparison which determines the branch to statements $\beta 1$, $\delta 1$, or $\gamma 1$, according as $z > n$, $z = n$, or $z < n$. The program represents a crude but effective process for determining $x = n^{2/3}$ for any positive cube n.

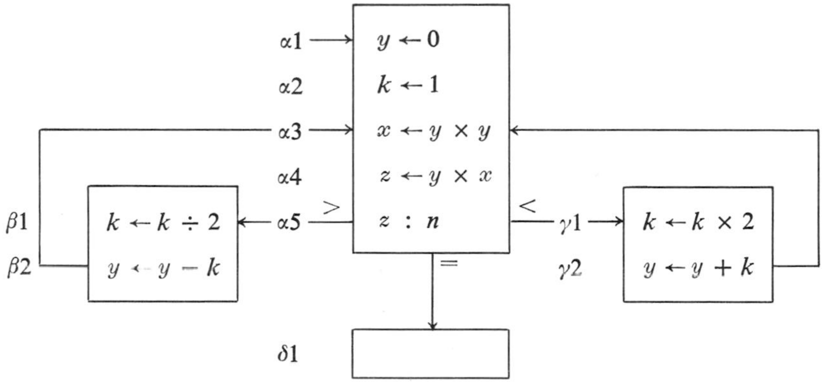

Program 1.3 Program for $x = n^{2/3}$

Program 1.4 shows the preceding program reorganized into a compact linear array and introduces two further conventions on the labeling of branch points. The listed successor of a branch statement is selected if none of the labeled conditions is met. Thus statement 6 follows statement 5 if neither of the arrows (to exit or to statement 8) are followed, i.e., if $z < n$. Moreover, any unlabeled arrow is always followed; e.g., statement 7 is invariably followed by statement 3, never by statement 8.

A program begins at a point indicated by an *entry arrow* (step 1) and ends at a point indicated by an *exit arrow* (step 5). There are two useful consequences of confining a program to the form of a linear array: the statements may be referred to by a unique serial index (statement number), and unnecessarily complex organization of the program manifests itself in crossing branch lines. The importance of the latter characteristic in developing clear and comprehensible programs is not sufficiently appreciated.

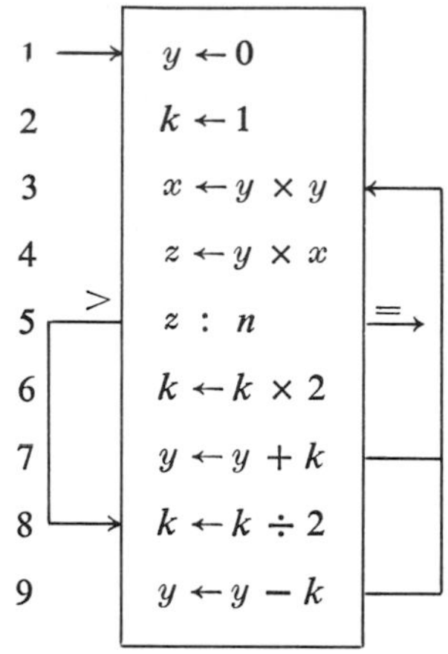

Program 1.4 Linear arrangement of Program 1.3

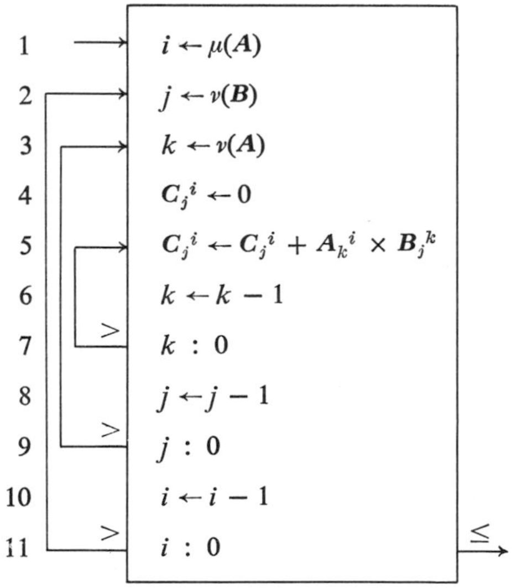

Program 1.5 Matrix multiplication

A process which is repeated a number of times is said to be *iterated*, and a process (such as Program 1.4) which includes one or more iterated subprocesses is said to be *iterative*. Program 1.5 shows an iterative process for the matrix multiplication

$$\mathbf{C} \leftarrow \mathbf{AB}$$

defined in the usual way as

$$C_j^i = \sum_{k=1}^{\nu(A)} A_k^i \times B_j^k, \qquad \begin{cases} i = 1, 2, \ldots, \mu(A), \\ j = 1, 2, \ldots, \nu(B), \end{cases}$$

where the dimension of an $m \times n$ rectangular matrix X (of m rows and n columns) is denoted by $\mu(X) \times \nu(X)$.

Program 1.5. Steps 1–3 initialize the indices, and the loop 5–7 continues to add successive products to the partial sum until k reaches zero. When this occurs, the process continues through step 8 to decrement j and to repeat the entire summation for the new value of j, providing that it is not zero. If j is zero, the branch to step 10 decrements i and the entire process over j and k is repeated from $j = \nu(B)$, providing that i is not zero. If i is zero, the process is complete, as indicated by the exit arrow.

In all examples used in this chapter, emphasis will be placed on clarity of description of the process, and considerations of efficient execution by a computer or class of computers will be subordinated. These considerations can often be introduced later by relatively routine modifications of the program. For example, since the execution of a computer operation involving an indexed variable is normally more costly than the corresponding operation upon a nonindexed variable, the substitution of a variable s for the variable C_j^i specified by statement 5 of Program 1.5 would accelerate the execution of the loop. The variable s would be initialized to zero before each entry to the loop and would be used to specify C_j^i at each termination.

The practice of first setting an index to its maximum value and then decrementing it (e.g., the index k in Program 1.5) permits the termination comparison to be made with zero. Since zero often occurs in comparisons, it is convenient to omit it. Thus, if a variable stands alone at a branch point, comparison with zero is implied. Moreover, since a comparison on an index frequently occurs immediately after it is modified, a branch at the point of modification will denote branching upon comparison of the indicated index with zero, the comparison occurring *after* modification. Designing programs to execute decisions immediately after modification of the controlling variable results in efficient execution as well as notational elegance, since the variable must be present in a central register for both operations.

Since the sequence of execution of statements is indicated by connecting arrows as well as by the order of listing, the latter can be chosen arbitrarily. This is illustrated by the functionally identical Programs 1.3 and 1.4. Certain principles of ordering may yield advantages such as clarity or simplicity of the pattern of connections. Even though the advantages of a particular organizing principle are not particularly marked, the uniformity resulting from its consistent application will itself be a boon. The scheme here adopted is called the *method of leading decisions:* the decision on each parameter is placed as early in the program as practicable, normally just before the operations indexed by the parameter. This arrangement groups at the head of each iterative segment the initialization, modification, and the termination test of the controlling parameter. Moreover, it tends to avoid program flaws occasioned by unusual values of the arguments. For

1	$i \leftarrow \mu(A) + 1$
2	$i \leftarrow i - 1$
3	$j \leftarrow \nu(B) + 1$
4	$j \leftarrow j - 1$
5	$k \leftarrow \nu(A) + 1$
6	$C_j{}^i \leftarrow 0$
7	$k \leftarrow k - 1$
8	$C_j{}^i \leftarrow C_j{}^i + A_k{}^i \times B_j{}^k$

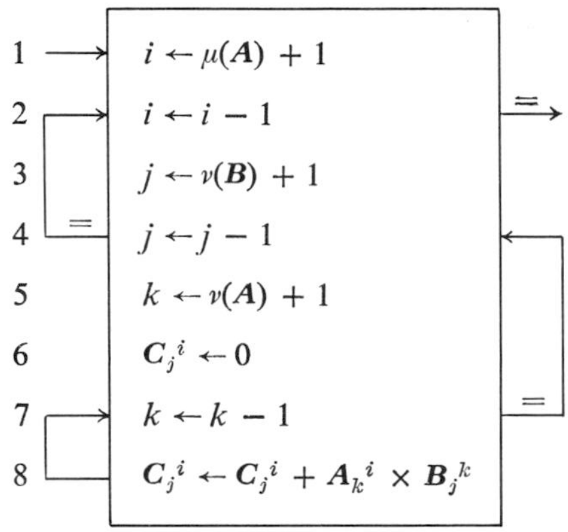

Program 1.6   Matrix multiplication using leading decisions

example, Program 1.6 (which is such a reorganization of Program 1.5) behaves properly for matrices of dimension zero, whereas Program 1.5 treats every matrix as if it were of dimension one or greater.

Although the labeled arrow representation of program branches provides a complete and graphic description, it is deficient in the following respects: (1) a routine translation to another language (such as a computer code) would require the tracing of arrows, and (2) it does not permit programmed modification of the branches.

The following alternative form of a branch statement will therefore be used as well:

$$x : y, \quad r \to s.$$

This denotes a branch to statement number s_i of the program if the relation $x r_i y$ holds. The parameters r and s may themselves be defined and re-defined in other parts of the program. The *null element* $\circ$ will be used to denote the relation which complements the remaining relations r_i; in particular, $(\circ) \to (s)$, or simply $\to s$, will denote an unconditional branch to statement s. Program 1.7 shows the use of these conventions in a reformulation of Program 1.6. More generally, two or more otherwise independent programs may interact through a statement in one program specifying a branch in a second. The statement number occurring in the branch must then be augmented by the name of the program in which the branch is effected. Thus the statement $(\circ) \rightarrow$ Program 2.24 executed in Program 1 causes a branch to step 24 to occur in Program 2.

1	$i \leftarrow \mu(\boldsymbol{A}) + 1$
2	$i \leftarrow i - 1, (\neq, =) \rightarrow (3, 9)$
3	$j \leftarrow \nu(\boldsymbol{B}) + 1$
4	$j \leftarrow j - 1, (\neq, =) \rightarrow (5, 2)$
5	$k \leftarrow \nu(\boldsymbol{A}) + 1$
6	$C_j^i \leftarrow 0$
7	$k \leftarrow k - 1, (\neq, =) \rightarrow (8, 4)$
8	$C_j^i \leftarrow C_j^i + A_k^i \times B_j^k, \rightarrow 7$

Program 1.7 A reformulation of Program 1.6, using an algebraic statement of the branching

One statement in a program can be modified by another statement which changes certain of its parameters, usually indices. More general changes in statements can be effected by considering the program itself as a vector $\boldsymbol{p}$ whose components are the individual, serially numbered statements. All the operations to be defined on general vectors can then be applied to the statements themselves. For example, the jth statement can be respecified by the ith through the occurrence of the statement $\boldsymbol{p}_j \leftarrow \boldsymbol{p}_i$.

The interchange of two quantities y and x (that is, x specifies y and the *original* value of y specifies x) will be denoted by the statement $y \leftrightarrow x$.

1.3 STRUCTURE OF THE LANGUAGE

Conventions

The Summary of Notation at the end of the book summarizes the notation developed in this chapter. Although intended primarily for reference, it supplements the text in several ways. It frequently provides a more concise alternative definition of an operation discussed in the text, and it also contains important but easily grasped extensions not treated explicitly in the text. By grouping the operations into related classes it displays their family relationships.

A concise programming language must incorporate families of operations whose members are related in a systematic manner. Each family will be denoted by a specific operation symbol, and the particular member of the family will be designated by an associated *controlling parameter* (scalar, vector, matrix, or tree) which immediately precedes the main operation symbol. The operand is placed immediately after the main operation symbol. For example, the operation $k \uparrow \boldsymbol{x}$ (left rotation of $\boldsymbol{x}$ by k places) may be viewed as the kth member of the set of rotation operators denoted by the symbol $\uparrow$.

Operations involving a single operand and no controlling parameter (such as $\lfloor x \rfloor$, or $\lceil x \rceil$) will be denoted by a pair of operation symbols which enclose the operand. Operations involving two operands and a controlling parameter (such as the mask operation $/\boldsymbol{a}, \boldsymbol{u}, \boldsymbol{b}/$) will be denoted by a pair of operation symbols enclosing the entire set of variables, and the controlling parameter will appear between the two operands. In these cases the operation symbols themselves serve as grouping symbols.

In interpreting a compound operation such as $k \uparrow (j \downarrow \boldsymbol{x})$ it is important to recognize that the operation symbol and its associated controlling parameter together represent an indivisible operation and must not be separated. It would, for example, be incorrect to assume that $j \uparrow (k \downarrow \boldsymbol{x})$ were equivalent to $k \uparrow (j \downarrow \boldsymbol{x})$, although it can be shown that the complete operations $j \downarrow$ and $k \uparrow$ do commute, that is, $k \uparrow (j \downarrow \boldsymbol{x}) = j \downarrow (k \uparrow \boldsymbol{x})$.

The need for parentheses will be reduced by assuming that compound statements are, except for intervening parentheses, executed from right to left. Thus $k \uparrow j \downarrow \boldsymbol{x}$ is equivalent to $k \uparrow (j \downarrow \boldsymbol{x})$, not to $(k \uparrow j) \downarrow \boldsymbol{x}$.

Structured operands such as vectors and matrices, together with a systematic component-by-component generalization of elementary operations, provide an important subordination of detail in the description of algorithms. The use of structured operands will be facilitated by *selection operations* for extracting a specified portion of an operand, *reduction operations* for extending an operation (such as logical or arithmetic multiplication) over all components, and *permutation operations* for reordering components. Operations defined on vectors are extended to matrices: the extended operation is called a *row* operation if the underlying vector operation is applied to each row of the matrix and a *column* operation if it is applied to each column. A column operation is denoted by doubling the symbol employed for the corresponding row (and vector) operation.

A distinct typeface will be used for each class of operand as detailed in

Table 1.8. Special quantities (such as the prefix vectors $\boldsymbol{\alpha}^j$ defined in Sec. 1.7) will be denoted by Greek letters in the appropriate typeface. For mnemonic reasons, an operation closely related to such a special quantity

Type of Operand	Representation	
	Printed	Typed
Literal		
Alphabetic	Roman, u.c. and l.c.	Circled u.c. and l.c. roman.
Numeric	Standard numeral	Standard numeral
Variable		
Alphabetic	Italic, u.c. and l.c.	Unmarked
Numeric	Italic numeral	Underscore
Vector	l.c. boldface italic	Underscore
Matrix	u.c. boldface italic	Underscore
Tree	u.c. boldface roman	Wavy underscore

Table 1.8 Typographic conventions for classes of operands

will be denoted by the same Greek letter. For example, $\alpha/\boldsymbol{u}$ denotes the maximum prefix (Sec. 1.10) of the logical vector $\boldsymbol{u}$. Where a Greek letter is indistinguishable from a Roman, sanserif characters will be used, e.g., **E** and **I** for the capitals epsilon and iota.

Literals and variables

The power of any mathematical notation rests largely on the use of symbols to represent general quantities which, in given instances, are further specified by other quantities. Thus Program 1.4 represents a general process which determines $x = n^{2/3}$ for any suitable value of n. In a specific case, say $n = 27$, the quantity x is specified as the number 9.

Each operand occurring in a meaningful process must be specified ultimately in terms of commonly accepted concepts. The symbols representing such accepted concepts will be called *literals*. Examples of literals are the integers, the characters of the various alphabets, punctuation marks, and miscellaneous symbols such as \$ and %. The literals occurring in Program 1.4 are 0, 1, and 2.

It is important to distinguish clearly between general symbols and literals. In ordinary algebra this presents little difficulty, since the only literals occurring are the integers and the decimal point, and each general symbol employed includes an alphabetic character. In describing more general processes, however, alphabetic literals (such as proper names) also appear. Moreover, in a computer program, numeric symbols (register addresses) are used to represent the variables.

In general, then, alphabetic literals, alphabetic variables, numeric literals, and numeric variables may all appear in a complex process and must be clearly differentiated. The symbols used for literals will be roman letters (enclosed in quotes when appearing in text) and standard numerals. The symbols used for variables will be italic letters, italic numerals, and boldface letters as detailed in Table 1.8. Miscellaneous signs and symbols when used as literals will be enclosed in quotes in both programs and text.

It is sometimes desirable (e.g., for mnemonic reasons) to denote a variable by a string of alphabetic or other symbols rather than by a single symbol. The monolithic interpretation of such a string will be indicated by the *tie* used in musical notation, thus: $\underset{\smile}{\mathit{inv}}$, $\underset{\smile}{\boldsymbol{inv}}$, and $\underset{\smile}{\boldsymbol{INV}}$ may denote the variable "inventory," a vector of inventory values, and a matrix of inventory values, respectively.

In the set of alphabetic characters, the *space* plays a special role. For other sets a similar role is usually played by some one element, and this element is given the special name of *null element*. In the set of numeric digits, the *zero* plays a dual role as both null element and numeric quantity. The null element will be denoted by the degree symbol $\circ$.

In any determinate process, each operand must be specified ultimately in terms of literals. In Program 1.4, for example, the quantity k is specified in terms of known arithmetic operations (multiplication and division) involving the literals 1 and 2. The quantity n, on the other hand, is not determined within the process and must presumably be specified within some larger process which includes Program 1.4. Such a quantity is called an *argument* of the process.

Domain and range

The class of arguments and the class of results of a given operator are called its *domain* and *range*, respectively. Thus the domain and range of the magnitude operation ($|x|$) are the real numbers and the nonnegative real numbers, respectively.

A variable is classified according to the range of values it may assume: it is *logical*, *integral*, or *numerical*, according as the range is the set of logical variables (that is, 0 and 1), the set of integers, or the set of real numbers. Each of the foregoing classes is clearly a subclass of each class following it, and any operation defined on a class clearly applies to any of its subclasses. A variable which is nonnumeric will be called *arbitrary*. In the Summary of Notation, the range and domain of each of the operators defined is specified in terms of the foregoing classes according to the conventions shown in Sec. S.1.

1.4 ELEMENTARY OPERATIONS

The elementary operations employed include the ordinary arithmetic operations, the elementary operations of the logical calculus, and the residue and related operations arising in elementary number theory. In defining operations in the text, the symbol $\Leftrightarrow$ will be used to denote equivalence of the pair of statements between which it occurs.

Arithmetic operations

The ordinary arithmetic operations will be denoted by the ordinary symbols $+$, $-$, $\times$, and $\div$ and defined as usual except that the domain and range of multiplication will be extended slightly as follows. If one of the factors is a logical variable (0 or 1), the second may be arbitrary and the product then assumes the value of the second factor or zero according as the value of the first factor (the logical variable) is 1 or 0. Thus if the arbitrary factor is the literal "q," then

$$0 \times \mathrm{q} = \mathrm{q} \times 0 = 0$$

and

$$1 \times \mathrm{q} = \mathrm{q} \times 1 = \mathrm{q}.$$

According to the usual custom in ordinary algebra, the multiplication symbol may be elided.

Logical operations

The elementary logical operations *and*, *or*, and *not* will be denoted by $\wedge$, $\vee$, and an overbar and are defined in the usual way as follows:

$$w \leftarrow u \wedge v \Leftrightarrow w = 1 \quad \text{if and only if} \quad u = 1 \text{ and } v = 1,$$

$$w \leftarrow u \vee v \Leftrightarrow w = 1 \quad \text{if and only if} \quad u = 1 \text{ or } v = 1,$$

$$w \leftarrow \bar{u} \quad \Leftrightarrow w = 1 \quad \text{if and only if} \quad u = 0.$$

If x and y are numerical quantities, then the expression $x < y$ implies that the quantity x stands in the relation "less than" to the quantity y. More generally, if α and β are arbitrary entities and $\mathscr{R}$ is any relation defined on them, the *relational statement* $(\alpha\mathscr{R}\beta)$ is a logical variable which is true (equal to 1) if and only if α stands in the relation $\mathscr{R}$ to β. For example, if x is any real number, then the function

$$(x > 0) - (x < 0)$$

(commonly called the *sign function* or sgn x) assumes the values 1, 0, or -1 according as x is strictly positive, 0, or strictly negative. Moreover, the magnitude function $|x|$ may be defined as $|x| = x \times \operatorname{sgn} x = x \times ((x > 0) - (x < 0))$.

The relational statement is a useful generalization of the Kronecker delta, that is, $\delta_j^{\,i} = (i = j)$. Moreover, it provides a convenient expression for a number of familiar logical operations. The *exclusive or*, for example, may be denoted by $(u \neq v)$, and its negation (i.e., the equivalence function) may be denoted by $(u = v)$.

Residues and congruence

For each set of integers n, j, and b, with $b > 0$, there exists a unique pair of integers q and r such that

$$n = bq + r, \quad j \leq r < j + b.$$

The quantity r is called the *j-residue of n modulo b* and is denoted by $b \,|_j\, n$. For example, $3 \,|_0\, 9 = 0$, $3 \,|_1\, 9 = 3$, and $3 \,|_0\, 10 = 1$. Moreover, if $n \geq 0$, then $b \,|_0\, n$ is the remainder obtained in dividing n by b and q is the integral part of the quotient. A number n is said to be of *even parity* if its 0-residue modulo 2 is zero and of *odd parity* if $2 \,|_0\, n = 1$.

If two numbers n and m have the same j-residue modulo b, they differ by an integral multiple of b and therefore have the same k-residue modulo b for any k. If $b \,|_j\, n = b \,|_j\, m$, then m and n are said to be *congruent mod b*. Congruency is transitive and reflexive and is denoted by

$$m \equiv n \pmod{b}.$$

In classical treatments, such as Wright (1939), only the 0-residue is considered. The use of 1-origin indexing (cf. Sec. 1.5) accounts for the interest of the 1-residue.

A number represented in a positional notation (e.g., in a base ten or a base two number system) must, in practice, employ only a finite number of digits. It is therefore often desirable to approximate a number x by an integer. For this purpose two functions are defined:

1. the *floor of* x (or integral part of x), denoted by $\lfloor x \rfloor$ and defined as the largest integer not exceeding x,
2. the *ceiling of* x, denoted by $\lceil x \rceil$ and defined as the smallest integer not exceeded by x.

Thus

$$\lceil 3.14 \rceil = 4, \qquad \lfloor 3.14 \rfloor = 3, \qquad \lfloor -3.14 \rfloor = -4,$$
$$\lceil 3.00 \rceil = 3, \qquad \lfloor 3.00 \rfloor = 3, \qquad \lfloor -3.00 \rfloor = -3.$$

Clearly $\lceil x \rceil = -\lfloor -x \rfloor$ and $\lfloor x \rfloor \leq x \leq \lceil x \rceil$. Moreover, $n = b\lfloor n \div b \rfloor + b \,|_0\, n$ for all integers n. Hence the integral quotient $\lfloor n \div b \rfloor$ is equivalent to the quantity q occurring in the definition of the j-residue for the case $j = 0$.

1.5 STRUCTURED OPERANDS

Elementary operations

Any operation defined on a single operand can be generalized to apply to each member of an array of related operands. Similarly, any binary operation (defined on two operands) can be generalized to apply to pairs of corresponding elements of two arrays. Since algorithms commonly incorporate processes which are repeated on each member of an array of operands, such generalization permits effective subordination of detail in their description. For example, the accounting process defined on the data of an individual bank account treats a number of distinct operands within the account, such as account number, name, and balance. Moreover, the over-all process is defined on a large number of similar accounts, all represented in a common format. Such structured arrays of variables will be called *structured operands*, and extensive use will be made of three types, called *vector*, *matrix*, and *tree*. As indicated in Sec. S.1 of the Summary of Notation, a structured operand is further classified as *logical*, *integral*, *numerical*, or *arbitrary*, according to the type of elements it contains.

A *vector* $\boldsymbol{x}$ is the ordered array of elements $(\boldsymbol{x}_1, \boldsymbol{x}_2, \boldsymbol{x}_3, \ldots, \boldsymbol{x}_{\nu(\boldsymbol{x})})$. The variable $\boldsymbol{x}_i$ is called the ith *component* of the vector $\boldsymbol{x}$, and the number of components, denoted by $\nu(\boldsymbol{x})$ (or simply ν when the determining vector is clear from context), is called the *dimension* of $\boldsymbol{x}$. Vectors and their components will be represented in lower case boldface italics. A numerical vector $\boldsymbol{x}$ may be multiplied by a numerical quantity k to produce the *scalar multiple* $k \times \boldsymbol{x}$ (or $k\boldsymbol{x}$) defined as the vector $\boldsymbol{z}$ such that $\boldsymbol{z}_i = k \times \boldsymbol{x}_i$.

All elementary operations defined on individual variables are extended consistently to vectors as component-by-component operations. For example,

$$\boldsymbol{z} = \boldsymbol{x} + \boldsymbol{y} \Leftrightarrow \boldsymbol{z}_i = \boldsymbol{x}_i + \boldsymbol{y}_i,$$

$$\boldsymbol{z} = \boldsymbol{x} \times \boldsymbol{y} \Leftrightarrow \boldsymbol{z}_i = \boldsymbol{x}_i \times \boldsymbol{y}_i,$$

$$\boldsymbol{z} = \boldsymbol{x} \div \boldsymbol{y} \Leftrightarrow \boldsymbol{z}_i = \boldsymbol{x}_i \div \boldsymbol{y}_i,$$

$$\boldsymbol{z} = \lceil \boldsymbol{x} \rceil \Leftrightarrow \boldsymbol{z}_i = \lceil \boldsymbol{x}_i \rceil,$$

$$\boldsymbol{w} = \boldsymbol{u} \wedge \boldsymbol{v} \Leftrightarrow \boldsymbol{w}_i = \boldsymbol{u}_i \wedge \boldsymbol{v}_i,$$

$$\boldsymbol{w} = (\boldsymbol{x} < \boldsymbol{y}) \Leftrightarrow \boldsymbol{w}_i = (\boldsymbol{x}_i < \boldsymbol{y}_i).$$

Thus if $\boldsymbol{x} = (1, 0, 1, 1)$ and $\boldsymbol{y} = (0, 1, 1, 0)$ then $\boldsymbol{x} + \boldsymbol{y} = (1, 1, 2, 1)$, $\boldsymbol{x} \wedge \boldsymbol{y} = (0, 0, 1, 0)$, and $(\boldsymbol{x} < \boldsymbol{y}) = (0, 1, 0, 0)$.

Matrices

A matrix $\boldsymbol{M}$ is the ordered two-dimensional array of variables

$$\begin{pmatrix} M_1^{\;1}, & M_2^{\;1}, & \ldots, & M_{\nu(M)}^1 \\ M_1^{\;2}, & M_2^{\;2}, & \ldots, & M_{\nu(M)}^2 \\ \cdot & & \cdot & \\ M_1^{\mu(M)}, & & \ldots, & M_{\nu(M)}^{\mu(M)} \end{pmatrix}.$$

The vector $(M_1^{\;i}, M_2^{\;i}, \ldots, M_\nu^{\;i})$ is called the *i*th *row vector* of $\boldsymbol{M}$ and is denoted by M^i. Its dimension $\nu(M)$ is called the *row dimension* of the matrix. The vector $(M_j^{\;1}, M_j^{\;2}, \ldots, M_j^{\;\mu})$ is called the *j*th *column vector* of $\boldsymbol{M}$ and is denoted by M_j. Its dimension $\mu(M)$ is called the *column dimension* of the matrix.

The variable $M_j^{\;i}$ is called the (i, j)th *component* or *element* of the matrix. A matrix and its elements will be represented by upper case boldface italics. Operations defined on each element of a matrix are generalized component by component to the entire matrix. Thus, if $\bigcirc$ is any binary operator,

$$P = M \bigcirc N \Leftrightarrow P_j^{\;i} = M_j^{\;i} \odot N_j^{\;i}.$$

Index systems

The subscript appended to a vector to designate a single component is called an *index*, and the indices are normally chosen as a set of successive integers beginning at 1, that is, $x = (x_1, x_2, \ldots, x_\nu)$. It is, however, convenient to admit more general *j-origin indexing* in which the set of successive integers employed as indices in any structured operand begin with a specified integer *j*.

The two systems of greatest interest are the common 1-origin system, which will be employed almost exclusively in this chapter, and the 0-origin system. The latter system is particularly convenient whenever the index itself must be represented in a positional number system and will therefore be employed exclusively in the treatment of computer organization in Chapter 2.

1.6 ROTATION

The *left rotation* of a vector x is denoted by $k \uparrow x$ and specifies the vector obtained by a cyclical left shift of the components of x by k places. Thus if $a = (1, 2, 3, 4, 5, 6)$, and $b = (\text{c, a, n, d, y})$, then $2 \uparrow a = (3, 4, 5, 6, 1, 2)$, and $3 \uparrow b = 8 \uparrow b = (\text{d, y, c, a, n})$. Formally,*

$$z = k \uparrow x \Leftrightarrow z_i = x_j, \qquad \text{where } j = \nu|_1(i + k).$$

* Restating the relation in terms of the 0-residue will illustrate the convenience of the 1-residue used here.

Right rotation is denoted by $k \downarrow \boldsymbol{x}$ and is defined analogously. Thus

$$\boldsymbol{z} = k \downarrow \boldsymbol{x} \Leftrightarrow \boldsymbol{z}_i = \boldsymbol{x}_j, \qquad \text{where } j = \nu|_1(i - k).$$

If $k = 1$, it may be elided. Thus $\uparrow \boldsymbol{b} = $ (a, n, d, y, c).

Left rotation is extended to matrices in two ways as follows:

$$\boldsymbol{A} \leftarrow \boldsymbol{j} \uparrow \boldsymbol{B} \Leftrightarrow \boldsymbol{A}^i = \boldsymbol{j}_i \uparrow \boldsymbol{B}^i$$
$$\boldsymbol{C} \leftarrow \boldsymbol{k} \Uparrow \boldsymbol{B} \Leftrightarrow \boldsymbol{C}_j = \boldsymbol{k}_j \uparrow \boldsymbol{B}_j.$$

The first operation is an extension of the basic vector rotation to each row of the matrix and is therefore called *row rotation*. The second operation is the corresponding column operation and is therefore denoted by the doubled operation symbol $\Uparrow$. For example, if

$$\boldsymbol{k} = (0, 1, 2),$$

and

$$\boldsymbol{B} = \begin{pmatrix} a & b & c \\ d & e & f \\ g & h & i \end{pmatrix}$$

then

$$\boldsymbol{k} \uparrow \boldsymbol{B} = \begin{pmatrix} a & b & c \\ e & f & d \\ i & g & h \end{pmatrix} \quad \text{and} \quad \boldsymbol{k} \Uparrow \boldsymbol{B} = \begin{pmatrix} a & e & i \\ d & h & c \\ g & b & f \end{pmatrix}.$$

Right rotation is extended analogously.

1.7 SPECIAL VECTORS

Certain special vectors warrant special symbols. In each of the following definitions, the parameter n will be used to specify the dimension. The *interval vector* $\boldsymbol{\iota}^j(n)$ is defined as the vector of integers beginning with j. Thus $\boldsymbol{\iota}^0(4) = (0, 1, 2, 3)$, $\boldsymbol{\iota}^1(4) = (1, 2, 3, 4)$, and $\boldsymbol{\iota}^{-7}(5) = (-7, -6, -5, -4, -3)$. Four types of logical vectors are defined as follows. The jth *unit vector* $\boldsymbol{\epsilon}^j(n)$ has a one in the jth position, that is, $(\boldsymbol{\epsilon}^j(n))_k = (k = j)$. The *full vector* $\boldsymbol{\epsilon}(n)$ consists of all ones. The vector consisting of all zeros is denoted both by 0 and by $\overline{\boldsymbol{\epsilon}}(n)$. The *prefix vector of weight j* is denoted by $\boldsymbol{\alpha}^j(n)$ and possesses ones in the first k positions, where k is the lesser of j and n. The *suffix vector* $\boldsymbol{\omega}^j(n)$ is defined analogously. Thus $\boldsymbol{\epsilon}^2(3) = (0, 1, 0)$, $\boldsymbol{\epsilon}(4) = (1, 1, 1, 1)$, $\boldsymbol{\alpha}^3(5) = (1, 1, 1, 0, 0)$, $\boldsymbol{\omega}^3(5) = (0, 0, 1, 1, 1)$, and $\boldsymbol{\alpha}^7(5) = \boldsymbol{\alpha}^5(5) = (1, 1, 1, 1, 1)$. Moreover, $\boldsymbol{\omega}^j(n) = j \uparrow \boldsymbol{\alpha}^j(n)$, and $\boldsymbol{\alpha}^j(n) = j \downarrow \boldsymbol{\omega}^j(n)$.

A logical vector of the form $\boldsymbol{\alpha}^h(n) \wedge \boldsymbol{\omega}^i(n)$ is called an *infix vector*. An infix vector can also be specified in the form $j \downarrow \boldsymbol{\alpha}^k(n)$, which displays its weight and location more directly.

An operation such as $\boldsymbol{x} \wedge \boldsymbol{y}$ is defined only for *compatible* vectors $\boldsymbol{x}$ and $\boldsymbol{y}$, that is, for vectors of like dimension. Since this compatibility requirement can be assumed to specify implicitly the dimension of one of the operands, elision of the parameter n may be permitted in the notation for the special vectors. Thus, if $\boldsymbol{y} = (3, 4, 5, 6, 7)$, the expressions $\boldsymbol{\epsilon} \times \boldsymbol{y}$ and $\boldsymbol{\epsilon}^j \times \boldsymbol{y}$ imply that the dimensions of $\boldsymbol{\epsilon}$ and $\boldsymbol{\epsilon}^j$ are both 5. Moreover, elision of j will be permitted for the interval vector $\boldsymbol{\iota}^j(n)$ (or $\boldsymbol{\iota}^j$), and for the residue operator $|_j$ when j is the index origin in use.

It is, of course, necessary to specify the index origin in use at any given time. For example, the unit vector $\boldsymbol{\epsilon}^3(5)$ is $(0, 0, 1, 0, 0)$ in a 1-origin system and $(0, 0, 0, 1, 0)$ in a 0-origin system, even though the definition (that is, $(\boldsymbol{\epsilon}^j(n))_k = (k = j)$) remains unchanged. The prefix and suffix vectors are, of course, independent of the index origin. Unless otherwise specified, 1-origin indexing will be assumed.

The vector $\boldsymbol{\epsilon}(0)$ is a vector of dimension zero and will be called the *null vector*. It should not be confused with the special null element $\circ$.

1.8 REDUCTION

An operation (such as summation) which is applied to all components of a vector to produce a result of a simpler structure is called a *reduction*. The $\odot$-reduction of a vector $\boldsymbol{x}$ is denoted by $\odot/\boldsymbol{x}$ and defined as

$$z \leftarrow \odot/\boldsymbol{x} \Leftrightarrow z = (\cdots((\boldsymbol{x}_1 \odot \boldsymbol{x}_2) \odot \boldsymbol{x}_3) \odot \cdots) \odot \boldsymbol{x}_\nu),$$

where $\odot$ is any binary operator with a suitable domain. Thus $+/\boldsymbol{x}$ is the sum, $\times/\boldsymbol{x}$ is the product, and $\vee/\boldsymbol{x}$ is the logical sum of the components of a vector $\boldsymbol{x}$. For example, $\times/\boldsymbol{\iota}^1(5) = 1 \times 2 \times 3 \times 4 \times 5$, $\times/\boldsymbol{\iota}^1(n) = n!$, and $+/\boldsymbol{\iota}^1(n) = n(n + 1)/2$.

As a further example, De Morgan's law may be expressed as $\wedge/\boldsymbol{u} = \overline{\vee/\overline{\boldsymbol{u}}}$, where $\boldsymbol{u}$ is a logical vector of dimension two. Moreover, a simple inductive argument (Exercise 1.10) shows that the foregoing expression is the valid generalization of De Morgan's law for a logical vector $\boldsymbol{u}$ of arbitrary dimension.

A relation $\mathscr{R}$ incorporated into a relational statement $(x\mathscr{R}y)$ becomes, in effect, an operator on the variables x and y. Consequently, the reduction $\mathscr{R}/\boldsymbol{x}$ can be defined in a manner analogous to that of $\odot/\boldsymbol{x}$, that is,

$$\mathscr{R}/\boldsymbol{x} = (\cdots((\boldsymbol{x}_1\mathscr{R}\boldsymbol{x}_2)\mathscr{R}\boldsymbol{x}_3)\mathscr{R} \cdots)\mathscr{R}\boldsymbol{x}_\nu).$$

The parentheses now imply relational statements as well as grouping.

The relational reductions of practical interest are $\neq/\boldsymbol{u}$, and $=/\boldsymbol{u}$, the *exclusive-or* and the *equivalence* reduction, respectively.

The inductive argument of Exercise 1.10 shows that $\neq/\boldsymbol{u} = 2 \mid_0 (+/\boldsymbol{u})$. For example, if $\boldsymbol{u} = (1, 0, 1, 1, 0)$, then

$$\begin{aligned}\neq/\boldsymbol{u} &= ((((1 \neq 0) \neq 1) \neq 1) \neq 0)\\ &= (((1 \neq 1) \neq 1) \neq 0)\\ &= ((0 \neq 1) \neq 0)\\ &= (1 \neq 0) = 1,\end{aligned}$$

and $2 \mid_0 (+/\boldsymbol{u}) = 2 \mid_0 3 = 1$. Similarly, $=/\boldsymbol{u} = \overline{2 \mid_0 (+/\overline{\boldsymbol{u}})}$, and as a consequence,

$$\neq/\boldsymbol{u} = \overline{=/\overline{\boldsymbol{u}}},$$

a useful companion to De Morgan's law.

To complete the system it is essential to define the value of $\odot/\boldsymbol{\epsilon}(0)$, the reduction of the null vector of dimension zero, as the identity element of the operator or relation $\odot$. Thus $+/\boldsymbol{\epsilon}(0) = \vee/\boldsymbol{\epsilon}(0) = 0$, and $\times/\boldsymbol{\epsilon}(0) = \wedge/\boldsymbol{\epsilon}(0) = 1$.

A reduction operation is extended to matrices in two ways. A *row reduction* of a matrix $\boldsymbol{X}$ by an operator $\odot$ is denoted by

$$\boldsymbol{y} \leftarrow \odot/\boldsymbol{X}$$

and specifies a vector $\boldsymbol{y}$ of dimension $\mu(\boldsymbol{X})$ such that $\boldsymbol{y}_i = \odot/\boldsymbol{X}^i$. A *column reduction* of $\boldsymbol{X}$ is denoted by $\boldsymbol{z} \leftarrow \odot//\boldsymbol{X}$ and specifies a vector $\boldsymbol{z}$ of dimension $\nu(\boldsymbol{X})$ such that $\boldsymbol{z}_j = \odot/\boldsymbol{X}_j$.

For example, if

$$\boldsymbol{U} = \begin{pmatrix} 1 & 0 & 1 & 0 \\ 0 & 0 & 1 & 1 \\ 1 & 1 & 1 & 0 \end{pmatrix}$$

then $+/\boldsymbol{U} = (2, 2, 3)$, $+//\boldsymbol{U} = (2, 1, 3, 1)$, $\wedge//\boldsymbol{U} = (0, 0, 1, 0)$, $\neq/\boldsymbol{U} = (0, 0, 1)$, $=//\boldsymbol{U} = (0, 1, 1, 1)$, and $+/(=//\boldsymbol{U}) = 3$.

1.9 SELECTION

Compression

The effective use of structured operands depends not only on generalized operations but also on the ability to specify and select certain elements or groups of elements. The selection of single elements can be indicated by indices, as in the expressions $\boldsymbol{v}_i$, $\boldsymbol{M}^i$, $\boldsymbol{M}_j$, and $\boldsymbol{M}_j^i$. Since selection is a binary operation (i.e., to select or not to select), more general selection is conveniently specified by a logical vector, each unit component indicating selection of the corresponding component of the operand.

The selection operation defined on an arbitrary vector $\boldsymbol{a}$ and a compatible (i.e., equal in dimension) logical vector $\boldsymbol{u}$ is denoted by $\boldsymbol{c} \leftarrow \boldsymbol{u}/\boldsymbol{a}$ and is defined as follows: the vector $\boldsymbol{c}$ is obtained from $\boldsymbol{a}$ by suppressing from $\boldsymbol{a}$ each component $\boldsymbol{a}_i$ for which $\boldsymbol{u}_i = 0$. The vector $\boldsymbol{u}$ is said to *compress* the vector $\boldsymbol{a}$. Clearly $\nu(\boldsymbol{c}) = +/\boldsymbol{u}$. For example, if $\boldsymbol{u} = (1, 0, 0, 0, 1, 1)$ and $\boldsymbol{a} = (\text{M, o, n, d, a, y})$, then $\boldsymbol{u}/\boldsymbol{a} = (\text{M, a, y})$. Moreover, if n is even and $\boldsymbol{v} = (2\boldsymbol{\epsilon}) \,|_0\, \boldsymbol{\iota}^1(n) = (1, 0, 1, 0, 1, \ldots)$, then $\boldsymbol{v}/\boldsymbol{\iota}^1(n) = (1, 3, 5, \ldots, n - 1)$, and $+/(\boldsymbol{v}/\boldsymbol{\iota}^1(n)) = (n/2)^2$.

Row compression of a matrix, denoted by $\boldsymbol{u}/\boldsymbol{A}$, compresses each row vector $\boldsymbol{A}^i$ to form a matrix of dimension $\mu(\boldsymbol{A}) \times +/\boldsymbol{u}$. *Column compression*, denoted by $\boldsymbol{u}//\boldsymbol{A}$, compresses each column vector $\boldsymbol{A}_j$ to form a matrix of dimension $+/\boldsymbol{u} \times \nu(\boldsymbol{A})$. Compatibility conditions are $\nu(\boldsymbol{u}) = \nu(\boldsymbol{A})$ for row compression, and $\nu(\boldsymbol{u}) = \mu(\boldsymbol{A})$ for column compression. For example, if $\boldsymbol{A}$ is an arbitrary 3×4 matrix, $\boldsymbol{u} = (0, 1, 0, 1)$ and $\boldsymbol{v} = (1, 0, 1)$; then

$$\boldsymbol{u}/\boldsymbol{A} = \begin{pmatrix} A_2^1 & A_4^1 \\ A_2^2 & A_4^2 \\ A_2^3 & A_4^3 \end{pmatrix}, \quad \boldsymbol{v}//\boldsymbol{A} = \begin{pmatrix} A_1^1 & A_2^1 & A_3^1 & A_4^1 \\ A_1^3 & A_2^3 & A_3^3 & A_4^3 \end{pmatrix},$$

and

$$\boldsymbol{u}/\boldsymbol{v}//\boldsymbol{A} = \boldsymbol{v}//\boldsymbol{u}/\boldsymbol{A} = \begin{pmatrix} A_2^1 & A_4^1 \\ A_2^3 & A_4^3 \end{pmatrix}$$

It is clear that *row* compression *suppresses columns* corresponding to zeros of the logical vector and that *column* compression *suppresses rows*. This illustrates the type of confusion in nomenclature which is avoided by the convention adopted in Sec. 1.3: an operation is called a *row operation* if the underlying operation from which it is generalized is applied to the row vectors of the matrix, and a *column operation* if it is applied to columns.

Example 1.1. A bank makes a quarterly review of accounts to produce the following four lists:

1. the name, account number, and balance for each account with a balance less than two dollars.

2. the name, account number, and balance for each account with a negative balance exceeding one hundred dollars.

3. the name and account number of each account with a balance exceeding one thousand dollars.

4. all unassigned account numbers.

The ledger may be described by a matrix

$$L = (L_1, L_2, L_3) = \begin{pmatrix} L^1 \\ \cdot \\ \cdot \\ \cdot \\ L^m \end{pmatrix}$$

with column vectors L_1, L_2, and L_3 representing names, account numbers, and balances, respectively, and with row vectors $L^1, L^2, \ldots, L^m$ representing individual accounts. An unassigned account number is identified by the word "none" in the name position. The four output lists will be denoted by the matrices P, Q, R, and S, respectively. They can be produced by Program 1.9.

Program 1.9. Since L_3 is the vector of balances, and 2ϵ is a compatible vector each of whose components equals two, the relational statement $(L_3 < 2\epsilon)$ defines a logical vector having unit components corresponding to those accounts to be

1 →	$P \leftarrow (L_3 < 2\,\epsilon)//L$
2	$Q \leftarrow (L_3 < -100\,\epsilon)//L$
3	$R \leftarrow (L_3 > 1000\,\epsilon)//\alpha^2/L$
4	$S \leftarrow (L_1 = \text{none}\,\epsilon)//\epsilon^2/L$ →

L	Bank ledger.
L^k	kth account.
$L_3{}^k$	Balance of kth account.
$L_2{}^k$	Account number of kth account.
$L_1{}^k$	Name of kth account or "none" if account number $L_2{}^k$ unused.

Legend

Program 1.9 Selection on bank ledger L (Example 1.1)

included in the list P. Consequently, the column compression of step 1 selects the appropriate rows of L to define P. Step 2 is similar, but step 3 incorporates an additional row compression by the compatible prefix vector $\alpha^2 = (1, 1, 0)$ to select columns one and two of L. Step 4 represents the comparison of the name (in column L_1) with the literal "none," the selection of each row which shows agreement, and the suppression of all columns but the second. The expression "none ϵ" occurring in step 4 illustrates the use of the extended definition of multiplication.

Mesh, mask, and expansion

A logical vector u and the two vectors $a = \bar{u}/c$ and $b = u/c$, obtained by compressing a vector c, collectively determine the vector c. The operation which specifies c as a function of a, b, and u is called a *mesh* and

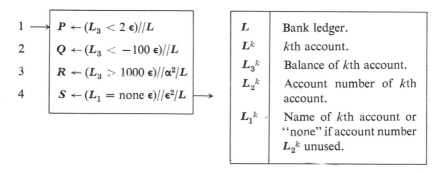

is defined as follows: If $\boldsymbol{a}$ and $\boldsymbol{b}$ are arbitrary vectors and if $\boldsymbol{u}$ is a logical vector such that $+/\overline{\boldsymbol{u}} = \nu(\boldsymbol{a})$ and $+/\boldsymbol{u} = \nu(\boldsymbol{b})$, then the *mesh of* $\boldsymbol{a}$ *and* $\boldsymbol{b}$ *on* $\boldsymbol{u}$ is denoted by $\backslash \boldsymbol{a}, \boldsymbol{u}, \boldsymbol{b} \backslash$ and is defined as the vector $\boldsymbol{c}$ such that $\overline{\boldsymbol{u}}/\boldsymbol{c} = \boldsymbol{a}$ and $\boldsymbol{u}/\boldsymbol{c} = \boldsymbol{b}$. The mesh operation is equivalent to choosing successive components of $\boldsymbol{c}$ from $\boldsymbol{a}$ or $\boldsymbol{b}$ according as the successive components of $\boldsymbol{u}$ are 0 or 1. If, for example, $\boldsymbol{a} =$ (s, e, k), $\boldsymbol{b} =$ (t, a), and $\boldsymbol{u} = (0, 1, 0, 1, 0)$, then $\backslash \boldsymbol{a}, \boldsymbol{u}, \boldsymbol{b} \backslash =$ (s, t, e, a, k). As a further example, Program 1.10*a*

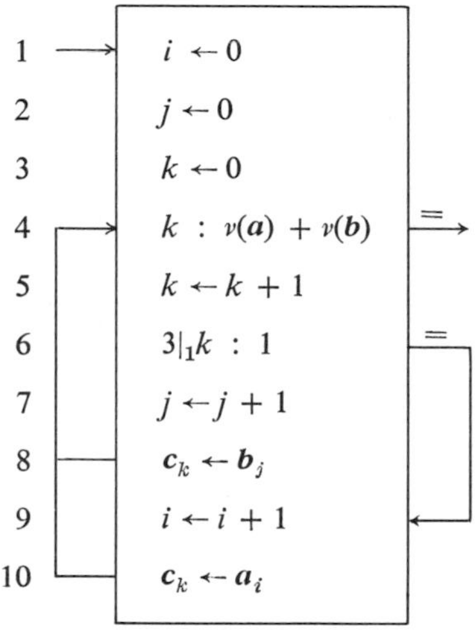

(*a*)

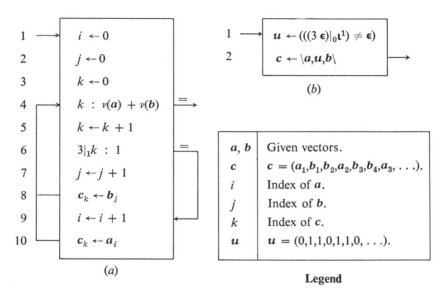

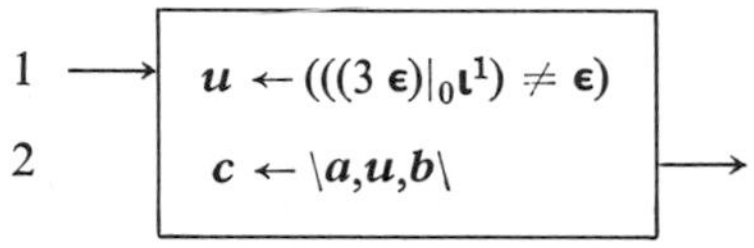

(*b*)

$\boldsymbol{a}, \boldsymbol{b}$	Given vectors.
$\boldsymbol{c}$	$\boldsymbol{c} = (a_1, b_1, b_2, a_2, b_3, b_4, a_3, \ldots)$.
i	Index of $\boldsymbol{a}$.
j	Index of $\boldsymbol{b}$.
k	Index of $\boldsymbol{c}$.
$\boldsymbol{u}$	$\boldsymbol{u} = (0,1,1,0,1,1,0, \ldots)$.

Legend

Program 1.10 Interfiling program

(which describes the merging of the vectors $\boldsymbol{a}$ and $\boldsymbol{b}$, with the first and every third component thereafter chosen from $\boldsymbol{a}$) can be described alternatively as shown in Program 1.10*b*. Since $\iota^1 = (1, 2, 3, 4, 5, 6, \ldots)$, then $(3\epsilon)\,|_0\,\iota^1 = (1, 2, 0, 1, 2, 0, \ldots)$, and consequently the vector $\boldsymbol{u}$ specified by step 1 is of the form $\boldsymbol{u} = (0, 1, 1, 0, 1, 1, 0, \ldots)$.

Mesh operations on matrices are defined analogously, row mesh and column mesh being denoted by single and double reverse virgules, respectively.

The *catenation* of vectors $\boldsymbol{x}, \boldsymbol{y}, \ldots, \boldsymbol{z}$ is denoted by $\boldsymbol{x} \oplus \boldsymbol{y} \oplus \cdots \oplus \boldsymbol{z}$ and is defined by the relation

$$\boldsymbol{x} \oplus \boldsymbol{y} \oplus \cdots \oplus \boldsymbol{z} = (x_1, x_2, \ldots, x_{\nu(\boldsymbol{x})}, y_1, y_2, \ldots, z_{\nu(\boldsymbol{z})}).$$

Catenation is clearly associative and for two vectors $\boldsymbol{x}$ and $\boldsymbol{y}$ it is a special case of the mesh $\backslash \boldsymbol{x}, \boldsymbol{u}, \boldsymbol{y} \backslash$ in which $\boldsymbol{u}$ is a suffix vector.

In numerical vectors (for which addition of two vectors is defined), the effect of the general mesh operation can be produced as the sum of two meshes, each involving one zero vector. Specifically,

$$\begin{aligned} \backslash \boldsymbol{x}, \boldsymbol{u}, \boldsymbol{y} \backslash &= \backslash \boldsymbol{x}, \boldsymbol{u}, 0 \backslash + \backslash 0, \boldsymbol{u}, \boldsymbol{y} \backslash \\ &= \backslash 0, \overline{\boldsymbol{u}}, \boldsymbol{x} \backslash + \backslash 0, \boldsymbol{u}, \boldsymbol{y} \backslash. \end{aligned}$$

The operation $\backslash 0, \boldsymbol{u}, \boldsymbol{y} \backslash$ proves very useful in numerical work and will be called *expansion* of the vector $\boldsymbol{y}$, denoted by $\boldsymbol{u} \backslash \boldsymbol{y}$. Compression of $\boldsymbol{u} \backslash \boldsymbol{y}$ by $\boldsymbol{u}$ and by $\overline{\boldsymbol{u}}$ clearly yield $\boldsymbol{y}$ and 0, respectively. Moreover, any numerical vector $\boldsymbol{x}$ can be *decomposed* by a compatible vector $\boldsymbol{u}$ according to the relation

$$\boldsymbol{x} = \overline{\boldsymbol{u}} \backslash \overline{\boldsymbol{u}} / \boldsymbol{x} + \boldsymbol{u} \backslash \boldsymbol{u} / \boldsymbol{x}.$$

The two terms are vectors of the same dimension which have no nonzero components in common. Thus if $\boldsymbol{u} = (1, 0, 1, 0, 1)$, the decomposition of $\boldsymbol{x}$ appears as

$$\boldsymbol{x} = (0, x_2, 0, x_4, 0) + (x_1, 0, x_3, 0, x_5).$$

Row expansion and column expansion of matrices are defined and denoted analogously. The decomposition relations become

$$\boldsymbol{X} = \overline{\boldsymbol{u}} \backslash \overline{\boldsymbol{u}} / \boldsymbol{X} + \boldsymbol{u} \backslash \boldsymbol{u} / \boldsymbol{X},$$

and

$$\boldsymbol{X} = \overline{\boldsymbol{u}} \backslash\backslash \overline{\boldsymbol{u}} // \boldsymbol{X} + \boldsymbol{u} \backslash\backslash \boldsymbol{u} // \boldsymbol{X}.$$

The *mask* operation is defined formally as follows:

$$\boldsymbol{c} \leftarrow /\boldsymbol{a}, \boldsymbol{u}, \boldsymbol{b}/ \Leftrightarrow \overline{\boldsymbol{u}}/\boldsymbol{c} = \overline{\boldsymbol{u}}/\boldsymbol{a}, \quad \text{and} \quad \boldsymbol{u}/\boldsymbol{c} = \boldsymbol{u}/\boldsymbol{b}.$$

The vectors $\boldsymbol{c}$, $\boldsymbol{a}$, $\boldsymbol{u}$, and $\boldsymbol{b}$ are clearly of a common dimension and $c_i = a_i$ or b_i according as $u_i = 0$ or $u_i = 1$. Moreover, the compress, expand, mask, and mesh operations on vectors are related as follows:

$$\begin{aligned} /\boldsymbol{a}, \boldsymbol{u}, \boldsymbol{b}/ &= \backslash \overline{\boldsymbol{u}}/\boldsymbol{a}, \boldsymbol{u}, \boldsymbol{u}/\boldsymbol{b} \backslash, \\ \backslash \boldsymbol{a}, \boldsymbol{u}, \boldsymbol{b} \backslash &= /\overline{\boldsymbol{u}} \backslash \boldsymbol{a}, \boldsymbol{u}, \boldsymbol{u} \backslash \boldsymbol{b}/. \end{aligned}$$

Analogous relations hold for the row mask and row mesh and for the column mask and column mesh.

Certain selection operations are controlled by logical matrices rather than by logical vectors. The *row compression* $\boldsymbol{U}/\boldsymbol{A}$ selects elements of $\boldsymbol{A}$ corresponding to the nonzero elements of $\boldsymbol{U}$. Since the nonzero elements of $\boldsymbol{U}$ may occur in an arbitrary pattern, the result must be construed as a vector rather than a matrix. More precisely, $\boldsymbol{U}/\boldsymbol{A}$ denotes the catenation of the vectors $\boldsymbol{U}^i/\boldsymbol{A}^i$ obtained by row-by-row compression of $\boldsymbol{A}$ by $\boldsymbol{U}$.

The *column compression* $U//A$ denotes the catenation of the vectors U_j/A_j. If, for example,

$$U = \begin{pmatrix} 0 & 1 & 0 & 1 & 1 \\ 1 & 1 & 0 & 0 & 0 \\ 0 & 1 & 1 & 0 & 0 \end{pmatrix}$$

then $$U/A = (A_2^1, A_4^1, A_5^1, A_1^2, A_2^2, A_2^3, A_3^3),$$

and $$U//A = (A_1^2, A_2^1, A_2^2, A_2^3, A_3^3, A_4^1, A_5^1).$$

Compression by the full matrix $\mathbf{E}$ (defined by $\overline{\mathbf{E}} = 0$) produces either a *row list* ($\mathbf{E}/A$) or a *column list* ($\mathbf{E}//A$) of the matrix A. Moreover, a numerical matrix $\boldsymbol{X}$ can be represented jointly by the logical matrix $\boldsymbol{U}$ and the row list $\boldsymbol{U}/\boldsymbol{X}$ (or the column list $\boldsymbol{U}//\boldsymbol{X}$), where $\boldsymbol{U} = (\boldsymbol{X} \neq 0)$. If the matrix $\boldsymbol{X}$ is sparse (i.e., the components are predominantly zero), this provides a compact representation which may reduce the computer storage required for $\boldsymbol{X}$.

The compression operations controlled by matrices also generate a group of corresponding mesh and mask operations as shown in Sec. S.9.

1.10 SELECTION VECTORS

The logical vector $\boldsymbol{u}$ involved in selection operations may itself arise in various ways. It may be a prefix vector $\boldsymbol{\alpha}^j$, a suffix $\boldsymbol{\omega}^j$, or an infix $(i \downarrow \boldsymbol{\alpha}^j)$; the corresponding compressed vectors $\boldsymbol{\alpha}^j/\boldsymbol{x}$, $\boldsymbol{\omega}^j/\boldsymbol{x}$, and $(i \downarrow \boldsymbol{\alpha}^j)/\boldsymbol{x}$ are called a *prefix*, *suffix*, and *infix* of $\boldsymbol{x}$, respectively.

Certain selection vectors arise as functions of other vectors, e.g., the vector $(\boldsymbol{x} \geq 0)$ can be used to select all nonnegative components of $\boldsymbol{x}$, and $(\boldsymbol{b} \neq *\boldsymbol{\epsilon})$ serves to select all components of $\boldsymbol{b}$ which are not equal to the literal "$*$." Two further types are important: the selection of the longest unbroken prefix (or suffix) of a given logical vector, and the selection of the set of distinct components occurring in a vector. The first is useful in left (or right) justification or in a corresponding compression intended to eliminate leading or trailing "filler components" of a vector (such as left zeros in a number or right spaces in a short name).

For any logical vector $\boldsymbol{u}$, the *maximum prefix* of $\boldsymbol{u}$ is denoted by $\alpha/\boldsymbol{u}$ and defined as follows:

$$\boldsymbol{v} \leftarrow \alpha/\boldsymbol{u} \Leftrightarrow \boldsymbol{v} = \boldsymbol{\alpha}^j,$$

where j is the maximum value for which $\wedge/(\boldsymbol{\alpha}^j/\boldsymbol{u}) = 1$. The maximum suffix is denoted by $\omega/\boldsymbol{u}$ and is defined analogously. If, for example, $\boldsymbol{u} = (1, 1, 1, 0, 1, 1, 0, 0, 1, 1)$, then $\alpha/\boldsymbol{u} = (1, 1, 1, 0, 0, 0, 0, 0, 0, 0)$, $\omega/\boldsymbol{u} = (0, 0, 0, 0, 0, 0, 0, 0, 1, 1)$, $+/\alpha/\boldsymbol{u} = 3$, and $+/\omega/\boldsymbol{u} = 2$.

The leading zeros of a numerical vector $\boldsymbol{x}$ can clearly be removed either by compression:

$$\boldsymbol{y} \leftarrow \overline{(\alpha/(\boldsymbol{x} = 0))}/\boldsymbol{x},$$

or by left justification (normalization):

$$\boldsymbol{z} \leftarrow (+/\alpha/(\boldsymbol{x} = 0)) \uparrow \boldsymbol{x}.$$

The extension of the maximum prefix operation to the rows of a logical matrix $\boldsymbol{U}$ is denoted by $\alpha/\boldsymbol{U}$ and defined as the compatible logical matrix $\boldsymbol{V}$, such that $\boldsymbol{V}^i = \alpha/\boldsymbol{U}^i$. The corresponding maximum column prefix operation is denoted by $\alpha//\boldsymbol{U}$. Right justification of a numerical matrix $\boldsymbol{X}$ is achieved by the rotation $\boldsymbol{k} \downarrow \boldsymbol{X}$, where $\boldsymbol{k} = +/\omega/(\boldsymbol{X} = 0)$, and *top justification* is achieved by the rotation $(+//\alpha//(\boldsymbol{X} = 0)) \Uparrow \boldsymbol{X}$ (see Sec. S.6.)

A vector whose components are all distinct will be called an *ordered set*. The *forward set selector* on $\boldsymbol{b}$ is a logical vector denoted by $\sigma/\boldsymbol{b}$ and defined as follows: the statement $\boldsymbol{v} \leftarrow \sigma/\boldsymbol{b}$ implies that $\boldsymbol{v}_j = 1$ if and only if $\boldsymbol{b}_j$ differs from all preceding components of $\boldsymbol{b}$. Hence $\boldsymbol{v}/\boldsymbol{b}$ is a set which contains all distinct components of $\boldsymbol{b}$, and $+/\boldsymbol{v}/\boldsymbol{\iota}$ is a minimum. For example, if $\boldsymbol{c}$ = (C, a, n, a, d, a), then $(\sigma/\boldsymbol{c})/\boldsymbol{c}$ = (C, a, n, d) is a list of the distinct letters in $\boldsymbol{c}$ in order of occurrence. Clearly $(\sigma/\boldsymbol{b})/\boldsymbol{b} = \boldsymbol{b}$ if and only if $\boldsymbol{b}$ is a set.

The backward set selector $\tau/\boldsymbol{b}$ is defined analogously (e.g., $(\tau/\boldsymbol{c})/\boldsymbol{c}$ = (C, n, d, a)). Forward and backward set selection are extended to matrices by both rows ($\sigma/\boldsymbol{B}$, and $\tau/\boldsymbol{B}$) and columns ($\sigma//\boldsymbol{B}$, and $\tau//\boldsymbol{B}$) in the established manner.

1.11 THE GENERALIZED MATRIX PRODUCT

The ordinary matrix product of matrices $\boldsymbol{X}$ and $\boldsymbol{Y}$ is commonly denoted by $\boldsymbol{XY}$ and defined as follows:

$$\boldsymbol{Z} \leftarrow \boldsymbol{XY} \Leftrightarrow \boldsymbol{Z}_j^i = \sum_{k=1}^{\nu(\boldsymbol{X})} \boldsymbol{X}_k^i \times \boldsymbol{Y}_j^k, \quad \begin{cases} i = 1, 2, \ldots \mu(\boldsymbol{X}) \\ j = 1, 2, \ldots \nu(\boldsymbol{Y}). \end{cases}$$

It can be defined alternatively as follows:

$$(\boldsymbol{XY})_j^i = +/(\boldsymbol{X}^i \times \boldsymbol{Y}_j).$$

This formulation emphasizes the fact that matrix multiplication incorporates two elementary operations $(+, \times)$ and suggests that they be displayed explicitly. The ordinary matrix product will therefore be written as $\boldsymbol{X} \overset{+}{\underset{\times}{}} \boldsymbol{Y}$.

More generally, if $\bigcirc_1$ and $\bigcirc_2$ are any two operators (whose domains include the relevant operands), then the *generalized matrix product* $\boldsymbol{X} \overset{\bigcirc_1}{\underset{\bigcirc_2}{}} \boldsymbol{Y}$ is defined as follows:

$$(\boldsymbol{X} \overset{\bigcirc_1}{\underset{\bigcirc_2}{}} \boldsymbol{Y})_j^i = \bigcirc_1/(\boldsymbol{X}^i \bigcirc_2 \boldsymbol{Y}_j), \quad \begin{cases} i = 1, 2, \ldots, \mu(\boldsymbol{X}) \\ j = 1, 2, \ldots, \nu(\boldsymbol{Y}) \end{cases}.$$

For example, if

$$\boldsymbol{A} = \begin{pmatrix} 1 & 3 & 2 & 0 \\ 2 & 1 & 0 & 1 \\ 4 & 0 & 0 & 2 \end{pmatrix} \quad \text{and} \quad \boldsymbol{B} = \begin{pmatrix} 4 & 1 \\ 0 & 3 \\ 0 & 2 \\ 2 & 0 \end{pmatrix}$$

then

$$\boldsymbol{A} \overset{+}{\underset{\times}{}} \boldsymbol{B} = \begin{pmatrix} 4 & 14 \\ 10 & 5 \\ 20 & 4 \end{pmatrix}, \quad \boldsymbol{A} \overset{\wedge}{\underset{=}{}} \boldsymbol{B} = \begin{pmatrix} 0 & 1 \\ 0 & 0 \\ 1 & 0 \end{pmatrix},$$

$$\boldsymbol{A} \overset{\vee}{\underset{\neq}{}} \boldsymbol{B} = \begin{pmatrix} 1 & 0 \\ 1 & 1 \\ 0 & 1 \end{pmatrix}, \quad \text{and} \quad (\boldsymbol{A} \neq 0) \overset{+}{\underset{/}{}} \boldsymbol{B} = \begin{pmatrix} 4 & 6 \\ 6 & 4 \\ 6 & 1 \end{pmatrix}.$$

The generalized matrix product and the selection operations together provide an elegant formulation in several established areas of mathematics. A few examples will be chosen from two such areas, symbolic logic and matrix algebra.

In symbolic logic, De Morgan's laws ($\wedge/\boldsymbol{u} = \overline{\vee/\overline{\boldsymbol{u}}}$ and $=/\boldsymbol{u} = \overline{\neq/\overline{\boldsymbol{u}}}$) can be applied directly to show that

$$\boldsymbol{U} \overset{\neq}{\underset{\wedge}{}} \boldsymbol{V} = \overline{\overline{\boldsymbol{U}} \overset{=}{\underset{\vee}{}} \overline{\boldsymbol{V}}}.$$

In matrix algebra, the notion of partitioning a matrix into submatrices of contiguous rows and columns can be generalized to an arbitrary partitioning specified by a logical vector $\boldsymbol{u}$. The following easily verifiable identities are typical of the useful relations which result:

$$\boldsymbol{X} \overset{+}{\underset{\times}{}} \boldsymbol{Y} = (\overline{\boldsymbol{u}}/\boldsymbol{X}) \overset{+}{\underset{\times}{}} (\overline{\boldsymbol{u}}//\boldsymbol{Y}) + (\boldsymbol{u}/\boldsymbol{X}) \overset{+}{\underset{\times}{}} (\boldsymbol{u}//\boldsymbol{Y}),$$

$$\boldsymbol{u}/(\boldsymbol{X} \overset{+}{\underset{\times}{}} \boldsymbol{Y}) = \boldsymbol{X} \overset{+}{\underset{\times}{}} (\boldsymbol{u}/\boldsymbol{Y}),$$

$$\boldsymbol{u}//(\boldsymbol{X} \overset{+}{\underset{\times}{}} \boldsymbol{Y}) = (\boldsymbol{u}//\boldsymbol{X}) \overset{+}{\underset{\times}{}} \boldsymbol{Y}.$$

The first identity depends on the commutativity and associativity of the operator $+$ and can clearly be generalized to other associative commutative operators, such as $\wedge$, $\vee$, and $\neq$.

The generalized matrix product applies directly (as does the ordinary matrix product $X \overset{+}{\times} Y$) to vectors considered as row (that is, $1 \times n$) or as column matrices. Thus:

$$z \leftarrow X \overset{\bigcirc_1}{\bigcirc_2} y \Leftrightarrow z_i = \bigcirc_1/(X^i \bigcirc_2 y),$$

$$z \leftarrow y \overset{\bigcirc_1}{\bigcirc_2} X \Leftrightarrow z_j = \bigcirc_1/(y \bigcirc_2 X_j),$$

$$z \leftarrow y \overset{\bigcirc_1}{\bigcirc_2} x \Leftrightarrow z = \bigcirc_1/(y \bigcirc_2 x).$$

The question of whether a vector enters a given operation as a row vector or as a column vector is normally settled by the requirement of conformability, and no special indication is required. Thus y enters as a column vector in the first of the preceding group of definitions and as a row vector in the last two. The question remains, however, in the case of the two vector operands, which may be considered with the pre-operand either as a row (as in the scalar product $y \overset{+}{\times} x$) or as a column. The latter case produces a matrix Z and will be denoted by

$$Z \leftarrow y \overset{\circ}{\bigcirc_2} x,$$

where $Z_j^i = y_i \bigcirc_2 x_j$, $\mu(Z) = \nu(y)$, and $\nu(Z) = \nu(x)$.* For example, if each of the vectors indicated is of dimension three, then

$$\epsilon \overset{\circ}{\times} y = \begin{pmatrix} y_1, & y_2, & y_3 \\ y_1, & y_2, & y_3 \\ y_1, & y_2, & y_3 \end{pmatrix}; \qquad y \overset{\circ}{\times} \epsilon = \begin{pmatrix} y_1, & y_1, & y_1 \\ y_2, & y_2, & y_2 \\ y_3, & y_3, & y_3 \end{pmatrix};$$

$$\alpha^2(3) \overset{\circ}{\wedge} \alpha^2(3) = \begin{pmatrix} 1 & 1 & 0 \\ 1 & 1 & 0 \\ 0 & 0 & 0 \end{pmatrix}.$$

1.12 TRANSPOSITIONS

Since the generalized matrix product is defined on columns of the post-operand and rows of the pre-operand, convenient description of corresponding operations on the rows of the post-operand and columns of the pre-operand demands the ability to *transpose* a matrix B, that is, to specify a matrix C such that $C_i^j = B_j^i$. In ordinary matrix algebra this type of transposition suffices, but in more general work transpositions

* Since each "vector" $y_i \bigcirc_2 x_j$ is of dimension one, no scan operator $\bigcirc_1$ is required, and the symbol $\circ$ may be interpreted as a "null" scan.

about either diagonal and about the horizontal and the vertical are also useful. Each of these transpositions of a matrix $\boldsymbol{B}$ is denoted by a superior arrow whose inclination indicates the axis of the transposition. Thus:

$$\left.\begin{array}{ll} \boldsymbol{C} \leftarrow \overset{\nwarrow}{\boldsymbol{B}} & \boldsymbol{C}_i^{\,j} = \boldsymbol{B}_j^{\,i} \\ \boldsymbol{C} \leftarrow \overset{\nearrow}{\boldsymbol{B}} & \boldsymbol{C}_i^{\,j} = \boldsymbol{B}_{\nu+1-j}^{\mu+1-i} \\ \boldsymbol{C} \leftarrow \overset{\rightarrow}{\boldsymbol{B}} & \boldsymbol{C}_j^{\,i} = \boldsymbol{B}_j^{\mu+1-i} \\ \boldsymbol{C} \leftarrow \overset{\uparrow}{\boldsymbol{B}} & \boldsymbol{C}_j^{\,i} = \boldsymbol{B}_{\nu+1-j}^{i} \end{array}\right\} \begin{array}{l} i = 1,2, \ldots, \mu(\boldsymbol{B}) \\ j = 1,2, \ldots, \nu(\boldsymbol{B}) \end{array}$$

For a vector $\boldsymbol{x}$, either $\overset{\rightarrow}{\boldsymbol{x}}$ or $\overset{\uparrow}{\boldsymbol{x}}$ will denote reversal of the order of the components. For ordinary matrix transposition (that is, $\overset{\nwarrow}{\boldsymbol{B}}$), the commonly used notation $\tilde{\boldsymbol{B}}$ will also be employed.

Since transpositions can effect any one or more of three independent alternatives (i.e., interchange of row and column indices or reversal of order of row or of column indices), repeated transposition can produce eight distinct configurations. There are therefore seven distinct transformations possible; all can be generated by any pair of transpositions having nonperpendicular axes.*

1.13 SPECIAL LOGICAL MATRICES

Certain of the special logical vectors introduced in Sec. 1.7 have useful analogs in logical matrices. Dimensions will again be indicated in parentheses (with the column dimension first) and may be elided whenever the dimension is determined by context. If not otherwise specified, a matrix is assumed to be square.

Cases of obvious interest are the *full* matrix $\mathbf{E}(m \times n)$, defined by $\bar{\mathbf{E}}(m \times n) = 0$, and the *identity* matrix $\mathbf{I}(m \times n)$, defined by $\mathbf{I}_j^{\,i} = (i = j)$. More generally, *superdiagonal* matrices ${}^k\mathbf{I}(m \times n)$ are defined such that ${}^k\mathbf{I}_j^{\,i}(m \times n) = (j = i + k)$, for $k \geq 0$. Clearly ${}^0\mathbf{I} = \mathbf{I}$. Moreover, for square matrices ${}^h\mathbf{I} \overset{+}{\underset{\times}{}} {}^k\mathbf{I} = {}^{(h+k)}\mathbf{I}$.

Four *triangular* matrices will be defined, the geometrical symbols employed for each indicating the (right-angled isosceles) triangular area of

* These transpositions generate the rotation group of the square [cf. Birkhoff and MacLane (1941) Chap. VI]. A pair of transpositions commute if and only if their axes are perpendicular. Hence the pair $\leftarrow$ and $\uparrow$ may be written unambiguously as $\overset{\uparrow}{\leftarrow}$. Moreover, $\overset{\uparrow}{\leftarrow} = \overset{\nwarrow}{\nearrow}$. The remaining two transformations can be denoted by $\overset{\nearrow}{\leftarrow}$ and $\overset{\nwarrow}{\leftarrow}$, with the convention that the operator nearest the operand (i.e., the horizontal) is executed first.

the $m \times n$ rectangular matrix which is occupied by *ones*. Thus

$$\left.\begin{array}{l} C \leftarrow \Box(m \times n) \Leftrightarrow C_j^i \\ C \leftarrow \Box(m \times n) \Leftrightarrow C_{\nu+1-j}^i \\ C \leftarrow \Box(m \times n) \Leftrightarrow C_j^{\mu+1-i} \\ C \leftarrow \Box(m \times n) \Leftrightarrow C_{\nu+1-j}^{\mu+1-i} \end{array}\right\} = (i + j \leq \min(m, n)) \quad \begin{array}{l}\text{for } i = 1, 2, \ldots, m \\ \text{and } j = 1, 2, \ldots, n.\end{array}$$

The use of the matrices $\mathbf{E}$ and $\mathbf{I}$ will be illustrated briefly. The relation $u \overset{\neq}{\wedge} v = 2 \,|_0\, (u \overset{+}{\times} v)$ can be extended to logical matrices as follows:

$$U \overset{\neq}{\wedge} V = (2\mathbf{E}) \,|_0\, (U \overset{+}{\times} V);$$

the trace of a square numerical matrix X may be expressed as $t = +/\mathbf{I}/X$. The triangular matrices are employed in the succeeding section.

1.14 POLYNOMIALS AND POSITIONAL NUMBER SYSTEMS

Any positional representation of a number n in a base b number system can be considered as a numerical vector $\boldsymbol{x}$ whose *base b value* is the quantity $n = \boldsymbol{w} \overset{+}{\times} \boldsymbol{x}$, where the *weighting vector* $\boldsymbol{w}$ is defined by $\boldsymbol{w} = (b^{\nu(\boldsymbol{x})-1}, b^{\nu(\boldsymbol{x})-2}, \ldots, b^2, b^1, 1)$. More generally, $\boldsymbol{x}$ may represent a number in a mixed-radix system in which the successive radices (from high to low order) are the successive components of a *radix vector* $\boldsymbol{y}$.

The *base* $\boldsymbol{y}$ *value of* $\boldsymbol{x}$ is a scalar denoted by $\boldsymbol{y} \perp \boldsymbol{x}$ and defined as the scalar product $\boldsymbol{y} \perp \boldsymbol{x} = \boldsymbol{w} \overset{+}{\times} \boldsymbol{x}$, where $\boldsymbol{w} = \Box \overset{\times}{/} \boldsymbol{y}$ is the weighting vector. For example, if $\boldsymbol{y} = (7, 24, 60, 60)$ is the radix vector for the common temporal system of units, and if $\boldsymbol{x} = (0, 2, 1, 18)$ represents elapsed time in days, hours, minutes, and seconds, then

$$t = \boldsymbol{w} \overset{+}{\times} \boldsymbol{x} = (86400, 3600, 60, 1) \overset{+}{\times} (0, 2, 1, 18) = 7278$$

is the elapsed time in seconds, and the weighting vector $\boldsymbol{w}$ is obtained as the product

$$\Box \overset{\times}{/} \boldsymbol{y} = \begin{pmatrix} 0 & 1 & 1 & 1 \\ 0 & 0 & 1 & 1 \\ 0 & 0 & 0 & 1 \\ 0 & 0 & 0 & 0 \end{pmatrix} \overset{\times}{/} \begin{pmatrix} 7 \\ 24 \\ 60 \\ 60 \end{pmatrix} = \begin{pmatrix} \times/(24, & 60, & 60) \\ \times/(60, & 60) & \\ \times/(60) & & \\ \times/\epsilon(0) & & \end{pmatrix} = \begin{pmatrix} 86400 \\ 3600 \\ 60 \\ 1 \end{pmatrix}$$

If b is any integer, then the value of $\boldsymbol{x}$ in the fixed base b is denoted by $(b\boldsymbol{\epsilon}) \perp \boldsymbol{x}$. For example, $(2\boldsymbol{\epsilon}) \perp \boldsymbol{\alpha}^2(5) = 24$. More generally, if y is any real number, then $(y\boldsymbol{\epsilon}) \perp \boldsymbol{x}$ is clearly a polynomial in y with coefficients $\boldsymbol{x}_1$, $\boldsymbol{x}_2, \ldots, \boldsymbol{x}_\nu$, that is,

$$(y\boldsymbol{\epsilon}) \perp \boldsymbol{x} = \boldsymbol{x}_1 y^{\nu(\boldsymbol{x})-1} + \cdots + \boldsymbol{x}_{\nu-1} y + \boldsymbol{x}_\nu.$$

Writing the definition of $\boldsymbol{y} \perp \boldsymbol{x}$ in the form

$$\boldsymbol{y} \perp \boldsymbol{x} = (\square \overset{\times}{/} \boldsymbol{y}) \overset{+}{\times} \boldsymbol{x}$$

exhibits the fact that the operation $\perp$ is of the double operator type. Its use in the generalized matrix product therefore requires no secondary scan operator. This will be indicated by a null placed over the symbol $\perp$. Thus

$$\boldsymbol{Z} \leftarrow \boldsymbol{X} \overset{\circ}{\perp} \boldsymbol{Y} \Leftrightarrow \boldsymbol{Z}_j^i = \boldsymbol{X}^i \perp \boldsymbol{Y}_j.$$

For example, $(y\boldsymbol{\epsilon}) \overset{\circ}{\perp} \boldsymbol{X}$ represents a set of polynomials in y with coefficients $\boldsymbol{X}_1, \boldsymbol{X}_2, \ldots, \boldsymbol{X}_\nu$, and $\boldsymbol{Y} \overset{\circ}{\perp} \boldsymbol{x}$ represents a set of evaluations of the vector $\boldsymbol{x}$ in a set of bases $\boldsymbol{Y}^1, \boldsymbol{Y}^2, \ldots, \boldsymbol{Y}^\mu$.

1.15 SET OPERATIONS

In conventional treatments, such as Jacobson (1951) or Birkhoff and MacLane (1941), a *set* is defined as an unordered collection of distinct elements. A calculus of sets is then based on such elementary relations as set membership and on such elementary operations as *set intersection* and *set union*, none of which imply or depend on an ordering among members of a set. In the present context it is more fruitful to develop a calculus of *ordered sets*.

A vector whose components are all distinct has been called (Sec. 1.10) an *ordered set* and (since no other types are to be considered) will hereafter be called a *set*. In order to provide a closed system, all of the "set operations" will, in fact, be defined on vectors. However, the operations will, in the special case of sets, be analogous to classical set operations. The following vectors, the first four of which are sets, will be used for illustration throughout.

$$\boldsymbol{t} = (\text{t, e, a})$$
$$\boldsymbol{a} = (\text{a, t, e})$$
$$\boldsymbol{s} = (\text{s, a, t, e, d})$$
$$\boldsymbol{d} = (\text{d, u, s, k})$$
$$\boldsymbol{n} = (\text{n, o, n, s, e, t})$$
$$\boldsymbol{r} = (\text{r, e, d, u, n, d, a, n, t})$$

A variable z is a *member* of a vector $\boldsymbol{x}$ if $z = \boldsymbol{x}_i$ for some i. Membership is denoted by $z \in \boldsymbol{x}$. A vector $\boldsymbol{x}$ *includes* a vector $\boldsymbol{y}$ (denoted by either

$\boldsymbol{x} \supseteq \boldsymbol{y}$ or $\boldsymbol{y} \subseteq \boldsymbol{x}$) if each element y_i is a member of $\boldsymbol{x}$. If both $\boldsymbol{x} \supseteq \boldsymbol{y}$ and $\boldsymbol{x} \subseteq \boldsymbol{y}$, then $\boldsymbol{x}$ and $\boldsymbol{y}$ are said to be *similar*. Similarity of $\boldsymbol{x}$ and $\boldsymbol{y}$ is denoted by $\boldsymbol{x} \equiv \boldsymbol{y}$. For example, $\boldsymbol{t} \subseteq \boldsymbol{s}$, $\boldsymbol{t} \subseteq \boldsymbol{r}$, $\boldsymbol{t} \subseteq \boldsymbol{a}$, $\boldsymbol{a} \subseteq \boldsymbol{t}$, $\boldsymbol{t} \equiv \boldsymbol{a}$, and $\boldsymbol{t} \not\equiv \boldsymbol{r}$. If $\boldsymbol{x} \subseteq \boldsymbol{y}$ and $\boldsymbol{x} \not\equiv \boldsymbol{y}$, then $\boldsymbol{x}$ is *strictly* included in $\boldsymbol{y}$. Strict inclusion is denoted by $\boldsymbol{x} \subset \boldsymbol{y}$.

The *characteristic vector* of $\boldsymbol{x}$ on $\boldsymbol{y}$ is a logical vector denoted by $\boldsymbol{\epsilon}_y^{\,x}$, and defined as follows:

$$\boldsymbol{u} = \boldsymbol{\epsilon}_y^{\,x} \Leftrightarrow \nu(\boldsymbol{u}) = \nu(\boldsymbol{y}), \text{ and } u_j = (y_j \in \boldsymbol{x}).$$

For example, $\boldsymbol{\epsilon}_s^{\,t} = (0, 1, 1, 1, 0)$, $\boldsymbol{\epsilon}_t^{\,s} = (1, 1, 1)$, $\boldsymbol{\epsilon}_s^{\,d} = (1, 0, 0, 0, 1)$, $\boldsymbol{\epsilon}_d^{\,s} = (1, 0, 1, 0)$, and $\boldsymbol{\epsilon}_n^{\,r} = (1, 0, 1, 0, 1, 1)$.

The intersection of $\boldsymbol{y}$ with $\boldsymbol{x}$ is denoted by $\boldsymbol{y} \cap \boldsymbol{x}$, and defined as follows:

$$\boldsymbol{y} \cap \boldsymbol{x} = \boldsymbol{\epsilon}_y^{\,x}/\boldsymbol{y}.$$

For example, $\boldsymbol{s} \cap \boldsymbol{d} = (\text{s, d})$, $\boldsymbol{d} \cap \boldsymbol{s} = (\text{d, s})$, $\boldsymbol{s} \cap \boldsymbol{r} = (\text{a, t, e, d})$ and $\boldsymbol{r} \cap \boldsymbol{s} = (\text{e, d, d, a, t})$. Clearly, $\boldsymbol{x} \cap \boldsymbol{y} \equiv \boldsymbol{y} \cap \boldsymbol{x}$, although $\boldsymbol{x} \cap \boldsymbol{y}$ is not, in general, equal to $\boldsymbol{y} \cap \boldsymbol{x}$, since the components may occur in a different order and may be repeated a differing number of times. The vector $\boldsymbol{x} \cap \boldsymbol{y}$ is said to be *ordered* on $\boldsymbol{x}$. Thus $\boldsymbol{a}$ is ordered on $\boldsymbol{s}$. If $\boldsymbol{x}$ and $\boldsymbol{y}$ contain no common elements (that is, $(\boldsymbol{x} \cap \boldsymbol{y}) = \boldsymbol{\epsilon}(0)$), they are said to be *disjoint*.

The *set difference* of $\boldsymbol{y}$ and $\boldsymbol{x}$ is denoted by $\boldsymbol{y} \,\Delta\, \boldsymbol{x}$ and defined as follows:

$$\boldsymbol{y} \,\Delta\, \boldsymbol{x} = \overline{\boldsymbol{\epsilon}}_y^{\,x}/\boldsymbol{y}.$$

Hence $\boldsymbol{y} \,\Delta\, \boldsymbol{x}$ is obtained from $\boldsymbol{y}$ by suppressing those components which belong to $\boldsymbol{x}$. For example, $\overline{\boldsymbol{\epsilon}}_s^{\,t} = (1, 0, 0, 0, 1)$ and $\boldsymbol{s} \,\Delta\, \boldsymbol{t} = (\text{s, d})$. Moreover, $\overline{\boldsymbol{\epsilon}}_t^{\,s} = (0, 0, 0)$ and $\boldsymbol{t} \,\Delta\, \boldsymbol{s} = \boldsymbol{\epsilon}(0)$.

The *union* of $\boldsymbol{y}$ and $\boldsymbol{x}$ is denoted by $\boldsymbol{y} \cup \boldsymbol{x}$ and defined as follows:* $\boldsymbol{y} \cup \boldsymbol{x} = \boldsymbol{y} \oplus (\boldsymbol{x} \,\Delta\, \boldsymbol{y})$. For example, $\boldsymbol{s} \cup \boldsymbol{d} = (\text{s, a, t, e, d, u, k})$, $\boldsymbol{d} \cup \boldsymbol{s} = (\text{d, u, s, k, a, t, e})$, $\boldsymbol{s} \cup \boldsymbol{a} = \boldsymbol{s} \cup \boldsymbol{t} = \boldsymbol{s}$, and $\boldsymbol{n} \cup \boldsymbol{t} = (\text{n, o, n, s, e, t, a})$. In general, $\boldsymbol{x} \cup \boldsymbol{y} \equiv \boldsymbol{y} \cup \boldsymbol{x}$, and $\boldsymbol{x} \equiv (\boldsymbol{x} \cap \boldsymbol{y}) \cup (\boldsymbol{x} \,\Delta\, \boldsymbol{y})$. If $\boldsymbol{x}$ and $\boldsymbol{y}$ are disjoint, their union is equivalent to their catenation, that is, $\boldsymbol{x} \cap \boldsymbol{y} = \boldsymbol{\epsilon}(0)$ implies that $\boldsymbol{x} \cup \boldsymbol{y} = \boldsymbol{x} \oplus \boldsymbol{y}$.

In the foregoing development, the concepts of inclusion and similarity are equivalent to the concepts of inclusion and equality in the conventional treatment of (unordered) sets. The remaining definitions of intersection, difference, and union differ from the usual formulation in that the result of any of these operations on a pair of ordered sets is again an *ordered* set. With respect to *similarity*, these operations satisfy the same identities as do the analogous conventional set operations on unordered sets with respect to equality.

* The symbols $\cup$ and $\cap$ (and the operations they denote) are commonly called *cup* and *cap*, respectively.

The forward selection $\sigma/\boldsymbol{b}$ and the backward selection $\tau/\boldsymbol{b}$ defined in Sec. 1.10 can both be used to reduce any vector $\boldsymbol{b}$ to a similar set, that is,

$$(\sigma/\boldsymbol{b})/\boldsymbol{b} \equiv (\tau/\boldsymbol{b})/\boldsymbol{b} \equiv \boldsymbol{b}.$$

Moreover, if $\boldsymbol{f} = (\sigma/\boldsymbol{x})/\boldsymbol{x}$, $\boldsymbol{g} = (\sigma/\boldsymbol{y})/\boldsymbol{y}$, and $\boldsymbol{h} = (\sigma/\boldsymbol{z})/\boldsymbol{z}$, then $\boldsymbol{x} = \boldsymbol{y} \cap \boldsymbol{z}$ implies that $\boldsymbol{f} = \boldsymbol{g} \cap \boldsymbol{h}$, and $\boldsymbol{x} = \boldsymbol{y} \cup \boldsymbol{z}$ implies that $\boldsymbol{f} = \boldsymbol{g} \cup \boldsymbol{h}$.

The unit vector $\boldsymbol{\epsilon}^j(n)$ will be recognized as a special case of the characteristic vector $\boldsymbol{\epsilon}_y^x$ in which $\boldsymbol{x}$ consists of the single component j, and $\boldsymbol{y} = \boldsymbol{\iota}^h(n)$, where h is the index origin in use. In fact, the notation $\boldsymbol{\epsilon}^j_{\iota^h}$ can be used to make explicit the index origin h assumed for $\boldsymbol{\epsilon}^j$.

If $\boldsymbol{z}$ is any vector of dimension two such that $\boldsymbol{z}_1 \in \boldsymbol{x}$ and $\boldsymbol{z}_2 \in \boldsymbol{y}$, then $\boldsymbol{z}$ is said to belong to the *Cartesian product* of $\boldsymbol{x}$ and $\boldsymbol{y}$. Thus if $\boldsymbol{x} = (\text{a, b, c})$ and $\boldsymbol{y} = (0, 1)$, the rows of the matrix

$$A = \begin{pmatrix} \text{a} & 0 \\ \text{a} & 1 \\ \text{b} & 0 \\ \text{b} & 1 \\ \text{c} & 0 \\ \text{c} & 1 \end{pmatrix}$$

are a complete list of the vectors $\boldsymbol{z}$ belonging to the product set of $\boldsymbol{x}$ and $\boldsymbol{y}$. The matrix A will be called the Cartesian product of $\boldsymbol{x}$ and $\boldsymbol{y}$ and will be denoted by $\boldsymbol{x} \otimes \boldsymbol{y}$.

The foregoing definition by example will be formalized in a more general way that admits the Cartesian product of several vectors (that is, $\boldsymbol{u} \otimes \boldsymbol{v} \otimes \cdots \otimes \boldsymbol{y}$) which need not be sets, and which specifies a unique ordering of the rows of the resulting matrix. Consider a family of vectors $\boldsymbol{x}^1, \boldsymbol{x}^2, \ldots, \boldsymbol{x}^s$ of dimensions $\boldsymbol{d}_1, \boldsymbol{d}_2, \ldots, \boldsymbol{d}_s$. Then

$$A \leftarrow \boldsymbol{x}^1 \otimes \boldsymbol{x}^2 \otimes \cdots \otimes \boldsymbol{x}^s \Leftrightarrow A^{1+\boldsymbol{d}\perp(\boldsymbol{k}-\boldsymbol{\epsilon})} = (\boldsymbol{x}^1_{\boldsymbol{k}_1}, \boldsymbol{x}^2_{\boldsymbol{k}_2}, \ldots, \boldsymbol{x}^s_{\boldsymbol{k}_s}),$$

for all vectors $\boldsymbol{k}$ such that $1 \leq \boldsymbol{k}_i \leq \boldsymbol{d}_i$. Clearly $\nu(A) = s$, and $\mu(A) = \times/\boldsymbol{d}$. As illustrated by Table 1.11, the rows of the Cartesian product A are not distinct if any one of the vectors $\boldsymbol{x}^i$ is not a set.

If the vectors $\boldsymbol{x}^i$ are all of the same dimension, they may be considered as the columns of a matrix $\boldsymbol{X}$, that is, $\boldsymbol{X}_i = \boldsymbol{x}^i$. The product $\boldsymbol{x}^1 \otimes \boldsymbol{x}^2 \otimes \cdots \otimes \boldsymbol{x}^s = \boldsymbol{X}_1 \otimes \boldsymbol{X}_2 \otimes \cdots \otimes \boldsymbol{X}_s$ may then be denoted by $\otimes/\boldsymbol{X}$, or alternatively by $\otimes//\boldsymbol{Y}$, where $\boldsymbol{Y}$ is the transpose of $\boldsymbol{X}$. For example, if

$$\boldsymbol{X} = \boldsymbol{\iota}^0(2) \mathbin{\overset{\circ}{\wedge}} \boldsymbol{\epsilon}(3) = \begin{pmatrix} 0 & 0 & 0 \\ 1 & 1 & 1 \end{pmatrix},$$

then $\otimes/\boldsymbol{X}$ is the matrix of arguments of the truth table for three variables.

$$\begin{aligned} \boldsymbol{x}^1 &= (\text{a, b, a}) \\ \boldsymbol{x}^2 &= (\#, *) \\ \boldsymbol{x}^3 &= (0, 1) \\ \boldsymbol{d} &= (3, 2, 2) \end{aligned} \qquad \boldsymbol{A} = \begin{pmatrix} \text{a} & \# & 0 \\ \text{a} & \# & 1 \\ \text{a} & * & 0 \\ \text{a} & * & 1 \\ \text{b} & \# & 0 \\ \text{b} & \# & 1 \\ \text{b} & * & 0 \\ \text{b} & * & 1 \\ \text{a} & \# & 0 \\ \text{a} & \# & 1 \\ \text{a} & * & 0 \\ \text{a} & * & 1 \end{pmatrix}$$

Table 1.11 The Cartesian product $\boldsymbol{A} = \boldsymbol{x}^1 \otimes \boldsymbol{x}^2 \otimes \boldsymbol{x}^3$

1.16 RANKING

The *rank* or *index* of an element $c \in \boldsymbol{b}$ is called the $\boldsymbol{b}$ *index of* c and is defined as the smallest value of i such that $c = \boldsymbol{b}_i$. To establish a closed system, the $\boldsymbol{b}$ index of any element $a \notin \boldsymbol{b}$ will be defined as the null character $\circ$. The $\boldsymbol{b}$ index of any element c will be denoted by $\boldsymbol{b}\, \iota\, c$; if necessary, the index origin in use will be indicated by a subscript appended to the operator ι. Thus, if $\boldsymbol{b} = (\text{a, p, e})$, $\boldsymbol{b}\, \iota_0\, \text{p} = 1$, and $\boldsymbol{b}\, \iota_1\, \text{p} = 2$.

The $\boldsymbol{b}$ index of a vector $\boldsymbol{c}$ is defined as follows:

$$\boldsymbol{k} \leftarrow \boldsymbol{b}\, \iota\, \boldsymbol{c} \Leftrightarrow \boldsymbol{k}_i = \boldsymbol{b}\, \iota\, \boldsymbol{c}_i.$$

The extension to matrices may be either row by row or (as indicated by a doubled operator symbol $\iota\iota$) column by column, as follows:

$$\boldsymbol{J} \leftarrow \boldsymbol{B}\, \iota\, \boldsymbol{C} \Leftrightarrow \boldsymbol{J}^i = \boldsymbol{B}^i\, \iota\, \boldsymbol{C}^i,$$

$$\boldsymbol{K} \leftarrow \boldsymbol{B}\, \iota\iota\, \boldsymbol{C} \Leftrightarrow \boldsymbol{K}_j = \boldsymbol{B}_j\, \iota\, \boldsymbol{C}_j.$$

Use of the ranking operator in a matrix product requires no secondary scan and is therefore indicated by a superior null symbol. Moreover, since the result must be limited to a two-dimensional array (matrix), either the pre- or post-operand is required to be a vector. Hence

$$\boldsymbol{J} \leftarrow \boldsymbol{B} \overset{\circ}{\iota} \boldsymbol{c} \Leftrightarrow \boldsymbol{J}^i = \boldsymbol{B}^i\, \iota\, \boldsymbol{c},$$

$$\boldsymbol{K} \leftarrow \boldsymbol{b} \overset{\circ}{\iota} \boldsymbol{C} \Leftrightarrow \boldsymbol{K}_j = \boldsymbol{b}\, \iota\, \boldsymbol{C}_j.$$

The first of these ranks the components of $\boldsymbol{c}$ with respect to each of a set of vectors $\boldsymbol{B}^1, \boldsymbol{B}^2, \ldots, \boldsymbol{B}^\mu$, whereas the second ranks each of the vectors $\boldsymbol{C}_1, \boldsymbol{C}_2, \ldots, \boldsymbol{C}_\nu$ with respect to the fixed vector $\boldsymbol{b}$.

The use of the ranking operation can be illustrated as follows. Consider the vector $\boldsymbol{b} = (\text{a, b, c, d, e})$ and the set of all 3^5 three-letter sequences (vectors) formed from its components. If the set is ordered lexically, and if $\boldsymbol{x}$ is the ith member of the set (counting from zero), then

$$j = (\nu(\boldsymbol{b})\boldsymbol{\epsilon}) \perp (\boldsymbol{b} \,\iota_0\, \boldsymbol{x}).$$

For example, if $\boldsymbol{x} = (\text{c, a, b})$, then $(\boldsymbol{b} \,\iota_0\, \boldsymbol{x}) = (2, 0, 1)$, and $j = 51$.

1.17 MAPPING AND PERMUTATIONS

Reordering operations

The selection operations employed thus far do not permit convenient reorderings of the components. This is provided by the *mapping* operation defined as follows:*

$$\boldsymbol{c} \leftarrow \boldsymbol{a}_{\boldsymbol{k}} \Leftrightarrow c_i = a_{k_i}.$$

For example, if $\boldsymbol{a} = (\text{a, b}, \ldots, \text{z})$ and $\boldsymbol{k} = (6, 5, 4)$, then $\boldsymbol{c} = (\text{f, e, d})$.

The foregoing definition is meaningful only if the components of $\boldsymbol{k}$ each lie in the range of the indices of $\boldsymbol{a}$, and it will be extended by defining $\boldsymbol{a}_j$ as the null element $\circ$ if j does not belong to the index set of $\boldsymbol{a}$. Formally,

$$\boldsymbol{c} \leftarrow \boldsymbol{a}_{\boldsymbol{m}} \Leftrightarrow c_i = \begin{cases} a_{m_i} & \text{if } m_i \in \boldsymbol{\iota}^1(\nu(\boldsymbol{a})) \\ \circ & \text{if } m_i \notin \boldsymbol{\iota}^1(\nu(\boldsymbol{a})). \end{cases}$$

The ability to specify an arbitrary index origin for the vector $\boldsymbol{a}$ being mapped is provided by the following alternative notation for mapping:

$$\boldsymbol{c} \leftarrow \boldsymbol{m} \int_j \boldsymbol{a} \Leftrightarrow c_i = \begin{cases} a_{m_i} & \text{if } m_i \in \boldsymbol{\iota}^j(\nu(\boldsymbol{a})) \\ \circ & \text{if } m_i \notin \boldsymbol{\iota}^j(\nu(\boldsymbol{a})), \end{cases}$$

where j-origin indexing is assumed for the vector $\boldsymbol{a}$. For example, if $\boldsymbol{a}$ is the alphabet and $\boldsymbol{m} = (5, \circ, \circ, 4, 27, \circ, 3)$, then $\boldsymbol{c} = \boldsymbol{m} \int_0 \boldsymbol{a} = (\text{f}, \circ, \circ, \text{e}, \circ, \circ, \text{d})$, and $(\boldsymbol{c} \neq \circ\boldsymbol{\epsilon})/\boldsymbol{c} = (\text{f, e, d})$. Moreover, $\boldsymbol{m} \int_2 \boldsymbol{a} = (\text{d}, \circ, \circ, \text{c}, \text{z}, \circ, \text{b})$. Elision of j is permitted.

If $\boldsymbol{a} \subseteq \boldsymbol{b}$, and $\boldsymbol{m} = \boldsymbol{b} \,\iota_j\, \boldsymbol{a}$, then clearly $\boldsymbol{m} \int_j \boldsymbol{b} = \boldsymbol{a}$. If $\boldsymbol{a} \not\subseteq \boldsymbol{b}$, then $\boldsymbol{m} \int_j \boldsymbol{b}$ contains (in addition to certain nulls) those components common to $\boldsymbol{b}$ and $\boldsymbol{a}$, arranged in the order in which they occur in $\boldsymbol{a}$. In other words,

$$(\boldsymbol{m} \neq \circ\boldsymbol{\epsilon})/(\boldsymbol{m} \int_j \boldsymbol{b}) = \boldsymbol{a} \cap \boldsymbol{b}.$$

* For the purposes of describing algorithms, this notation is superior to the classical "disjoint cycles" notation for permutations [cf. Birkhoff and MacLane, (1941)] because (1) the direction of the transformation (from $\boldsymbol{a}$ to $\boldsymbol{c}$) is unequivocally indicated, and (2) the notation directly indicates a straightforward and efficient method for actual execution, namely, indirect addressing.

Consequently, if $\boldsymbol{p}, \boldsymbol{q}, \ldots, \boldsymbol{t}$ are vectors, each contained in $\boldsymbol{b}$, then each can be represented jointly by the vector $\boldsymbol{b}$ and a mapping vector. If, for example, $\boldsymbol{b}$ is a glossary and $\boldsymbol{p}$, $\boldsymbol{q}$, etc., are texts, the total storage required for $\boldsymbol{b}$ and the mapping vectors might be considerably less than for the entire set of texts.

Mapping may be shown to be associative, that is, $\boldsymbol{m}^1 \int_i (\boldsymbol{m}^2 \int_j \boldsymbol{a}) = (\boldsymbol{m}^1 \int_i \boldsymbol{m}^2) \int_j \boldsymbol{a}$. Mapping is not, in general, commutative.

Mapping is extended to matrices as follows:

$$\boldsymbol{A} \leftarrow \boldsymbol{M} \int_h \boldsymbol{B} \Leftrightarrow \boldsymbol{A}^i = \boldsymbol{M}^i \int_h \boldsymbol{B}^i,$$

$$\boldsymbol{C} \leftarrow \boldsymbol{M} \int\!\!\int_h \boldsymbol{B} \Leftrightarrow \boldsymbol{C}_j = \boldsymbol{M}_j \int_h \boldsymbol{B}_j.$$

Row and column mappings are associative. A row mapping ${}^1\boldsymbol{M}$ and a column mapping ${}^2\boldsymbol{M}$ do not, in general, commute, but do if all rows of ${}^1\boldsymbol{M}$ agree (that is, ${}^1\boldsymbol{M} = \boldsymbol{\epsilon} \overset{\circ}{\times} \boldsymbol{p}$), and if all columns of ${}^2\boldsymbol{M}$ agree (that is, ${}^2\boldsymbol{M} = \boldsymbol{q} \overset{\circ}{\times} \boldsymbol{\epsilon}$). The generalized matrix product is defined for the cases $\boldsymbol{m} \overset{\circ}{\int} \boldsymbol{A}$, and $\boldsymbol{M} \overset{\circ}{\int} \boldsymbol{a}$.

The alternative notation (that is, $\boldsymbol{c} = \boldsymbol{a}_{\boldsymbol{m}}$), which does not incorporate specification of the index origin, is particularly convenient for matrices and is extended as follows:

$$\boldsymbol{A} \leftarrow \boldsymbol{B}^{\boldsymbol{m}} \Leftrightarrow \boldsymbol{A}^i = \boldsymbol{B}^{\boldsymbol{m}_i},$$

$$\boldsymbol{A} \leftarrow \boldsymbol{B}_{\boldsymbol{m}} \Leftrightarrow \boldsymbol{A}_i = \boldsymbol{B}_{\boldsymbol{m}_i}.$$

Permutations

A vector $\boldsymbol{k}$ of dimension n is called a j-origin *permutation vector* if $\boldsymbol{k} \equiv \boldsymbol{\iota}^j(n)$. A permutation vector used to map any set of the same dimension produces a reordering of the set without either repetition or suppression of elements, that is, $\boldsymbol{k} \int_j \boldsymbol{a} \equiv \boldsymbol{a}$ for any set $\boldsymbol{a}$ of dimension $\nu(\boldsymbol{k})$. For example, if $\boldsymbol{a} = (\text{f}, 4, *, 6, \text{z})$, and $\boldsymbol{k} = (4, 2, 5, 1, 3)$, then $\boldsymbol{k} \int_1 \boldsymbol{a} = (6, 4, \text{z}, \text{f}, *)$.

If $\boldsymbol{p}$ is an h-origin permutation vector and $\boldsymbol{q}$ is any j-origin permutation vector of the same dimension, then $\boldsymbol{q} \int_j \boldsymbol{p}$ is an h-origin permutation vector.

Since

$$\boldsymbol{\iota}^j(\nu(\boldsymbol{a})) \int_j \boldsymbol{a} = \boldsymbol{a},$$

the interval vector $\boldsymbol{\iota}^j(n)$ will also be called the *j-origin identity permutation vector*. If $\boldsymbol{p}$ and $\boldsymbol{q}$ are two j-origin permutation vectors of the same dimension n and if $\boldsymbol{q} \int_j \boldsymbol{p} = \boldsymbol{\iota}^j(n)$, then $\boldsymbol{p} \int_j \boldsymbol{q} = \boldsymbol{\iota}^j(n)$ also and $\boldsymbol{p}$ and $\boldsymbol{q}$ are said to be *inverse* permutations. If $\boldsymbol{p}$ is any j-origin permutation vector, then $\boldsymbol{q} = \boldsymbol{p}\, \iota_j\, \boldsymbol{\iota}^j$ is inverse to $\boldsymbol{p}$.

The rotation operation $k \uparrow \boldsymbol{x}$ is a special case of permutation.

Function mapping

A function f which defines for each element $\boldsymbol{b}_i$ of a set $\boldsymbol{b}$ a unique correspondent $\boldsymbol{a}_k$ in a set $\boldsymbol{a}$ is called a *mapping from* $\boldsymbol{b}$ *to* $\boldsymbol{a}$. If $f(\boldsymbol{b}_i) = \boldsymbol{a}_k$, the element $\boldsymbol{b}_i$ is said to *map into* the element $\boldsymbol{a}_k$. If the elements $f(\boldsymbol{b}_i)$ exhaust the set $\boldsymbol{a}$, the function f is said to map $\boldsymbol{b}$ *onto* $\boldsymbol{a}$. If $\boldsymbol{b}$ maps onto $\boldsymbol{a}$ and the elements $f(\boldsymbol{b}_i)$ are all distinct, the mapping is said to be one-to-one or *biunique*. In this case, $\nu(\boldsymbol{a}) = \nu(\boldsymbol{b})$, and there exists an inverse mapping from $\boldsymbol{a}$ to $\boldsymbol{b}$ with the same correspondences.

A program for performing the mapping f from $\boldsymbol{b}$ to $\boldsymbol{a}$ must therefore determine for any given element $b \in \boldsymbol{b}$, the correspondent $a \in \boldsymbol{a}$, such that $a = f(b)$. Because of the convenience of operating upon integers (e.g., upon register addresses or other numeric symbols) in the automatic execution of programs, the mapping is frequently performed in three successive phases, determining in turn the following quantities:

1. the index $i = \boldsymbol{b}\ \iota\ b$,
2. the index k such that $\boldsymbol{a}_k = f(\boldsymbol{b}_i)$,
3. the element $\boldsymbol{a}_k$.

The three phases are shown in detail in Program 1.12*a*. The ranking is performed (steps 1–3) by scanning the set $\boldsymbol{b}$ in order and comparing each element with the argument b. The second phase is a permutation of the integers 1, 2, . . . , $\nu(\boldsymbol{b})$, which may be described by a permutation vector $\boldsymbol{j}$, such that $\boldsymbol{j}_i = k$. The selection of $\boldsymbol{j}_i$ (step 4) then defines k, which, in turn, determines the selection of $\boldsymbol{a}_k$ on step 5.

Example 1.2. If

$$\boldsymbol{b} = (\text{apple, booty, dust, eye, night}),$$
$$\boldsymbol{a} = (\text{Apfel, Auge, Beute, Nacht, Staub})$$

are, respectively, a set of English words and a set of German correspondents (both in alphabetical order), and if the function required is the mapping of a given English word b into its German equivalent a according to the dictionary correspondences:

English:	apple	booty	dust	eye	night
German:	Apfel	Beute	Staub	Auge	Nacht

then $\boldsymbol{j} = (1, 3, 5, 2, 4)$. If $\boldsymbol{b}$ = "night," then $i = 5$, $\boldsymbol{j}_i = 4$, and $a = \boldsymbol{a}_4$ = Nacht.

If $\boldsymbol{k}$ is a permutation vector inverse to $\boldsymbol{j}$, then Program 1.12*b* describes a mapping inverse to that of Program 1.12*a*. If $\boldsymbol{j} = (1, 3, 5, 2, 4)$, then $\boldsymbol{k} = (1, 4, 2, 5, 3)$. The inverse mapping can also be described in terms of $\boldsymbol{j}$, as is done in Program 1.12*c*. The selection of the ith component of the permutation vector is then necessarily replaced by a scan of its components. Programs 1.12*d* and 1.12*e* show alternative formulations of Program 1.12*a*.

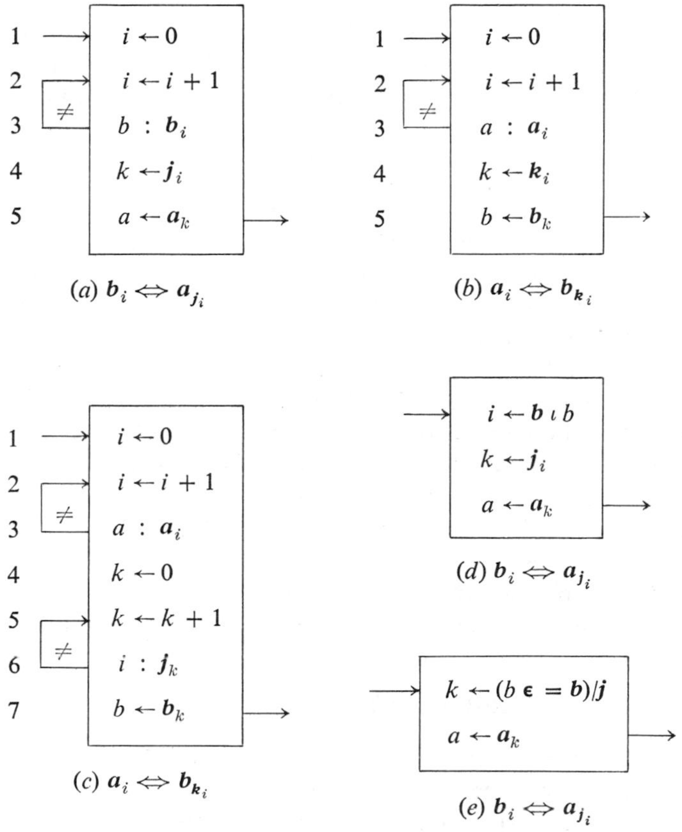

$\boldsymbol{a}$	Set of correspondents in Programs (a, d, e) and set of arguments in Programs (b, c).
$\boldsymbol{b}$	Set of arguments in Programs (a, d, e) and set of correspondents in Programs (b, c).
$\boldsymbol{j}, \boldsymbol{k}$	Mutually inverse permutation vectors.

Legend

Program 1.12 Mapping defined by a permutation vector $\boldsymbol{j}$

Ordering vector

If $\boldsymbol{x}$ is a numeric vector and $\boldsymbol{k}$ is a j-origin permutation vector such that the components of $\boldsymbol{y} = \boldsymbol{k} \int_j \boldsymbol{x}$ are in ascending order, then $\boldsymbol{k}$ is said to *order* $\boldsymbol{x}$. The vector $\boldsymbol{k}$ can be determined by an ordering operation defined as follows:

$$\boldsymbol{k} \leftarrow \theta_j / \boldsymbol{x}$$

implies that $\boldsymbol{k}$ is a j-origin permutation vector, and that if $\boldsymbol{y} = \boldsymbol{k} \int_j \boldsymbol{x}$, then either $y_i < y_{i+1}$ or $y_i = y_{i+1}$ and $k_i < k_{i+1}$. The resulting vector $\boldsymbol{k}$ is unique and preserves the original relative order among equal components. For example, if $\boldsymbol{x} = (7, 3, 5, 3)$, then $\theta_1/\boldsymbol{x} = (2, 4, 3, 1)$.

The ordering operation is extended to arbitrary vectors by treating all nonnumeric quantities as equal and as greater than any numeric quantity. For example, if $\boldsymbol{a} = (7, \circ, 3, \circ, 5, 3)$, then $\theta_1/\boldsymbol{a} = (3, 6, 5, 1, 2, 4)$, and if $\boldsymbol{b}$ is any vector with no numerical components, then $\theta_j/\boldsymbol{b} = \boldsymbol{\iota}^j(\nu(\boldsymbol{b}))$.

Ordering of a vector $\boldsymbol{a}$ with respect to a vector $\boldsymbol{b}$ is achieved by ordering the $\boldsymbol{b}$-index of $\boldsymbol{a}$. For example, if $\boldsymbol{a} = $ (e, a, s, t, 4, 7, t, h), and $\boldsymbol{b}$ is the alphabet, then $\boldsymbol{m} = \boldsymbol{b}\ \iota_1\ \boldsymbol{a} = (5, 1, 19, 20, \circ, \circ, 20, 8)$ and $\theta_1/\boldsymbol{m} = (2, 1, 8, 3, 4, 7, 5, 6)$.

The ordering operation is extended to matrices by the usual convention. If $\boldsymbol{K} = \theta_j // \boldsymbol{A}$, then each column of the matrix $\boldsymbol{B} = \boldsymbol{K} \int\!\!\int_j \boldsymbol{A}$ is in ascending order.

1.18 MAXIMIZATION

In determining the maximum m over components of a numerical vector $\boldsymbol{x}$, it is often necessary to determine the indices of the maximum components as well. The maximization operator is therefore defined so as to determine a logical vector $\boldsymbol{v}$ such that $\boldsymbol{v}/\boldsymbol{x} = m\boldsymbol{\epsilon}$.

Maximization over the entire vector $\boldsymbol{x}$ is denoted by $\boldsymbol{\epsilon}\lceil \boldsymbol{x}$, and is defined as follows: if $\boldsymbol{v} = \boldsymbol{\epsilon}\lceil \boldsymbol{x}$, then there exists a quantity m such that $\boldsymbol{v}/\boldsymbol{x} = m\boldsymbol{\epsilon}$ and such that all components of $\overline{\boldsymbol{v}}/\boldsymbol{x}$ are strictly less than m. The maximum is assumed by a single component of $\boldsymbol{x}$ if and only if $+/\boldsymbol{v} = 1$. The actual value of the maximum is given by the first (or any) component of $\boldsymbol{v}/\boldsymbol{x}$. Moreover, the j-origin indices of the maximum components are the components of the vector $\boldsymbol{v}/\boldsymbol{\iota}^j$.

More generally, the maximization operation $\boldsymbol{v} \leftarrow \boldsymbol{u}\lceil \boldsymbol{x}$ will be defined so as to determine the maximum over the subvector $\boldsymbol{u}/\boldsymbol{x}$ only, but to express the result $\boldsymbol{v}$ with respect to the entire vector $\boldsymbol{x}$. More precisely,

$$\boldsymbol{v} \leftarrow \boldsymbol{u}\lceil \boldsymbol{x} \Leftrightarrow \boldsymbol{v} = \boldsymbol{u}\backslash(\boldsymbol{\epsilon}\lceil(\boldsymbol{u}/\boldsymbol{x})).$$

The operation may be visualized as follows—a horizontal plane punched at points corresponding to the zeros of $\boldsymbol{u}$ is lowered over a plot of the components of $\boldsymbol{x}$, and the positions at which the plane first touches them are the positions of the unit components of $\boldsymbol{v}$. For example, maximization over the negative components of $\boldsymbol{x}$ is denoted by

$$\boldsymbol{v} \leftarrow (\boldsymbol{x} < 0)\lceil \boldsymbol{x}$$

and if $\boldsymbol{x} = (2, -3, 7, -5, 4, -3, 6)$, then $(\boldsymbol{x} < 0) = (0, 1, 0, 1, 0, 1, 0)$, $\boldsymbol{v} = (0, 1, 0, 0, 0, 1, 0)$, $\boldsymbol{v}/\boldsymbol{x} = (-3, -3)$, $(\boldsymbol{v}/\boldsymbol{x})_1 = -3$, and $\boldsymbol{v}/\boldsymbol{\iota}^1 = (2, 6)$. Minimization is defined analogously and is denoted by $\boldsymbol{u}\lfloor \boldsymbol{x}$.

The extension of maximization and minimization to arbitrary vectors is the same as for the ordering operation, i.e., all nonnumeric quantities are treated as equal and as exceeding all numeric quantities. The extensions to matrices are denoted and defined as follows:

$$\boldsymbol{V} \leftarrow \boldsymbol{U} \lceil \boldsymbol{X} \Leftrightarrow \boldsymbol{V}^i = \boldsymbol{U}^i \lceil \boldsymbol{X}^i,$$
$$\boldsymbol{V} \leftarrow \boldsymbol{U} \lceil\!\lceil \boldsymbol{X} \Leftrightarrow \boldsymbol{V}_j = \boldsymbol{U}_j \lceil \boldsymbol{X}_j,$$
$$\boldsymbol{V} \leftarrow \boldsymbol{U} \overset{\circ}{\lceil} \boldsymbol{x} \Leftrightarrow \boldsymbol{V}^i = \boldsymbol{U}^i \lceil \boldsymbol{x},$$
$$\boldsymbol{V} \leftarrow \boldsymbol{u} \overset{\circ}{\lceil} \boldsymbol{X} \Leftrightarrow \boldsymbol{V}_j = \boldsymbol{u} \lceil \boldsymbol{X}_j.$$

As in the case of the ordering operation, maximization in a vector $\boldsymbol{a}$ with respect to order in a set $\boldsymbol{b}$ is achieved by maximizing over the $\boldsymbol{b}$-index of $\boldsymbol{a}$. Thus if

$$\boldsymbol{H} = \begin{pmatrix} \text{d c h d h s h d c h c h d} \\ \text{a 6 k q 4 3 5 k 8 2 j 9 2} \end{pmatrix}$$

represents a hand of thirteen playing cards, and if

$$\boldsymbol{B} = \begin{pmatrix} \text{c}, & \text{d}, & \text{h}, & \text{s}, & \circ, & \circ, & \circ, & \circ, & \circ, & \circ, & \circ, & \circ, & \circ \\ 2, & 3, & 4, & 5, & 6, & 7, & 8, & 9, & 10, & \text{j}, & \text{q}, & \text{k}, & \text{a} \end{pmatrix},$$

then

$$\boldsymbol{B}\, \iota_0\, \boldsymbol{H} = \begin{pmatrix} 1, & 0, & 2, & 1, & 2, & 3, & 2, & 1, & 0, & 2, & 0, & 2, & 1 \\ 12, & 4, & 11, & 10, & 2, & 1, & 3, & 11, & 6, & 0, & 9, & 7, & 0 \end{pmatrix},$$

$$(4, 13) \overset{\circ}{\perp} (\boldsymbol{B}\, \iota_0\, \boldsymbol{H}) = (25, 4, 37, 23, 28, 40, 29, 24, 6, 26, 9, 33, 13),$$

and

$$(\boldsymbol{\epsilon}\lceil((4, 13) \overset{\circ}{\perp} (\boldsymbol{B}\, \iota_0\, \boldsymbol{H})))/\boldsymbol{H} = (\text{s}, 3)$$

is the highest ranking card in the hand.

1.19 INVERSE FUNCTIONS

To every biunique* function f there corresponds an *inverse* function g such that $g(f(x)) = x$ for each argument x in the domain of the function f.

* If the function f is many-to-one, the specification of a unique inverse g is achieved by restricting the range of g to some set of "principal" values, as is done, for example, for the inverse trigonometric functions.

It is common practice either to introduce a distinct symbolism for the inverse function, as for the inverse functions of logarithm ($\log_b x$) and exponentiation (b^3), or to use a superscript -1, as in $\sin^{-1} x$ or $f^{-1}(x)$.

The first alternative doubles the number of distinct operator symbols required and obscures the relation between pairs of inverse functions; the second raises other difficulties. The solution adopted here is that of *implicit* specification; i.e., a statement is permitted to specify not only a variable but also any function of that variable. Functions may therefore appear on both sides of the specification arrow in a statement. For example,

$$(2\boldsymbol{\epsilon}) \perp \boldsymbol{x} \leftarrow z$$

specifies the variable $\boldsymbol{x}$ as the vector whose base two value is the number z.

Certain ambiguities remain in the foregoing statement. First, the dimension of $\boldsymbol{x}$ is not specified. For example, if $z = 12$, $\boldsymbol{x} = (1, 1, 0, 0)$ is an admissible solution, but so are $(0, 1, 1, 0, 0)$ and $(0, 0, 0, 1, 1, 0, 0)$. This could be clarified by compatibility with a specified dimension of $\boldsymbol{\epsilon}$. Thus the statement

$$(2\boldsymbol{\epsilon}(5)) \perp \boldsymbol{x} \leftarrow z$$

specifies $\boldsymbol{x}$ unambiguously as $(0, 1, 1, 0, 0)$. More generally, however, any previously specified auxiliary variables will be listed to the right of the main statement, with a semicolon serving as a separation symbol. The current example could therefore be written as

$$\nu(\boldsymbol{x}) \leftarrow 5$$

$$(2\boldsymbol{\epsilon}) \perp \boldsymbol{x} \leftarrow z; \quad \nu(\boldsymbol{x}).$$

The second ambiguity concerns the permissible range of the individual components of $\boldsymbol{x}$. For example, the base two value of $\boldsymbol{x} = (5, 2)$ is also twelve. For certain functions it is therefore necessary to adopt some obvious conventions concerning the range of the result. The assumption implicit in the preceding paragraph is that each component of $\boldsymbol{x}$ is limited to the range of the residues modulo the corresponding radix. This convention will be adopted. Hence the pair of statements

$$\boldsymbol{y} \leftarrow (7, 24, 60, 60)$$

$$\boldsymbol{y} \perp \boldsymbol{x} \leftarrow 7278; \quad \boldsymbol{y}$$

determines $\boldsymbol{x}$ unambiguously as the vector $(0, 2, 1, 18)$.

It is also convenient, though not essential, to use selection operations on the left of a statement. Thus the statement

$$\boldsymbol{u}/\boldsymbol{b} \leftarrow \boldsymbol{a}$$

is understood to respecify only the selected components of $\boldsymbol{b}$ and to leave all others unchanged. It is therefore equivalent to the statement

$$\boldsymbol{b} \leftarrow \backslash \overline{\boldsymbol{u}}/\boldsymbol{b}, \boldsymbol{u}, \boldsymbol{a}\backslash.$$

Similarly,

$$\boldsymbol{u}/\boldsymbol{b} \leftarrow \boldsymbol{u}/\boldsymbol{a}$$

is equivalent to

$$\boldsymbol{b} \leftarrow /\boldsymbol{b}, \boldsymbol{u}, \boldsymbol{a}/.$$

1.20 LEVELS OF STRUCTURE

Vectors and matrices are arrays which exhibit one level and two levels of structure, respectively. Although in certain fields, such as tensor analysis, it is convenient to define more general arrays whose *rank* specifies the number of levels of structure (i.e., zero for a scalar, one for a vector of scalars, two for a vector of vectors (matrix), three for a vector of matrices, etc.), the notation will here be limited to the two levels provided by the matrix.* The present section will, however, indicate methods for removing this limitation.

The only essential particularization to two levels occurs in the provision of single and double symbols (e.g., "/" and "//", "$\perp$" and "$\perp\!\!\perp$") for row and column operations, respectively, and in the use of superscripts and subscripts for denoting rows and columns, respectively. In applications requiring multiple levels, the former can be generalized by adjoining to the single symbol an index which specifies the coordinate (e.g., "$/_1$" and "$/_2$", for row and for column compression, and, in general, "$/_j$".) The latter can be generalized by using a vector index subscript possessing one component index for each coordinate.

The generalized notation can be made compatible with the present notation for vectors and matrices by adopting the name *tensor* and a symbol class (such as capital italics) for the general array of arbitrary rank.

1.21 SUBROUTINES

Detail can be subordinated in a more general manner by the use of subroutines. The name of one program appearing as a single statement in a second program implies execution of the named program at that point; the named program is called a *subroutine* of the second program. If, for example, "Cos" is the name of a program which specifies z as the cosine of

* Further levels can, of course, be handled by considering a family of matrices $^1\boldsymbol{M}$, $^2\boldsymbol{M}, \ldots, {}^n\boldsymbol{M}$, or families of families $_j^i\boldsymbol{M}$.

the angle between the vectors $\boldsymbol{x}$ and $\boldsymbol{y}$, then Program 1.13*a* uses the program "Cos" as a subroutine to determine r as the cosine of the angle between the vectors $\boldsymbol{p}$ and $\boldsymbol{q}$.

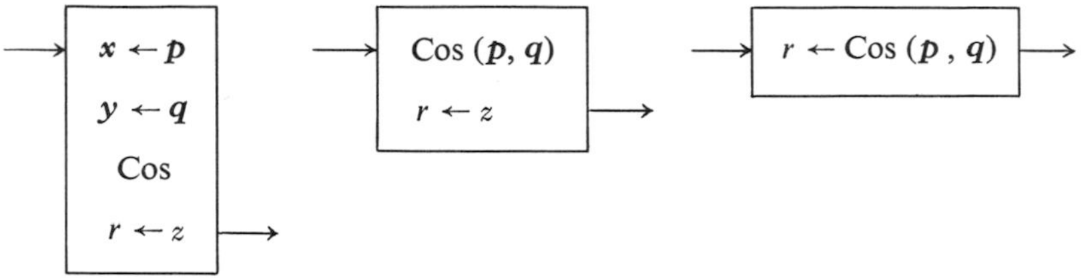

(*a*) (*b*) (*c*)

Program 1.13 Modes of subroutine reference

It is sometimes convenient to include the names of the arguments or results or both in the name of the subroutine as dummy variables. Thus if "Cos ($\boldsymbol{x}$, $\boldsymbol{y}$)" is the name of a subroutine which determines z as the cosine of the angle between $\boldsymbol{x}$ and $\boldsymbol{y}$, then Program 1.13*b* uses Cos ($\boldsymbol{x}$, $\boldsymbol{y}$) as a subroutine to determine r as the cosine of the angle between $\boldsymbol{p}$ and $\boldsymbol{q}$. Similarly, the program "$z \leftarrow$ Cos ($\boldsymbol{x}$, $\boldsymbol{y}$)" can be used as in Program 1.13*c* to produce the same result.

1.22 FILES

Many devices used for the storage of information impose certain restrictions upon its insertion or withdrawal. The items recorded on a magnetic tape, for example, may be read from the tape much more quickly in the order in which they appear physically on the tape than in some other prescribed order.

Certain storage devices are also self-indexing in the sense that the item selected in the next read from the device will be determined by the current state or position of the device. The next item read from a magnetic tape, for example, is determined by the position in which the tape was left by the last preceding read operation.

To allow the convenient description of algorithms constrained by the characteristics of storage devices, the following notation will be adopted. A *file* is a representation of a vector $\boldsymbol{x}$ arranged as follows:

$$p_1, x_1, p_2, x_2, \ldots, x_{\nu(\boldsymbol{x})}, p_{\nu(\boldsymbol{x})+1}, \circ, p_{\nu(\boldsymbol{x})+2}, \circ, \ldots, p_{\nu(\boldsymbol{p})}.$$

The null elements denote the "unused" portion of the file not employed in representing $\boldsymbol{x}$. Each *partition* $\boldsymbol{p}_j$ determines a *position* (position j) in the file. If a file Φ is in position j, then a *forward read*, denoted by

$$x, p \leftarrow {}_0\Phi,$$

specifies x by the component $\boldsymbol{x}_j$, the auxiliary variable p by the succeeding partition $\boldsymbol{p}_{j+1}$, and stops the file in the position $j + 1$.

The position of a file Φ will be denoted by $\pi(\Phi)$. Thus the statement $j \leftarrow \pi(\Phi)$ specifies j as the position of Φ, whereas $\pi(\Phi) \leftarrow j$ *positions* the file to j. In particular, $\pi(\Phi) \leftarrow 1$ denotes the *rewinding* of the file and $\pi(\Phi) \leftarrow \nu$ denotes *winding*, i.e., positioning to the extreme end of the file. Any file for which the general positioning operation $\pi(\Phi) \leftarrow j$ is to be avoided as impossible or inefficient is called a *serial* or *serial-access* file.

Each terminal partition (that is, $\boldsymbol{p}_1$ and $\boldsymbol{p}_{\nu(\boldsymbol{p})}$) assumes a single fixed value denoted by λ. Each nonterminal partition $\boldsymbol{p}_j$ may assume one of several values denoted by $\boldsymbol{\lambda}_1, \boldsymbol{\lambda}_2, \ldots, \boldsymbol{\lambda}_{\nu(\boldsymbol{\lambda})}$, the partitions with larger indices normally demarking larger subgroups of components within the file. Thus if $\boldsymbol{x}$ were the row list of a matrix, the last component might be followed by the partition $\boldsymbol{\lambda}_3$, the last component of each of the preceding rows by $\boldsymbol{\lambda}_2$, and the remaining components by $\boldsymbol{\lambda}_1$. The auxiliary variable p specified by the partition symbol during the read of a file is normally used to control a subsequent branch.

A file may be produced by a sequence of *forward record* statements:

$${}_0\Phi \leftarrow \boldsymbol{x}_i, p \qquad \text{for } i \in \boldsymbol{\iota}^1(\nu(\boldsymbol{x})),$$

where p is the partition symbol recorded after the component $\boldsymbol{x}_j$. As in reading, each forward record operation increments the position of the file by one. A file which is only recorded during a process is called an *output file* of the process; a file which is only read is called an *input file*.

Different files occurring in a process will be distinguished by righthand subscripts and superscripts, the latter being usually employed to denote major classes of files, such as input and output.

Example 1.3. A set of m input files $\Phi_i^{\,1}$, $i \in \boldsymbol{\iota}^1(m)$, each terminated by a partition $\boldsymbol{\lambda}_2$, is to be copied to a single output file $\Phi_1^{\,2}$ as follows. Successive items (components) are chosen in turn from files $\Phi_1^{\,1}, \Phi_2^{\,1}, \ldots, \Phi_m^{\,1}, \Phi_1^{\,1}, \Phi_2^{\,1}, \ldots$, always omitting from the sequence any exhausted file. A partition $\boldsymbol{\lambda}_2$ is to be recorded with the last item recorded on $\Phi_1^{\,2}$, and all files are to be rewound. The process is described by Program 1.14.

Program 1.14. Step 8 cycles k through the values 1 to m, and step 9 allows the read on step 10 to occur only if $\boldsymbol{u}_k = 0$. The logical vector $\boldsymbol{u}$ is of dimension m and designates the set of exhausted files. Its kth component is set to unity by step 11 when file k is exhausted, as indicated by the occurrence of the partition $\boldsymbol{\lambda}_2$. Each read is normally followed by step 13, which records on the output file the

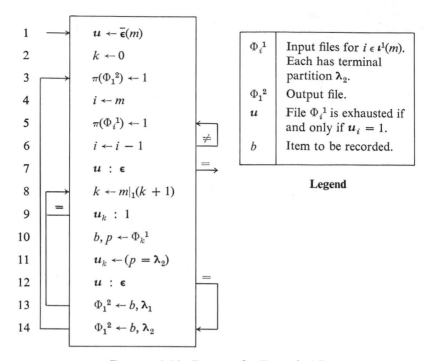

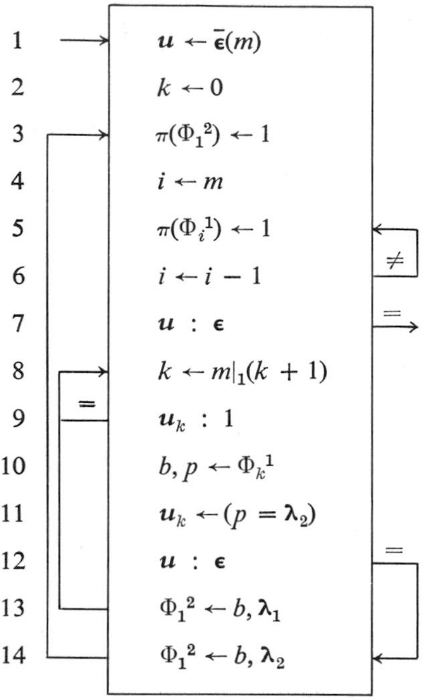

Φ_i^1	Input files for $i \in \iota^1(m)$. Each has terminal partition λ_2.
Φ_1^2	Output file.
u	File Φ_i^1 is exhausted if and only if $u_i = 1$.
b	Item to be recorded.

Legend

Program 1.14 Program for Example 1.3

item read. However, when the last file becomes exhausted, step 14 is executed instead to record the last item, together with the final partition λ_2.

Steps 1–6 initialize the parameters u and k and rewind all files. After the last item is recorded by step 14, the file rewinds are repeated before the final termination on step 7.

It is sometimes convenient to suppress explicit reference to the partition symbol read from a file by using a statement of the form

$$\xleftarrow{\lambda_1}\Big| \; x \leftarrow {}_0\Phi \; \Big|\xrightarrow{\lambda_2},$$

where the indicated branches depend on the value of the partition p_{j+1} which terminates the read. Thus the left or the right branch is taken according to whether $p_{j+1} = \lambda_1$ or $p_{j+1} = \lambda_2$. Certain files (such as the IBM 7090 tape files) permit only such "immediate" branching and do not permit the partition symbol to be stored for use in later operations, as was done in Program 1.14.

In recording, the lowest level partition λ_1 may be elided. Thus statement 13 of Program 1.14 may be written as

$$\Phi_1^2 \leftarrow b.$$

A file may be read or recorded backward as well as forward. A backward read is denoted by

$$x, p \leftarrow {}_1\Phi,$$

and if Φ is initially in position $j + 1$, then $x = \boldsymbol{x}_j$, $p = \boldsymbol{p}_j$, and the final position becomes j. Backward recording is defined analogously. The zero prescript may be omitted from the symbol ${}_0\Phi$ for both forward reading and recording.

The conventions used for matrices can be applied in an obvious way to an array of files $\Phi_j^{\,i}$. For example, the statement

$$\pi(\Phi^i) \leftarrow \boldsymbol{\epsilon}$$

denotes the rewinding of the *row of files* $\Phi_j^{\,i}$, $j \in \iota^1(\nu(\Phi))$; the statement

$$\pi(\Phi_j) \leftarrow \boldsymbol{\epsilon}$$

denotes the rewinding of the *column of files* $\Phi_j^{\,i}$, $i \in \iota^1(\mu(\Phi))$; and the statement

$$\boldsymbol{u}/\Phi^i \leftarrow \boldsymbol{u}/\boldsymbol{x},\ \boldsymbol{u}/\boldsymbol{p}$$

denotes the recording of the vector component $\boldsymbol{x}_j$ on file $\Phi_j^{\,i}$ together with partition $\boldsymbol{p}_j$ for all j such that $\boldsymbol{u}_j = 1$.

As for vectors and matrices, j-origin indexing may be used and will apply to the indexing of the file positions and the partition vector $\boldsymbol{\lambda}$ as well as to the array indices. However, the prescripts (denoting direction of read and record) are independent of index origin. 0-origin indexing is used in the following example.

Example 1.4. Files $\Phi_0^{\,0}$ and $\Phi_1^{\,0}$ contain the vectors $\boldsymbol{x}$ and $\boldsymbol{y}$, respectively, each of dimension n. In the first phase, the components are to be merged in the order $\boldsymbol{x}_0, \boldsymbol{y}_0, \boldsymbol{x}_1, \boldsymbol{y}_1, \ldots, \boldsymbol{x}_{\nu-1}, \boldsymbol{y}_{\nu-1}$, and the first n components of the resulting vector are to be recorded on file $\Phi_0^{\,1}$, and the last n on file $\Phi_1^{\,1}$. In other words, the vectors $\boldsymbol{x}^1 = \boldsymbol{\alpha}^n/\boldsymbol{z}$, and $\boldsymbol{y}^1 = \boldsymbol{\omega}^n/\boldsymbol{z}$ are to be recorded on $\Phi_0^{\,1}$ and $\Phi_1^{\,1}$, respectively, where $\boldsymbol{z} = \backslash \boldsymbol{x}, \boldsymbol{u}, \boldsymbol{y} \backslash$, and $\boldsymbol{u} = (0, 1, 0, 1, \ldots, 0, 1)$. In the next phase, the roles of input and output files are reversed, and the same process is performed on $\boldsymbol{x}^1$ and $\boldsymbol{y}^1$, that is, $\boldsymbol{x}^2 = \boldsymbol{\alpha}^n/(\backslash \boldsymbol{x}^1, \boldsymbol{u}, \boldsymbol{y}^1 \backslash)$, and $\boldsymbol{y}^2 = \boldsymbol{\omega}^n/(\backslash \boldsymbol{x}^1, \boldsymbol{u}, \boldsymbol{y}^1 \backslash)$ are recorded on files $\Phi_0^{\,0}$ and $\Phi_1^{\,0}$, respectively. The process is to be continued through m phases.

Program 1.15. The program for Example 1.4 begins with the rewind of the entire 2×2 array of files. To obviate further rewinding, the second (and each subsequent even-numbered) execution is performed by reading and recording all files in the backward direction. Step 6 performs the essential read and record operation under control of the logical vector $\boldsymbol{u}$, whose components $\boldsymbol{u}_0$, $\boldsymbol{u}_1$, $\boldsymbol{u}_2$ determine, respectively, the subscript of the file to be read, the subscript of the file to be recorded, and the direction of read and record. The file superscripts (determining which classes serve as input and output in the current repetition) are also determined by $\boldsymbol{u}_2$, the input being $\boldsymbol{u}_2$ and the output $\overline{\boldsymbol{u}}_2$. The loop 6–8 copies

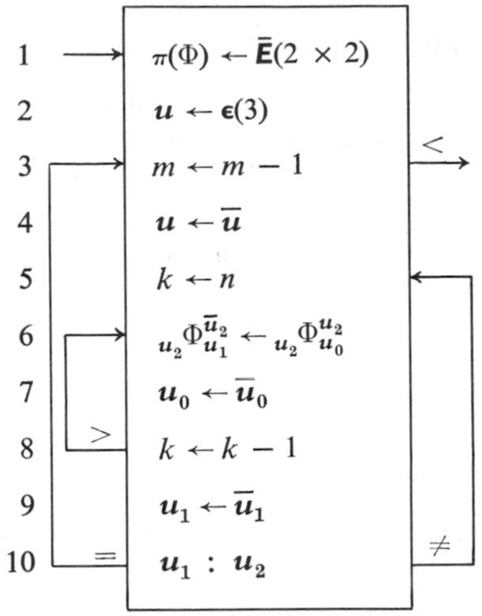

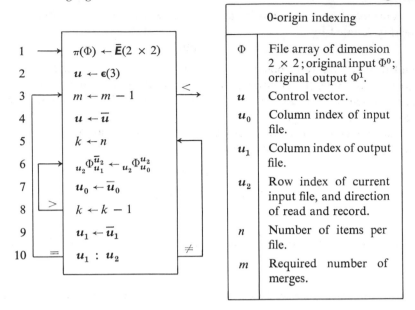

0-origin indexing	
Φ	File array of dimension 2×2; original input Φ^0; original output Φ^1.
$\boldsymbol{u}$	Control vector.
u_0	Column index of input file.
u_1	Column index of output file.
u_2	Row index of current input file, and direction of read and record.
n	Number of items per file.
m	Required number of merges.

Legend

Program 1.15 Program for Example 1.4

n items, alternating the input files through the negation of u_0 on step 7. When the loop terminates, u_1 is negated to interchange the outputs, and the loop is repeated unless $u_1 = u_2$. Equality occurs and causes a branch to step 3 if and only if all $2n$ items of the current phase have already been copied.

Step 3 decrements m and is followed by the negation of $\boldsymbol{u}$ on step 4. The component u_2 must, of course, be negated to reverse direction, but the need to negate u_0 and u_1 is not so evident. It arises because the copying order was prescribed for the forward direction, beginning always with the operation

$${}_0\Phi_0{}^p \leftarrow {}_0\Phi_0{}^{\overline{p}}.$$

An equivalent backward copy must therefore begin with the operation

$${}_1\Phi_1{}^p \leftarrow {}_1\Phi_1{}^{\overline{p}}.$$

Not all computer files have the very general capabilities indicated by the present notation. Some files, for example, can be read and recorded in the forward direction only and, except for rewind, cannot be positioned directly. Positioning to an arbitrary position k must then be performed by a rewind and a succession of $(k - 1)$ subsequent reads. In some files, recording can be performed in the forward direction only, and the positions are defined only by the recorded data. Consequently, recording in position k makes unreliable the data in all subsequent positions, and recording must always proceed through all successive positions until terminated.

1.23 ORDERED TREES

Directed graphs

For many processes it is convenient to use a structured operand with the treelike structure suggested by Fig. 1.16. It is helpful to begin with a more

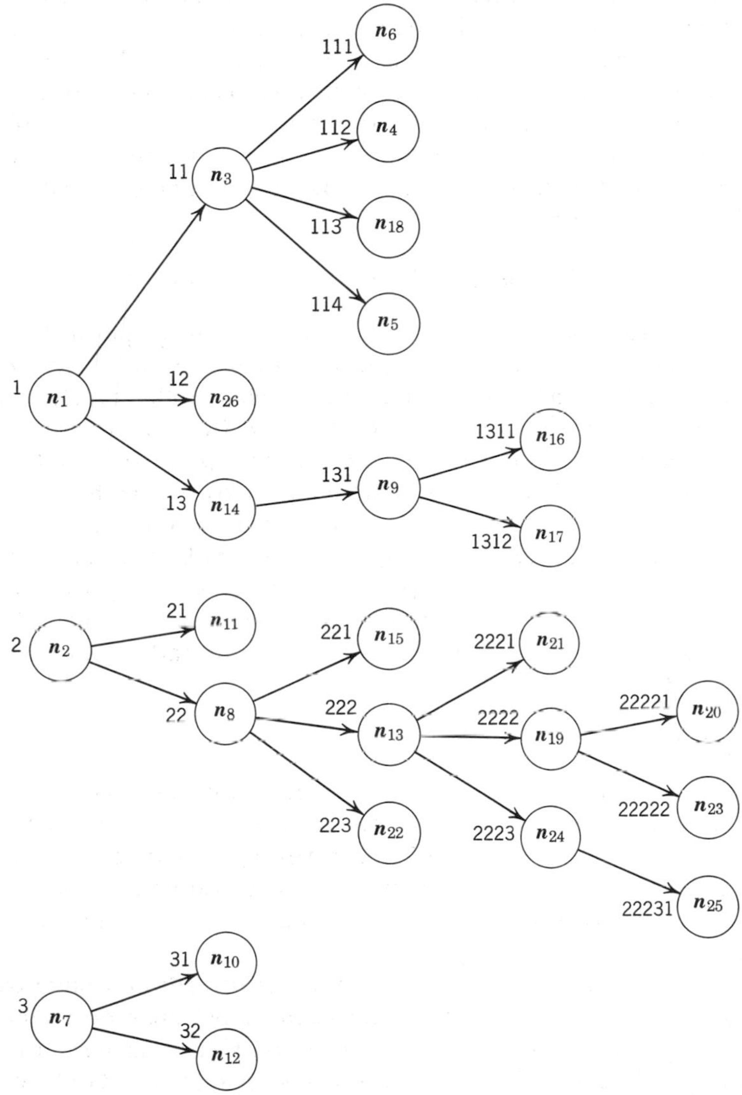

Figure 1.16 A general triply rooted tree with $\lambda(\mathbf{T}) = 16$, $\boldsymbol{\nu}(\mathbf{T}) = (3, 3, 4, 3, 2)$, $\nu(\mathbf{T}) = 5$, $\boldsymbol{\mu}(\mathbf{T}) = (3, 7, 8, 5, 3)$, and $\mu(\mathbf{T}) = 26$

general structure (such as Fig. 1.17) in which a unidirectional association may be specified between any pair of its components.

A *directed graph* comprises a vector $\boldsymbol{n}$ and an arbitrary set of unilateral associations specified between pairs of its components. The vector $\boldsymbol{n}$ is called a *node vector* and its components are also called *nodes*. The associations are conveniently specified by a (logical) *connection matrix* $\boldsymbol{U}$ of dimension $\nu(\boldsymbol{n}) \times \nu(\boldsymbol{n})$ with the following convention: there is an association, called a *branch*, from node i to node j if and only if $\boldsymbol{U}_j^i = 1$.

A directed graph admits of a simple graphical interpretation, as illustrated by Fig. 1.17. The nodes might, for example, represent places, and the lines, connecting streets. A two-way street is then represented by a pair of oppositely directed lines, as shown between nodes 3 and 4.

If $\boldsymbol{k}$ is any mapping vector such that

$$U_{\boldsymbol{k}_i}^{\boldsymbol{k}_{i-1}} = 1 \qquad \text{for } i = 2, 3, \ldots, \nu(\boldsymbol{k}),$$

then the vector $\boldsymbol{p} = \boldsymbol{k}\int\boldsymbol{n}$ is called a *path vector* of the graph $(\boldsymbol{n}, \boldsymbol{U})$. The dimension of a path vector is also called its *length*. Nodes $\boldsymbol{k}_1$ and $\boldsymbol{k}_\nu$ are called the *initial* and *final* nodes, respectively; both are also called *terminal* nodes. If $\boldsymbol{j}$ is any infix of $\boldsymbol{k}$, then $\boldsymbol{q} = \boldsymbol{j}\int\boldsymbol{n}$ is also a path. It is called a subpath of $\boldsymbol{p}$ and is said to be *contained* in $\boldsymbol{p}$. If $\nu(\boldsymbol{q}) < \nu(\boldsymbol{p})$, then $\boldsymbol{q}$ is a *proper* subpath of $\boldsymbol{p}$. If $\boldsymbol{k}_1 = \boldsymbol{k}_\nu$ and $\boldsymbol{p} = \boldsymbol{k}\int\boldsymbol{n}$ is a path of a length exceeding one, $\boldsymbol{p}$ is called a *circuit*. For example, if $\boldsymbol{k} = (6, 1, 7, 7, 2, 6, 1, 5)$, then $\boldsymbol{p} = (\boldsymbol{n}_6, \boldsymbol{n}_1, \boldsymbol{n}_7, \boldsymbol{n}_7, \boldsymbol{n}_2, \boldsymbol{n}_6, \boldsymbol{n}_1, \boldsymbol{n}_5)$ is a path vector of the graph of Fig. 1.17, which contains the proper subpaths $(\boldsymbol{n}_7, \boldsymbol{n}_2, \boldsymbol{n}_6)$, $(\boldsymbol{n}_1, \boldsymbol{n}_7, \boldsymbol{n}_7, \boldsymbol{n}_2, \boldsymbol{n}_6, \boldsymbol{n}_1)$, and $(\boldsymbol{n}_7, \boldsymbol{n}_7)$, the last two of which are circuits. Node j is said to be *reachable* from node i if there exists a path from node i to node j.

Ordered trees

A graph (such as Fig. 1.16) which contains no circuits and which has at most one branch entering each node is called a *tree*. Since each node is entered by at most one branch, a path existing between any two nodes in a tree is unique, and the length of path is also unique. Moreover, if any two paths have the same final node, one is a subpath of the other.

Since a tree contains no circuits, the length of path in a finite tree is bounded. There therefore exist *maximal paths* which are proper subpaths of no longer paths. The initial and final nodes of a maximal path are called a *root* and *leaf* of the tree, respectively. A root is said to lie on the *first level* of the tree, and, in general, a node which lies at the end of a path of length j from a root, lies in the jth *level* of the tree.

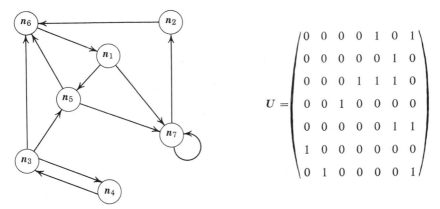

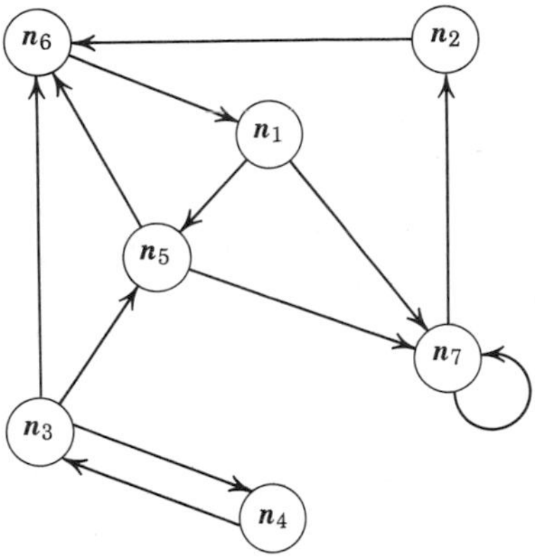

$$U = \begin{pmatrix} 0 & 0 & 0 & 0 & 1 & 0 & 1 \\ 0 & 0 & 0 & 0 & 0 & 1 & 0 \\ 0 & 0 & 0 & 1 & 1 & 1 & 0 \\ 0 & 0 & 1 & 0 & 0 & 0 & 0 \\ 0 & 0 & 0 & 0 & 0 & 1 & 1 \\ 1 & 0 & 0 & 0 & 0 & 0 & 0 \\ 0 & 1 & 0 & 0 & 0 & 0 & 1 \end{pmatrix}$$

Figure 1.17 A graphical representation of the directed graph $(\boldsymbol{n}, U)$.

A tree which contains n roots is said to be *n-tuply rooted.* The sets of nodes reachable from each of the several roots are disjoint, for if any node is reachable by paths from each of two disjoint roots, one is a proper subpath of the other and is therefore not maximal. Similarly, any node of a tree defines a *subtree* of which it is the root, consisting of itself and all nodes reachable from it, with the same associations as the parent tree.

If for each level j, a simple ordering is assigned to each of the disjoint sets of nodes reachable from each node of the preceding level, and if the roots are also simply ordered, the tree is said to be *ordered.* Attention will henceforth be restricted to ordered trees, which will be denoted by uppercase boldface roman characters. The *height* of a tree **T** is defined as the length of the longest path in **T** and is denoted by $\nu(\mathbf{T})$. The number of nodes on level j is called the *moment of level j* and is denoted by $\boldsymbol{\mu}_j(\mathbf{T})$. The vector $\boldsymbol{\mu}(\mathbf{T})$ is called the *moment vector*. The total number of nodes in **T** is called the moment of **T** and is denoted by $\mu(\mathbf{T})$. Clearly, $\nu(\boldsymbol{\mu}(\mathbf{T})) = \nu(\mathbf{T})$, and $+/\boldsymbol{\mu}(\mathbf{T}) = \mu(\mathbf{T}) = \nu(\boldsymbol{n})$. The number of roots is equal to $\boldsymbol{\mu}_1(\mathbf{T})$, and the number of leaves will be denoted by $\lambda(\mathbf{T})$.

The number of branches leaving a node is called its *branching ratio* or *degree*, and the maximum degree occurring in a tree **T** is denoted by $\delta(\mathbf{T})$. The *dispersion vector* of a tree **T** is denoted by $\boldsymbol{\nu}(\mathbf{T})$ and is defined as follows: $\boldsymbol{\nu}_1(\mathbf{T}) = \boldsymbol{\mu}_1(\mathbf{T})$, and for $j = 2, 3, \ldots, \nu(\mathbf{T})$, $\boldsymbol{\nu}_j(\mathbf{T})$ is equal to the maximum over the branching ratios of the nodes on level $j - 1$. For the tree of Fig. 1.16, $\boldsymbol{\nu}(\mathbf{T}) = (3, 3, 4, 3, 2)$. The number of roots possessed by a tree **T** (that is, $\boldsymbol{\nu}_1(\mathbf{T})$) is called its *dispersion.* A tree possessing unity dispersion is called *rooted* or *singular.*

Each node $\boldsymbol{n}_i$ of a graph (and hence of a tree) may be identified by its index i. Since a tree admits of more convenient index vectors, the underlying index i will henceforth be referred to as the *graph* index.

In an ordered tree, any path of length k from a root can be uniquely specified by an *index vector* $\boldsymbol{i}$ of dimension k, where $\boldsymbol{i}_1$ specifies the particular root, and the remaining components specify the (unique) path as follows: the path node on level j is the $\boldsymbol{i}_j$th element of the set of nodes on level j reachable from the path node on level j-1. The node at the end of the path can therefore be designated uniquely by the index vector $\boldsymbol{i}$. The degree of node $\boldsymbol{i}$ will be denoted by $\delta(\boldsymbol{i}, \mathbf{T})$. The index vectors are shown to the left of each node in Fig. 1.16.

The path from a root whose terminal node is $\boldsymbol{i}$ will be denoted by $\mathbf{T}^{\boldsymbol{i}}$. In Fig. 1.16, for example, $\mathbf{T}^{\boldsymbol{i}} = (\boldsymbol{n}_2, \boldsymbol{n}_8, \boldsymbol{n}_{13}, \boldsymbol{n}_{24})$ if $\boldsymbol{i} = (2, 2, 2, 3)$. A vector $\boldsymbol{i}$ is said to be an *index* of $\mathbf{T}$ if it is the index of some node in $\mathbf{T}$.

The subtree of $\mathbf{T}$ rooted in node $\boldsymbol{i}$ will be denoted by $\mathbf{T}_{\boldsymbol{i}}$. Thus in Fig. 1.16, $\mathbf{P} = \mathbf{T}_{(2,2,2)}$ is a rooted subtree with $\boldsymbol{\nu}(\mathbf{P}) = (1, 3, 2)$, and $\boldsymbol{\mu}(\mathbf{P}) = (1, 3, 3)$. A path in $\mathbf{T}_{\boldsymbol{i}}$ is denoted by $(\mathbf{T}_{\boldsymbol{i}})^{\boldsymbol{j}}$. For example, if $\mathbf{G}$ is an ascending genealogical tree* with the sword and distaff sides denoted by the indices 1 and 2, respectively, then any individual x and the nearest $(n - 1)$ paternal male ancestors are represented by the path vector $(\mathbf{G}_{\boldsymbol{i}})^{\boldsymbol{\epsilon}(n)}$, where $\boldsymbol{i}$ is the index of x in $\mathbf{G}$.

Example 1.5. Determine the index $\boldsymbol{i}$ such that the path $\mathbf{T}^{\boldsymbol{i}}$ is equal to a given argument $\boldsymbol{x}$ and is the "first" such path in $\mathbf{T}$; that is, the function

$$(\boldsymbol{\alpha}^{\nu(\boldsymbol{x})}/\boldsymbol{\nu}(\mathbf{T})) \perp \boldsymbol{i}$$

is a minimum.

Program 1.18. The index vector $\boldsymbol{i}$ specifies the path currently under test. Its last component is incremented repeatedly by step 7 until the loop 6–8 is terminated. If the path $\mathbf{T}^{\boldsymbol{i}}$ agrees with the corresponding prefix of the argument $\boldsymbol{x}$, termination occurs through the branch to step 9, which tests for completion before step 10 augments $\boldsymbol{i}$ by a final zero component. Step 5 then respecifies d as the degree of the penultimate node of the set of d paths next to be tested by the loop. Termination by a branch from step 6 to step 2 occurs if all d possible paths are exhausted without finding agreement on step 8. In this event, retraction by one level occurs on step 2, and d is again respecified. If $\nu(\boldsymbol{i}) = 1$, the paths to be searched comprise the roots of the tree and d must therefore be specified as the number of roots. This is achieved by executing step 3 and skipping step 5. Retraction to a vector $\boldsymbol{i}$ of dimension zero occurs only if all roots have been exhausted, and final termination from step 4 indicates that the tree possesses no path equal to the argument $\boldsymbol{x}$.

* Although such a genealogical tree is not necessarily a tree in the mathematical sense, it will be assumed so for present purposes.

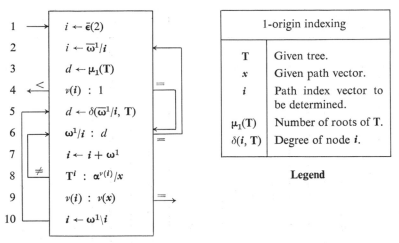

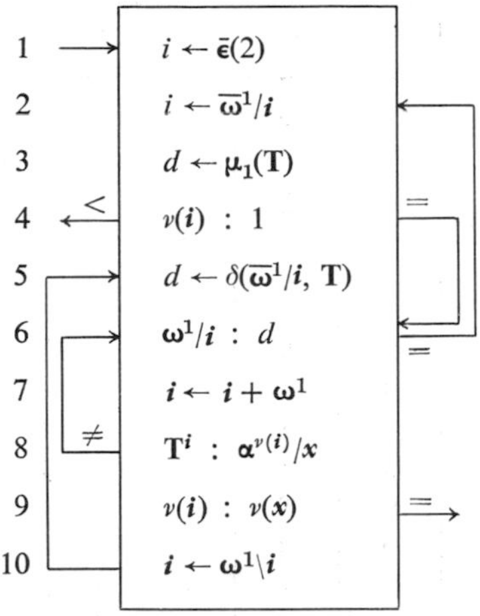

1-origin indexing	
T	Given tree.
x	Given path vector.
i	Path index vector to be determined.
$\mu_1(\mathbf{T})$	Number of roots of T.
$\delta(i, \mathbf{T})$	Degree of node i.

Legend

Program 1.18 Determination of i such that $\mathbf{T}^i = x$

If d is a vector of dimension $\nu(n)$ such that d_i is the degree of node n_i of a tree T, then d is called the *degree vector associated with* n. In Fig. 1.16, for example,

$$d = (3, 2, 4, 0, 0, 0, 2, \ldots, 1, 0, 0).$$

Moreover, if n is itself the alphabet (that is, $n = (\text{a, b, c}, \ldots, \text{z})$), then the vector n' of Table 1.19*a* is a permutation of n, and d' is the associated degree vector. Table 1.19*b* shows another such pair, n'' and d''.

The degree vector provides certain useful information most directly. For example, since each leaf is of degree zero, $\lambda(\mathbf{T}) = +/(d = 0)$. Moreover, the number of roots is equal to the number of nodes less the total of the degrees, that is, $\mu_1(\mathbf{T}) = \nu(d) - +/d$, and the maximum degree occurring in T is given by $\delta(\mathbf{T}) = ((\epsilon\lceil d)/d)_1$. Finally, the degree vector and the node vector together can, in certain permutations (those of Table 1.19), provide a complete and compact description of the tree.

Right and left list matrices

If each one of the $\mu(\mathbf{T})$ index vectors i of a tree T is listed together with its associated node $(\mathbf{T}^i)_{\nu(i)}$, the list determines the tree completely. Since the index vectors are, in general, of different dimensions, it is convenient to append null components* to extend each to the common maximum dimension $\nu(\mathbf{T})$. They may then be combined in an *index matrix* of

* In the 1-origin indexing system used here it would be possible to use the numeric zero to represent the null. In 0-origin indexing, however, zeros occur as components of index vectors and must be distinguishable from the nulls used.

d'	n'	I'						d''	n''	I''				
3	a	1	∘	∘	∘	∘	1	3	a	∘	∘	∘	∘	1
4	c	1	1	∘	∘	∘	2	2	b	∘	∘	∘	∘	2
0	f	1	1	1	∘	∘	3	2	g	∘	∘	∘	∘	3
0	d	1	1	2	∘	∘	4	4	c	∘	∘	∘	1	1
0	r	1	1	3	∘	∘	5	0	z	∘	∘	∘	1	2
0	e	1	1	4	∘	∘	6	1	n	∘	∘	∘	1	3
0	z	1	2	∘	∘	∘	7	0	k	∘	∘	∘	2	1
1	n	1	3	∘	∘	∘	8	3	h	∘	∘	∘	2	2
2	i	1	3	1	∘	∘	9	0	j	∘	∘	∘	3	1
0	p	1	3	1	1	∘	10	0	l	∘	∘	∘	3	2
0	q	1	3	1	2	∘	11	0	f	∘	∘	1	1	1
2	b	2	∘	∘	∘	∘	12	0	d	∘	∘	1	1	2
0	k	2	1	∘	∘	∘	13	0	r	∘	∘	1	1	3
3	h	2	2	∘	∘	∘	14	0	e	∘	∘	1	1	4
0	o	2	2	1	∘	∘	15	2	i	∘	∘	1	3	1
3	m	2	2	2	∘	∘	16	0	o	∘	∘	2	2	1
0	u	2	2	2	1	∘	17	3	m	∘	∘	2	2	2
2	s	2	2	2	2	∘	18	0	v	∘	∘	2	2	3
0	t	2	2	2	2	1	19	0	p	∘	1	3	1	1
0	w	2	2	2	2	2	20	0	q	∘	1	3	1	2
1	x	2	2	2	3	∘	21	0	u	∘	2	2	2	1
0	y	2	2	2	3	1	22	2	s	∘	2	2	2	2
0	v	2	2	3	∘	∘	23	1	x	∘	2	2	2	3
2	g	3	∘	∘	∘	∘	24	0	t	2	2	2	2	1
0	j	3	1	∘	∘	∘	25	0	w	2	2	2	2	2
0	l	3	2	∘	∘	∘	26	0	y	2	2	2	3	1

Full left list matrix [T (*a*) — Full right list matrix]T (*b*)

Table 1.19 Full list matrices of the tree of Fig. 1.16

dimension $\mu(\mathbf{T}) \times \nu(\mathbf{T})$, which, together with the associated node vector, completely describes the tree, If, for example, the node vector $\boldsymbol{n}$ is the alphabet, the tree of Fig. 1.16 is described by the node vector $\boldsymbol{n}'$ and index matrix $\boldsymbol{I}'$ of Table 1.19*a* or, alternatively, by $\boldsymbol{n}''$ and $\boldsymbol{I}''$ of Table 1.19*b*.

Because of the utility of the degree vector, it will be annexed to the array of node vector and index matrix, as shown in Table 1.19*a*, to form a *full list matrix* of the tree. The degree vector and node vector together will be called a *list matrix*. As remarked, the list matrix can, in certain permutations, alone describe the tree.

Formally, the full list matrix $\boldsymbol{M}$ of a tree $\mathbf{T}$ is defined as follows: $\bar{\boldsymbol{\alpha}}^2/\boldsymbol{M}$ is an index matrix of the tree, $\boldsymbol{M}_1$ is the associated degree vector, and $\boldsymbol{M}_2$

is the associated node vector. Thus for each $k \in \iota^1(\mu(\mathbf{T}))$, $\boldsymbol{M}_1^k = \delta(\boldsymbol{i}, \mathbf{T})$, and $\boldsymbol{M}_2^k = (\mathbf{T}^{\boldsymbol{i}})_{\nu(\boldsymbol{i})}$, where $\boldsymbol{i}$ is the nonnull portion of $\overline{\boldsymbol{\alpha}}^2/\boldsymbol{M}^k$, that is, $\boldsymbol{i} = ((\overline{\boldsymbol{\alpha}}^2/\boldsymbol{M}^k) \neq {}^\circ\boldsymbol{\epsilon})/\overline{\boldsymbol{\alpha}}^2/\boldsymbol{M}^k)$. The corresponding list matrix is $\boldsymbol{\alpha}^2/\boldsymbol{M}$.

Since a full list matrix provides a complete description of a tree regardless of the order in which the nodes occur in the list, any column permutation $\boldsymbol{M}^{\boldsymbol{p}}$ (that is, any reordering among the rows) is also a full list matrix. Two particular arrangements of the full list matrix are of prime interest because each possesses the following properties: (1) the nodes are grouped in useful ways, and (2) the list matrix (i.e., the degree vector and node vector) alone describes the tree without reference to the associated index matrix. They are called the full *left* list matrix and full *right* list matrix and are denoted by [**T** and]**T**, respectively. Table 1.19 shows the full left and full right lists of the tree of Fig. 1.16.

The left list index matrix $\boldsymbol{I}$ is left justified,* that is, the null elements are appended at the right of each index. The rows $\boldsymbol{I}^j$ are arranged in increasing order on their values as decimal (or rather $(\delta(\mathbf{T}) + 1)$-ary) fractions with the radix point at the left and the nulls replaced by zeros. More precisely, the rows are arranged in increasing order on the function $(\nu(\boldsymbol{a})\boldsymbol{\epsilon}) \perp (\boldsymbol{a}\ \iota_0\ \boldsymbol{I}^j)$, where $\boldsymbol{a} = (\circ, 1, 2, \ldots, \delta(\mathbf{T}))$.†

The right list matrix is right justified and is ordered on the same function, namely $(\nu(\boldsymbol{a})\boldsymbol{\epsilon}) \perp (\boldsymbol{a}\ \iota_0\ \boldsymbol{I}^j)$. The rows are therefore ordered on their values as integers, i.e., with the decimal point at the right. From the example of Table 1.19*b* it is clear that the right list groups the nodes by levels, i.e., level j is represented by the infix $(i \downarrow \boldsymbol{\alpha}^k)//(]\mathbf{T})$, where $k = \boldsymbol{\mu}_j(\mathbf{T})$, and $i = +/\boldsymbol{\alpha}^{j-1}/\boldsymbol{\mu}(\mathbf{T})$. In Table 1.19*b*, for example, $\boldsymbol{\mu}(\mathbf{T}) = (3, 7, 8, 5, 3)$, and if $j = 3$, then $k = 8$, $i = 10$, and level j is represented by rows $i + 1 = 11$ to $i + k = 18$. The right list is therefore useful in executing processes (such as the *p*th degree selection sort) which require a scan of successive levels of the tree.

The left list groups the nodes by subtrees, i.e., any node $\boldsymbol{i}$ is followed immediately by the remaining nodes of its subtree $\mathbf{T}_{\boldsymbol{i}}$. Formally, if $\boldsymbol{I} = \overline{\boldsymbol{\alpha}}^2/[\mathbf{T}$, and if $\boldsymbol{i} = (\boldsymbol{I}^k \neq {}^\circ\boldsymbol{\epsilon})/\boldsymbol{I}^k$, then the tree $\mathbf{T}_{\boldsymbol{i}}$ is represented by the infix $((k - 1) \downarrow \boldsymbol{\alpha}^{\mu(\mathbf{T}_i)})//[\mathbf{T}$. In Fig. 1.19*a*, for example, if $k = 16$, then $\boldsymbol{i} = (2, 2, 2)$, $\mu(\mathbf{T}_{\boldsymbol{i}}) = 7$, and $\mathbf{T}_{\boldsymbol{i}}$ is represented by rows 16 to 22 of [**T**. The left list is therefore useful in processes (such as the construction of a Huffman code and the evaluation of a compound statement) which require a treatment of successive subtrees.

The row index of a node in a right (left) list matrix is a graph index of the node and will be called the *right* (*left*) *list index*.

* The term *left list* and the notation [**T** are both intended to suggest left justification.

† These statements hold only for 1-origin indexing. In 0-origin indexing, $\boldsymbol{a} = (\circ, 0, 1, \ldots, \delta(\mathbf{T}) - 1)$.

Well formation

A two-column matrix which forms the right list of some tree is said to be a *well formed right list*. Since the ordering of the nodes in a right list of a given tree is unique, the right list of a given tree is unique. Conversely, any well formed right list specifies a unique tree according to the algorithm of Program 1.20.

Identical remarks apply to the left list, except that Program 1.20 is replaced by Program 1.21. Moreover, the necessary and sufficient conditions for the well formation of a left list are identical with those for a right list and are derived by virtually identical arguments. The case will be stated for the right list only.

If $\boldsymbol{R}$ is a well formed right list representing a tree $\mathbf{T}$, then the dispersion (i.e., the number of roots) $\boldsymbol{\nu}_1(\mathbf{T}) = \nu(\boldsymbol{R}_1) - (+/\boldsymbol{R}_1)$ must be strictly positive. Moreover, if $\boldsymbol{S} = \bar{\boldsymbol{\alpha}}^j//\boldsymbol{R}$ is any suffix of $\boldsymbol{R}$, then $\boldsymbol{S}$ is a right list of the tree obtained by deleting from $\mathbf{T}$ the first j nodes of the original list. For, such level-by-level deletion always leaves a legitimate tree with the degrees of the remaining nodes unchanged. Consequently, the number of roots determined by every suffix of $\boldsymbol{R}_1$ must also be strictly positive. In other words, all components of the *suffix dispersion vector* $\boldsymbol{s}$ defined by

$$s_j = \nu(\bar{\boldsymbol{\alpha}}^{j-1}/\boldsymbol{R}_1) - (+/\bar{\boldsymbol{\alpha}}^{j-1}/\boldsymbol{R}_1), \quad j \in \boldsymbol{\iota}^1(\nu(\boldsymbol{R}_1))$$

must be strictly positive. The condition is also sufficient.

Sufficiency is easily established by induction on the column dimension of $\boldsymbol{R}$. The condition is clearly sufficient for $\nu(\boldsymbol{R}_1) = 1$. Assume it sufficient for dimension $\nu(\boldsymbol{R}_1) - 1$. If $\boldsymbol{s}$, the suffix dispersion vector of $\boldsymbol{R}$, is strictly positive, then $\bar{\boldsymbol{\alpha}}^1/\boldsymbol{s}$, the suffix dispersion vector of $\bar{\boldsymbol{\alpha}}^1//\boldsymbol{R}$, is also positive, and by hypothesis $\bar{\boldsymbol{\alpha}}^1//\boldsymbol{R}$ represents a tree $\mathbf{G}$ possessing s_2 roots. Moreover,

$$0 < s_1 = s_2 + (1 - R_1^{\,1})$$

implies that $s_2 \geq R_1^{\,1}$, and the number of roots possessed by $\mathbf{G}$ therefore fulfills the number of branches required by the added node $R_2^{\,1}$. A legitimate tree corresponding to $\boldsymbol{R}$ can therefore be formed by joining the last $R_1^{\,1}$ roots of $\mathbf{G}$ to the node $R_2^{\,1}$.

Tests for well formation can therefore be incorporated in any algorithm defined on a right or left list matrix $\boldsymbol{M}$ by computing the components of the suffix dispersion vector $\boldsymbol{s}$. The recursion $s_{i-1} = s_i + 1 - M_1^{i-1}$ is convenient in a backward scan of $\boldsymbol{M}$, and the equivalent recursion $s_i = s_{i-1} - 1 + M_1^{i-1}$ serves for a forward scan. The starting condition for a forward scan is $s_1 = \nu(\boldsymbol{M}_1) - (+/\boldsymbol{M}_1)$, and for a backward scan is $s_\nu = 1 - M_1^{\,\mu}$. Since the criteria of well formation are identical for right and left lists, a matrix may be characterized simply as well or ill formed.

The purpose served by the degree vector $\boldsymbol{d}$ in the description of a tree is sometimes served instead [e.g., Burks et al. (1954)] by the vector $g = \boldsymbol{\epsilon} - \boldsymbol{d}$. It is somewhat more convenient in the analysis of well formation, since the expression for the suffix dispersion vector then simplifies to

$$s_{j+1} = (+/\overline{\boldsymbol{\alpha}}^{j}/g), \qquad \text{or} \qquad s = (\boldsymbol{I} + \square)^{+}_{/}/g.$$

The index matrix as a function of the degree vector

The complete determination of the tree corresponding to a given list matrix $\boldsymbol{M}$ is best described as the determination of the associated index matrix $\boldsymbol{I}$. For both left and right lists this can be achieved by a single forward scan of the rows of $\boldsymbol{M}$ and of $\boldsymbol{I}$.

For a right list $\boldsymbol{R}$ it is first necessary to determine r, the number of roots. The first r components of $\boldsymbol{R}$ are then the roots of the tree in order, the next $\boldsymbol{R}_1^{\,1}$ components of $\boldsymbol{R}$ are the second-level nodes reachable from the first root, and so forth. Programs 1.20 and 1.21 describe the processes for a right list and a left list, respectively.

Program 1.20. In each execution of the main loop 13–16, the ith row of the right list $\boldsymbol{R}$ is examined to determine the index vector of each node on the succeeding level which is directly reachable from it. The number of such nodes is controlled by the parameter d, initialized to the degree of the ith node by step 12. The (right list) index of the nodes reachable from node i is determined by j, which is incremented on step 14 as the index vector of each node is determined. The index vectors of the successive nodes reachable from node i have the final components 1, 2, 3, . . . , and each must be prefixed by the index vector of node i. This assignment is effected by the vector $\boldsymbol{v}$, which is initialized by the index vector of node i rotated left by one (step 11), and which is incremented by step 15 before each assignment occurring on step 16. At the outset, $\boldsymbol{v}$ is set to zero and d is set to the number of roots as determined by step 4.

Since j is, at step 10, equal to the current number of roots r augmented by the cumulative degrees of the first $i - 1$ nodes, then $r = j - i + 1$ and the exit on step 10 therefore occurs always and only in the event of ill formation. Alternatively, the test can be viewed as an assurance that each row of the matrix $\boldsymbol{I}$ is specified before it is itself used in specification.

When step 5 is first reached, the index matrix $\boldsymbol{I}$ is complete but is expressed in 1-origin indexing with zeros representing the null elements. Steps 5–7 translate the matrix to the origin ϕ and mask in the necessary null elements.

Program 1.21. The index vectors $\boldsymbol{I}^j$ are determined in order under control of the parameter j. The loop 5–18 traces a continuous path through the tree, determining the index of each successive node of the path by rotating the index of the preceding node (step 17) and adding one to the last component (step 13), and maintaining in the connection vector $\boldsymbol{c}$ a record $\boldsymbol{c}_{i+1}$ of the index j of the successor of node i in the path traced. The path is interrupted by the occurrence of a leaf (that is, $\boldsymbol{L}_1^{\,j} = 0$ on step 18), and the degree vector $\boldsymbol{L}_1$ is then scanned by the loop

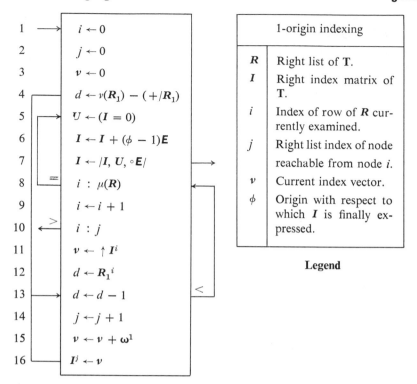

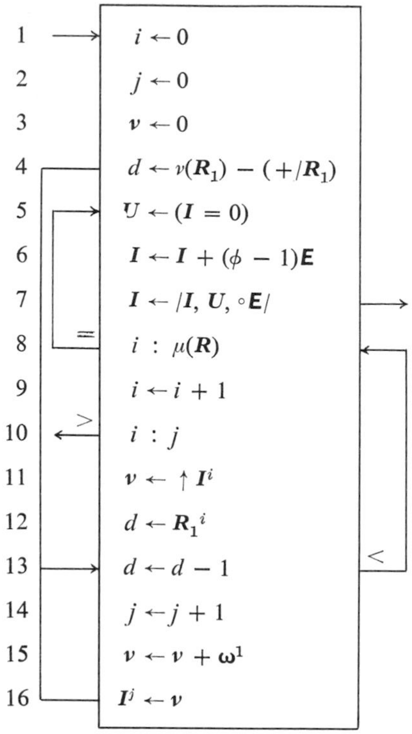

	1-origin indexing
R	Right list of **T**.
I	Right index matrix of **T**.
i	Index of row of R currently examined.
j	Right list index of node reachable from node i.
v	Current index vector.
ϕ	Origin with respect to which I is finally expressed.

Legend

1     $i \leftarrow 0$
2     $j \leftarrow 0$
3     $v \leftarrow 0$
4     $d \leftarrow v(R_1) - (+/R_1)$
5     $U \leftarrow (I = 0)$
6     $I \leftarrow I + (\phi - 1)E$
7     $I \leftarrow /I, U, \circ E/$
8     $i : \mu(R)$
9     $i \leftarrow i + 1$
10    $i : j$
11    $v \leftarrow \uparrow I^i$
12    $d \leftarrow R_1{}^i$
13    $d \leftarrow d - 1$
14    $j \leftarrow j + 1$
15    $v \leftarrow v + \omega^1$
16    $I^j \leftarrow v$

Program 1.20 Determination of the index matrix I associated with a right list matrix R

(19–20) to determine the index i of the last preceding node whose branches remain incompleted. Steps 22–23 then respecify v as the index vector of the node following node i in the path last traced, and step 21 decrements the component $L_1{}^i$ of the degree vector. The branch from step 19 to step 22 occurs at the completion of each rooted subtree. The test for well formation (step 12) is the same as that applied to the right list in Program 1.20, except that the notation for the relevant parameters differs. The concluding operations (6–9) include left justification on step 7.

Tree, path, and level compression

The *tree compression*

$$\mathbf{P} \leftarrow \mathbf{U}/\mathbf{T}$$

specifies a tree **P** obtained from **T** by suppressing those nodes corresponding to zeros of the logical tree **U**, and reconnecting so that for every pair of nodes x, y of **P**, x belongs to the subtree of **P** rooted in y if and only if x belongs to the subtree of **T** rooted in y. If, for example, **T** is the tree of

1	$i \leftarrow 0$
2	$j \leftarrow 0$
3	$\boldsymbol{\nu} \leftarrow 0$
4	$r \leftarrow \nu(\boldsymbol{L}_1) - (+/\boldsymbol{L}_1)$
5	$j : \mu(\boldsymbol{L})$
6	$\boldsymbol{U} \leftarrow (\boldsymbol{I} = 0)$
7	$\boldsymbol{I} \leftarrow (+/\alpha/\overline{\boldsymbol{U}}) \uparrow \boldsymbol{I}$
8	$\boldsymbol{I} \leftarrow \boldsymbol{I} + (\phi - 1)\mathbf{E}$
9	$\boldsymbol{I} \leftarrow /\boldsymbol{I}, \boldsymbol{U}, \circ\mathbf{E}/$
10	$j \leftarrow j + 1$
11	$r \leftarrow r + \boldsymbol{L}_1{}^j$
12	$j : r$
13	$\boldsymbol{\nu} \leftarrow \boldsymbol{\nu} + \boldsymbol{\omega}^1$
14	$\boldsymbol{I}^j \leftarrow \boldsymbol{\nu}$
15	$\boldsymbol{c}_{i+1} \leftarrow j$
16	$i \leftarrow j$
17	$\boldsymbol{\nu} \leftarrow \uparrow \boldsymbol{\nu}$
18	$\boldsymbol{L}_1{}^j : 0$
19	$i \leftarrow i - 1$
20	$\boldsymbol{L}_1{}^i : 1$
21	$\boldsymbol{L}_1{}^i \leftarrow \boldsymbol{L}_1{}^i - 1$
22	$k \leftarrow \boldsymbol{c}_{i+1}$
23	$\boldsymbol{\nu} \leftarrow \boldsymbol{I}^k$

1-origin indexing	
$\boldsymbol{L}$	Left list of **T**.
$\boldsymbol{I}$	Left index matrix of **T**.
j	Index of row of $\boldsymbol{I}$ being determined.
i	Left list index of path node preceding node j in current path (Step 16), or index of last previous node whose branches remain unexhausted (step 22).
$\boldsymbol{c}_{i+1}$	Index of node following node i in last path traced from i.
r	Parameter for testing well formation.
$\boldsymbol{\nu}$	Current index vector.
ϕ	Origin with respect to which $\boldsymbol{I}$ is expressed.

Legend

Program 1.21 Determination of the index matrix $\boldsymbol{I}$ associated with a left list matrix $\boldsymbol{L}$

Fig. 1.16 with $\boldsymbol{n}$ as the alphabet, and **U** is the tree of Fig. 1.22*a*, then **P** is the tree of Fig. 1.22*b*. The new indices are shown to the left of each node of **P**. The set of nodes 221, 222, . . . , 226, are all on the same level of **P** although they have been shown with branches of different lengths to permit easy identification with the nodes of the original tree **T**.

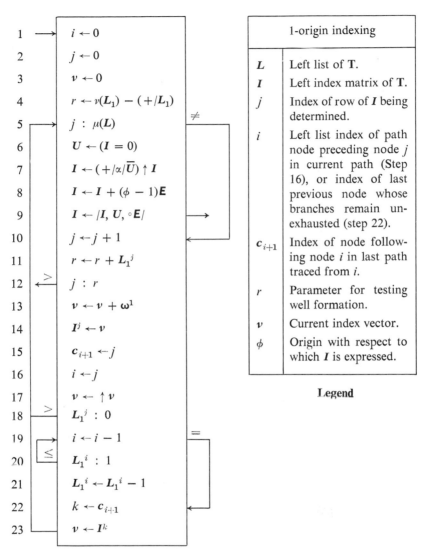

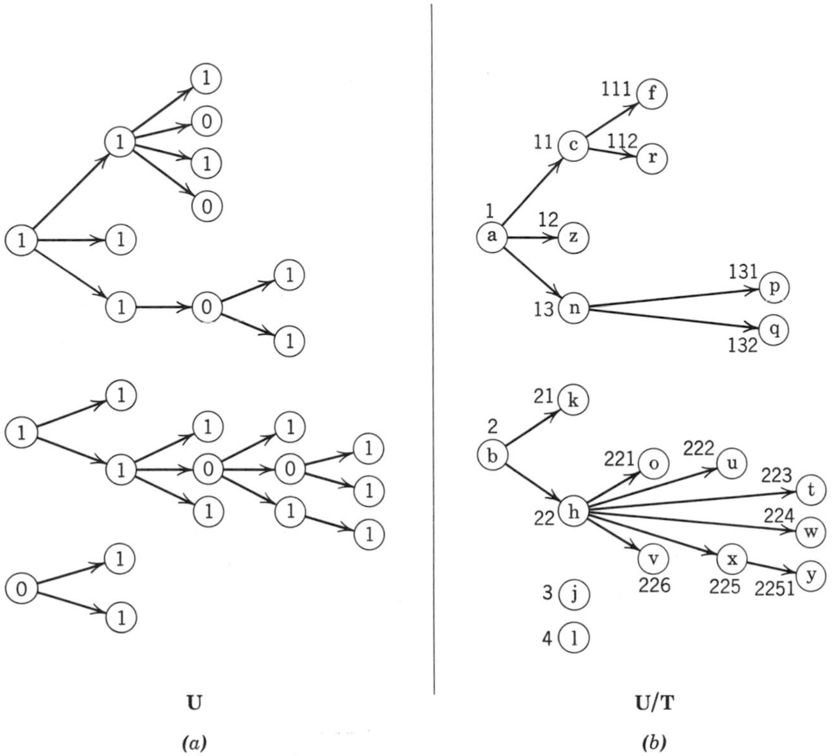

Figure 1.22 Compression of tree **T** of Fig. 1.16 (with $\boldsymbol{n}$ = alphabet)

The compress operation is best executed on the left list because of the grouping by subtrees. Program 1.23 gives a suitable algorithm which also serves as a formal definition of the compress operation.

Program 1.23. The vector $\boldsymbol{u}$ is specified as the node vector of the left list of the controlling logical tree **U** and controls the subsequent process. Step 4 determines j as the index of the first zero component of $\boldsymbol{u}$. Steps 6 and 7 then delete the corresponding nodes of $\boldsymbol{u}$ and of the left list of **T**, but only after step 5 has determined d as the change in degree which this deletion will occasion to the root of the smallest subtree containing the deleted node. Steps 9–11 perform a backward scan of the degree vector to determine j as the index of the root of the subtree, and step 12 effects the requisite change in its degree. The exit on step 9 occurs only if the node deleted is a root of the original tree, in which event no change is produced in the degree of any other node.

Two further compress operations controlled by logical vectors are defined as follows. *Path compression* is denoted by

$$\mathbf{P} \leftarrow \boldsymbol{u}/\mathbf{T}.$$

1	$u \leftarrow ([U)_2$
2	$L \leftarrow \alpha^2 /([T)$
3	$u \;:\; \epsilon$
4	$j \leftarrow (+/\alpha/u) + 1$
5	$d \leftarrow L_1{}^j - 1$
6	$u \leftarrow \bar{\epsilon}^j/u$
7	$L \leftarrow \bar{\epsilon}^j//L$
8	$r \leftarrow 1$
9	$j \leftarrow j - 1$
10	$r \leftarrow r - L_1{}^j + 1$
11	$r \;:\; 1$
12	$L_1{}^j \leftarrow L_1{}^j + d$

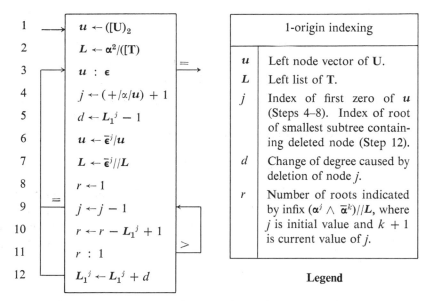

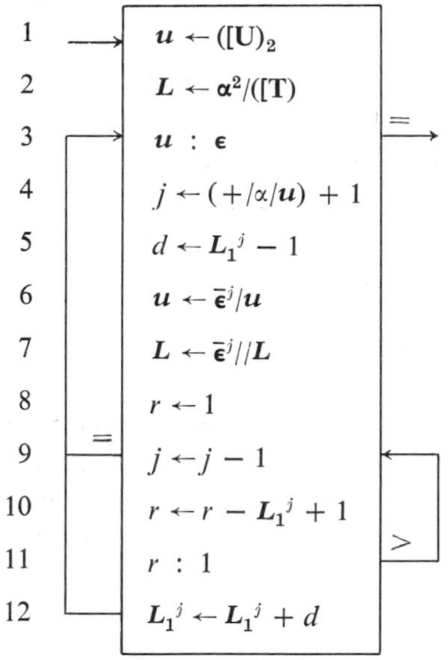

1-origin indexing	
u	Left node vector of **U**.
L	Left list of **T**.
j	Index of first zero of u (Steps 4–8). Index of root of smallest subtree containing deleted node (Step 12).
d	Change of degree caused by deletion of node j.
r	Number of roots indicated by infix $(\alpha^j \wedge \bar{\alpha}^k)//L$, where j is initial value and $k + 1$ is current value of j.

Legend

Program 1.23   Determination of the left list $L = \alpha^2/[(U/T)$

P is obtained from **T** by suppressing every node on level j if $u_j = 0$, and reconnecting as in tree compression. *Level compression* is denoted by

$$\mathbf{P} \leftarrow u//\mathbf{T},$$

and **P** is obtained from **T** by deleting each rooted subtree $\mathbf{T}_i$ for which $u_i = 0$.

Path compression by a unit vector ϵ^j produces a tree of height one. Such a tree is, in effect, a vector and will be treated as one.

Two related special logical trees are defined: the *path tree* ${}^{u}\mathbf{E}$ such that $\bar{u}/{}^{u}\mathbf{E} = 0$ and $u/{}^{u}\mathbf{E}$ is the full tree **E** whose nodes are all unity, and the *level tree* ${}_{u}\mathbf{E}$ such that $\bar{u}//{}_{u}\mathbf{E} = 0$, and $u//{}_{u}\mathbf{E} = \mathbf{E}$.

Extension of other operations to trees

Two trees are *compatible* if they have the same structure. Elementary binary operations are extended node by node to compatible trees. For example,

$$\mathbf{Z} \leftarrow \mathbf{X} \times \mathbf{Y}$$

implies that node i of **Z** is the product of node i of **X** and node i of **Y** for all i. Similarly,

$$\mathbf{M} \leftarrow b \, \iota_j \, \mathbf{T}$$

specifies **M** as a tree (of the same structure as **T**) such that node $\boldsymbol{i}$ of **M** is the j-origin $\boldsymbol{b}$-index of node $\boldsymbol{i}$ of **T**.

The mapping operation is extended to trees so as to permute the rooted subtrees of a tree. Formally

$$\mathbf{P} \leftarrow \boldsymbol{m} \int_j \mathbf{T}$$

implies that $\boldsymbol{\mu}_1(\mathbf{P}) = \nu(\boldsymbol{m})$, that $\mathbf{P}_i$ is a single null character if $m_i \notin \boldsymbol{\iota}^j(\boldsymbol{\mu}_1(\mathbf{T}))$, and otherwise $\mathbf{P}_i = \mathbf{T}_{m_i}$, where j-origin indexing is used for **T**.

Permutation of the subtrees rooted in node $\boldsymbol{i}$ of **T** can be effected as follows:

$$\overline{\boldsymbol{\alpha}}^1/\mathbf{T}_i \leftarrow \boldsymbol{m} \int (\overline{\boldsymbol{\alpha}}^1/\mathbf{T}_i).$$

The notation $\odot//\mathbf{T}$ will denote the application of the binary operator or relation $\odot$ to the nodes of **T** in right list order (i.e., *down* successive levels) and $\odot/\mathbf{T}$ will denote the same application in left list order (i.e., *across* paths). If the operator is symmetric (i.e., its operands commute), then $\odot//\mathbf{T} = \odot/\mathbf{T}$.

Maximization ($\mathbf{U}\lceil\mathbf{T}$) and minimization ($\mathbf{U}\lfloor\mathbf{T}$) are extended to trees in the obvious way.

The operations $\alpha/\boldsymbol{u}$, $\omega/\boldsymbol{u}$, $\sigma/\boldsymbol{a}$, and $\tau/\boldsymbol{a}$ are each extended in two ways: across paths and down levels. Examples of each appear in Fig. 1.24. Operations extending down levels are denoted by double virgules and represent an application of the corresponding vector operation to each level of the tree considered as a vector. For example, the statement

$$\mathbf{V} \leftarrow \sigma//\mathbf{A}$$

implies that each level of **V** is the forward set selection of the corresponding level of **A**, that is, $\boldsymbol{\epsilon}^j/\mathbf{V} = \sigma/\boldsymbol{\epsilon}^j/\mathbf{A}$. Operations extending across paths are denoted by single virgules and are defined in terms of subtrees. Thus

$$\mathbf{V} \leftarrow \alpha/\mathbf{U}$$

implies that **V** is obtained from the logical tree **U** by setting to zero all nodes of any subtree rooted in a zero node, and

$$\mathbf{V} \leftarrow \omega/\mathbf{U}$$

implies that **V** is obtained from **U** by setting to zero every node whose subtree contains a zero node. The definitions of $\sigma/\mathbf{U}$ and $\tau/\mathbf{U}$ are analogous.

Homogeneous trees

If, for all j, every node on level j of a tree **T** is either of degree zero or of degree $\boldsymbol{\nu}_{j+1}(\mathbf{T})$, then the tree **T** is said to be *uniform*. If all leaves of a uniform tree **T** lie in the same level (necessarily the top), then the tree is said to be *homogeneous*. The structure of a homogeneous tree is completely characterized by its dispersion vector $\boldsymbol{\nu}(\mathbf{T})$. All maximal paths in a homogeneous tree are clearly of the same length, namely $\nu(\mathbf{T}) = \nu(\boldsymbol{\nu}(\mathbf{T}))$. Figure 1.25 shows a homogeneous tree and its associated dispersion vector.

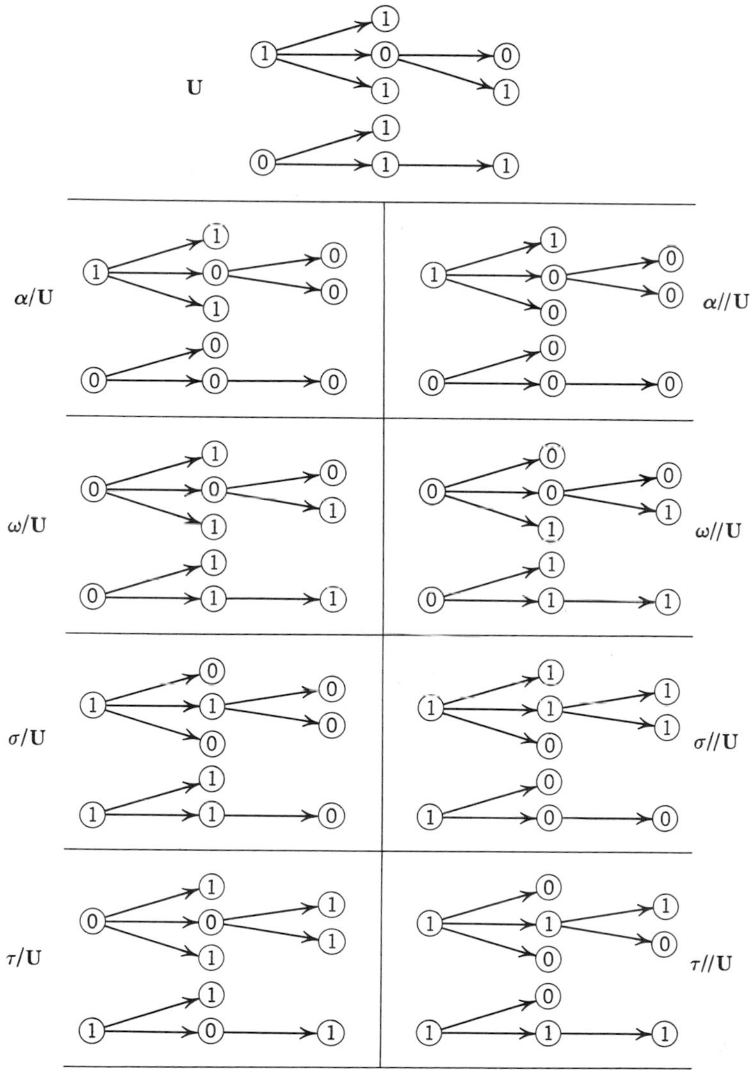

Figure 1.24 Set selection and maximum prefix and suffix operations

A tree $\mathbf{T}$ for which $\boldsymbol{\nu}(\mathbf{T}) = m\boldsymbol{\epsilon}$ is called an *m-way tree*, and a tree for which $\boldsymbol{\nu}_1(\mathbf{T}) = 1$ and $\bar{\boldsymbol{\alpha}}^1/\boldsymbol{\nu}(\mathbf{T}) = m\boldsymbol{\epsilon}$ is called a *singular m-way tree.*

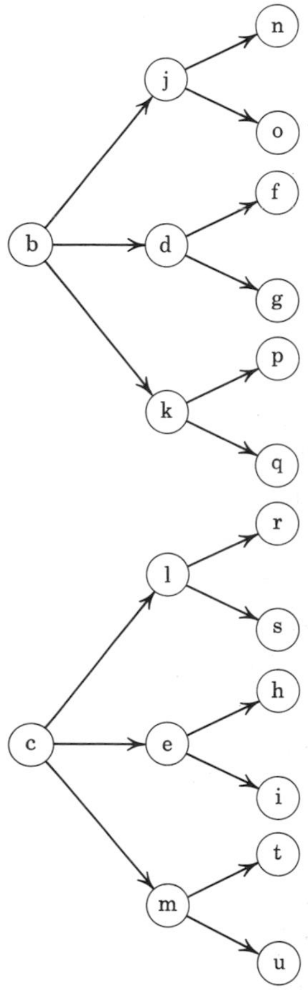

$\nu(\mathbf{H}) = (2, 3, 2)$
$\mu(\mathbf{H}) = (2, 6, 12)$

Figure 1.25 Homogeneous tree $\mathbf{H}$ and dispersion and moment vectors

The jth component of the moment vector of a homogeneous tree is clearly equal to the product of the first j components of the dispersion vector, that is, $\boldsymbol{\mu}(\mathbf{T}) = (\boxdot + \boldsymbol{I})^{\times}_{/}\ \boldsymbol{\nu}(\mathbf{T})$. The dispersion vector is, in turn, uniquely determined by the moment vector. The total number of nodes is given by $\mu(\mathbf{T}) = +/\boldsymbol{\mu}(\mathbf{T})$, and it can also be shown that $\mu(\mathbf{T}) = \boldsymbol{y} \perp \boldsymbol{y}$, where $\boldsymbol{y}$ is the dispersion vector in reverse order.

Tree compression of a homogeneous tree $\mathbf{H}$ (that is, $\mathbf{U}/\mathbf{H}$) does not generally produce a homogeneous tree, and, in fact, any tree $\mathbf{P}$ of arbitrary structure can be represented by a pair of homogeneous trees $\mathbf{U}$ and $\mathbf{H}$ such that $\mathbf{P} = \mathbf{U}/\mathbf{H}$. On the other hand, both path and level compression of homogeneous trees produce homogeneous trees. Moreover, if $\mathbf{P} = \boldsymbol{u}/\mathbf{H}$, then $\boldsymbol{\nu}(\mathbf{P}) = \boldsymbol{u}/\boldsymbol{\nu}(\mathbf{H})$, and if $\mathbf{P} = \boldsymbol{u}//\mathbf{H}$, then $\boldsymbol{\nu}(\mathbf{P}) = \boldsymbol{\nu}(\mathbf{H}) - (+/\bar{\boldsymbol{u}})\boldsymbol{\alpha}^1$.

Since the structure of a homogeneous tree is completely specified by its dispersion vector $\boldsymbol{k}$, the structure of the special logical trees can be specified in the forms $\mathsf{E}(\boldsymbol{k})$, ${}^{u}\mathsf{E}(\boldsymbol{k})$, and ${}_{u}\mathsf{E}(\boldsymbol{k})$.

In a homogeneous tree, the right list or left list index of a node can be determined as an explicit function of its index vector. Conversely, the index vector $\boldsymbol{i}$ can be determined directly from the corresponding left list index, to be denoted by $l(\boldsymbol{i})$, or from the right list index $r(\boldsymbol{i})$. In developing the relations between indices it will be convenient to use 0-origin indexing throughout.

The right list index is given by

$$r(\boldsymbol{i}) = f(\boldsymbol{i}) + g(\boldsymbol{i}),$$

where $$f(\boldsymbol{i}) = +/\boldsymbol{\alpha}^{\nu(\boldsymbol{i})-1}/\boldsymbol{\mu}(\mathbf{T})$$

is the number of nodes in the first $\nu(\boldsymbol{i}) - 1$ levels, and

$$g(\boldsymbol{i}) = (\boldsymbol{\alpha}^{\nu(\boldsymbol{i})}/\boldsymbol{\nu}(\mathbf{T})) \perp \boldsymbol{i}$$

is the rank of node $\boldsymbol{i}$ in the $\nu(\boldsymbol{i})$th level. For example, if $\boldsymbol{i} = (1, 0, 1)$ in the tree of Fig. 1.25, then $\boldsymbol{\mu}(\mathbf{H}) = (2, 6, 12)$, $f(\boldsymbol{i}) = +/(2, 6) = 8$, and $g(\boldsymbol{i}) = (2, 3, 2) \perp (1, 0, 1) = 7$.

Since $f(\boldsymbol{i})$ depends only on $\nu(\boldsymbol{i})$, the index $\boldsymbol{i}$ may be determined from r by first determining $\nu(\boldsymbol{i})$ as the largest value for which $f(\boldsymbol{i}) \leq r$, and then determining $\boldsymbol{i}$ such that

$$(\boldsymbol{\alpha}^{\nu(\boldsymbol{i})}/\boldsymbol{\nu}(\mathbf{T})) \perp \boldsymbol{i} = r - f(\boldsymbol{i}).$$

In tracing a path through a tree, the kth node of the set reachable from node $\boldsymbol{i}$ is the node $\boldsymbol{j} = \boldsymbol{i} \oplus (k)$. It is therefore useful to express $r(\boldsymbol{j})$ as a function of $r(\boldsymbol{i})$. Clearly

$$f(\boldsymbol{j}) = f(\boldsymbol{i}) + (\boldsymbol{\mu}(\mathbf{T}))_{\nu(\boldsymbol{i})-1},$$

$$g(\boldsymbol{j}) = g(\boldsymbol{i}) \times (\boldsymbol{\nu}(\mathbf{T}))_{\nu(\boldsymbol{i})} + \boldsymbol{j}_{\nu-1}.$$

In the special case of a singular homogeneous m-way tree,

$$f(\boldsymbol{i}) = 1 + m + m^2 + \cdots + m^{\nu(\boldsymbol{i})-2} = (m\boldsymbol{\epsilon}) \perp \boldsymbol{\epsilon}(\nu(\boldsymbol{i}) - 1)$$

$$= \frac{m^{\nu(\boldsymbol{i})-1} - 1}{m - 1}.$$

Hence $f(\boldsymbol{j}) = 1 + m \times f(\boldsymbol{i})$, and $g(\boldsymbol{j}) = m \times g(\boldsymbol{i}) + \boldsymbol{j}_{\nu-1}$. Recursion can therefore be performed simply upon the single function $r(\boldsymbol{i})$ as follows:

$$r(\boldsymbol{j}) = m \times r(\boldsymbol{i}) + 1 + \boldsymbol{j}_{\nu-1}.$$

The left list index $l(\boldsymbol{i})$ is most conveniently expressed as a function of $\nu(\boldsymbol{i})$ and of the vector $\boldsymbol{z}(\boldsymbol{i})$ (zero extension of $\boldsymbol{i}$), where $\boldsymbol{z} = \boldsymbol{\alpha}^{\nu(\boldsymbol{i})}(\nu(\mathbf{T}))\backslash\boldsymbol{i}$. Clearly $\nu(\boldsymbol{z}) = \nu(\mathbf{T})$ and $\boldsymbol{z}$ is the index of the "earliest" leaf reachable from node $\boldsymbol{i}$. In Fig. 1.25, for example, $\boldsymbol{z}((1, 2)) = (1, 2, 0)$.

The zero extension has the obvious property that every node above the path $\mathbf{T}^{\boldsymbol{z}(\boldsymbol{i})}$ precedes node $\boldsymbol{i}$ in the left list, and every node below the path follows it. The number of nodes in the path which precede node $\boldsymbol{i}$ is $\nu(\boldsymbol{i}) - 1$.

The number of leaves above the path $\mathbf{T}^{\boldsymbol{z}(\boldsymbol{i})}$ is $\boldsymbol{\nu}(\mathbf{T}) \perp \boldsymbol{z}(\boldsymbol{i})$, and more generally, the number of $(j - 1)$th level nodes above it is given by $(\boldsymbol{\alpha}^j/\boldsymbol{\nu}(\mathbf{T})) \perp (\boldsymbol{\alpha}^j/\boldsymbol{z}(\boldsymbol{i}))$. Consequently,

$$l(\boldsymbol{i}) = \nu(\boldsymbol{i}) - 1 + \sum_{j=1}^{\nu(\mathbf{T})} (\boldsymbol{\alpha}^j/\boldsymbol{\nu}(\mathbf{T})) \perp (\boldsymbol{\alpha}^j/\boldsymbol{z}(\boldsymbol{i})).$$

For example, if $\boldsymbol{i} = (1, 0)$ in Fig. 1.25, then $\boldsymbol{z}(\boldsymbol{i}) = (1, 0, 0)$ and

$$l(\boldsymbol{i}) = \nu(\boldsymbol{i}) - 1 + (2) \perp (1) + (2, 3) \perp (1, 0) + (2, 3, 2) \perp (1, 0, 0) = 11.$$

The foregoing result may be written alternatively as

$$l(\boldsymbol{i}) = \nu(\boldsymbol{i}) - 1 + \boldsymbol{w} \overset{+}{\underset{\times}{}} \boldsymbol{z}(\boldsymbol{i}),$$

where $\boldsymbol{w}_\nu = 1$, and $\boldsymbol{w}_{i-1} = 1 + (\boldsymbol{w}_i \times \boldsymbol{\nu}_i(\mathbf{T}))$. In the foregoing example, $\boldsymbol{w} = (10, 3, 1)$, and $\boldsymbol{w} \overset{+}{\underset{\times}{}} \boldsymbol{z}(\boldsymbol{i}) = 10$. This form is most convenient for determining $\boldsymbol{i}$ as a function of l, for since $\boldsymbol{w} \overset{+}{\underset{\times}{}} \boldsymbol{z} = l + 1 - \nu(\boldsymbol{i})$, then $\boldsymbol{z}_0(\boldsymbol{i}) = \lfloor l \div \boldsymbol{w}_0 \rfloor$, $\boldsymbol{z}_1(\boldsymbol{i}) = \lfloor ((\boldsymbol{w}_0 \mid l) - 1) \div \boldsymbol{w}_1 \rfloor$, etc. for all positive values of the quotient, and all components thereafter are zero. The dimension $\nu(\boldsymbol{i})$ is then determined from the relation $\nu(\boldsymbol{i}) = l + 1 - \boldsymbol{w} \overset{+}{\underset{\times}{}} \boldsymbol{z}(\boldsymbol{i})$.

REFERENCES

Birkhoff, G., and S. MacLane (1941), *A Survey of Modern Algebra*, Macmillan, New York.

Burks, A. W., D. W. Warren, and J. B. Wright (1954), "An Analysis of a Logical Machine Using Parenthesis-free Notation," *Mathematical Tables and Other Aids to Computation*, vol. VIII, pp. 53–57.

Dickson, L. E. (1939), *New First Course in the Theory of Equations*, Wiley, New York.

Garner, Harvey L. (1959), "The Residue Number System," *IRE Transactions*, vol. EC-8, pp. 140–147.

Goldstine, H. H., and J. von Neumann (1947), "Planning and Coding of Problems for an Electronic Computing Instrument," *Report on the Mathematical and Logical Aspects of an Electronic Computing Instrument*, Part II, vol. 1, Institute for Advanced Study, Princeton.

Iverson, K. E. (1954), "Machine Solutions of Linear Differential Equations," Doctoral Thesis, Harvard University.

Jacobson, N. (1951), *Lectures in Abstract Algebra*, vol. 1, Van Nostrand, New York.

Kunz, K. S. (1957), *Numerical Analysis*, McGraw-Hill, New York.

Margenau, H., and G. M. Murphy (1943), *The Mathematics of Physics and Chemistry*, Van Nostrand, New York.

Phister, M. (1958), *Logical Design of Digital Computers*, Wiley, New York.

Richards, R. K. (1955), *Arithmetic Operations in Digital Computers*, Van Nostrand, New York.

Riordan, J. (1958), *An Introduction to Combinatorial Analysis*, Wiley, New York.

Rutishauser, H. (1959), "Zur Matrizeninversion nach Gauss-Jordan," *Zeitschrift für Angewandte Mathematik und Physik*, vol. X, pp. 281–291.

Wright, H. N. (1939), *First Course in Theory of Numbers*, Wiley, New York.

EXERCISES

Organize each of the programs according to the method of leading decisions. Except where otherwise indicated, use 1-origin indexing. The conventions of Sec. S.1 of the Summary of Notation will be used in the statement of each of the exercises.

1.1 Let $\boldsymbol{d}$ = (a, 2, 3, 4, 5, 6, 7, 8, 9, 10, j, q, k), $\boldsymbol{s}$ = (c, d, h, s), $\boldsymbol{u}$ = (1, 0, 1, 0, 1), $\boldsymbol{v}$ = (0, 1, 1, 1, 0), $\boldsymbol{x}$ = (16, 8, 4, 2, 1), and $\boldsymbol{y}$ = (2, 3, 4, 5, 6). Determine

(a) the dimensions $\nu(\boldsymbol{d})$, $\nu(\boldsymbol{s})$, and $\nu(\boldsymbol{x})$.
(b) the vectors $\boldsymbol{x} + \boldsymbol{y}$, $\boldsymbol{x} - \boldsymbol{y}$, $\boldsymbol{x} \times \boldsymbol{y}$, $\boldsymbol{x} \div \boldsymbol{y}$, and $\boldsymbol{u} + \boldsymbol{v}$.
(c) the logical vectors $\boldsymbol{u} \wedge \boldsymbol{v}$, $\boldsymbol{u} \vee \boldsymbol{v}$, $(\boldsymbol{u} \neq \boldsymbol{v})$, and $(\boldsymbol{u} = \boldsymbol{v})$.
(d) the reductions $+/\boldsymbol{x}$, $\times/\boldsymbol{y}$, $\wedge/\boldsymbol{u}$, and $\vee/\boldsymbol{v}$.
(e) the base two values of $\boldsymbol{u}$ and of $\boldsymbol{v}$, that is, $+/(\boldsymbol{x} \times \boldsymbol{u})$, and $+/(\boldsymbol{x} \times \boldsymbol{v})$.
(f) the rotated vectors $2 \downarrow \boldsymbol{d}$, $4 \uparrow \boldsymbol{s}$, and $\uparrow \boldsymbol{y}$.
(g) the unit vector $\boldsymbol{\epsilon}^1(5)$ in a 1-origin system, and $\boldsymbol{\epsilon}^3(5)$ in a 0-origin system.
(h) the infixes $(\boldsymbol{\alpha}^5(7) \wedge \boldsymbol{\omega}^5(7))$ and $2 \downarrow \boldsymbol{\alpha}^3(7)$.

1.2 Show that

(a) $\times/\iota^1(n) = n!$ (Include the case $n = 0$.)
(b) $+/\iota^j(n) = n(n + 2j - 1) \div 2$.
(c) $\times/(k \uparrow \boldsymbol{x}) = \times/\boldsymbol{x}$.
(d) $(k \uparrow \boldsymbol{x}) + (k \uparrow \boldsymbol{y}) = k \uparrow (\boldsymbol{x} + \boldsymbol{y})$.

1.3 Write detailed (i.e., component-by-component) programs for the following operations. Include tests for compatibility of the operands.

(a) $\boldsymbol{w} \leftarrow \boldsymbol{u} \wedge \boldsymbol{v}$.
(b) $\boldsymbol{W} \leftarrow \boldsymbol{U} \vee \boldsymbol{V}$.
(c) $\boldsymbol{b} \leftarrow \boldsymbol{u}/\boldsymbol{a}$.
(d) $\boldsymbol{B} \leftarrow \boldsymbol{u}/\boldsymbol{A}$.
(e) $\boldsymbol{B} \leftarrow \boldsymbol{u}/\boldsymbol{v}//\boldsymbol{A}$.
(f) $\boldsymbol{x} \leftarrow (\boldsymbol{x} > 0)/\boldsymbol{x}$.
(g) $\boldsymbol{u} \leftarrow \alpha^j(k)$.
(h) $\boldsymbol{u} \leftarrow i \downarrow \alpha^j(k)$.
(i) $\boldsymbol{c} \leftarrow \backslash \boldsymbol{a}, \boldsymbol{u}, \boldsymbol{b} \backslash$.
(j) $\boldsymbol{c} \leftarrow /\boldsymbol{a}, \boldsymbol{u}, \boldsymbol{b}/$.
(k) $\boldsymbol{c} \leftarrow \boldsymbol{u} \backslash \boldsymbol{a}$.

1.4 Establish the identities

(a) $/\boldsymbol{a}, \boldsymbol{u}, \boldsymbol{b}/ = \backslash \bar{\boldsymbol{u}}/\boldsymbol{a}, \boldsymbol{u}, \boldsymbol{u}/\boldsymbol{b} \backslash$.
(b) $\backslash \boldsymbol{a}, \boldsymbol{u}, \boldsymbol{b} \backslash = /\bar{\boldsymbol{u}} \backslash \boldsymbol{a}, \boldsymbol{u}, \boldsymbol{u} \backslash \boldsymbol{b}/$.

1.5 The classic "rings-*o*-seven" puzzle can be posed as follows: an ordered collection of n rings is to be placed on (removed from) a bar under the following constraints:

(i) ring n may be placed on or removed at will.
(ii) ring k may be placed on or removed only if ring $(k + 1)$ is on and all succeeding rings are off.

The state of the rings can be described by a logical vector $\boldsymbol{u}$, with $\boldsymbol{u}_k = 1$ if ring k is on. Write programs on $\boldsymbol{u}$ which describe the removal of the rings beginning with

(a) $\boldsymbol{u} = \boldsymbol{\epsilon}$ [The successive values of $\boldsymbol{u}$ represent a *reflected Gray code*; see Phister (1958).]
(b) $\boldsymbol{u}$ arbitrary.

1.6 The ordered array of variables used to represent a variable x in some coding system may be considered as a *vector representation* of x, denoted by $\rho(x)$. In the 8421 code for decimal digits, for example, $\rho(0) = (0, 0, 0, 0)$, $\rho(1) = (0, 0, 0, 1)$, and, in general, $\rho(x)$ is defined by the relation $+/[\boldsymbol{w} \times \rho(x)] = x$, where $\boldsymbol{w} = (8, 4, 2, 1)$. For each of the following coding systems, (see Richards, pp. 183–184 for definitions), write a concise expression for $\rho(x)$:

(a) the excess-three code for decimal digits.
(b) any chosen two-out-of-five code.
(c) any chosen biquinary code.
(d) the semaphore code for the alphabet (see any good dictionary). Denote each code by a two-component vector $\rho(x) \subseteq \iota^0(8)$. Use $\boldsymbol{a}\,\iota\,x$, where $\boldsymbol{a} = $ (a, b, c, . . . , z).

1.7 Let $\boldsymbol{X}$ be a square sparse matrix represented by the logical matrix $\boldsymbol{U} = (\boldsymbol{X} \neq 0)$ and either or both of the vectors $\boldsymbol{r} = \boldsymbol{U}/\boldsymbol{X}$, and $\boldsymbol{c} = \boldsymbol{U}//\boldsymbol{X}$. Write programs to determine the product $\boldsymbol{Y} = \boldsymbol{X} \overset{+}{\underset{\times}{}} \boldsymbol{X}$, using the arguments

(a) $\boldsymbol{r}$, $\boldsymbol{c}$, and $\boldsymbol{U}$.
(b) $\boldsymbol{r}$ and $\boldsymbol{U}$.
(c) $\boldsymbol{c}$ and $\boldsymbol{U}$.

1.8 Prove that

(a) $\lceil x \rceil = -\lfloor -x \rfloor$.

(b) $\lfloor \lfloor a \div b \rfloor \div c \rfloor = \lfloor a \div bc \rfloor$ for all positive integers a, b, and c.

1.9 Let $\boldsymbol{r} = \mathbf{E}/\boldsymbol{A}$, and $\boldsymbol{c} = \mathbf{E}//\boldsymbol{A}$ be the row list and column list, respectively, of the matrix $\boldsymbol{A}$, and let r_h, A_j^i, and c_k be corresponding elements of the three representations of $\boldsymbol{A}$. Determine:

(a) h as a function of k, $\nu(\boldsymbol{A})$, and $\mu(\boldsymbol{A})$.

(b) k as a function of h, $\nu(\boldsymbol{A})$, and $\mu(\boldsymbol{A})$.

(c) the permutation vector $\boldsymbol{h}$ such that $\boldsymbol{c} = \boldsymbol{h} \int \boldsymbol{r}$.

1.10 Show that

(a) $\wedge/\boldsymbol{u} = \overline{\vee/\bar{\boldsymbol{u}}}$ (Use De Morgan's law for two variables and induction.)

(b) $\neq/\boldsymbol{u} = 2 \,|_0\, +/\boldsymbol{u}$ (Use induction.)

(c) $=/\boldsymbol{u} = \overline{2 \,|_0\, +/\bar{\boldsymbol{u}}}$.

(d) $\neq/\boldsymbol{u} = \overline{=/\bar{\boldsymbol{u}}}$.

(e) $\boldsymbol{U} \,{}^{\neq}_{\wedge}\, \boldsymbol{v} = (2\boldsymbol{\epsilon}) \,|_0\, (\boldsymbol{U} \,{}^{+}_{\times}\, \boldsymbol{v})$.

(f) $\boldsymbol{U} \,{}^{\neq}_{\wedge}\, \boldsymbol{V} = \overline{\bar{\boldsymbol{U}} \,{}^{=}_{\vee}\, \bar{\boldsymbol{V}}}$.

(g) $(\boldsymbol{t} \,{}^{\circ}_{\wedge}\, \boldsymbol{u}) \wedge (\boldsymbol{v} \,{}^{\circ}_{\wedge}\, \boldsymbol{w}) = (\boldsymbol{t} \,{}^{\circ}_{\wedge}\, \boldsymbol{w}) \wedge (\boldsymbol{v} \,{}^{\circ}_{\wedge}\, \boldsymbol{u})$.

1.11 (a) Show that $+/\boldsymbol{x} = +/(\bar{\boldsymbol{u}}/\boldsymbol{x}) + +/(\boldsymbol{u}/\boldsymbol{x})$. (Include the case $\boldsymbol{u} = 0$.) (b) What properties are required of an operator $\bigcirc$ that it satisfy the relation established for $+$ in part (a)?

1.12 Show that

(a) $\boldsymbol{X} \,{}^{+}_{\times}\, \boldsymbol{Y} = (\bar{\boldsymbol{u}}/\boldsymbol{X}) \,{}^{+}_{\times}\, (\bar{\boldsymbol{u}}//\boldsymbol{Y}) + (\boldsymbol{u}/\boldsymbol{X}) \,{}^{+}_{\times}\, (\boldsymbol{u}//\boldsymbol{Y})$.

(b) $\boldsymbol{u}/(\boldsymbol{X} \,{}^{+}_{\times}\, \boldsymbol{Y}) = \boldsymbol{X} \,{}^{+}_{\times}\, (\boldsymbol{u}/\boldsymbol{Y})$.

(c) $\boldsymbol{u}//(\boldsymbol{X} \,{}^{+}_{\times}\, \boldsymbol{Y}) = (\boldsymbol{u}//\boldsymbol{X}) \,{}^{+}_{\times}\, \boldsymbol{Y}$.

(d) $(\boldsymbol{u} \wedge \boldsymbol{v})/\boldsymbol{a} = (\boldsymbol{u}/\boldsymbol{v})/(\boldsymbol{u}/\boldsymbol{a})$.

1.13 Use the result of Exercise 1.11(b) to extend the results of Exercise 1.12(a–c) to logical operators.

1.14 Write programs to determine:

(a) the value of the polynomial $\boldsymbol{x}$ at the point a, that is, to evaluate $(y\boldsymbol{\epsilon}) \perp \boldsymbol{x}$ for $y = a$. Use no more than $\nu(\boldsymbol{x})$ multiplications.

(b) the derivative of the polynomial $\boldsymbol{x}$, that is, the vector $\boldsymbol{z}$ such that

$$(y\boldsymbol{\epsilon}) \perp \boldsymbol{z} = \frac{d}{dy}((y\boldsymbol{\epsilon}) \perp \boldsymbol{x}), \text{ and } \nu(\boldsymbol{z}) = \nu(\boldsymbol{x}).$$

(c) the integral $\boldsymbol{z}$ of the polynomial $\boldsymbol{x}$ satisfying the boundary condition

$$(a\boldsymbol{\epsilon}) \perp \boldsymbol{z} = b.$$

(d) the quotient $\boldsymbol{q}$ and remainder $\boldsymbol{r}$ obtained in dividing the polynomial $\boldsymbol{n}$ by the polynomial $\boldsymbol{d}$, for $\nu(\boldsymbol{d}) \leq \nu(\boldsymbol{n})$.

(e) the value of the polynomial $\boldsymbol{n}$ at the point a by using part (d) with $\boldsymbol{d} = (1, -a)$.

(f) the value of $\dfrac{d}{dy}((y\boldsymbol{\epsilon}) \perp \boldsymbol{n})$ at the point a by two applications of part (e).

(g) an approximate real root of the equation $(y\boldsymbol{\epsilon}) \perp \boldsymbol{x} = 0$, using parts (e) and (f) and the Newton-Raphson formula [Kunz (1957)].

1.15 Let the components of the vector $\boldsymbol{r}$ be the real roots of a polynomial $\boldsymbol{x}$. Write a program to

(a) determine the symmetric functions of $\boldsymbol{r}$. [Dickson (1939), Ch. X.]
(b) determine $\boldsymbol{x}$ as a function of $\boldsymbol{r}$.

1.16 Write a program to determine the polynomial $\boldsymbol{x}$ consisting of the first n terms of the exponential series $1 + y + y^2/2! + \cdots$.

1.17 Write a program to determine the moduli of all roots of the polynomial $\boldsymbol{x}$, using the Graeffe method [Kunz (1957)]. Assume that operations for the logarithm and exponential functions are available as subroutines.

1.18 List all the 1-origin permutation vectors of dimension four which are self-inverse.

1.19 Using 1-origin indexing, write programs to derive

(a) the permutation $\boldsymbol{k}$ which is inverse to the permutation $\boldsymbol{j}$.
(b) a permutation $\boldsymbol{j}$ which transforms a given logical vector $\boldsymbol{u}$ to a prefix vector.

1.20 A square logical matrix $\boldsymbol{U}$ such that $+/\boldsymbol{U} = +//\boldsymbol{U} = \boldsymbol{\epsilon}$ is sometimes called a *permutation matrix*, since premultiplication of a numerical vector $\boldsymbol{x}$ determines a permutation of $\boldsymbol{x}$. Write programs to determine

(a) the permutation matrix $\boldsymbol{U}$ corresponding to the 1-origin permutation vector $\boldsymbol{k}$, that is, determine $\boldsymbol{U}$ such that $\boldsymbol{U} \overset{+}{\underset{\times}{}} \boldsymbol{x} = \boldsymbol{k} \int_1 \boldsymbol{x}$.
(b) the permutation $\boldsymbol{k}$ corresponding to a given permutation matrix $\boldsymbol{U}$.
(c) the permutation $\boldsymbol{V}$ which is inverse to the permutation $\boldsymbol{U}$.

1.21 Let $\boldsymbol{p}$ be the vector representation of a permutation and let $\boldsymbol{c}$ be the standard representation in terms of disjoint cycles, including all cycles of one [Jacobson (1951), p. 34.] Each cycle of $\boldsymbol{c}$ is enclosed in square brackets, each half-bracket being considered as a component of $\boldsymbol{c}$. For example, if $\boldsymbol{c}$ = ([, 1, 3, 5,], [, 2, 4,], [, 6,]), then $\boldsymbol{p} = (3, 4, 5, 2, 1, 6)$, $\nu(\boldsymbol{c}) = 12$, and $\nu(\boldsymbol{p}) = 6$, and, in general, $\nu(\boldsymbol{c}) = \nu(\boldsymbol{p}) + 2k$ where k is the number of disjoint cycles in $\boldsymbol{p}$. The usual elision of cycles of one would give $\boldsymbol{c}$ = ([, 1, 3, 5,], [, 2, 4,]), but this determines a unique correspondent $\boldsymbol{p}$ only if the dimension of $\boldsymbol{p}$ is otherwise specified, and inclusion of all cycles of one will therefore be assumed. If each infix of numerical components in $\boldsymbol{c}$ is preceded by a left bracket and followed by a right bracket, and if $\boldsymbol{c}$ determines a legitimate permutation vector $\boldsymbol{p}$, then $\boldsymbol{c}$ is said to be *well formed*.

(a) Write a program to determine $\boldsymbol{p}$ as a function of a well formed permutation $\boldsymbol{c}$. Include determination of the dimension of $\boldsymbol{p}$.
(b) Modify the program of part (a) to incorporate checks on the well formation of $\boldsymbol{c}$. If $\boldsymbol{c}$ is ill formed, the vector $\boldsymbol{p}$ is to be defined as the literal "ill formed."
(c) Modify part (b) to process a sequence of vectors $\boldsymbol{c}^1, \boldsymbol{c}^2, \ldots$, each pair being separated by a single null element, and the end of the sequence being indicated by a pair of successive null elements, i.e., to process $\boldsymbol{z} = \boldsymbol{c}^1 \oplus (\circ) \oplus \boldsymbol{c}^2 \oplus \cdots \oplus \boldsymbol{c}^r \oplus (\circ, \circ)$. Include checks on the well formation of each permutation.
(d) Write a program to determine the parity [Jacobson (1951), p. 36] of a permutation vector $\boldsymbol{p}$.

1.22 Write detailed programs for the following processes:

(a) $k \leftarrow \theta_1/x$
(b) $y \leftarrow m \int_1 x$
(c) $v \leftarrow u \lceil x$
(d) $V \leftarrow u \mathring{\lceil} X$
(e) $v \leftarrow \alpha/u$
(f) $V \leftarrow \omega//U$
(g) $v \leftarrow \sigma/b$
(h) $V \leftarrow \tau//B$
(i) $m \leftarrow b\, \iota_0\, a$
(j) $M \leftarrow B\, \mathring{\iota}_0\, a$
(k) $u \leftarrow \epsilon_b^{\,a}$
(l) $c \leftarrow b \cap a$
(m) $c \leftarrow b \triangle a$
(n) $c \leftarrow b \cup a$
(o) $C \leftarrow a \otimes b$

1.23 (a) Copy onto file $\Phi_1^{\,2}$ successive groups of items from the row of files Φ^1 in cyclic order, omitting any exhausted files. The end of each group is demarked by a partition λ_2, and the end of each file by a partition λ_3.
(b) A file which is always recorded in the forward direction and read in the backward direction functions as a *stack*. Using file $\Phi_2^{\,2}$ as a stack, modify the program of part (a) so as to reverse (in the output file $\Phi_1^{\,2}$) the order of the items within each group.

1.24 The accompanying node vector n and connection matrix C together specify a directed graph ($C_j^{\,i} = 1$ indicates a branch from node i to node j) which is, in fact, a tree.

$$n = (a, b, c, d, e, f, g)$$

$$C = \begin{pmatrix} 0 & 0 & 0 & 0 & 1 & 1 & 0 \\ 0 & 0 & 0 & 0 & 0 & 0 & 0 \\ 1 & 0 & 0 & 1 & 0 & 0 & 0 \\ 0 & 0 & 0 & 0 & 0 & 0 & 0 \\ 0 & 0 & 0 & 0 & 0 & 0 & 0 \\ 0 & 0 & 0 & 0 & 0 & 0 & 0 \\ 0 & 1 & 0 & 0 & 0 & 0 & 0 \end{pmatrix}$$

(a) Draw one of the possible ordered trees represented by n and C.
(b) For the tree **T** of part (a) show the full left list [**T**.
(c) Show the full right list]**T**.

1.25 Write programs which include tests on compatibility and which determine
(a) L = [**T** from R =]**T**
(b) S =](u/**T**) from μ(**T**),]**T**, and u
(c) M = [(u//**T**) from L = [**T** and u
(d) M = [($k \int_1$ **T**) from L = [**T** and k

1.26 (a) Give an example of a well formed right list which demonstrates that a *prefix* of a right list is not, in general, well formed.
(b) Show clearly where the argument used in establishing the well formation of any suffix of a well formed list breaks down when applied to a prefix.

1.27 Give formal proofs for the facts that

(a) a left list groups nodes by subtrees.

(b) a right list groups nodes by levels.

(c) $\boldsymbol{\mu}_1(\mathbf{T}) = \nu(\boldsymbol{d}) - +/\boldsymbol{d}$, where $\boldsymbol{d}$ is the degree vector of $\mathbf{T}$.

1.28 Write programs to determine $\boldsymbol{\mu}(\mathbf{T})$ as a function of

(a) the left list degree vector of **T**.

(b) the right list degree vector of **T**.

1.29 Trace Programs 1.20 and 1.21 for the tree of Exercise 1.24.

1.30 Show that for a homogeneous tree **H**, $\mu(\mathbf{H}) = \boldsymbol{y} \perp \boldsymbol{y}$, where $\vec{\boldsymbol{y}} = \boldsymbol{\nu}(\mathbf{H})$.

1.31 If **H** is homogeneous, $\boldsymbol{\nu}(\mathbf{H}) = (3, 2, 3, 4)$, and $\boldsymbol{i} = (1, 0, 2)$, determine, in a 0-origin system

(a) the left list index $l(\boldsymbol{i})$.

(b) the right list index $r(\boldsymbol{i})$.

(c) the index $\boldsymbol{j}$ of the node whose left list index is 27.

1.32 (a) If $\boldsymbol{K} = \boldsymbol{\iota}^0(n) \downarrow (\boldsymbol{\epsilon}(n) \overset{\circ}{\times} \boldsymbol{\iota}^0(n))$, show that $\boldsymbol{K} + \tilde{\boldsymbol{K}} = n(\mathsf{E} - \mathsf{I})$.

(b) If $\boldsymbol{y}$ is any permutation of $\boldsymbol{x}$ and $\nu(\boldsymbol{x}) = n$, show that $\boldsymbol{x} \overset{+}{\times} \boldsymbol{K} \overset{+}{\times} \boldsymbol{x} = \boldsymbol{y} \overset{+}{\times} \boldsymbol{K} \overset{+}{\times} \boldsymbol{y}$.

1.33 Using the Euclidean algorithm, write programs to determine:

(a) d as the greatest common divisor of positive integers x and y.

(b) $\boldsymbol{d}$ as the g.c.d. of $\boldsymbol{x}$ and $\boldsymbol{y}$ where $\boldsymbol{d}$, $\boldsymbol{x}$, and $\boldsymbol{y}$ represent polynomials in z (e.g., $(z\boldsymbol{\epsilon}) \perp \boldsymbol{x}$).

1.34 To assure uniqueness, the number of different digits (symbols) used in a base b number system must not exceed b. The limitation to the particular range $0 \leq a_i < b$ is, however, not essential. For example, a base three system can be constructed using digits -1, 0, and 1, for which it is convenient to adopt the symbols $-$, 0, and $+$, respectively. The positive numbers beginning at zero are then represented by the sequence 0, $+$, $+-$, $+0$, $++$, $+--$, $+-0$, $+-+$, $+0-$, $+00$, etc. The negative numbers beginning at zero are 0, $-$, $-+$, -0, $--$, $-++$, $-+0$, $-+-$, $-0+$, -00, etc.

(a) Construct addition and multiplication tables for this number system and calculate the sum and the product of the numbers $0-$ and $--$. Use the decimal system to check all results.

(b) Negative numbers are represented in this system without the attachment of a special sign position. Special rules regarding sign are therefore banished except that it is necessary to formulate a rule for changing the sign of a number, i.e., to multiply by minus one. Formulate such a rule.

1.35 For any integer n, let $x_2 = 2 \mid_0 n$, $x_3 = 3 \mid_0 n$, $x_5 = 5 \mid_0 n$, and $x_7 = 7 \mid_0 n$. As shown by Garner (1959), the ordered array (x_2, x_3, x_5, x_7) provides a representation of the integer n in a so-called *residue* number system.

(a) Write the residue representations of the first ten nonnegative integers.

(b) For integers n in the range $0 \leq n < (2 \times 3 \times 5 \times 7)$ show:

(1) that the representation is unique.

(2) that an addition algorithm may be defined which treats the several

columns independently, i.e., there are no carries. (The sums must also lie within the specified range.)

(c) Discuss the choice of moduli for extending the range of the representation.

(d) Show that the algorithm derived in part (b) is valid for all positive and negative integers in the range $-a/2 \leq n < a/2$ for $a = 2 \times 3 \times 5 \times 7$.

(e) Derive an algorithm for obtaining $-n$ from n.

(f) Derive an algorithm for multiplication.

(g) The sign of the number (i.e., its relation to zero) is not displayed directly by this representation. Convince yourself that its determination is nontrivial.

1.36 Let $\boldsymbol{x}$, $\boldsymbol{y}$, and $\boldsymbol{z}$ be the positional representations of the numbers x, y, and z respectively. Using the floor and residue operations, write programs to determine $\boldsymbol{z}$ as a function of $\boldsymbol{x}$ and $\boldsymbol{y}$, where $z = x + y$ and the representation in use is

(a) base b.

(b) mixed base $\boldsymbol{b}$.

(c) the $+$, $-$, 0 base three system (of Exercise 1.34).

(d) the residue number system (of Exercise 1.35).

1.37 Write programs for the multiplication $z = x \times y$ for each of the cases of Exercise 1.36.

1.38 Write programs to convert in each direction between the following pairs of number systems:

(a) base b_1 and base b_2.

(b) base $\boldsymbol{b}^1$ and base $\boldsymbol{b}^2$.

(c) base three and the $+$, $-$, 0 base three of Exercise 1.34.

(d) residue and base b (Exercise 1.35).

1.39 (a) Show that the superdiagonal matrices satisfy ${}^{j}\boldsymbol{I} \overset{+}{\times} {}^{k}\boldsymbol{I} = {}^{(j+k)}\boldsymbol{I}$.

(b) A matrix of the form $\boldsymbol{J} = (x\boldsymbol{I} + {}^{1}\boldsymbol{I})$ is called a *Jordan box*. Write the expansion of the nth power of $\boldsymbol{J}$.

(c) Show that $\boldsymbol{X} \overset{+}{\times} \boldsymbol{Y} = \boldsymbol{X}_1 \overset{\circ}{\times} \boldsymbol{Y}^1 + \boldsymbol{X}_2 \overset{\circ}{\times} \boldsymbol{Y}^2 + \cdots + \boldsymbol{X}_{\nu(\boldsymbol{X})} \overset{\circ}{\times} \boldsymbol{Y}^{\nu(\boldsymbol{X})}$.

(d) Determine an explicit solution to the set of linear equations $\boldsymbol{A} \overset{+}{\times} \boldsymbol{x} = \boldsymbol{y}$, where $\boldsymbol{u}/\boldsymbol{x} = \boldsymbol{a}$ and $\boldsymbol{v}/\boldsymbol{y} = \boldsymbol{b}$ are known and where $+/\boldsymbol{u} + +/\boldsymbol{v} = \nu(\boldsymbol{A}) = \mu(\boldsymbol{A})$. State the conditions for the existence of a unique solution.

1.40 Any nonsingular matrix $\boldsymbol{A}$ can be reduced to the identity $\boldsymbol{I}$ by a sequence of *row operations* of the form $\boldsymbol{A}^i \leftarrow x\boldsymbol{A}^i + y\boldsymbol{A}^i$, or $\boldsymbol{A}^i \leftrightarrow \boldsymbol{A}^j$. The process which accomplishes this (using row operations only) by reducing successive column vectors to the successive unit vectors is called *Jordan* or *complete* elimination. If the same sequence of row operations is executed upon the identity matrix, it will be transformed to the matrix $\boldsymbol{B}$ such that $\boldsymbol{B} \overset{+}{\times} \boldsymbol{A} = \boldsymbol{I}$. The inverse of $\boldsymbol{A}$ can therefore be obtained by performing Jordan elimination on the matrix $\boldsymbol{M} = \boldsymbol{A} \oplus \boldsymbol{I}$ so as to reduce the first $\nu(\boldsymbol{A})$ columns to the identity. The last $\nu(\boldsymbol{A})$ columns are then the inverse of $\boldsymbol{A}$.

(a) Write a program to determine the inverse of $\boldsymbol{A}$ by Jordan elimination.

(b) The sequence of operations which reduce the ith column of $\boldsymbol{A}$ to $\boldsymbol{\epsilon}^i$ is called the ith *step* of the process, and the ith diagonal element at the beginning of the ith step is called the ith pivot element. Modify the program of part (a) so that each step is preceded by a column permutation which yields the largest (in absolute value) pivot element possible. This modification tends to reduce the accumulation of round-off errors.

(c) In the Jordan elimination of part (a), it is unnecessary to store the identity matrix explicitly, and, since the ith column is first affected at the ith step, only one new column need be brought in at each step. Moreover, the ith column of $\boldsymbol{A}$ may be discarded after its reduction to $\boldsymbol{\epsilon}^i$ on the ith step, and it is therefore necessary to store only a square matrix at all times. Show that by shifting all columns to the left and by moving the rows upward cyclically, a very uniform process results, with the pivot element in the leading position at every step [Iverson (1954) or Rutishauser (1959)]. Write a program for the process.

(d) Modify part (c) to allow the choice of pivot elements as in part (b). The effects of the permutation on the not explicitly recorded identity cannot be indicated directly, but the performance of the same set of permutations in reverse order upon the *rows* of the resulting inverse produces the same result. Verify this and program the process.

1.41 (a) Show that a group [Jacobson (1951)] can be represented by a square matrix $\boldsymbol{M}$ such that each row and each column is a permutation vector.

(b) Show that $\boldsymbol{M}^i = \boldsymbol{M}_i = \boldsymbol{\iota}^1$ for some i.

(c) What are the necessary and sufficient conditions that the group represented by $\boldsymbol{M}$ be Abelian?

(d) Write a program to determine all cyclic subgroups of a group represented by $\boldsymbol{M}$.

1.42 If $\boldsymbol{U}$ is a logical matrix whose rows are each nonzero, mutually disjoint, and collectively exhaustive (that is, $(+/\boldsymbol{U} \geq \boldsymbol{\epsilon}) = \boldsymbol{\epsilon}$, and $+//\boldsymbol{U} = \boldsymbol{\epsilon}$), then $\boldsymbol{U}$ defines an *m-way partition* of n, where $m = \mu(\boldsymbol{U})$, and $n = \nu(\boldsymbol{U})$. The partition is more commonly represented by the vector $\boldsymbol{p} = +/\boldsymbol{U}$ [Riordan (1958), p. 107]. Clearly $+/\boldsymbol{p} = n$. Write a program to generate

(a) all partitions $\boldsymbol{U}$ of a given integer n.

(b) all distinct partitions of n, where $\boldsymbol{U}$ and $\boldsymbol{V}$ are considered equivalent if $\boldsymbol{p} = +/\boldsymbol{U}$ is a permutation of $\boldsymbol{q} = +/\boldsymbol{V}$.

1.43 Let $\boldsymbol{x}$ be a *space* vector (i.e., of dimension three), and let $\boldsymbol{R}(\boldsymbol{x})$ be the square matrix $\boldsymbol{\iota} \uparrow (\boldsymbol{\epsilon} \underset{\wedge}{\circ} \boldsymbol{x})$. Show that

(a) $+/\boldsymbol{R}(\boldsymbol{x} \times \boldsymbol{y}) = (\boldsymbol{x} \underset{\times}{+} \boldsymbol{y}) \times \boldsymbol{\epsilon}$

(b) $\boldsymbol{\epsilon} \underset{\times}{+} (\boldsymbol{x} \times \boldsymbol{y}) = \boldsymbol{x} \underset{\times}{+} \boldsymbol{y}$

(c) $(+/\boldsymbol{R}(\boldsymbol{x} \times \boldsymbol{y})) \underset{\times}{+} (\boldsymbol{w} \times \boldsymbol{z}) = (\boldsymbol{x} \underset{\times}{+} \boldsymbol{y}) \times (\boldsymbol{w} \underset{\times}{+} \boldsymbol{z})$

(d) $(\boldsymbol{x} \underset{\times}{+} \boldsymbol{y}) \times (\boldsymbol{x} \underset{\times}{+} \boldsymbol{y}) = (\boldsymbol{x} \times \boldsymbol{y}) \underset{\times}{+} (\boldsymbol{x} \times \boldsymbol{y}) + 2(\downarrow\boldsymbol{x} \times \uparrow\boldsymbol{y}) \underset{\times}{+} (\downarrow\boldsymbol{x} \times \uparrow\boldsymbol{y})$.

1.44 Let $\boldsymbol{x} \cdot \boldsymbol{y} = (\uparrow\boldsymbol{x} \times \downarrow\boldsymbol{y}) - (\downarrow\boldsymbol{x} \times \uparrow\boldsymbol{y})$ be the *vector product* of $\boldsymbol{x}$ and $\boldsymbol{y}$ for vectors of dimension three. Show that

(a) this agrees with the usual definition [Margenau and Murphy (1943)].

(b) $\boldsymbol{x} \cdot \boldsymbol{y} = -(\boldsymbol{y} \cdot \boldsymbol{x})$

(c) $x \cdot y$ is perpendicular to x, that is, $x \overset{+}{\underset{\times}{.}} (x \cdot y) = 0$. (Use the fact that $\downarrow x = 2\uparrow x$ for a vector of dimension three.)

1.45 Let $[x] = \sqrt{(x \overset{+}{\underset{\times}{.}} x)}$ be the *length of* x, let $x \,\gamma\, y = \dfrac{x \overset{+}{\underset{\times}{.}} y}{[x] \times [y]}$ be the cosine of the angle between x and y, and let $x \,\sigma\, y = \sqrt{1 - (x \,\gamma\, y)^2}$ be the sine of the angle. Use the results of Exercises 1.43 and 1.44 to show that for space vectors

(a) $[x \cdot y] = [x] \times [y] \times (x \,\sigma\, y)$. Note that $[x \cdot y]$ is the area enclosed by the parallelogram defined by x and y.

(b) $(x \cdot y) \cdot z = (x \overset{+}{\underset{\times}{.}} z) \times y - (y \overset{+}{\underset{\times}{.}} z) \times x$

(c) $(x \cdot y) \overset{+}{\underset{\times}{.}} z = x \overset{+}{\underset{\times}{.}} (y \cdot z)$.

chapter 2

MICROPROGRAMMING

The algorithms to be executed by an automatic computer must be described in the restricted set of operations (called *instructions* or *commands*) provided in a given computer, and an algorithm so described is called a *computer program.* Since computer instructions are relatively complex, they may be described in turn by *microprograms* employing more elementary operations.

Microprograms may be used to define a computer instruction set for the programmer, to define the detailed algorithms by which the computer circuits produce the operations of the instruction set, or for a variety of other purposes. In the design and development of a computer, for example, it is important to maintain precise and complete communication between the computer programmer, the computer (or *system*) designer, and the logical circuit (or *hardware*) designer. The system designer will, in fact, ordinarily begin with a description at the programmer's level and proceed through increasing detail to the hardware designer's level. Meanwhile, the programmers concerned with evaluating potential performance and with developing systems of metaprograms (so-called automatic programming systems) should be enabled to follow and to influence the evolving design.

The use of microprogramming will be illustrated by a description of the IBM 7090 computer (to be called the 7090) at a level approximately suited to the programmer and the system designer. The final section treats some problems in the extension to the hardware design level.

The programs together with the lists of operands constitute a self-contained description of the 7090 which, to readers already familiar with computer organization and with the relevant sections (1.1 to 1.11 and 1.14) of Chapter 1, should prove readable without reference to the text. The text serves only to elucidate the microprograms and does not treat all of the instructions described by them. Tables 2.1, 2.13, and 2.14 summarize the dimensions, format, and significance of the various operands and should be consulted as each is first encountered. 0-origin indexing will be used throughout.

2.1 INSTRUCTION PREPARATION

The operation of an automatic digital computer splits naturally into two phases which normally alternate: the *instruction fetch and preparation* and the *instruction execution*. The former involves the selection from some information store (*memory*) of the next instruction to be executed, its transfer to one or more *control registers*, and perhaps some modification of the instruction introduced into the control registers through so-called indexing, indirect addressing, or relocation. The execution phase begins with the *decoding* of the *operation code* segment of the instruction in the control registers to select the particular execution microprogram to be employed, and continues through the execution of the selected microprogram upon variables in certain *central registers* and in certain memory registers determined by the *address* portion or portions of the control registers.

The main memory of the 7090 will be denoted by a logical matrix $\boldsymbol{M}$ of dimension $2^{15} \times 36$. Selection from $\boldsymbol{M}$ is limited to the selection of a row $\boldsymbol{M}^i$; each such row is called a *word*, and $\boldsymbol{M}^i$ is called *word i* or *register i*.

		Dimension
Memory	$\boldsymbol{M}$	$2^{15} \times 36$
Index accumulators	$\boldsymbol{I}$	3×15
Sequence vector	$\boldsymbol{s}$ (instruction counter)	15
Command vector	$\boldsymbol{c}$	36
Upper accumulator	$\boldsymbol{u}$ $(s, q, p, 1, 2, \ldots, 35)$	38
Lower accumulator (Quotient register)	$\boldsymbol{l}$ $(s, 1, 2, \ldots, 35)$	36
Upper accumulator overflow	u	
Lower accumulator overflow	l	
Trapping mode indicator	t	
Instruction fetch mode	f 0: normal 1: skip channel trap 2: skip trap and fetch phase	
Indexing class	$k^0(\boldsymbol{c})$ 0: no indexing 1: normal indexing (15 bit) 2: restricted indexing (9 bit)	
Indirect addressing class	$k^1(\boldsymbol{c})$ 0: no indirect addressing 1: indirect addressing	
Console start signal (run)	r	
Binary representation of z	$\rho(z)$	

Table 2.1 Central computer operands

Each instruction is a full word selected from $\boldsymbol{M}$, and the sequence in which instructions are selected is controlled by a control register called the instruction counter or *sequence register*. This register represents a logical vector $\boldsymbol{s}$ of dimension 15 whose base two value determines the word i to be selected in the next instruction phase. The quantity* $\perp \boldsymbol{s}$ is incremented after each instruction fetch and therefore selects instruction words in natural ascending sequence. The value of $\boldsymbol{s}$ may, however, be respecified by the execution of certain *branch* instructions.

$$\boldsymbol{c} \leftarrow \boldsymbol{M}^{\perp \boldsymbol{s}}$$

$$\perp \boldsymbol{s} \leftarrow 2^{15} \mid (1 + \perp \boldsymbol{s})$$

Program 2.2 Basic instruction fetch

The current instruction will be denoted by $\boldsymbol{c}$. It is stored in a 36-bit *command register*.

The basic instruction fetch involves only the variables $\boldsymbol{M}$, $\boldsymbol{s}$, and $\boldsymbol{c}$, and is described by Program 2.2. The second step shows that the incrementation of $\perp \boldsymbol{s}$ is reduced modulo 2^{15} and that the selection of instructions from the 2^{15} word memory is therefore cyclic.

Additive indexing

It is convenient to the programmer to be able to add (or subtract) an index quantity i to (from) the address portion of an instruction in the command register $\boldsymbol{c}$ before its execution. This quantity is represented in base two by a logical vector $\boldsymbol{a}$ and is stored in a special *index register*. In the 7090, the data address portion of $\boldsymbol{c}$ is the fifteen-bit suffix $\boldsymbol{\omega}^{15}/\boldsymbol{c}$ and the indexing is subtractive:

$$\perp \boldsymbol{\omega}^{15}/\boldsymbol{c} \leftarrow 2^{15} \mid (\perp \boldsymbol{\omega}^{15}/\boldsymbol{c} - \perp \boldsymbol{a}).$$

The reduction modulo 2^{15} again indicates cyclic treatment of addresses.

The 7090 contains three index registers or *index accumulators* which may be used independently or jointly. They will be denoted by the *index matri* $\boldsymbol{I}$ of dimension 3×15. One or more (or none) of the index registers $\boldsymbol{I}^j$ are selected according to the value of the vector $\boldsymbol{i} = (18 \downarrow \boldsymbol{\alpha}^3)/\boldsymbol{c}$, the three-bit index tag portion of the command, as follows:

$$\perp \boldsymbol{\omega}^{15}/\boldsymbol{c} \leftarrow 2^{15} \mid (\perp \boldsymbol{\omega}^{15}/\boldsymbol{c} - \perp(((18 \downarrow \boldsymbol{\alpha}^3)/\boldsymbol{c}) \overset{\vee}{\underset{\wedge}{}} \boldsymbol{I})).$$

The address in the command register is clearly decremented by the base

* Since number bases other than two will be used but rarely in the present chapter, the elided form $\perp \boldsymbol{x}$ will be used instead of $(2\boldsymbol{\epsilon}) \perp \boldsymbol{x}$.

two value of the vector obtained by *or*ing together the selected rows of $\boldsymbol{I}$. The *or*ing of the index accumulators permits simple circuits for their selection. It is, however, of questionable value to the programmer, and the 7090 index registers are normally used individually.

Indirect addressing

It is often convenient (as in the execution of a permutation) for a programmer to specify a data address indirectly, i.e., to specify the address of the word containing the desired data address. Such indirect addressing could proceed through several levels, but in the 7090 it is limited to one.

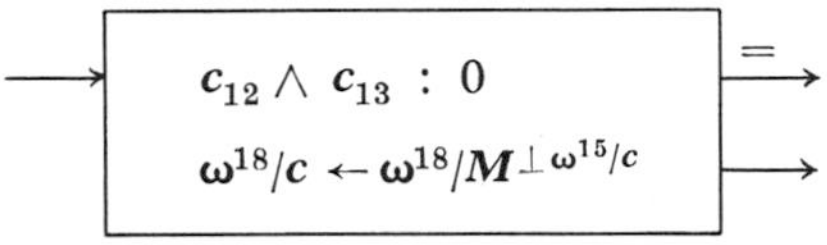

Program 2.3 Indirect addressing

Only the last half of $\boldsymbol{c}$ is respecified by the corresponding portion of the selected word, as described by Program 2.3. The occurrence of indirect addressing is determined by components c_{12} and c_{13} of the operation code.

Dynamic relocation

The correct execution of any computer program requires that each instruction and each operand be stored in the register assigned in the construction of the program. A program can, however, be *relocated* by an integral amount n if each word originally assigned to address j is assigned to address $j + n$, and if each address in the program is also incremented by n. The incrementation of program addresses can be performed explicitly by an assembler or other metaprogram, or it can be performed *dynamically* by an additive index register containing the number n. An index register employed exclusively for this purpose is called a *base address register.*

More generally, the provision of a table of base addresses permits independent dynamic relocation of different blocks of a program, where each block is confined to a set of successive registers. This is equivalent to one-level indirect addressing in which a certain portion of the address (e.g., $\boldsymbol{v}/(\boldsymbol{\omega}^{15}/\boldsymbol{c})$) selects from memory one of a table of base addresses to respecify the same portion $\boldsymbol{v}/(\boldsymbol{\omega}^{15}/\boldsymbol{c})$ thus:

$$\boldsymbol{v}/(\boldsymbol{\omega}^{15}/\boldsymbol{c}) \leftarrow \boldsymbol{v}/(\boldsymbol{\omega}^{15}/\boldsymbol{M}^{\perp \boldsymbol{v}/(\boldsymbol{\omega}^{15}/\boldsymbol{c})}).$$

If, for example, $\boldsymbol{v} = \boldsymbol{\alpha}^7$, and the format is otherwise as in the 7090, then columns 21–27 of registers 0 to $(2^7 - 1)$ provide the base addresses for successive blocks of 2^8 registers each. The 7090 provides no dynamic relocation.

Branching, interruption, and trapping

The normal sequence of instructions (fetched from successive memory registers) can be interrupted by respecifying the sequence register $\mathbf{s}$. Such respecification is performed in the execution phase of certain instructions, primarily those called *transfers*, and *skips*. The simplest branch is the TRA* (transfer), whose execution effects the following operation

$$\mathbf{s} \leftarrow \boldsymbol{\omega}^{15}/\mathbf{c}.$$

The normal sequence can also be broken by the *insertion* of an instruction in the command register without disturbing the sequence register. Unless the inserted instruction is itself a branch, the normal sequence is resumed immediately.

If just before a branch (or insertion) the present value of $\mathbf{s}$ is stored in some chosen memory register i, then the data in register i can be used in a subsequent branch to reestablish the original sequence at the point reached before the first branch. The storage of $\mathbf{s}$ and immediate branch are jointly called an *interruption*. An interruption which is performed automatically upon the occurrence of certain special conditions is called a *trap*. A trap provides a convenient device for inserting in the normal program sequence a subprogram demanded by the occurrence of the special conditions.

In the 7090, the so-called *channel trap* is controlled by an 8×3 logical matrix $\boldsymbol{T}$ whose elements are determined by three different conditions existing in each of the 8 *input-output channels* of the computer. A corresponding *enable matrix* $\boldsymbol{E}$ (also 8×3) and an *enable toggle* e determine which elements of $\boldsymbol{T}$ are effective.

The channel trap is effected in the first phase of the instruction fetch (Program 2.4) as described by steps 2–8. If the matrix $e\boldsymbol{E} \wedge \boldsymbol{T}$ is zero, the branch on step 2 skips the trap operation and begins the normal fetch on step 9. If not, step 3 determines j as the index of the first nonzero row, step 4 stores $\mathbf{s}$ in a memory register determined by j, and step 5 stores the nonzero row (which indicates the particular condition causing the interruption) in another portion of the same register. Step 6 resets the indicators which occasioned the trap. Step 7 resets the enable toggle e and hence (as is clear from step 2) prevents the occurrence of further traps until e is again set to one by the execution of a special *enable* instruction ENB. (The reset of e to zero prevents the uncontrolled interruption of interruptions.) Step 8 performs the actual insertion by transferring to the

* 7090 instructions will be referred to by the mnemonic codes used in the *IBM Manual* (1960).

command register the content of a second memory register determined by j. The sequence register is undisturbed.

The 7090 can also be operated in a special *trap mode* which effectively converts all transfer instructions (but not skip instructions) into interruptions. Discussion of this type of trapping will be deferred since it is not relevant to the instruction fetch phase.

Complete instruction fetch

The complete instruction fetch comprises three phases: channel trapping, the fetch proper, and the instruction preparation by indirect addressing and indexing. They are described by steps 2–8, 9–10, and 11–18, respectively, of Program 2.4.

Certain of the three phases may be skipped according to the setting of the *fetch mode indicator* f. In the normal case ($f = 0$) none are skipped. If $f = 1$, the trap phase only is skipped. This case occurs after execution of an instruction such as the RDS (read select), which must be followed by a certain auxiliary instruction within a fixed time limit. If $f = 2$ (a case which occurs only after execution of the XEC (execute) instruction), the trap and the fetch proper are both skipped, and the command already in $\boldsymbol{c}$ is merely prepared by indexing and indirect addressing. In every case, f is reset to its normal zero value by step 11.

Not all instructions are subject to indexing. The indexability of a command $\boldsymbol{c}$ is determined by a *class* function $k^0(\boldsymbol{c})$, which assumes the values 0, 1, or 2, according to whether $\boldsymbol{c}$ is subject to no indexing, normal indexing (affecting all fifteen bits of the address), or restricted indexing (affecting the last nine bits of the address), respectively. This behavior is determined by the branch on step 13.

A second class function $k^1(\boldsymbol{c})$ determines whether the instruction $\boldsymbol{c}$ is of a type subject to indirect addressing. Actual indirect addressing of any particular instruction of the appropriate type is initiated by the configuration $\boldsymbol{c}_{12} = 1$ and $\boldsymbol{c}_{13} = 1$. The function $k^1(\boldsymbol{c})$ is itself independent of $\boldsymbol{c}_{12}$ and $\boldsymbol{c}_{13}$.

The class functions $k^0(\boldsymbol{c})$ and $k^1(\boldsymbol{c})$ will themselves be specified by prefacing the mnemonic code of each instruction described by a pair of digits. Thus,

11 CLA

indicates that *clear and add* is subject to both indexing and indirect addressing, and

10 CHS

indicates that *change sign* is subject to indexing but not to indirect addressing.

1	$f : 1$
2	$eE \wedge T : 0$
3	$j \leftarrow +/\alpha/\wedge/\overline{(eE \wedge T)}$
4	$M^{10+2j} \leftarrow \omega^{15}(36)\backslash s$
5	$(15 \downarrow \alpha^3)/M^{10+2j} \leftarrow (eE \wedge T)^j$
6	$T^j \leftarrow 0$
7	$e \leftarrow 0$
8	$c \leftarrow M^{11+2j}$
9	$c \leftarrow M^{\perp s}$
10	$\perp s \leftarrow 2^{15} \mid (1 + \perp s)$
11	$f \leftarrow 0$
12	$a \leftarrow k^1(c) \wedge c_{12} \wedge c_{13}$
13	$k^0(c) : 1$
14	$\perp\omega^{15}/c \leftarrow 2^{15} \mid (\perp\omega^{15}/c - \perp(i \,{}^{\vee}_{\wedge}\, I))$
15	$\perp\omega^{9}/c \leftarrow 2^{9} \mid (\perp\omega^{9}/c - \perp(i \,{}^{\vee}_{\wedge}\, \omega^9/I))$
16	$a : 0$
17	$\omega^{18}/c \leftarrow \omega^{18}/M^{\perp\omega^{15}/c}$
18	$a \leftarrow 0$

$i = (18 \downarrow \alpha^3)/c$

Program 2.4 Complete instruction fetch

The phases of instruction preparation are performed in the following order:

indexing (if indicated); indirect addressing (if indicated).

Moreover, if indirect addressing is performed, the new address is itself re-indexed (if indicated). As shown by steps 12, 16, and 18, the indirect addressing is limited to a single level.

2.2 INSTRUCTION EXECUTION

The execution phase begins with the "decoding" of the operation part of the command c to select the appropriate microprogram to be executed.

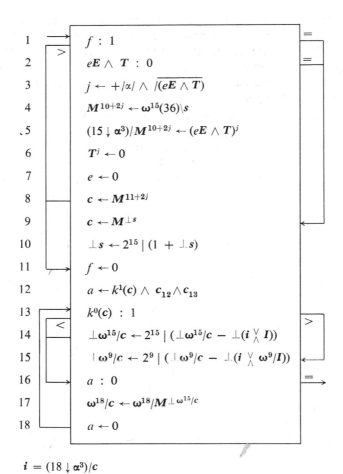

Except for the format of the operation code* (which in the common case occupies the prefix $\boldsymbol{\alpha}^{12}/\boldsymbol{c}$) the details of the decoding are, however, of no interest to the programmer, and attention will be confined to the execution microprograms. These may be grouped into a small number of families; for the 7090 they are *load and store*, *branch*, *logical*, *arithmetic*, *shift*, *convert*, and *input-output*.

Certain of the arguments and results of the computer instructions are represented by three central data registers to be denoted by $\boldsymbol{l}$, $\boldsymbol{u}$, and $\boldsymbol{d}$. The registers $\boldsymbol{u}$ and $\boldsymbol{l}$ serve as accumulators in the addition and other arithmetic operations, and, since $\boldsymbol{u}$ and $\boldsymbol{l}$ jointly represent double precision numbers (i.e., carries are in some operations propagated between the high order end of $\boldsymbol{l}$ and the low order end of $\boldsymbol{u}$), they will be called the *upper* and *lower* accumulator, respectively. Since $\boldsymbol{l}$ receives the multiplier in a multiplication and the quotient in division, it is called (in the 7090 manual) the Multiplier-Quotient or MQ register, and the letter Q occurs in the mnemonic code for instructions affecting it.

Signed numeric quantities are represented in base two with the sign in the first component, i.e., register i represents the quantity $y = (1 - 2\,\boldsymbol{M}_0{}^i) \times (\perp \overline{\boldsymbol{\alpha}}^1/\boldsymbol{M}^i)$. The lower accumulator $\boldsymbol{l}$ is, like each memory register, of dimension 36, and the sign of a numeric quantity is represented by $\boldsymbol{l}_0$. The upper accumulator is of dimension 38 and represents the number $(1 - 2\boldsymbol{u}_0) \times (\perp \overline{\boldsymbol{\alpha}}^1/\boldsymbol{u})$. The two extra components $\boldsymbol{u}_1$ and $\boldsymbol{u}_2$ are called *overflow* positions and are excluded from normal transfers of data from $\boldsymbol{u}$ to the memory. The component $\boldsymbol{u}_2$ (called the p-bit) is, however, included instead of the sign bit $\boldsymbol{u}_0$ in certain *logical* instructions. The component $\boldsymbol{u}_1$ (called the q-bit) is made accessible only by certain *shift* operations.

The register $\boldsymbol{d}$ (distributor) serves only as intermediary in transfers between main memory and the central data registers $\boldsymbol{u}$ and $\boldsymbol{l}$ and is not accessible to the programmer.

Load and store

In each member of the family of basic load and store instructions (Program 2.5), the memory word involved is selected by $\boldsymbol{\omega}^{15}/\boldsymbol{c}$, the address portion of the instruction. The instruction STA stores only the address part of $\boldsymbol{u}$, and STD stores the *decrement* part, so called because it is used in certain instructions to specify the amount of decrement to be applied to an index register. The STP stores the p-bit and the first two digits of the magnitude part of $\boldsymbol{u}$; that is, the three-bit prefix of the *logical part* of $\boldsymbol{u}$ which enters into logical operations. The STO instruction stores the

* The operation code representing instruction x is a logical vector to be denoted by $\rho(x)$. Thus $\rho(\text{CLA}) = (000101000000)$.

Load Q	11	LDQ →	$\boldsymbol{l} \leftarrow \boldsymbol{M}^{\perp \omega^{15}/\boldsymbol{c}}$ →
Store Q	11	STQ →	$\boldsymbol{M}^{\perp \omega^{15}/\boldsymbol{c}} \leftarrow \boldsymbol{l}$ →
Store left half Q	11	SLQ →	$\alpha^{18}/\boldsymbol{M}^{\perp \omega^{15}/\boldsymbol{c}} \leftarrow \alpha^{18}/\boldsymbol{l}$ →
Store	11	STO →	$\boldsymbol{M}^{\perp \omega^{15}/\boldsymbol{c}} \leftarrow (\downarrow \overline{\alpha}^{2})/\boldsymbol{u}$ →
Store zero	11	STZ →	$\boldsymbol{M}^{\perp \omega^{15}/\boldsymbol{c}} \leftarrow 0$ →
Store address	11	STA →	$\omega^{15}/\boldsymbol{M}^{\perp \omega^{15}/\boldsymbol{c}} \leftarrow \omega^{15}/\boldsymbol{u}$ →
Store decrement	11	STD →	$(3 \downarrow \alpha^{15})/\boldsymbol{M}^{\perp \omega^{15}/\boldsymbol{c}} \leftarrow (5 \downarrow \alpha^{15})/\boldsymbol{u}$ →
Store prefix	11	STP →	$\alpha^{3}/\boldsymbol{M}^{\perp \omega^{15}/\boldsymbol{c}} \leftarrow (2 \downarrow \alpha^{3})/\boldsymbol{u}$ →
Store tag	11	STT →	$(18 \downarrow \alpha^{3})/\boldsymbol{M}^{\perp \omega^{15}/\boldsymbol{c}} \leftarrow (20 \downarrow \alpha^{3})/\boldsymbol{u}$ →
Store instruction location counter	11	STL →	$\omega^{15}/\boldsymbol{M}^{\perp \omega^{15}/\boldsymbol{c}} \leftarrow \boldsymbol{s}$ →
Store logical word	11	SLW →	$\boldsymbol{M}^{\perp \omega^{15}/\boldsymbol{c}} \leftarrow \overline{\alpha}^{2}/\boldsymbol{u}$ →

Program 2.5 Load and store instructions

normal numeric part of $\boldsymbol{u}$ (that is, all but the overflow bits), whereas SLW (store logical word) stores the p-bit instead of the sign.

The instructions which load and store the index accumulators (Program 2.6) are of four types, as indicated by the leading letter of each of the mnemonic codes, *L* for load index from memory, *S* for store index in memory, *A* for load index from the address of the command register, and *P* for place the index in the upper accumulator or the upper accumulator in the index. The portion of memory, command register, or upper accumulator involved in each of the ten instructions which specify the index is shown in steps 1–10. The last five of these differ from the corresponding members of the first five only by complementation on 2^{15}, as shown in step 11. Since the subtraction occurring in indexing (step 14 of Program 2.4) is reduced modulo 2^{15}, the effect of complementation is to add rather than subtract the quantity used to load the index accumulator.

Step 12 shows that the index accumulators specified are selected by the three-bit tag vector $\boldsymbol{i} = (18 \downarrow \alpha^{3})/\boldsymbol{c}$ and that each receives the same specifying quantity. Since the tag vector is used to select the index registers to be specified, it cannot also be used to specify indexing of the instruction itself, and, consequently, none of the load and store index instructions are indexable. Neither do they permit indirect addressing.

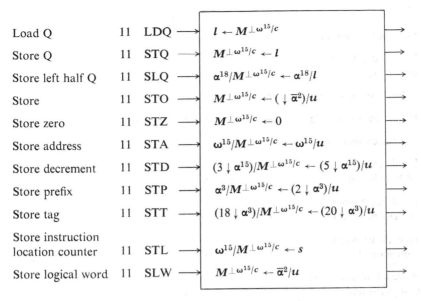

Load index from address	00	LXA →	$x \leftarrow \omega^{15}/M^{\perp\omega^{15}/c}$	1
Load index from decrement	00	LXD →	$x \leftarrow (3 \downarrow \alpha^{15})/M^{\perp\omega^{15}/c}$	2
Address to index true	00	AXT →	$x \leftarrow \omega^{15}/c$	3
Place address in index	00	PAX →	$x \leftarrow \omega^{15}/u$	4
Place decrement in index	00	PDX →	$x \leftarrow (5 \downarrow \alpha^{15})/u$	5
Load complement of address in index	00	LAC →	$x \leftarrow \omega^{15}/M^{\perp\omega^{15}/c}$	6
Load complement of decrement in index	00	LDC →	$x \leftarrow (3 \downarrow \alpha^{15})/M^{\perp\omega^{15}/c}$	7
Address to index complemented	00	AXC →	$x \leftarrow \omega^{15}/c$	8
Place address in index complemented	00	PAC →	$x \leftarrow \omega^{15}/u$	9
Place decrement in index complemented	00	PDC →	$x \leftarrow (5 \downarrow \alpha^{15})/u$	10
			$\perp x \leftarrow 2^{15} \mid (-\perp x)$	11
		←	$i//I \leftarrow \epsilon(+/i) \overset{\circ}{\wedge} x$	12
Store index in address	00	SXA →	$\omega^{15}/M^{\perp\omega^{15}/c} \leftarrow i \overset{\vee}{\wedge} I$	13
Store index in decrement	00	SXD →	$(3 \downarrow \alpha^{15})/M^{\perp\omega^{15}/c} \leftarrow i \overset{\vee}{\wedge} I$	14
Place index in address	00	PXA →	$u \leftarrow \omega^{15}(38)\backslash(i \overset{\vee}{\wedge} I)$	15
Place index in decrement	00	PXD →	$u \leftarrow (5 \downarrow \alpha^{15}(38))\backslash(i \overset{\vee}{\wedge} I)$	16

$(i = (18 \downarrow \alpha^3)/c)$

Program 2.6 Load and store index instructions

The last four steps show the storing of the index accumulators. The quantity stored is the *or* function of the accumulators selected by the tag $(18 \downarrow \alpha^3)/c$.

Branch instructions

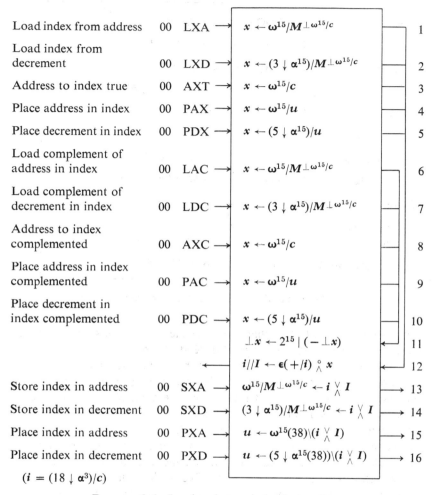

The basic branch instructions are of two main types, the *transfer* (denoted by a leading *T* in the mnemonic code) and the *skip*. The behavior of the skip instructions is shown in steps 1–10 of Program 2.7, and is typified by the PBT (*p*-bit test) of steps 1 and 10. If the *p*-bit of the upper accumulator is not zero, the sequence vector is incremented so as to skip the next instruction in the sequence; if the p-bit is zero, the instruction has no effect. The various skip instructions differ in the particular tests made, and the last two (CAS and LAS) differ also in providing three alternatives,

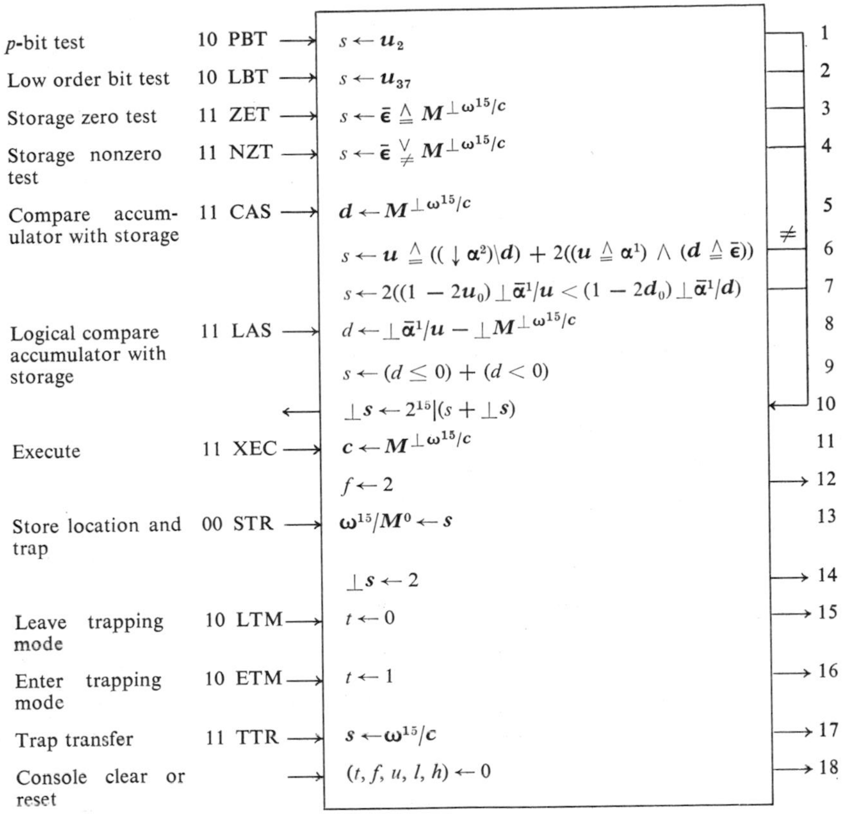

Program 2.7 Skip type and other special branches

skipping 2, 1, or 0 instructions according to whether the quantities compared stand in the relation $<$, $=$, or $>$, respectively.

When operating in the nontrapping mode ($t = 0$), the essential operation of the transfer type of branch (Program 2.8) is the (conditional) respecification of the sequence vector $\boldsymbol{s}$ by the address portion of $\boldsymbol{c}$. The HTR (halt and transfer) also suspends operation of the computer until a *run* signal is received from the console (steps 27–29).

In the trapping mode, all transfer operations are converted to interruptions; the sequence vector is first stored in register zero, and a

Transfer on index high	00 TXH	$b \leftarrow (\perp(\boldsymbol{i} \overset{\vee}{\wedge} \boldsymbol{I}) > \perp(3 \downarrow \boldsymbol{\alpha}^{15})/\boldsymbol{c})$	1
Transfer on index low or equal	00 TXL	$b \leftarrow (\perp(\boldsymbol{i} \overset{\vee}{\wedge} \boldsymbol{I}) \leq \perp(3 \downarrow \boldsymbol{\alpha}^{15})/\boldsymbol{c})$	2
Transfer on index	00 TIX	$b \leftarrow (\perp(\boldsymbol{i} \overset{\vee}{\wedge} \boldsymbol{I}) > \perp(3 \downarrow \boldsymbol{\alpha}^{15})/\boldsymbol{c})$	3
		$y \leftarrow \perp(\boldsymbol{i} \overset{\vee}{\wedge} \boldsymbol{I}) - \perp(3 \downarrow \boldsymbol{\alpha}^{15})/\boldsymbol{c}$	4
		$\perp \boldsymbol{i}//\boldsymbol{I} \leftarrow (2^{15}\|y)\boldsymbol{\epsilon}(+/\boldsymbol{i})$	5
Transfer on no index	00 TNX	$b \leftarrow (\perp(\boldsymbol{i} \overset{\vee}{\wedge} \boldsymbol{I}) \leq \perp(3 \downarrow \boldsymbol{\alpha}^{15})/\boldsymbol{c})$	6
Transfer with index incremented	00 TXI	$y \leftarrow \perp(\boldsymbol{i} \overset{\vee}{\wedge} \boldsymbol{I}) + \perp(3 \downarrow \boldsymbol{\alpha}^{15})/\boldsymbol{c}$	7
		$\perp \boldsymbol{i}//\boldsymbol{I} \leftarrow (2^{15}\|y)\boldsymbol{\epsilon}(+/\boldsymbol{i})$	8
Transfer and set index	00 TSX	$\perp \boldsymbol{i}//\boldsymbol{I} \leftarrow (2^{15}\|(-\perp \boldsymbol{s}))\boldsymbol{\epsilon}(+/\boldsymbol{i})$	9
Transfer Halt and transfer	11 TRA 11 HTR	$b \leftarrow 1$	10
Transfer on zero	11 TZE	$b \leftarrow (\bar{\boldsymbol{\alpha}}^1/\boldsymbol{u}) \overset{\wedge}{=} \bar{\boldsymbol{\epsilon}}$	11
Transfer on nonzero	11 TNZ	$b \leftarrow (\bar{\boldsymbol{\alpha}}^1/\boldsymbol{u}) \overset{\vee}{\neq} \bar{\boldsymbol{\epsilon}}$	12
Transfer on plus	11 TPL	$b \leftarrow \bar{\boldsymbol{u}}_0$	13
Transfer on minus	11 TMI	$b \leftarrow \boldsymbol{u}_0$	14
Transfer on overflow	11 TOV	$(b, u) \leftarrow (u, 0)$	15
Transfer on no overflow	11 TNO	$(b, u) \leftarrow (\bar{u}, 0)$	16
Transfer on Q plus	11 TQP	$b \leftarrow \bar{\boldsymbol{l}}_0$	17
Transfer on Quotient overflow	11 TQO	$(b, l) \leftarrow (l, 0)$	18
Transfer on low Q	11 TLQ	$b \leftarrow ((1 - 2\boldsymbol{l}_0) \perp \bar{\boldsymbol{\alpha}}^1/\boldsymbol{l} < (1 - 2\boldsymbol{u}_0) \perp \bar{\boldsymbol{\alpha}}^1/\boldsymbol{u})$	19
		$b \leftarrow b \vee ((\boldsymbol{l} \overset{\wedge}{=} \boldsymbol{\alpha}^1) \wedge (\boldsymbol{u} \overset{\wedge}{=} \bar{\boldsymbol{\epsilon}}))$	20
		$t : 1$	21
$(\boldsymbol{i} = (18 \downarrow \boldsymbol{\alpha}^3)/\boldsymbol{c})$		$b : 0$	22
		$\boldsymbol{s} \leftarrow \boldsymbol{\omega}^{15}/\boldsymbol{c}$	23
		$\boldsymbol{\omega}^{15}/\boldsymbol{M}^0 \leftarrow \boldsymbol{s}$	24
		$b : 0$	25
		$\perp \boldsymbol{s} \leftarrow 1$	26
		$\boldsymbol{\alpha}^{12}/\boldsymbol{c} : \rho(\text{HTR})$	27
		$r \leftarrow 0$	28
		$r : 0$	29

Program 2.8 Basic transfer type branches

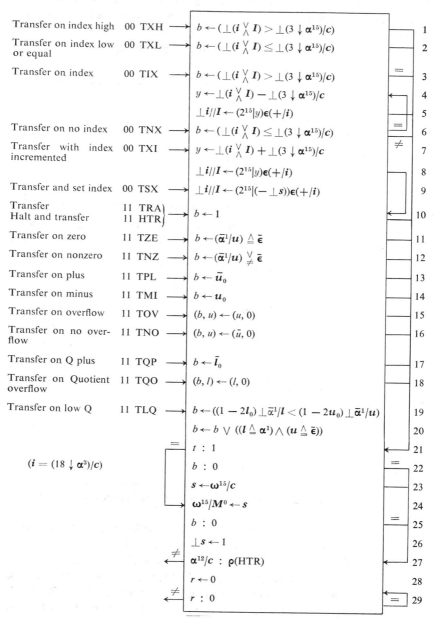

(conditional) branch is made to register one. This behavior is useful in trace programs. The conditions for the various transfers are indicated in the setting of the logical variable b. Special indicators (such as the overflow toggle u) are reset by the transfer instructions which they control.

Transfers based on the condition of the index accumulators (steps 1–9) are combined with modification of the index registers. The quantity from the index accumulators is again the *or* function of the accumulators selected by $(18 \downarrow \boldsymbol{\alpha}^3)/\boldsymbol{c}$. This quantity is compared with the decrement part of the command (that is, $(3 \downarrow \boldsymbol{\alpha}^{15})/\boldsymbol{c}$) to control the conditional branches and is decremented or augmented by the decrement part to modify the selected index accumulators.

The TSX (transfer and set index) inserts the complement (on 2^{15}) of the sequence vector into the selected index accumulators before effecting an unconditional transfer. This instruction is convenient for incorporating closed subroutines or other interruptions, since a subsequent TRA (transfer) with a zero address and indexed by the same index register restores the program sequence to the point of interruption.

As shown in Program 2.7, only the TTR (trap transfer) is exempt from trapping. The trap indicator is set by the ETM (enter trap mode) and is reset by the LTM (leave trap mode) as well as by a console clear or reset. The XEC (execute) instruction performs no operation upon the central data registers but inserts in the normal instruction sequence (without breaking it) the instruction in the register specified by the data address accompanying the XEC. This is effected by simply loading the specified register into $\boldsymbol{c}$ and (by setting $f = 2$) skipping the trap and the fetch proper of the instruction fetch phase.

Logical instructions

The logical operations (Program 2.9) concern the logical part of $\boldsymbol{u}$, which differs from the numeric part by including the p-bit rather than the sign, and hence comprises $\overline{\boldsymbol{\alpha}}^2/\boldsymbol{u}$. The first instruction of the family (ORS) produces the *logical or* of the word selected from storage with the vector $\overline{\boldsymbol{\alpha}}^2/\boldsymbol{u}$ and returns the result to the same location in storage. The instruction ANS (and to storage) is similar. In the ORA (or to accumulator) the result $\boldsymbol{u}$ is of dimension 38, and the second operand (that is, $\boldsymbol{M}^{\perp \boldsymbol{\omega}^{15}/\boldsymbol{c}}$) is expanded to this dimension by inserting two leading zeros before *or*ing it with $\boldsymbol{u}$. The instruction ANA is similar. It is easily verified that ORA leaves the extra bits unchanged and that ANA resets them. The ERA (exclusive or to accumulator) is anomalous in that it resets the extra bits.

The ACL (add and carry logical) is normally used only in certain parity check algorithms. It adds the selected word to the logical part of $\boldsymbol{u}$, treating both as 36-bit positive base two numbers, again adds any resulting

Or to storage	11	ORS	$\boldsymbol{M}^{\perp\omega^{15}/c} \leftarrow (\overline{\boldsymbol{\alpha}}^2/\boldsymbol{u}) \vee \boldsymbol{M}^{\perp\omega^{15}/c}$
Or to accumulator	11	ORA	$\boldsymbol{u} \leftarrow \boldsymbol{u} \vee (\overline{\boldsymbol{\alpha}}^2\backslash\boldsymbol{M}^{\perp\omega^{15}/c})$
And to storage	11	ANS	$\boldsymbol{M}^{\perp\omega^{15}/c} \leftarrow (\overline{\boldsymbol{\alpha}}^2/\boldsymbol{u}) \wedge \boldsymbol{M}^{\perp\omega^{15}/c}$
And to accumulator	11	ANA	$\boldsymbol{u} \leftarrow \boldsymbol{u} \wedge (\overline{\boldsymbol{\alpha}}^2\backslash\boldsymbol{M}^{\perp\omega^{15}/c})$
Exclusive or to accumulator	11	ERA	$\boldsymbol{u} \leftarrow (\boldsymbol{u} \neq (\overline{\boldsymbol{\alpha}}^2\backslash\boldsymbol{M}^{\perp\omega^{15}/c}))$
			$\overline{\boldsymbol{\alpha}}^2/\boldsymbol{u} \leftarrow 0$
Complement magnitude	10	COM	$\overline{\boldsymbol{\alpha}}^1/\boldsymbol{u} \leftarrow \overline{\boldsymbol{\alpha}}^1/\overline{\boldsymbol{u}}$
Clear magnitude	10	CLM	$\overline{\boldsymbol{\alpha}}^1/\boldsymbol{u} \leftarrow 0$
Change sign	10	CHS	$u_0 \leftarrow \overline{u}_0$
Set sign plus	10	SSP	$u_0 \leftarrow 0$
Set sign minus	10	SSM	$u_0 \leftarrow 1$
Store logical word	11	SLW	$\boldsymbol{M}^{\perp\omega^{15}/c} \leftarrow \overline{\boldsymbol{\alpha}}^2/\boldsymbol{u}$
Clear and add logical	11	CAL	$\boldsymbol{u} \leftarrow \overline{\boldsymbol{\alpha}}^2\backslash\boldsymbol{M}^{\perp\omega^{15}/c}$
Add and carry logical	11	ACL	$y \leftarrow \perp(\overline{\boldsymbol{\alpha}}^2/\boldsymbol{u}) + \perp\boldsymbol{M}^{\perp\omega^{15}/c}$
			$\perp\overline{\boldsymbol{\alpha}}^2/\boldsymbol{u} \leftarrow (2^{36} \mid y) + (y \geq 2^{36})$

Program 2.9 Logical operations

overflow to the low order end, and places the result (which will not exceed $2^{36} - 1$) in the logical part of $\boldsymbol{u}$. The behavior of the remaining logical instructions is evident from Program 2.9. As shown by the class functions k^0 and k^1, five of them do not permit indirect addressing.*

Arithmetic instructions

The description of arithmetic instructions will be illustrated by the family of fixed point† add instructions shown in Program 2.10. The CLA (clear and add) transfers the selected memory register to $\boldsymbol{u}$, resetting the two

* Since each of these five instructions involves the accumulator only, the normal address portion $\boldsymbol{\omega}^{15}/\boldsymbol{c}$ does not represent an address, and its last three components are used in representing the operation code itself. The possibility of indirect addressing would suggest to the programmer the nonexistent possibility of specifying an arbitrary indirect address in $\boldsymbol{\omega}^{15}/\boldsymbol{c}$.

† The 7090 incorporates three arithmetic functions: addition, multiplication, and division, each of which may be performed in either a fixed (radix) point or floating point mode.

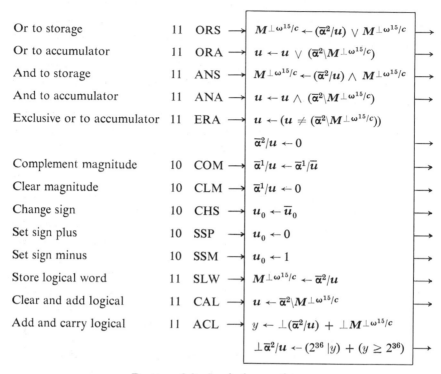

Instruction		Mnemonic	Statement	Step
Clear and add	11	CLA →	$\boldsymbol{u} \leftarrow (\downarrow \bar{\boldsymbol{\alpha}}^2) \backslash \boldsymbol{M}^{\perp \boldsymbol{\omega}^{15}/\boldsymbol{c}}$	→ 1
Clear and subtract	11	CLS →	$\boldsymbol{u} \leftarrow (\downarrow \bar{\boldsymbol{\alpha}}^2) \backslash (\boldsymbol{\alpha}^1 \neq \boldsymbol{M}^{\perp \boldsymbol{\omega}^{15}/\boldsymbol{c}})$	→ 2
Add	11	ADD →	$\boldsymbol{d} \leftarrow \boldsymbol{M}^{\perp \boldsymbol{\omega}^{15}/\boldsymbol{c}}$	3 (→ 8)
Subtract	11	SUB →	$\boldsymbol{d} \leftarrow (\boldsymbol{\alpha}^1 \neq \boldsymbol{M}^{\perp \boldsymbol{\omega}^{15}/\boldsymbol{c}})$	4 (→ 8)
Add magnitude	11	ADM →	$\boldsymbol{d} \leftarrow \bar{\boldsymbol{\alpha}}^1 \wedge \boldsymbol{M}^{\perp \boldsymbol{\omega}^{15}/\boldsymbol{c}}$	5 (→ 8)
Subtract magnitude	11	SBM →	$\boldsymbol{d} \leftarrow \boldsymbol{\alpha}^1 \vee \boldsymbol{M}^{\perp \boldsymbol{\omega}^{15}/\boldsymbol{c}}$	6 (→ 8)
Round	11	RND →	$\boldsymbol{d} \leftarrow \boldsymbol{u}_0 \boldsymbol{\alpha}^1 \vee \boldsymbol{l}_1 \boldsymbol{\omega}^1$	7 (→ 8)
			$z \leftarrow (1 - 2\boldsymbol{u}_0)(\perp \bar{\boldsymbol{\alpha}}^1/\boldsymbol{u}) + (1 - 2\boldsymbol{d}_0)(\perp \bar{\boldsymbol{\alpha}}^1/\boldsymbol{d})$	8
			$x \leftarrow \boldsymbol{u}_2$	9
			$\perp \bar{\boldsymbol{\alpha}}^1/\boldsymbol{u} \leftarrow 2^{37} \mid (\lvert z \rvert)$	10
			$u \leftarrow u \vee ((x \neq \boldsymbol{u}_2) \wedge (\boldsymbol{u}_0 = \boldsymbol{d}_0))$	11
			$\boldsymbol{u}_0 \leftarrow (z < 0) \vee (\boldsymbol{u}_0 \wedge (z = 0))$	12

Program 2.10 Add instructions

overflow positions. The CLS (clear and subtract) differs only in that the sign is reversed in transfer.

The instructions ADD, SUB, ADM, and SBM each transfer the selected word to $\boldsymbol{d}$ with an appropriate sign, add it to the number represented by $\boldsymbol{u}$ (including the overflow positions), and place the sum reduced modulo 2^{37} in $\boldsymbol{u}$. The sign of a zero result is (as indicated by step 12) the sign of the number originally contained in $\boldsymbol{u}$.

The overflow indicator u is set only by a carry (but not a borrow) from $\boldsymbol{u}_3$ to $\boldsymbol{u}_2$. This indicator controls, and is reset by, certain branch instructions.

The RND (round) instruction is used to round up the magnitude of the number represented jointly by the upper and lower accumulator by one unit in the high order position of the lower accumulator. As shown in Program 2.10, the content of the upper accumulator only is actually affected.

Shift instructions

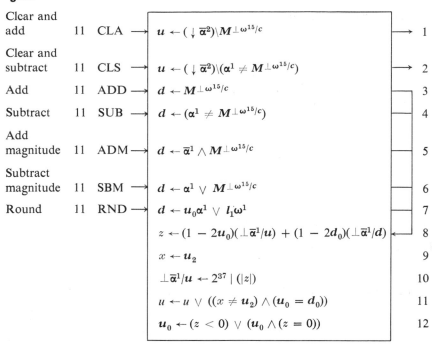

In describing computer instructions, the term *left shift* of a vector $\boldsymbol{x}$ by r places refers either to the left rotation $\boldsymbol{x} \leftarrow r \uparrow \boldsymbol{x}$ or to the left rotation combined with a reset to zero of the last r "vacated positions," that is,

$$x \leftarrow (r \uparrow x) \wedge \overline{\omega}^r.$$

Both types of shift occur in the 7090 and concern various portions of the entire accumulator $u \oplus l$, as shown in Program 2.11. The portion affected is determined by the mask vector m.

			$u \leftarrow u \vee (\alpha^r \overset{\vee}{\wedge} (m/(u \oplus l))$
			$m/(u \oplus l) \leftarrow (r \uparrow (m/(u \oplus l))) \wedge \overline{\omega}^r$
Accumulator left shift	10	ALS	$m \leftarrow \overline{\alpha}^1(38) \oplus \overline{\epsilon}(36)$
Long left shift	10	LLS	$m \leftarrow \overline{\alpha}^1(38) \oplus \overline{\alpha}^1(36)$
			$u_0 \leftarrow l_0$
Logical left shift	10	LGL	$m \leftarrow \overline{\alpha}^1(38) \oplus \epsilon(36)$
Accumulator right shift	10	ARS	$m \leftarrow \overline{\alpha}^1(38) \oplus \overline{\epsilon}(36)$
Long right shift	10	LRS	$m \leftarrow \overline{\alpha}^1(38) \oplus \overline{\alpha}^1(36)$
			$l_0 \leftarrow u_0$
Logical right shift	10	LGR	$m \leftarrow \overline{\alpha}^1(38) \oplus \epsilon(36)$
			$m/(u \oplus l) \leftarrow (r \downarrow (m/(u \oplus l))) \wedge \overline{\alpha}^r$
Rotate MQ	10	RQL	$l \leftarrow r \uparrow l$
Exchange accumulator and MQ	00	XCA	$(\downarrow \overline{\alpha}^2)/u \longleftrightarrow l$
			$(\downarrow \overline{\alpha}^2)/u \leftarrow 0$
Exchange logical accumulator and MQ	00	XCL	$\overline{\alpha}^2/u \longleftrightarrow l$
			$\alpha^2/u \leftarrow 0$

$r = \perp\omega^8/c$

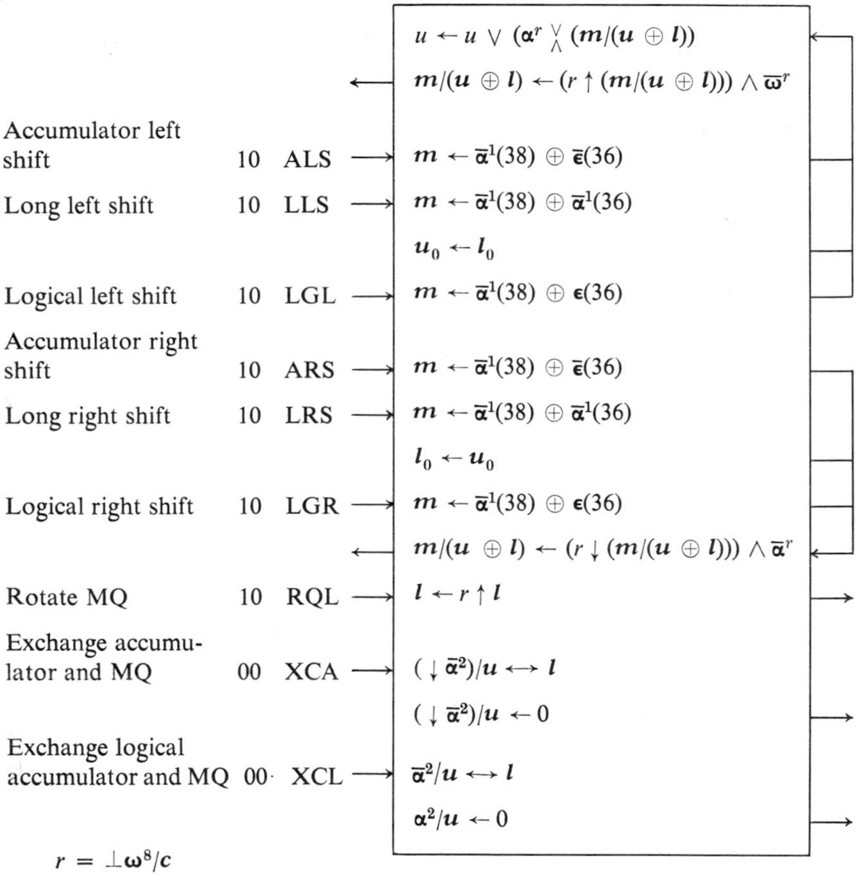

Program 2.11   Shift instructions

The first three instructions are left shifts. Each sets the accumulator overflow indicator if any nonzero bits are lost, i.e., if any of the first r positions of the affected portion are nonzero. The next three are analogous right shifts, which do not, however, set the overflow indicator. In the "long" shifts LLS and LRS, one sign position specifies the other, although the sign positions are otherwise excluded from the shift by the mask $\boldsymbol{m}$. The LGR shifts all positions save the sign of $\boldsymbol{u}$; RQL rotates MQ without resetting any positions; and XCA, which "exchanges" the accumulators, is effectively a rotation except that it resets the overflow bits. The amount of shift r is in each case determined by the base two value of $\boldsymbol{\omega}^8/\boldsymbol{c}$.

Convert instructions

Each convert instruction (Program 2.12) selects a six-bit infix of one of the accumulators, adds its base two value to a "base address" initially specified by the address portion of the instruction, and selects the memory register

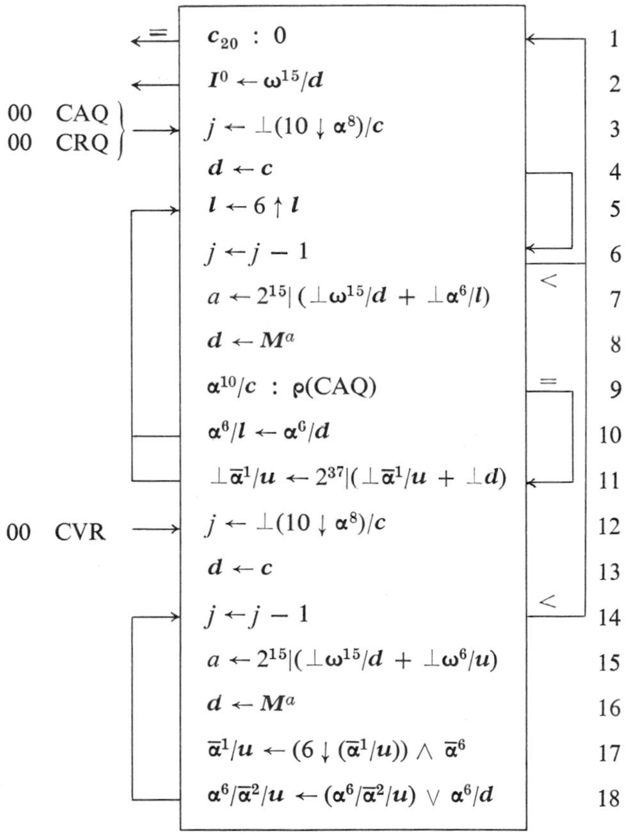

Program 2.12 Convert instructions

specified by the resulting address. Part of the selected register is used to respecify the base address and part to modify one or other of the accumulators. The process is reapplied to successive six-bit infixes in cyclic order a number of times determined by the base two value of $(10 \downarrow \boldsymbol{\alpha}^8)/\boldsymbol{c}$. If $c_{20} = 1$, the last fifteen bits of the last word selected in the operation are transferred to index accumulator $\boldsymbol{I}^0$.

Input-output instructions

Because the data transmission rates of input-output equipment serving a computer are much lower than those of the computer proper, computer systems are normally designed to permit concurrent operation of the computer and one or more input-output units. The units are therefore more or less autonomous.

In the 7090, the autonomy of input-output equipment is carried further by providing eight *data channels* which transmit data to, and are controlled by, the computer proper, and which in turn control and accept data from the individual input-output units. The entire input-output process therefore comprises three levels of microprograms: a semiautonomous input-output unit controlled by a semiautonomous data channel controlled by the computer proper.

Attention will be restricted to the magnetic tape input-output units of the 7090. Each unit is available to one specific data channel i (for $i = 0 - 7$), and a particular unit can be characterized as the file Φ_j^i. The unit is completely autonomous only in certain simple operations, such as *rewind*, *write end of file*, *backspace*, and *continue to end of record.* Except for these special operations, a given data channel can control only one of its files at a time. The eight data channels may, however, operate concurrently under control of the computer proper.

Each channel i behaves as a subcomputer with its own sequence vector $\boldsymbol{S}^i$, command vector $\boldsymbol{C}^i$, data register $\boldsymbol{D}^i$, and other miscellaneous operands, as shown in Table 2.13. The instructions of the subcomputer (listed in the matrix $\boldsymbol{K}$) are called *channel commands* and differ from the instructions of the computer proper in both format and function.

Tape Units. Each tape unit behaves as a file (Sec. 1.22); each recorded component is an alphanumeric character represented in a seven-bit odd-parity error-detecting code, the lowest level partition $\boldsymbol{\lambda}_0$ is represented by the intercharacter space on the tape, the second level partition $\boldsymbol{\lambda}_1$ (called an *end of record gap*) is a longer blank space on tape.

Each record gap is immediately preceded by a parity check character which is appended to the normal data of the record to permit an even parity "longitudinal" parity check on each of the seven-bit positions of the

			Dimension
Channel data registers	$\boldsymbol{D}$		8×36
Channel sequence vectors	$\boldsymbol{S}$		8×15
Channel command vectors	$\boldsymbol{C}$		8×36
Channel trap	$\boldsymbol{T}$	$\boldsymbol{T}_0{}^i$: End of file $\boldsymbol{\lambda}_2$ $\boldsymbol{T}_1{}^i$: Parity check $\boldsymbol{T}_2{}^i$: Channel command	8×3
Channel trap enabled	$\boldsymbol{E}$		8×3
Channel trap enabled	e		
Tape position limits	$\boldsymbol{L}$	$\boldsymbol{L}^i$: (Beginning, End)	8×2
Limit position on tape	$\boldsymbol{v}$	(Determined by reflective marker)	
Busy indicator	$\boldsymbol{b}$		8
Write or read indicator	$\boldsymbol{w}$		8
Tape unit index	$\boldsymbol{t}$		8
Functions	$\boldsymbol{f}$	0 : Normal read-write 1 : Backspace record or write end of file 2 : Backspace to file mark 3 : Rewind	8
Load channel waiting	$\boldsymbol{r}$	(reload)	8
Write record gap ($\boldsymbol{\lambda}_1$) next	$\boldsymbol{g}$		8
Current character	$\boldsymbol{X}$	$\boldsymbol{X}^i$ is the 7-bit representation	8×7
Current parity check	$\boldsymbol{Y}$		8×7
Interlock vector	$\boldsymbol{x}$	$\boldsymbol{x}_i = 1$ if character $\boldsymbol{X}^i$ is loaded	8
Current character selector	$\boldsymbol{V}$	$\boldsymbol{V}^i/\boldsymbol{D}^i$ is current character	8×36
End of file indicator	$\boldsymbol{Q}$	$\boldsymbol{Q}^i$: (Counter, Potential error)	8×2
Input-output indicator	h		
Channel commands	$\boldsymbol{K}$	$\begin{pmatrix} \text{c} & \text{d} \\ - & - \\ \text{r} & \text{p} \\ \text{r} & \text{t} \\ \text{c} & \text{p} \\ \text{c} & \text{t} \\ \text{s} & \text{p} \\ \text{s} & \text{t} \end{pmatrix} \begin{matrix} \text{IOCD} \\ \text{TCH} \\ \text{IORP} \\ \text{IORT} \\ \text{IOCP} \\ \text{IOCT} \\ \text{IOSP} \\ \text{IOST} \end{matrix}$	

Table 2.13 Channel operands

preceding record. The check character is recorded automatically and when read from the tape is used in the parity check but is not transmitted with the data of the preceding record.

The third and highest level partition (called *end of file*) is represented by a special recorded character $\boldsymbol{\lambda}_2$ which has the seven-bit representation $\boldsymbol{\rho}(\boldsymbol{\lambda}_2) = (0, 0, 0, 1, 1, 1, 1)$. It is recorded together with the appropriate check character (which, since the check is of even-parity is also $\boldsymbol{\lambda}_2$) as a separate record. The character $\boldsymbol{\lambda}_2$ alone is not recognized as an end of file partition; only the sequence $\boldsymbol{\lambda}_1, \boldsymbol{\lambda}_2, \boldsymbol{\lambda}_2, \boldsymbol{\lambda}_1$ is so recognized. Tapes are normally stopped only at a record gap so that, on restarting, the tape is fully accelerated before the end of the record gap (and hence data) is reached.

		Dimension
Character buffer	$\boldsymbol{Z}$	8 × # of units per channel
Partition buffer	$\boldsymbol{P}$	
Logical association (connection)	$\boldsymbol{A}$	
Busy indicator	$\boldsymbol{B}$	
Write-read status	$\boldsymbol{W}$	
Function status	$\boldsymbol{F}$	
End of file counter	$\boldsymbol{R}$	
File partitions	$\boldsymbol{\lambda}$	$\boldsymbol{\lambda}_0$ intercharacter gap $\boldsymbol{\lambda}_1$ inter-record gap $\boldsymbol{\lambda}_2$ end-of-file symbol (0001111)

Table 2.14 Input-output unit operands

The tape unit parameters are listed in Table 2.14, and the operation of tape unit Φ_j^i is described by Program 2.15. The unit idles at step 5 until its busy indicator $\boldsymbol{B}_j^i$ is turned on by data channel i. After a starting delay of about 650 microseconds required to accelerate the tape and reach the beginning of the record, one of four functions (listed under $\boldsymbol{f}$ in Table 2.13) is performed as determined by the function indicator $\boldsymbol{F}_j^i$.

If $\boldsymbol{F}_j^i = 0$, a normal read or write is performed under direct control of the data channel as detailed in steps 18–37. If $\boldsymbol{F}_j^i \neq 0$, one of the several completely autonomous operations is initiated. If $\boldsymbol{F}_j^i$ is not zero and $\boldsymbol{W}_j^i$ (write indicator) is unity, the autonomous function *write end of file* is performed by steps 1–3, after which the busy indicator is turned off and the unit returns to idle status. The *end limit indicator* $\boldsymbol{L}_1^i$ is set by step 3 if the tape position exceeds a limit ν set by a reflective marker attached to the tape a short way before its extreme end.

If $\boldsymbol{W}_j^i = 0$ and if $\boldsymbol{F}_j^i = 1$, 2, or 3, the unit backspaces to the next earlier record gap, to the next earlier end of file position, or to position zero, respectively. The last is called *rewind.* If, in backspacing, the tape becomes

1. $\Psi_j^i \leftarrow \lambda_2, \lambda_0$
2. $\Phi_j^i \leftarrow \lambda_2, \lambda_1$
3. $L_1^i \leftarrow L_1^i \vee (\pi(\Phi_j^i) > v)$
4. $B_j^i \leftarrow 0$
5. $B_j^i : 0$
6. starting delay
7. $F_j^i : 0$
8. $W_j^i : 1$
9. $R_j^i \leftarrow 3$
10. $\pi(\Phi_j^i) : 0$
11. $L_0^i \leftarrow L_0^i \vee (F_j^i \neq 3)$
12. $Z_j^i, P_j^i \leftarrow_1 \Phi_j^i$
13. $R_j^i : 0$
14. $R_j^i \leftarrow (Z_j^i = \lambda_2) \times (R_j^i - 1)$
15. $P_j^i : \lambda_0$
16. $F_j^i : 2$
17. $R_j^i : 1$
18. $g_i \leftarrow g_i \vee A_j^i$
19. $W_j^i : 1$
20. $Z_j^i, P_j^i \leftarrow \Phi_j^i$
21. $A_j^i : 0$
22. $p_i \leftarrow P_j^i$
23. $X^i \leftarrow \rho(Z_j^i)$
24. $x_i \leftarrow 1$
25. $P_j^i : \lambda_0$
26. record gap delay
27. $A_j^i : 1$
28. $\rho(Z_j^i) \leftarrow X^i$
29. $x_i \leftarrow 1$
30. $\Phi_j^i \leftarrow Z_j^i, \lambda_0$
31. $L_1^i \leftarrow L_1^i \vee (\pi(\Phi_j^i) > v)$
32. $g_i : 0$
33. $\rho(Z_j^i) \leftarrow Y^i$
34. $\Phi_j^i \leftarrow Z_j^i, \lambda_1$
35. $g_i \leftarrow 0$
36. record gap delay
37. $A_j^i : 1$

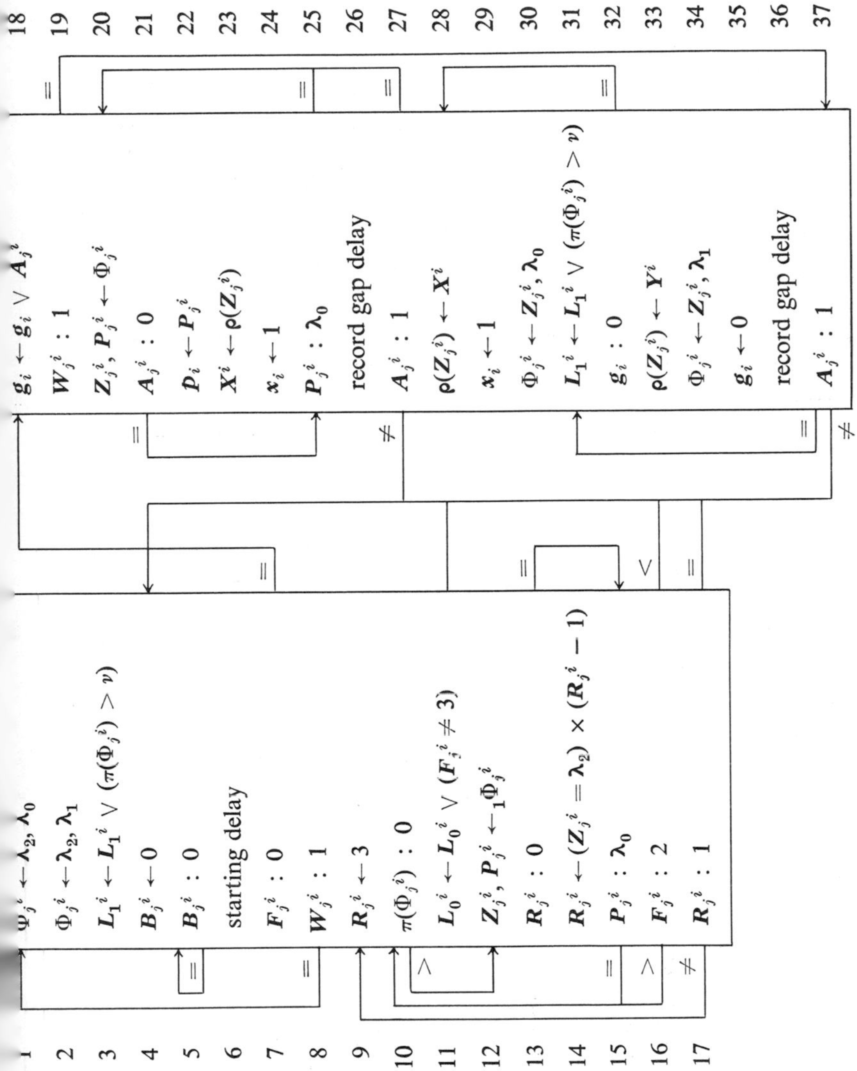

Program 2.15   Tape unit Φ_j^i

1 $T_2{}^i \leftarrow T_2{}^i \vee (\bar{r}_i \wedge (k_1 = \text{t}))$

2 $k_1 : \text{p}$

3 $r_i \wedge (k_1 = \text{t}) : 1$

4 $(b_i, A^i_{t_i}) \leftarrow 0$

5 $(\bar{b}_i \vee B^i_{t_i}) : 1$

6 $(B^i_{t_i}, F^i_{t_i}, W^i_{t_i}, x_i) \leftarrow (1, f_i, w_i, w_i)$

7 $f_i : 0$

8 delay

9 $r_i \leftarrow 0$

10 $r_i : 0$

11 $(p_i \oplus A^i_{t_i} \oplus Q^i) \leftarrow (\lambda_0, 1, 3, 0)$

12 $(g_i \oplus r_i \oplus Y^i) \leftarrow 0$

13 $C^i \leftarrow M^{\perp S^i}$

14 $\perp S^i \leftarrow 2^{15} | (1 + \perp S^i)$

15 $\alpha^3/C^i : \rho(\text{TCH})$

16 $S^i \leftarrow \omega^{15}/C^i$

17 $(\perp \alpha^{18}/C^i = 2^{17}) \vee (\perp \alpha^{18}/C^i = 6 \times 2^{15}) : 1$

35 $D^i \leftarrow 0$

36 $V^i \leftarrow \alpha^6 (36)$

37 $(k_0 \neq \text{r}) \wedge ((3 \downarrow \alpha^{15})/C^i \overset{\wedge}{=} \bar{\epsilon}) : 1$

38 $(k_0 \neq \text{c}) \wedge (p_i = \lambda_1) : 0$

39 $p_i \leftarrow \lambda_0$

40 $x_i : 0$

41 $x_i \leftarrow 0$

42 $Y^i \leftarrow (Y^i \neq X^i)$

43 $T_1{}^i \leftarrow T_1{}^i \vee (=/X^i)$

44 $(=/X^i) \wedge E_1{}^i : 1$

45 $Q_0{}^i : 0$

46 $Q_0{}^i \leftarrow (X^i \overset{\wedge}{=} \rho(\lambda_2)) \times (Q_0{}^i - 1)$

47 $Q_1{}^i \leftarrow Q_1{}^i \vee (Q_0{}^i > 0)$

48 $(Q_1{}^i = 1) \wedge (p_i = \lambda_1) : 0$

49 $T_0{}^i \leftarrow 1$

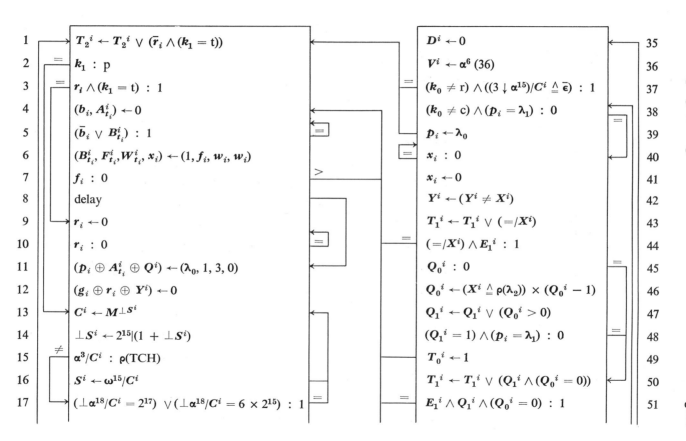

50 $T_1{}^i \leftarrow T_1{}^i \vee (Q_1{}^i \wedge (Q_0{}^i = 0))$

51 $E_1{}^i \wedge Q_1{}^i \wedge (Q_0{}^i = 0) : 1$

$C_{18}^{\ i} \ : \ 0$

$\boldsymbol{\omega}^{15}/\boldsymbol{C}^i \leftarrow \boldsymbol{\omega}^{15}/\boldsymbol{M}^{\perp \boldsymbol{\omega}^{15}/\boldsymbol{C}^i}$

$\boldsymbol{k} \leftarrow \boldsymbol{K}^{\perp \boldsymbol{\alpha}^3/\boldsymbol{C}^i}$

$w_i \ : \ 0$

$(3 \downarrow \boldsymbol{\alpha}^{15})/\boldsymbol{C}^i \ : \ 0$

$g_i \leftarrow (\boldsymbol{k}_0 = \mathrm{r})$

$g_i \ : \ 1$

$\boldsymbol{D}^i \leftarrow \boldsymbol{M}^{\perp \boldsymbol{\omega}^{15}/\boldsymbol{C}^i}$

$\perp\boldsymbol{\omega}^{15}/\boldsymbol{C}^i \leftarrow 2^{15} | (1 + \perp\boldsymbol{\omega}^{15}/\boldsymbol{C}^i)$

$\boldsymbol{V}^i \leftarrow \boldsymbol{\alpha}^6 \ (36)$

$x_i \ : \ 0$

$x_i \leftarrow 0$

$\boldsymbol{X}^i \leftarrow (\neq/\boldsymbol{V}^i/\boldsymbol{D}^i) \oplus \boldsymbol{V}^i/\boldsymbol{D}^i$

$\boldsymbol{Y}^i \leftarrow (\boldsymbol{Y}^i \neq \boldsymbol{X}^i)$

$\boldsymbol{V}^i \leftarrow 6 \downarrow \boldsymbol{V}^i$

$\boldsymbol{V}^i \ : \ \boldsymbol{\alpha}^6$

$\perp(3 \downarrow \boldsymbol{\alpha}^{15})/\boldsymbol{C}^i \leftarrow \perp(3 \downarrow \boldsymbol{\alpha}^{15})/\boldsymbol{C}^i - 1$

$p_i \ : \ \boldsymbol{\lambda}_0$

$\boldsymbol{Q}^i \leftarrow (3, 0)$

$T_1^{\ i} \leftarrow T_1^{\ i} \vee (\vee/\boldsymbol{Y}^i)$

$(\vee/\boldsymbol{Y}^i) \wedge E_1^{\ i} \ : \ 1$

$\boldsymbol{Y}^i \leftarrow 0$

$Q_0^{\ i} \ : \ 0$

$\boldsymbol{V}^i/\boldsymbol{D}^i \leftarrow \overline{\boldsymbol{\alpha}}^1/\boldsymbol{X}^i$

$\boldsymbol{V}^i \leftarrow 6 \downarrow \boldsymbol{V}^i$

$\boldsymbol{V}^i \ : \ \boldsymbol{\alpha}^6$

$(3 \downarrow \boldsymbol{\alpha}^{15})/\boldsymbol{C}^i \ : \ 0$

$\perp(3 \downarrow \boldsymbol{\alpha}^{15})/\boldsymbol{C}^i \leftarrow \perp(3 \downarrow \boldsymbol{\alpha}^{15})/\boldsymbol{C}^i - 1$

$C_{19}^{\ i} \ : \ 0$

$\boldsymbol{M}^{\perp \boldsymbol{\omega}^{15}/\boldsymbol{C}^i} \leftarrow \boldsymbol{D}^i$

$\perp\boldsymbol{\omega}^{15}/\boldsymbol{C}^i \leftarrow 2^{15} | (1 + \perp\boldsymbol{\omega}^{15}/\boldsymbol{C}^i)$

Program 2.16 Channel *i*

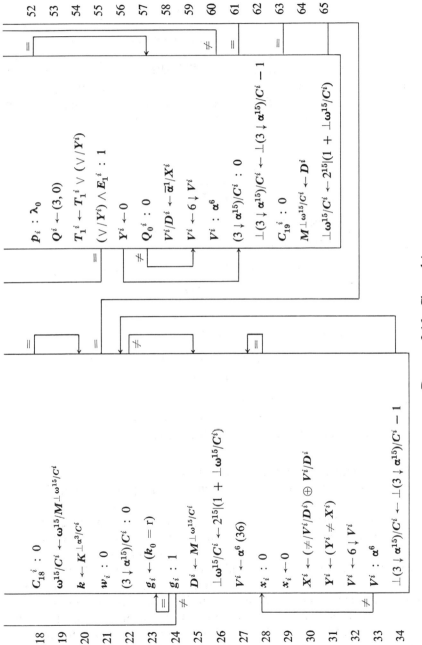

rewound before the appropriate partition is found, the process is terminated and the *beginning limit indicator* $\mathbf{L}_0{}^i$ is turned on (steps 10–11).

The file is read backward repeatedly by step 12. When a record gap occurs, step 16 is executed, and if $F_j{}^i = 1$, the branch to step 4 returns the unit to idle status. If $F_j{}^i = 3$, termination can occur only from step 11, at which point the tape is rewound. The counter $R_j{}^i$ is used to detect an end of file partition. It is reduced by one (step 14) if the character read is λ_2 or to zero if it is not. Since $R_j{}^i$ is set to 3 after each record gap, step 17 is reached with $R_j{}^i = 1$ if and only if the end of file sequence $\lambda_1, \lambda_2, \lambda_2, \lambda_1$ has occurred.

Entry	Statement	Branch	Step
20 WEF →	$k \leftarrow 4$	→ 5	1
20 BSR →	$k \leftarrow 1$	→ 5	2
20 BSF →	$k \leftarrow 2$	→ 5	3
20 REW →	$k \leftarrow 3$	→ 5	4
	$i \leftarrow (\perp(9 \uparrow \omega^4)/c) - 1$		5
	$b_i : 1$	= → 6	6
	$t_i \leftarrow \perp\omega^8/c$		7
	$f_i \leftarrow k - 3\ (k = 4)$		8
	$w_i \leftarrow (k = 4)$		9
	$b_i \leftarrow 1$	→	10

Program 2.17 Instructions for special tape unit functions

Before completing the discussion of the remaining functions of the tape unit, it may be helpful to follow through the entire process initiated by the BSR (back space record) instruction. The channel idles (Program 2.16) on step 5 with the busy indicator b_i off. The BSR instruction (Program 2.17) first determines the index i of the channel addressed, waits on step 6 until the selected channel becomes free, sets the tape index $t_i = j$ to select the particular unit $\Phi_j{}^i$, the function indicator f_i to unity, the write indicator w_i to zero, and the busy indicator b_i to unity. This last action initiates operation of channel i, which, as soon as unit $\Phi_j{}^i$ becomes free ($B_j{}^i = 0$), executes steps 6–7 and then (since $f_i > 0$) returns the channel immediately to idle status. Step 6 transfers to the parameters of the selected unit the relevant channel parameters which were themselves specified by the BSR instruction.

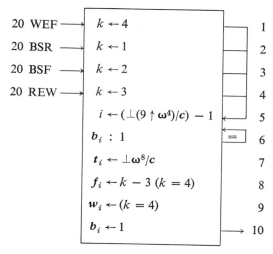

Step 6 also makes the selected unit busy ($\boldsymbol{B}_j{}^i = 1$), and hence starts it in operation.

The normal read-write functions of the tape unit are described by steps 18–37. They are initiated by a branch from step 7 in the event that the function indicator is zero. Over-all control by the channel is exercised primarily through the association indicator $\boldsymbol{A}_j{}^i$, which is equal to unity if unit j is logically associated with channel i, that is, if data are permitted to flow between them. If writing is in progress ($\boldsymbol{W}_j{}^i = 1$) and $\boldsymbol{A}_j{}^i$ becomes zero, the unit stops; if reading is in progress, the channel is freed immediately but the tape continues to a record gap.

Step 20 performs the read from tape, and if $\boldsymbol{A}_j{}^i = 1$, the partition read is transferred to $\boldsymbol{p}_i$, the seven-bit representation of the character read is transferred to $\boldsymbol{X}^i$ (both for use by the channel), and the channel-unit interlock $\boldsymbol{x}_i$ is set to unity to initiate appropriate disposition of the character by the channel. If $\boldsymbol{P}_j{}^i$ is not a record gap reading continues, the intercharacter delay (not shown) permitting time for the channel to dispose of the character before the next is actually read. If $\boldsymbol{P}_j{}^i$ is a record gap, the corresponding delay elapses before $\boldsymbol{A}_j{}^i$ is tested. If $\boldsymbol{A}_j{}^i = 0$, the branch to step 4 stops the unit. The tape stops only at a record gap although transmission of data may be discontinued earlier by step 21.

The writing process begins at step 37 and may be discontinued before any writing occurs (although the current record gap will be lengthened by a few inches of blank tape). The main writing is performed by the loop 28–32, employing the channel interlock $\boldsymbol{x}_i$. Step 31 sets the tape end limit indicator. The loop terminates (step 32) when the *write record gap* indicator $\boldsymbol{g}_i$ is set to unity by the channel. Steps 33–36 then write the longitudinal parity check character $\boldsymbol{Y}^i$ supplied by the channel, together with the inter-record gap partition $\boldsymbol{\lambda}_1$. The write loop is then re-entered unless $\boldsymbol{A}_j{}^i = 0$.

Channel operation. Operation of a channel is initiated either by one of the special functions (WEF, BSR, BSF, REW) already described, or by a WRS (write select), or an RDS (read select). The loading of the channel command $\boldsymbol{C}^i$ required to control the two latter functions is, however, controlled by a subsequent RCH (reset load channel), which transfers to $\boldsymbol{S}^i$ the address in memory of the desired channel command.

The WRS (Program 2.18) selects the channel i specified by a portion of its address, waits until the channel is free, sets its tape unit index $\boldsymbol{t}_i$ as specified by another portion of the address, sets the write indicator $\boldsymbol{w}_i$ to unity and the function indicator $\boldsymbol{f}_i$ to zero, and, finally, sets $\boldsymbol{b}_i$ to start the channel. The fetch mode indicator f is also set to *one* so as to skip the

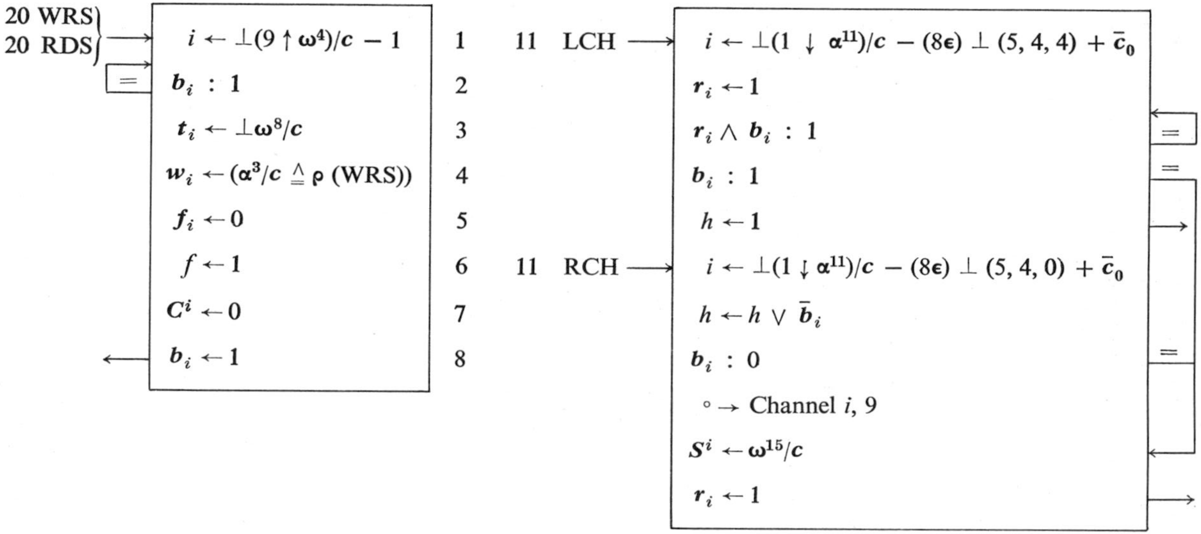

Program 2.18 Select unit and load channel instructions

channel trap on the next instruction fetch. This prevents a trap from intervening between the WRS and the following instruction (which is normally an RCH). The RDS differs only in the setting of $\boldsymbol{w}_i$ on step 4.

If the channel is not busy (i.e., not selected), the RCH instruction (Program 2.18) selects the channel specified by a portion of the operation code, sets the input-output indicator h, and copies the instruction address to the channel sequence vector $\boldsymbol{S}^i$. If the channel is busy, the RCH instruction sets the selected channel to its step 9, whereupon the channel waits on the interlock at step 10. Meanwhile, step 18 of the RCH sets $\boldsymbol{S}^i$ and step 19 sets the interlock $\boldsymbol{r}_i$ so that the channel may proceed.

Steps 13 and 14 of the channel operation load the channel command register $\boldsymbol{C}^i$ and increment the channel sequence register $\boldsymbol{S}^i$. If the command is a TCH (Transfer in Channel), step 16 causes a branch to a new sequence of commands. If not, the *word count*, represented by $(3 \downarrow \boldsymbol{\alpha}^{15})/\boldsymbol{C}^i$, is tested. If it is zero and if the current command is either an IOSP or IOCP, the branch to step 13 immediately fetches the next command in sequence. Otherwise, indirect addressing of the command occurs (step 19) unless C^i_{18} is zero.

Step 20 specifies $\boldsymbol{k}$ according to the class of the command being executed. The commands are listed in the matrix $\boldsymbol{K}$ of Table 2.13.

The first component $\boldsymbol{K}_0{}^i$ assumes the value c, r, or s according as the command having code i is terminated by a word count test, a record gap, or by either (signal). The second component $\boldsymbol{K}_1{}^i$ assumes the value d, p, or t according as the channel discontinues operation, proceeds to the next command in sequence (as determined by $\boldsymbol{S}^i$), or *transfers* to an LCH (Load Channel) instruction which may be awaiting execution by the computer proper. Execution of the LCH (Program 2.18) is delayed at step 11 and branches to step 18 (to respecify $\boldsymbol{S}^i$ in the manner of the RCH) only if the channel reaches step 3.

Channel operation continues on the right-hand segment (steps 35–65) if the operation is a *read* ($\boldsymbol{w}_i = 0$), and on the left (steps 22–34) if it is a *write*. In the latter case, a zero word count causes immediate termination of the current command.

The normal termination of a command in either read or write mode occasions a branch to step 1, where the tests for continuation begin. Step 1 sets the *Channel Command Trap* indicator $\boldsymbol{T}_2{}^i$ if the current command is of the transfer type and an LCH (Load Channel) is not awaiting execution in the computer proper. If the command is of the proceed type, step 2 branches to step 13, where the next command in sequence is fetched. If the command is of the transfer type and an LCH is waiting ($\boldsymbol{r}_i = 1$), step 3 branches to step 9 to reset parameters and permit the channel to be reloaded. In all other circumstances step 4 is executed to disassociate the unit from the channel and to return the channel to idle status. In read status, certain abnormal events—the occurrence of a parity error, or an end of file partition—return the channel to idle status immediately, regardless of the type of command being executed.

The write operation (steps 22–34) is relatively simple. If the word count in $(3 \downarrow \boldsymbol{\alpha}^{15})/C^i$ is zero, steps 23–24 terminate the current command but first initiate the writing of an end of record gap* if the command is of the "record" type (e.g., an IORP). If the word count is not zero, step 25 transfers to the channel data register $\boldsymbol{D}^i$ the memory word selected by the address portion of the command. The loop 28–33 transfers to the tape unit successive six-bit infixes of $\boldsymbol{D}^i$ and maintains the longitudinal parity check $\boldsymbol{Y}^i$ (originally reset on step 12). When all six have been transferred, the branch to step 34 decrements the word count and, unless it becomes zero, repeats the entire process from step 25.

The read operation (steps 35–65) begins by resetting $\boldsymbol{D}^i$ to zero and the infix selector $\boldsymbol{V}^i$ to $\boldsymbol{\alpha}^6$. Step 37 terminates the current command if it is of the count or signal type and the word count is zero. Steps 38–39 terminate the command if it is of the record or signal type and if the last file partition read is a record gap. The partition indicator $\boldsymbol{p}_i$ is reset to $\boldsymbol{\lambda}_0$ by step 39. Thus a record gap present when termination is caused by a zero count is still present on the first execution of the succeeding command, whereas a gap which itself causes termination is not present on the succeeding command.

Steps 40–43 show the data interlock, the determination of the longitudinal parity check, and the setting of the parity error trap $\boldsymbol{T}_1{}^i$ in the event of a parity error in the character. If the corresponding channel trap is enabled, step 44 causes immediate termination in the event of a parity error. Steps 45–48 detect an end of file configuration (using a counter, $\boldsymbol{Q}_0{}^i$ in a manner similar to that used in Program 2.15), set the indicator $\boldsymbol{Q}_1{}^i$ if a partition character $\boldsymbol{\lambda}_2$ appears at the beginning of a word, and cause termination (from step 49) with the end of file trap $\boldsymbol{T}_0{}^i$ set if an end of file configuration occurs. If the character $\boldsymbol{\lambda}_2$ occurring at the beginning of a word is not part of an end of file configuration, step 50 sets the tape error trap $\boldsymbol{T}_1{}^i$, and step 51 causes termination if the corresponding channel trap is enabled.

Steps 53–56 are executed only if $\boldsymbol{p}_i$ is a record gap. They reset the counters $\boldsymbol{Q}^i$ controlling the end of file test, test and reset the longitudinal parity vector $\boldsymbol{Y}^i$, and may cause termination in the event of an error. Step 57 causes the character transfer of step 58 to be skipped if the character is

* Since the partition $\boldsymbol{\lambda}_1$ is represented by a gap, the writing of one gap immediately following another, with no intervening data, has the effect (when subsequently read) of a single record gap.

$$\perp s \leftarrow 2^{15}|(1 + \perp s)$$

Input-output test   10 IOT $\longrightarrow$ $h : 0$

$$h \leftarrow 0$$

Beginning of tape test 10 BTT $\longrightarrow$ $k \leftarrow 0$

End of tape test   10 ETT $\longrightarrow$ $k \leftarrow 1$

$$i \leftarrow \perp(9 \uparrow \omega^6)/c - 1$$

$$L_k{}^i : 0$$

$$L_k{}^i \leftarrow 0$$

Transfer on channel   11 TEF $\longrightarrow$ $i \leftarrow \perp(1 \downarrow \alpha^{11})/c - (8\epsilon)\perp(3, 0) + c_0$
end of file

$$b \leftarrow T_0{}^i$$

$$T_0{}^i \leftarrow 0$$

Transfer on channel   11 TRC $\longrightarrow$ $i \leftarrow \perp(1 \downarrow \alpha^{11})/c - (8\epsilon)\perp(2, 2) + c_0$
redundancy

$$b \leftarrow T_1{}^i$$

$$T_1{}^i \leftarrow 0$$

Transfer on channel   11 TCO $\longrightarrow$ $k \leftarrow 0$
in operation

Transfer on channel   11 TCN $\longrightarrow$ $k \leftarrow 1$
not in operation

$$i \leftarrow \perp(1 \downarrow \alpha^{11})/c - (8\epsilon)\perp(6, 0)$$

$$b \leftarrow (b_i \neq k)$$

$$t : 1$$

$$b : 0$$

$$s \leftarrow \omega^{15}/c$$

$$M^0 \leftarrow \omega^{15}(36)\backslash s$$

$$b : 0$$

$$\perp s \leftarrow 1$$

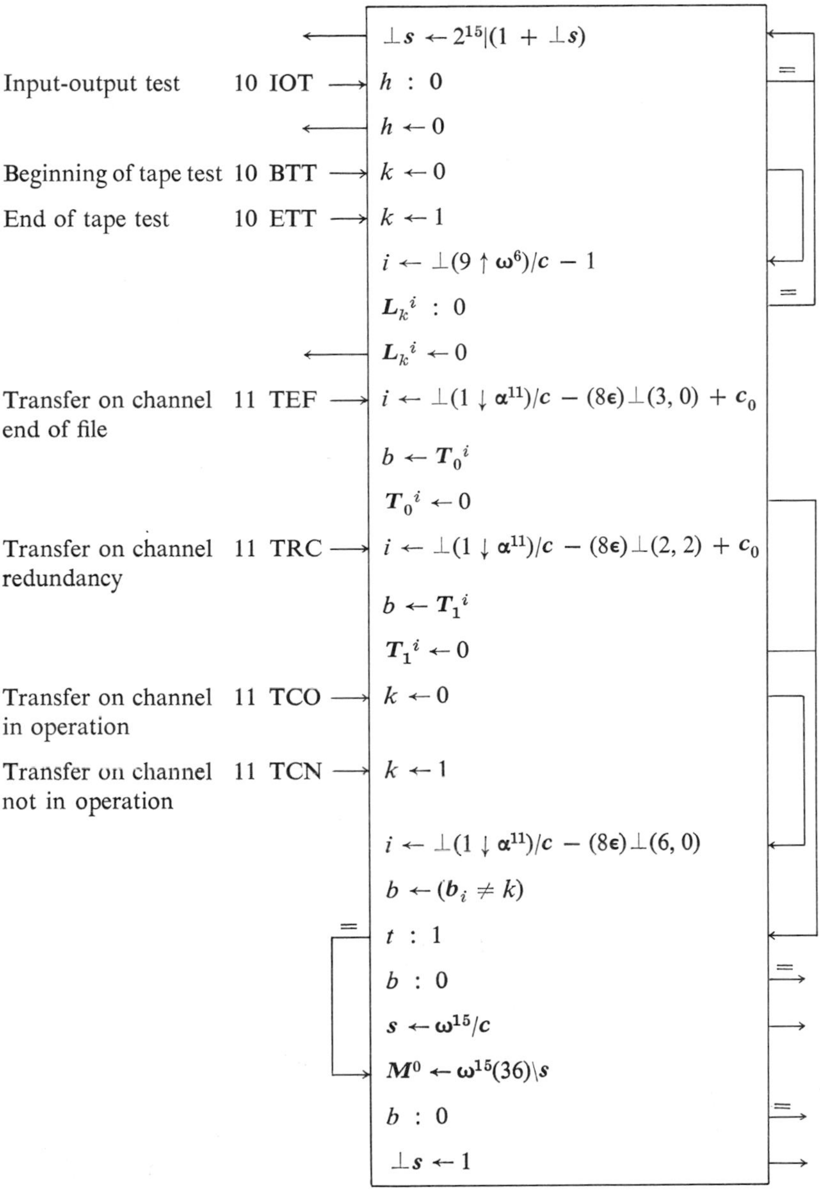

Program 2.19 Input-output branch operations

a potential end of file. Steps 62–65 decrement the word count and transfer completed words to successive memory locations unless C^i_{19} is zero. Step 61 suspends these operations when the word count reaches zero. Since step 56 is followed by step 61, the occurrence of a record gap occasions the (potential) transfer of a word to memory even though it is incomplete. Because of the reset of $\boldsymbol{D}^i$ on step 35, the incompleted part of the word is zero.

Auxiliary channel instructions. Program 2.19 shows those branch instructions which are controlled by indicators associated with the data channels. Each indicator tested is also reset. The last four instructions shown are subject to the trap mode.

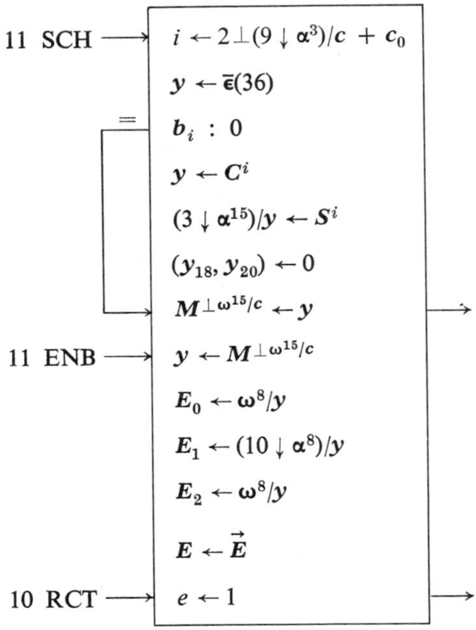

Program 2.20 Trap control and store channel

The channel indicators $\boldsymbol{T}$ may also cause interruptions as detailed in the instruction fetch phase. They are controlled by the enable matrix $\boldsymbol{E}$ and the enable trigger e which are set by the ENB (enable) and RCT (reset traps) instruction of Program 2.20. The instruction SCH (Program 2.20) permits storage of the channel registers.

2.3 DETAILED LOGICAL DESIGN

Although a description couched at the programmer's level specifies completely the functions of a computer, it requires considerable extension to provide a basis for the so-called *logical design* of circuits for realizing the computer. The extensions include: (1) the specification of sequence in the microprograms themselves; (2) further detailing of certain complex functions; (3) reduction of the number of operands (registers) required; and (4) economization in the underlying functions provided. The nature of these extensions will be indicated briefly.

In principle, the problem of sequence control in the microprograms does not differ from the sequence control in computer programs. However, the function served by the sequence vector $\boldsymbol{s}$ (a base two representation of the address of the succeeding instruction) is frequently served instead by a ring or combination of rings. A *ring* is a logical vector $\boldsymbol{r}$ of weight one (that is, $+/\boldsymbol{r} = 1$) capable of rotation ($\uparrow\boldsymbol{r}$ or $\downarrow\boldsymbol{r}$) and of resetting to one of several initial positions $\boldsymbol{p}_i$ (that is, $\boldsymbol{r} \leftarrow \boldsymbol{\epsilon}^{\boldsymbol{p}_i}$.)

Certain steps of a microprogram, which at the programmer's level may be considered as monolithic, must themselves be realized in circuitry as more detailed microprograms. The addition of two unsigned (positive) numbers represented in base two by the vectors $\boldsymbol{x}$ and $\boldsymbol{y}$ might, for example, be performed as in Program 2.21. The result $\boldsymbol{x}$ produced is correct only if the sum is less than $2^{\nu(\boldsymbol{x})}$.

Economization in the underlying functions provided is achieved by restricting the "data paths" provided between the various operands (i.e., registers) and by restricting the operands to which certain operations apply. Restriction of data paths implies that it is not possible for each operand to specify every other operand directly. For example, memory may be restricted to communicate only with the buffer register $\boldsymbol{d}$ so that any transfer from memory such as

$$\boldsymbol{c} \leftarrow \boldsymbol{M}^{\perp \boldsymbol{s}}$$

$$\boldsymbol{y} : 0 \quad (=\ \text{exit})$$
$$\boldsymbol{z} \leftarrow \boldsymbol{y}$$
$$\boldsymbol{y} \leftarrow \uparrow(\boldsymbol{x} \wedge \boldsymbol{z})$$
$$\boldsymbol{x} \leftarrow (\boldsymbol{x} \neq \boldsymbol{z})$$

Program 2.21 Base two addition

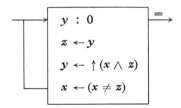

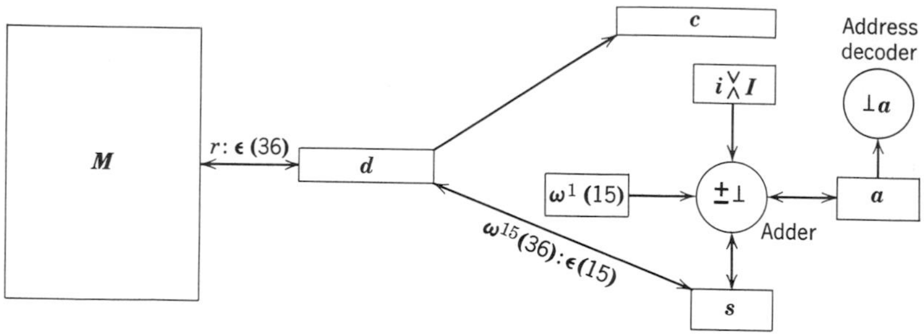

Figure 2.22 Data paths

must in fact be performed in two steps:

$$\mathbf{d} \leftarrow \mathbf{M}^{\perp \mathbf{s}}$$

$$\mathbf{c} \leftarrow \mathbf{d}.$$

An operation such as address decoding (i.e., conversion of the normal base two representation of an address i into a one-out-of-n code of the form $\boldsymbol{\epsilon}^i$ suitable for selecting word i from memory) is relatively costly and is not normally provided for all relevant operands (such as $\mathbf{s}$ and $\boldsymbol{\omega}^{15}/\mathbf{c}$ in the 7090). Instead, decoding may be provided on a single auxiliary operand $\mathbf{a}$; the selection of an instruction in the 7090 would then be executed in two steps:

$$\mathbf{a} \leftarrow \mathbf{s}$$

$$\mathbf{c} \leftarrow \mathbf{M}^{\perp \mathbf{a}}.$$

All microprograms specified at the programmer's level must, of course, be translated into equivalent microprograms which satisfy the path constraints. Path restrictions are perhaps best displayed as a "block diagram" showing the data paths provided between the various registers and operations units. Figure 2.22 illustrates a convenient representation in which the paths are shown as connecting lines with arrowheads indicating the possible directions of transfer. If the indicated paths are further restricted to selected components of the operands, this restriction may be indicated by a pair of selection vectors separated by a colon. Thus the notation

$$\boldsymbol{\omega}^{15}(36) : \boldsymbol{\epsilon}(15)$$

on the path between $\mathbf{d}$ and $\mathbf{s}$ of Fig. 2.22 indicates that transfers occur between $\boldsymbol{\omega}^{15}/\mathbf{d}$ and $\mathbf{s}$. The symbols r and c denote the selection of a matrix row and a matrix column, respectively, as illustrated by the path between $\mathbf{M}$ and $\mathbf{d}$. Permutations may be represented in the form $\mathbf{p}\int$. Thus if the vector d were to be transposed (reversed in order) in the transfer to c, the path would be labeled with the expression

$$p\int : \epsilon,$$

where $p = |\iota^{-35}(36)| = (35, 34, \ldots, 1, 0)$.

REFERENCES

Falkoff, A., (1962) "Algorithms for Parallel-Search Memories," *J.A.C.M.* (to appear).

IBM Reference Manual, 7090 *Data Processing System*, (1960), Form # A-22-6528, International Business Machines Corporation.

Phister, M., (1958), *Logical Design of Digital Computers*, Wiley, New York.

EXERCISES

2.1 Write 7090 programs for each of the following operations:

(a) $M^8 \leftarrow M^8 \vee M^9$

(b) $M^8 \leftarrow \overline{M}^8$

(c) $\begin{cases} \perp M^6 \leftarrow 2^{36} \mid (\perp M^8 + \perp M^9) \\ \perp M^7 \leftarrow ((\perp M^8 + \perp M^9) \geq 2^{36}) \end{cases}$

(d) $M^6 \leftarrow /M^7, \alpha^6, M^9/$

(e) $M^6 \leftarrow /M^7, \omega^6, M^9/$

(f) $M^6 \leftarrow /M^7, (8 \downarrow \alpha^{10}), M^9/$

(g) $M^6 \leftarrow /M^7, M^8, M^9/$ [Use $/x, u, y/ = (x \wedge \overline{u}) \vee (y \wedge u)$]

(h) $M^6 \leftarrow u_1\omega^1$

2.2 In the magnetic core technology employed in the 7090, logical disjunction (*or*) and negation are much easier to produce than conjunction (*and*). Limiting the logical functions employed to disjunction and negation, write microprograms for the following 7090 instructions:

(a) ANS (Use De Morgan's law, Sec. 1.8)

(b) ERA

2.3 In the magnetic core technology used in the 7090, each transfer of a quantity y into a register x is actually an *or* with the present content of the register, i.e., $x \leftarrow y \vee x$. A register may also be reset to zero. Subject to the foregoing restriction, write microprograms for

(a) the operation $l \leftarrow M^i$. (Use two steps.)

(b) the operations of Exercise 2.2(a).

2.4 Describe the main portion of the instruction fetch of the 7090 (steps 9–18 of Program 2.4) in an algorithm which satisfies the data path constraints of Fig. 2.22.

2.5 Repeat Exercise 2.4 so as to satisfy the constraints of Exercises 2.2 and 2.3 as well.

2.6 A vector p which permits only the following types of operation:

(i) $p \leftarrow \backslash p, \omega^1, x\backslash$

(ii) $\begin{cases} y \leftarrow \omega^1/p \\ p \leftarrow \overline{\omega}^1/p \end{cases}$

is called a *pushdown* or *stack* vector. If the successive components of a stack vector $\boldsymbol{p}$ are represented by successive memory registers, then the operations affecting it can be controlled by a single *address counter* $\boldsymbol{v}$, which is automatically incremented at each operation of type (i) (addition of a new final component) and is automatically decremented at each operation of type (ii) (reference to the final component accompanied by its deletion).

(a) Using the 7090 registers and formats augmented by an address counter $\boldsymbol{v}$ of dimension 15, write a microprogram for an operation LDS (load stack) which transfers $\boldsymbol{M}^{\perp \omega^{15}/c}$ to the top of the stack [operation type (i)].

(b) Write a microprogram for STS (store stack) which transfers the top of the stack to $\boldsymbol{M}^{\perp \omega^{15}/c}$ [operation type (ii)].

(c) Write a microprogram for an operation AND which produces the *and* function of the top two components of the stack, deletes them, and appends the result as a new final component. [The net reduction in $\nu(\boldsymbol{p})$ is *one*].

(d) The AND of part (c) has no associated address. Show that all 7090 instructions (other than input-output) can be redefined so that only the LDS and STS require associated addresses.

2.7 In the 7090, a decimal digit x is represented in direct binary coding in a six-bit logical vector $\boldsymbol{x}$, (that is, $\perp \boldsymbol{x} = x$), and each register accommodates six decimal digits. Use the *convert* instructions (Program 2.12) in a 7090 program to

(a) convert from binary to decimal.

(b) convert from decimal to binary.

(c) replace all leading zeros (i.e., all preceding the first significant digit) of a number represented in decimal.

2.8 Write a 7090 program to convert

(a) from a 36-bit binary code to a 36-bit reflected Gray code [see Phister (1958)].

(b) from a reflected Gray code to binary.

2.9 A memory $\boldsymbol{M}$ is called a *tag* or *associative* memory if for any argument $\boldsymbol{x}$ it yields a direct indication of the row or rows of $\boldsymbol{M}$ which agree with $\boldsymbol{x}$. If the resulting indication is in the form of a vector $\boldsymbol{s}$ such that the matrix $\boldsymbol{s}//\boldsymbol{M}$ contains the indicated rows, then $\boldsymbol{s} = \boldsymbol{M} \overset{\wedge}{=} \boldsymbol{x}$. More generally, a logical *mask vector* $\boldsymbol{m}$ is added to the system so that $\boldsymbol{m}/\boldsymbol{M}$ is compared with the argument $\boldsymbol{m}/\boldsymbol{x}$ and some desired function of $\boldsymbol{m}/\boldsymbol{M}^k$ is represented by $\overline{\boldsymbol{m}}/\boldsymbol{M}^k$ for each k. In the following exercises $\boldsymbol{M}$ is assumed to be a logical matrix.

(a) Use De Morgan's laws (Secs. 1.8 and 1.11 or Sec. 7.1) to derive from the relation $\boldsymbol{s} = \boldsymbol{M} \overset{\wedge}{=} \boldsymbol{x}$ an expression for $\boldsymbol{s}$ which would be suited to a circuit technology in which disjunction and negation are easier to perform than conjunction.

(b) Write a detailed algorithm using a row-by-row scan of $\boldsymbol{M}$ to determine $\boldsymbol{s} = (\boldsymbol{m}/\boldsymbol{M}) \overset{\wedge}{=} (\boldsymbol{m}/\boldsymbol{x})$.

(c) Repeat part (b) using a column-by-column scan of $\boldsymbol{M}$.

(d) Use a column-by-column scan of $\boldsymbol{M}$ to determine $\boldsymbol{s}$ such that $\boldsymbol{s}//\boldsymbol{M}$ contains the rows of $\boldsymbol{M}$ of maximum base two value [see Falkoff (1962)].

chapter 3

REPRESENTATION OF VARIABLES

3.1 ALLOCATION AND ENCODING

Although the abstract description of a program may be presented in any suitable language, its automatic execution must be performed on some specified representation of the relevant operands. The specification of this representation presents two distinct aspects—allocation and encoding.

An *allocation* specifies the correspondences between physical devices and the variables represented thereby. An *encoding* specifies the correspondences between the distinct states of the physical devices and the literals which they represent. If, for example, certain numerical data are to be represented by a set of 50 two-state devices, the two-out-of-five coding system of Exercise 1.6 might be chosen, and it would then remain to specify the allocation. The two-digit quantity "hours worked" might be allocated as follows: devices 31–35 represent components 1–5, respectively, of the first digit, and devices 29, 16, 17, 24, and 47 represent components 1, 2, 3, 4, 5, respectively, of the second digit.

The encoding of a variable will be specified by an *encoding matrix* C and associated *format vector* f such that the rows of $\bar{f}/C$ list the representands and the rows of f/C list the corresponding representations. The encoding is normally fixed and normally concerns the programmer only in the translation of input or output data. Even this translation is usually handled in a routine manner, and attention will therefore be restricted primarily to the problem of allocation.

However, the encoding of numeric quantities warrants special comment. It includes the representation of the sign and of the scale, as well as the representation of the significant digits. Small numbers, such as indices, admit not only of the usual positional representation but also of the use of the unit vector $\boldsymbol{\epsilon}^j$ to represent the number j (i.e., a one-out-of-n coding system), or of the use of a logical vector of weight j (i.e., a base 1 number system).

Allocation will be described in terms of the *physical vector* $\boldsymbol{\pi}$, which denotes the physical storage elements of the computer. Each component of $\boldsymbol{\pi}$ corresponds to one of the $\nu(\boldsymbol{\pi})$ similar physical devices available, its range of values is the set of physical states achievable by each device, and its index is the address of the device. Each component of $\boldsymbol{\pi}$ may correspond to a computer register, an individual character position in a register, or an individual binary digit within a character, depending on the degree of resolution appropriate to the allocation problem considered. The 0-origin indexing normally used for computer addresses will be used for the physical vector, but 1-origin indexing will, throughout this chapter, normally be employed for all other structured operands.

An index of the physical vector will be called an *address* and will itself be represented in the (perhaps mixed) radix appropriate to the given computer. The Univac, for example, employs base ten addressing for the registers, and (because of the use of 12-character words) a radix of twelve for finer resolution. The address of the fourth character of register 675 might therefore be written as 675.3. In computers which have two or more independent addressing systems (e.g., the independent addressing systems for main memory and for auxiliary storage in the IBM 705), superscripts may be used to identify the several physical vectors $\boldsymbol{\pi}^j$.

In general, the *representation* of a quantity x is a vector (to be denoted by $\boldsymbol{\rho}(x)$) whose components are chosen from the physical vector $\boldsymbol{\pi}$. Thus $\boldsymbol{\rho}(x) = \boldsymbol{k} \int \boldsymbol{\pi}$, where $\boldsymbol{k}$ is a mapping vector associated with x. The dimension of the representation (that is, $\nu(\boldsymbol{\rho}(x))$) is called the *dimension of x in $\boldsymbol{\pi}$*. If, for example, $\boldsymbol{\rho}(x) = (\pi_{10}, \pi_9, \pi_{17}, \pi_{18})$, then $\boldsymbol{k} = (10, 9, 17, 18)$, and the dimension of x in $\boldsymbol{\pi}$ is four. If $\boldsymbol{\rho}(x)$ is an infix of $\boldsymbol{\pi}$, then the representation of x is said to be *solid*. A solid representation can be characterized by two parameters, its dimension d and its *leading address* f, that is, the index in $\boldsymbol{\pi}$ of its first component. Then $\boldsymbol{\rho}(x) = (f \downarrow \boldsymbol{\alpha}^d)/\boldsymbol{\pi}$.

3.2 REPRESENTATION OF STRUCTURED OPERANDS

The grid matrix

If each component of a vector $\boldsymbol{x}$ has a solid representation, then the representation of the entire vector is said to be solid and may be characterized by the *grid matrix* $\boldsymbol{\Gamma}(\boldsymbol{x})$, of dimension $\nu(\boldsymbol{x}) \times 2$, defined as follows: $\boldsymbol{\Gamma}_1{}^i(\boldsymbol{x})$ is the leading address of $\boldsymbol{\rho}(\boldsymbol{x}_i)$, and $\boldsymbol{\Gamma}_2{}^i(\boldsymbol{x})$ is the dimension of $\boldsymbol{x}_i$ in $\boldsymbol{\pi}$. If, for example, the vector $\boldsymbol{x}$ is represented as shown in Fig. 3.1*a*, then

$$\boldsymbol{\Gamma}(\boldsymbol{x}) = \begin{pmatrix} 17 & 2 \\ 19 & 4 \\ 27 & 5 \\ 23 & 1 \\ 32 & 3 \end{pmatrix}.$$

Representand	x_1		x_2				x_4				x_3					x_5		
Physical vector	π_{17}	π_{18}	π_{19}	π_{20}	π_{21}	π_{22}	π_{23}	π_{24}	π_{25}	π_{26}	π_{27}	π_{28}	π_{29}	π_{30}	π_{31}	π_{32}	π_{33}	π_{34}

(*a*) Representation of a vector $\boldsymbol{x}$

Representand	Γ_1^1		Γ_2^1		Γ_1^2		Γ_2^2		Γ_1^3		Γ_2^3		Γ_1^4		Γ_2^4		Γ_1^5		Γ_2^5	
Physical vector	π_{40}	π_{41}	π_{42}	π_{43}	π_{44}	π_{45}	π_{46}	π_{47}	π_{48}	π_{49}	π_{50}	π_{51}	π_{52}	π_{53}	π_{54}	π_{55}	π_{56}	π_{57}	π_{58}	π_{59}
Actual value	1	7	0	2	1	9	0	4	2	7	0	5	2	3	0	1	3	2	0	3

(*b*) Linear representation of $\boldsymbol{\Gamma}(\boldsymbol{x})$ with $l = 34 + 4i + 2j$.

Figure 3.1

		X_1^1					X_1^2			X_2^1					X_2^2			
π_0	π_1	π_2	π_3	π_4	π_5	π_6	π_7	π_8	π_9	π_{10}	π_{11}	π_{12}	π_{13}	π_{14}	π_{15}	π_{16}	π_{17}	π_{18}

Figure 3.2 Linear representation of a matrix $\boldsymbol{X}$

Any structured operand can first be reduced to an equivalent vector, and the grid matrix therefore suffices for describing the representation of any construct, providing only that the representation of each of its elements is solid. Thus a matrix $\boldsymbol{X}$ may be represented by either the row-by-row list $\boldsymbol{r} = \mathbf{E}/\boldsymbol{X}$ or the column-by-column list $\boldsymbol{c} = \mathbf{E}//\boldsymbol{X}$, and a tree $\mathbf{T}$ may be represented by the left list matrix $[\mathbf{T}$ or the right list matrix $]\mathbf{T}$, either of which may be represented, in turn, by a vector.

If a process involves only a small number of variables, it is practical to make their allocation implicit in the algorithm, i.e., to incorporate in the algorithm the selection operations on the vector $\boldsymbol{\pi}$ necessary to extract the appropriate variables. This is the procedure usually employed, for example, in simple computer programs. In processes involving numerous variables, implicit allocation may become too cumbersome and confusing, and more systematic procedures are needed.

Linear representations

The representation of a structured operand is said to be *linear* if each component is represented by an infix of the form $(l \downarrow \boldsymbol{\alpha}^d)/\boldsymbol{\pi}$, where l is a linear function of the indices of the component. For example, the representation of the matrix $\boldsymbol{X}$ indicated by Fig. 3.2 is linear, with $d = 2$ and $l = -11 + 5i + 8j$.

A linear representation is solid and can clearly be characterized by a small number of parameters—the dimension d of each component and the coefficients in the linear expression l. The representation of a vector $\boldsymbol{x}$ is linear if and only if $\boldsymbol{\Gamma}_2(\boldsymbol{x}) = d\boldsymbol{\epsilon}$ and the difference $\delta = \boldsymbol{\Gamma}_1{}^i(\boldsymbol{x}) - \boldsymbol{\Gamma}_1^{i-1}(\boldsymbol{x})$ is constant for $i = 2, 3, \ldots, \nu(\boldsymbol{x})$.

If $l = p + qi + rj$ is the function defining a linear representation of a matrix $\boldsymbol{X}$ and if a is the leading address of a given element, then the leading address of the succeeding element in the row (or column) is simply $a + r$ (or $a + q$). Frequently, the succession must be cyclic, and the resulting sum must be reduced modulo $\nu(\boldsymbol{X}) \times r$ (or $\mu(\boldsymbol{X}) \times q$). The inherent convenience of linear representations is further enhanced by index registers, which provide efficient incrementation and comparison of addresses.

Linear representation of a structured operand requires that all components be of the same dimension in $\boldsymbol{\pi}$. This common dimension may, however, be achieved by appending null elements to the shorter components. The convenience of the linear representation must then be weighed against the waste occasioned by the null elements. Moreover, if several vectors or matrices are to be represented and if each is of unspecified total dimension in $\boldsymbol{\pi}$, it may be impossible to allot to each an infix sufficiently large to permit linear representation. Consequently, a linear representation is not always practicable.

Nonlinear representations

Since the use of the grid matrix imposes only the condition of solidity for each component, it permits an allocation which is sufficiently general for most purposes. The grid matrix serves in two distinct capacities: (1) as a useful conceptual device for describing an allocation even when the actual allocation is implicit in the program, and (2) as a parameter which enters directly into an algorithm and explicitly specifies the allocation.

If the grid matrix is used in a program as an explicit specification of the allocation, then the grid matrix must itself be represented by the physical vector. There remains, therefore, the problem of choosing a suitable allocation for the grid matrix itself; a linear allocation is illustrated by Fig. 3.1*b*.

If the grid matrix $\mathbf{\Gamma}(\boldsymbol{x})$ itself employs a linear representation, its use offers advantages over the direct use of a linear representation of $\boldsymbol{x}$ only if the total dimension of $\mathbf{\Gamma}$ in $\boldsymbol{\pi}$ is much less than the total dimension of $\boldsymbol{x}$ in $\boldsymbol{\pi}$ when linear representations are employed for both. This is frequently the case, since each element of a grid matrix belongs to the index set of $\boldsymbol{\pi}$ (that is, to $\boldsymbol{\iota}^0(\nu(\boldsymbol{\pi}))$), and the dimension of each element in $\boldsymbol{\pi}$ is therefore both uniform and relatively small. Program 3.3 shows the use of the grid matrix $\mathbf{\Gamma}(\boldsymbol{x})$ and the encoding matrix C in determining the kth component of the vector $\boldsymbol{x}$.

Program 3.3. A linear representation is assumed for $\mathbf{\Gamma}(\mathbf{x})$, with element $\mathbf{\Gamma}_j{}^i(\boldsymbol{x})$ represented by the infix $((p + qi + rj) \downarrow \boldsymbol{\alpha}^g)/\boldsymbol{\pi}$. Moreover, each element of $\mathbf{\Gamma}(\boldsymbol{x})$ is assumed to be represented in a base $\boldsymbol{b}$ number system. Step 1 determines the leading address of the representation of $\mathbf{\Gamma}_1{}^k(\boldsymbol{x})$. Step 2 specifies f as the base $\boldsymbol{b}$ value of this representation, i.e., as the leading address of $\boldsymbol{\rho}(\boldsymbol{x}_k)$. Steps 3 and 4 specify d as the dimension of $\boldsymbol{x}_k$ in $\boldsymbol{\pi}$, and step 5 therefore specifies $\boldsymbol{z}$ as the representation of $\boldsymbol{x}_k$.

Steps 7–9 perform the decoding of $\boldsymbol{z} = \boldsymbol{\rho}(\boldsymbol{x}_k)$ to obtain z as the actual value of $\boldsymbol{x}_k$. Since this process is normally performed by human or mechanical means (e.g., a printer) outside the purview of the programmer, it is here expressed directly in terms of the encoding matrix C rather than in terms of its representation. The left-pointing exit on step 7 is followed only if $\boldsymbol{z}$ does not occur as an entry in the encoding matrix.

The form chosen for the grid matrix is one of several possible. The two columns could, for example, represent the leading and final addresses of the corresponding representations or the dimensions and final addresses. The present choice of leading address f and dimension d is, however, the most convenient for use in conjunction with the notation adopted for infixes; the logical vector $(f \downarrow \boldsymbol{\alpha}^d)$ selects the appropriate infix.

	Program	
1 →	$l \leftarrow p + qk + r \times 1$	
2	$f \leftarrow \boldsymbol{b}\bot((l \downarrow \boldsymbol{\alpha}^g)/\boldsymbol{\pi})$	
3	$l \leftarrow l + r$	
4	$d \leftarrow \boldsymbol{b}\bot((l \downarrow \boldsymbol{\alpha}^g)/\boldsymbol{\pi})$	
5	$\boldsymbol{z} \leftarrow (f \downarrow \boldsymbol{\alpha}^d)/\boldsymbol{\pi}$	
6	$h \leftarrow \mu(\boldsymbol{C}) + 1$	
7 ← =	$h \leftarrow h - 1$	←
8	$\boldsymbol{z} : \boldsymbol{f}/\boldsymbol{C}^h$	≠
9	$z \leftarrow \bar{\boldsymbol{f}}/\boldsymbol{C}^h$	→

0-origin indexing for $\boldsymbol{\pi}$ only	
p, q, r	Constant, coefficient of row index, and coefficient of column index in the linear function for the representation of $\boldsymbol{\Gamma}(\boldsymbol{x})$.
$\boldsymbol{b}$	Base used in representing elements of $\boldsymbol{\Gamma}(\boldsymbol{x})$.
g	Dimension in $\boldsymbol{\pi}$ of each element of $\boldsymbol{\Gamma}(\boldsymbol{x})$.
f	Leading address of $\boldsymbol{\rho}(\boldsymbol{x}_k)$.
d	Dimension of $\boldsymbol{\rho}(\boldsymbol{x}_k)$ in $\boldsymbol{\pi}$.
$\boldsymbol{z}$	$\boldsymbol{\rho}(\boldsymbol{x}_k)$.
$\boldsymbol{C}$	Encoding matrix for components of $\boldsymbol{x}$.
$\boldsymbol{f}$	Format vector for $\boldsymbol{C}$.
z	Character encoded by $\boldsymbol{x}_k$.

Legend

Program 3.3 Determination of $\boldsymbol{z} = \boldsymbol{\rho}(\boldsymbol{x}_k)$ and $z = \boldsymbol{x}_k$ from a linear representation of the grid matrix $\boldsymbol{\Gamma}(\boldsymbol{x})$

Chained representations*

If a linear representation is used for a vector, then the deletion of a component (as in a compress operation) necessitates the moving (i.e., respecification) of the representations of each of the subsequent components. Similarly, mesh operations (insertion) and permutations necessitate extensive respecification. The use of a grid matrix $\boldsymbol{\Gamma}(\boldsymbol{x})$ obviates such respecification in $\boldsymbol{x}$, since appropriate changes can instead be made in $\boldsymbol{\Gamma}(\boldsymbol{x})$, where they may be much simpler to effect. If, for example, $\boldsymbol{x}$ is the vector represented as in Fig. 3.1*a*, and z is a quantity of dimension six in $\boldsymbol{\pi}$, then the mesh operation

$$\boldsymbol{x} \leftarrow \backslash \boldsymbol{x}, \boldsymbol{\epsilon}^3, z \backslash$$

may be effected by specifying the physical infix $(70 \downarrow \boldsymbol{\alpha}^6)/\boldsymbol{\pi}$ by $\boldsymbol{\rho}(z)$ and by

* Chained representations have received extensive treatment, frequently under the name "lists." See, for example, Shaw et al. (1958) and Blaauw (1959).

respecifying $\mathbf{\Gamma}(\boldsymbol{x})$ as follows:

$$\mathbf{\Gamma}(\boldsymbol{x}) = \begin{pmatrix} 17 & 2 \\ 19 & 4 \\ 70 & 6 \\ 27 & 5 \\ 23 & 1 \\ 32 & 3 \end{pmatrix}.$$

However, if the representation of $\mathbf{\Gamma}(\boldsymbol{x})$ is itself linear, then insertions, deletions, and permutations in $\boldsymbol{x}$ will occasion changes in all components of $\mathbf{\Gamma}(\boldsymbol{x})$ whose indices are affected. The need for a linear representation of the grid matrix (and hence for all linear representations) can be obviated by the use of a *chained representation* defined as follows.

Consider a vector $\boldsymbol{y}$, each of whose components $\boldsymbol{y}_k$ has a solid representation $\boldsymbol{\rho}(\boldsymbol{y}_k)$ whose infixes $(g \downarrow \boldsymbol{\alpha}^g)/\boldsymbol{\rho}(\boldsymbol{y}_k)$ and $\boldsymbol{\alpha}^g/\boldsymbol{\rho}(\boldsymbol{y}_k)$ are, respectively, the dimension of $\boldsymbol{\rho}(\boldsymbol{y}_k)$ in $\boldsymbol{\pi}$ and the leading address of the representation of the (cyclically) succeeding component of $\boldsymbol{y}$ (both in a base $\boldsymbol{b}$ system), and whose suffix $\overline{\boldsymbol{\alpha}}^{2g}/\boldsymbol{\rho}(\boldsymbol{y}_k)$ is the representation of the kth component of some vector $\boldsymbol{x}$. Then (the representation of) $\boldsymbol{y}$ is called a *chained representation of* $\boldsymbol{x}$. In other words, the representation of $\boldsymbol{y}$ incorporates its own grid matrix (with the address column $\mathbf{\Gamma}_1(\boldsymbol{y})$ rotated upward by one place) as well as the representation of the vector $\boldsymbol{x}$.

For example, if $g = 2$, $\boldsymbol{b} = 10\boldsymbol{\epsilon}$, and $\boldsymbol{x} = (365, 7, 24)$, then

$$\boldsymbol{\rho}(\boldsymbol{y}_1) = (\pi_{17}, \pi_{18}, \pi_{19}, \pi_{20}, \pi_{21}, \pi_{22}, \pi_{23}) = (6, 8, 0, 7, 3, 6, 5),$$
$$\boldsymbol{\rho}(\boldsymbol{y}_2) = (\pi_{68}, \pi_{69}, \pi_{70}, \pi_{71}, \pi_{72}) = (2, 6, 0, 5, 7),$$

and

$$\boldsymbol{\rho}(\boldsymbol{y}_3) = (\pi_{26}, \pi_{27}, \pi_{28}, \pi_{29}, \pi_{30}, \pi_{31}) = (1, 7, 0, 6, 2, 4),$$

is a suitable chained representation of $\boldsymbol{x}$.

The parameters required in executing an algorithm on a chained representation $\boldsymbol{y}$ are g, the common dimension in $\boldsymbol{\pi}$ of the elements of the grid matrix $\mathbf{\Gamma}(\boldsymbol{y})$; $\boldsymbol{b}$, the base of the number system employed in their representation; and f and h, the leading address and index, respectively, of the representation of some one component of $\boldsymbol{y}$. The parameters g and $\boldsymbol{b}$ are usually common to the entire set of chained representations in use. Program 3.4 illustrates the type of algorithm required to determine $\boldsymbol{\rho}(\boldsymbol{x}_k)$ from a given chained representation of $\boldsymbol{x}$.

Program 3.4. The loop (1–3) is executed $\nu(\boldsymbol{x}) \,|_0\, (k - h)$ times, with the result that at step 4 the parameter f is the leading address of $\boldsymbol{\rho}(\boldsymbol{y}_k)$. Step 4 therefore specifies d as the dimension of $\boldsymbol{\rho}(\boldsymbol{y}_k)$, that is, as the base $\boldsymbol{b}$ value of $\mathbf{\Gamma}_2{}^k(\boldsymbol{y})$. Step 5

1	$h \leftarrow \nu(\boldsymbol{x}) \,\vert_1\, (h + 1)$
2	$f \leftarrow \boldsymbol{b} \perp ((f \downarrow \boldsymbol{\alpha}^g)/\boldsymbol{\pi})$
3	$\rightarrow h : k$ ($\neq$ → 1)
4	$d \leftarrow \boldsymbol{b} \perp ((f + g) \downarrow \boldsymbol{\alpha}^g)/\boldsymbol{\pi}$
5	$\boldsymbol{z} \leftarrow (f \downarrow \boldsymbol{\alpha}^d)/\boldsymbol{\pi}$
6	$\boldsymbol{\rho}(\boldsymbol{x}_k) \leftarrow \overline{\boldsymbol{\alpha}}^{2g}/\boldsymbol{z}$ →

0-origin indexing for $\boldsymbol{\pi}$ only	
h, f	f is the leading address of the hth component of the chained representation of $\boldsymbol{x}$.
$\boldsymbol{b}$	Base used for representation of the elements of the grid matrix.
g	Dimension in $\boldsymbol{\pi}$ of elements of the grid matrix.
d	Dimension in $\boldsymbol{\pi}$ of kth component of the chained representation of $\boldsymbol{x}$.
$\boldsymbol{z}$	kth component of the chained representation of $\boldsymbol{x}$.

Legend

Program 3.4 Determination of $\boldsymbol{\rho}(\boldsymbol{x}_k)$ from a chained representation of $\boldsymbol{x}$

then specifies $\boldsymbol{z}$ as $\boldsymbol{\rho}(\boldsymbol{y}_k)$. Step 6 deletes those components of $\boldsymbol{z}$ which represent the elements of the grid matrix, leaving $\boldsymbol{\rho}(\boldsymbol{x}_k)$.

The parameters f and h are themselves respecified in the execution of the algorithm so that h becomes k and f becomes, appropriately, the leading address of $\boldsymbol{\rho}(\boldsymbol{y}_k)$. A subsequent execution then begins from this new initial condition.

The chained representation used thus far is cyclic and contains no internal identification of the first or the last components. Such an identification can be incorporated by adding a null component between the last and first components of $\boldsymbol{x}$. Alternatively the identification may be achieved without augmenting the dimension but by sacrificing the end-around chaining, i.e., by replacing the last component of $\uparrow\boldsymbol{\Gamma}_1(\boldsymbol{y})$ by a null element. Moreover, a chained representation may be entered (i.e., the scan may be begun) at any one of several points, provided only that the index h and corresponding leading address f are known for each of the points.

The number of components of a chained representation scanned (steps 1–3 of Program 3.4) in selecting the kth component of $\boldsymbol{x}$ is given by $\nu(\boldsymbol{x}) \,\vert_0\, (k - h)$, where h is the index of the component last selected. The selection operation is therefore most efficient when the components are selected in ascending order on the index. The chaining is effective in the forward direction only, and the component $(h - 1)$ would be obtained only by a complete cyclic forward scan of $\nu(\boldsymbol{x}) - 1$ components. The representation is therefore called a *forward chain.* A *backward chain* can be formed by incorporating the vector $\downarrow\boldsymbol{\Gamma}_1(\boldsymbol{y})$ instead of $\uparrow\boldsymbol{\Gamma}_1(\boldsymbol{y})$, and a *double chain* results from incorporating both.

A vector $\boldsymbol{x}$ which is respecified only by either deleting the final component or by adding a new final component (i.e., by operations of the form $\boldsymbol{x} \leftarrow \bar{\boldsymbol{\omega}}^1/\boldsymbol{x}$, or $\boldsymbol{x} \leftarrow \boldsymbol{x} \oplus (z)$) behaves as a *stack* (cf. Exercise 2.6). A backward-chained representation is clearly convenient for such a stack.

A simple example of the use of a chained stack occurs in representing the available (i.e., unused) segments of the physical vector $\boldsymbol{\pi}$. This will be illustrated by a program for the vector compression

$$\boldsymbol{x} \leftarrow \boldsymbol{v}/\boldsymbol{x}$$

executed on a forward-chained representation of $\boldsymbol{x}$. The unused segments representing the components of $\bar{\boldsymbol{v}}/\boldsymbol{x}$ are returned to a backward-chained stack or *pool* of available components. A linear representation can usually be used for logical control vectors such as $\boldsymbol{v}$; in any case the problems involved in their representation are relatively trivial and will be subordinated by expressing each operation directly in terms of the logical vectors and not in terms of the physical components representing them.

Program 3.5. In the major loop (6–23), k determines the index of the current component $\boldsymbol{v}_k$, and i and j determine the leading addresses of $\boldsymbol{\rho}(\boldsymbol{x}_k)$ and $\boldsymbol{\rho}(\boldsymbol{x}_{k+1})$, respectively. These three parameters are cycled through successive values by steps 7, 8, and 12 and are initialized by steps 2, 5, and 12. If $\boldsymbol{v}_k = 0$, the infix $\boldsymbol{\rho}(\boldsymbol{x}_k)$ is returned to the pool by steps 21, 22, 23, and 6 so as to construct a backward chain.

The parameter x specifies the leading address of $\boldsymbol{\rho}(\boldsymbol{x}_1)$ unless $\nu(\boldsymbol{x}) = 0$, in which case x is null. Step 1 terminates the process if $\nu(\boldsymbol{x}) = 0$, and otherwise step 4 respecifies x as the null element. If $\boldsymbol{v} = 0$, this null value of x remains; if not, the first nonzero component of $\boldsymbol{v}$ causes a branch to step 14. Since $x = \circ$, step 15 is executed to respecify x as the leading address of $\boldsymbol{\rho}((\boldsymbol{v}/\boldsymbol{x})_1)$. Step 16 then specifies h, the leading address of the last completed component of $\boldsymbol{v}/\boldsymbol{x}$. Step 15 is never again executed.

Components of $\boldsymbol{v}/\boldsymbol{x}$ other than the first must each be chained (in a forward chain) to the preceding one. Hence the leading address i of a newly added component must be inserted in the last preceding component (whose leading address is h). This is normally done by steps 18, 19, and 6; step 20 respecifies h. If, however, the component $\boldsymbol{x}_{k-1}$ were also included, it would appear as the last completed component of $\boldsymbol{v}/\boldsymbol{x}$ and would already be chained to the new component $\boldsymbol{x}_k$. This situation is recognized by step 17 and occasions a branch to step 16. Step 16 then respecifies h and repeats the loop without executing steps 18, 19, and 6.

The process terminates when the cycle through the chained representation of $\boldsymbol{x}$ is completed, that is, when i returns to the original value of x, preserved as t by step 3. Step 10 is then executed, terminating the process directly if $\nu(\boldsymbol{v}/\boldsymbol{x}) = 0$.

Otherwise, step 11 is executed to close the chain of $\boldsymbol{v}/\boldsymbol{x}$, that is, to insert x, the leading address of $\rho((\boldsymbol{v}/\boldsymbol{x})_1)$, in the representation of the last component of $\boldsymbol{v}/\boldsymbol{x}$.

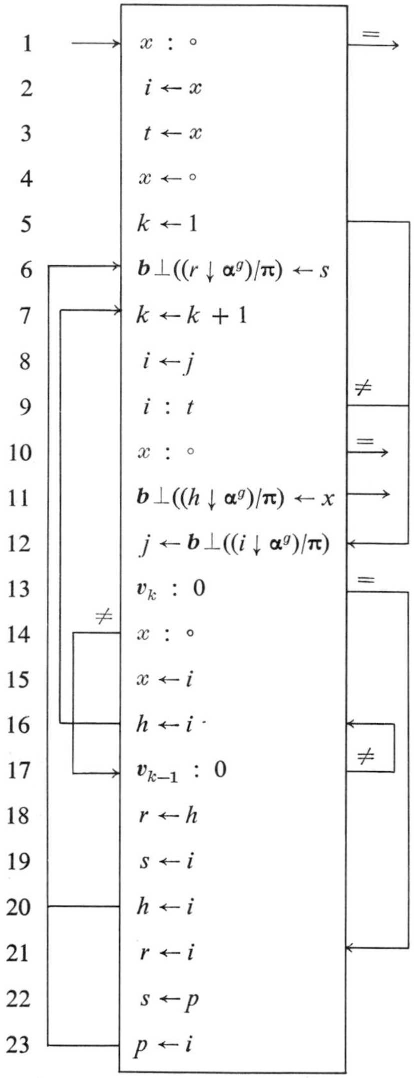

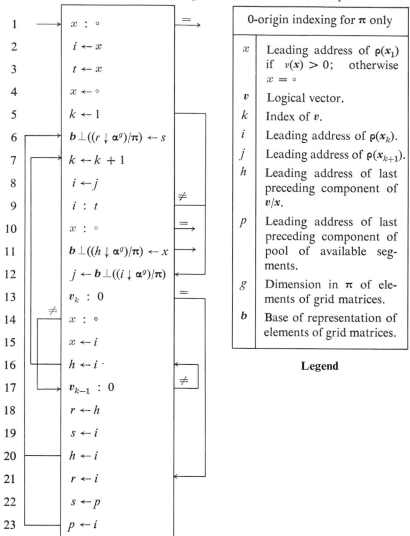

0-origin indexing for π only	
x	Leading address of $\rho(\boldsymbol{x}_1)$ if $\nu(\boldsymbol{x}) > 0$; otherwise $x = \circ$
$\boldsymbol{v}$	Logical vector.
k	Index of $\boldsymbol{v}$.
i	Leading address of $\rho(\boldsymbol{x}_k)$.
j	Leading address of $\rho(\boldsymbol{x}_{k+1})$.
h	Leading address of last preceding component of $\boldsymbol{v}/\boldsymbol{x}$.
p	Leading address of last preceding component of pool of available segments.
g	Dimension in π of elements of grid matrices.
$\boldsymbol{b}$	Base of representation of elements of grid matrices.

Legend

Program 3.5 Program for $\boldsymbol{x} \leftarrow \boldsymbol{v}/\boldsymbol{x}$ on a forward chained representation of $\boldsymbol{x}$ and a backward chained stack of available segments

A chained representation can be generalized to allow the direct representation of more complex constructs, such as trees, by incorporating the address of each of the successor components associated with a given component. This notion is formalized in the chain list matrix of Sec. 3.4. The same scheme can also be employed to produce an efficient combined representation of two or more vectors which share certain common components. If, for example, $\boldsymbol{x}_j = \boldsymbol{z}_k$, and chained representations are used for both $\boldsymbol{x}$ and $\boldsymbol{z}$, then $\boldsymbol{x}$ may be represented in standard form except that component $\boldsymbol{x}_j$ incorporates a secondary address, which is the leading address of $\boldsymbol{z}_{k+1}$. Moreover $\boldsymbol{z}$ has a standard representation except that $\boldsymbol{z}_{k-1}$ is chained to $\boldsymbol{x}_j$, with an indicator to show that the secondary address of the succeeding component is to be used. Deletion of any vector component in such a shared system must occasion only the corresponding change in the address chain of the vector, the actual representation of the component being deleted only when no associated address remains.

Partitions

If the set $\boldsymbol{a}$ is the range of the components of the physical vector $\boldsymbol{\pi}$, and if some element, say $\boldsymbol{a}_1$, is reserved as a *partition symbol* and is excluded from use in the normal representation of quantities, it can be inserted to demark the end (or beginning) of an infix of $\boldsymbol{\pi}$. If the vector $\boldsymbol{y}$ is represented by a single infix of $\boldsymbol{\pi}$ such that the beginning of component $\boldsymbol{y}_{j+1}$ follows immediately after the terminal partition of $\boldsymbol{y}_j$, then the structure of $\boldsymbol{y}$ is completely represented by the partitions, and $\boldsymbol{y}$ is called a *partitioned representation*. A partitioned representation can be used for more complex operands, such as matrices, if a set of two or more distinct partition symbols are provided, one for each level of structure. The distinct partition symbols can, of course, be represented by multiple occurrences of a single symbol $\boldsymbol{a}_1$ rather than by distinct members of $\boldsymbol{a}$.

A partitioned representation is similar to a double-chained representation without end-around chaining in the following particular: beginning from component $\boldsymbol{y}_i$, the component $\boldsymbol{y}_j$ can be reached only by scanning all intervening components between i and j in increasing or decreasing order according as $i < j$ or $i > j$. The file notation introduced in Sec. 1.22 clearly provides the operations appropriate to a partitioned representation of a vector, with conventions which suppress all inessential references to the partitions themselves.

The use of a partition to demark the end of an infix is particularly convenient when the infix must be processed component by component for other reasons, as in the use of magnetic tape or other serial storage. The partition also appears to be more economical than the grid matrix, which it replaces. This apparent economy is, however, somewhat illusory, since the reservation of a special partition symbol reduces the information content of each nonpartition component by the factor $\log_2 (\nu(\boldsymbol{a}) - 1) \div \log_2 \nu(\boldsymbol{a})$, where $\boldsymbol{a}$ is the range of the components of $\boldsymbol{\pi}$.

Partitions can be employed in chained representations. For example, the dimension in $\boldsymbol{\pi}$ of each component of a chained representation $\boldsymbol{y}$ can be specified implicitly by terminal partitions instead of explicitly by the vector $\boldsymbol{\Gamma}_2(\boldsymbol{y})$ of the grid matrix. Thus if the elements of $\boldsymbol{\Gamma}_1(\boldsymbol{y})$ are of dimension g in $\boldsymbol{\pi}$, then $\boldsymbol{\omega}^1/\boldsymbol{\rho}(\boldsymbol{y}_j) = \boldsymbol{a}_1$, and $(\overline{\boldsymbol{\alpha}}^g \wedge \overline{\boldsymbol{\omega}}^1)/\boldsymbol{\rho}(\boldsymbol{y}_j) = \boldsymbol{\rho}(\boldsymbol{x}_j)$, where $\boldsymbol{x}$ is the vector represented by $\boldsymbol{y}$. Program 3.6 shows the determination of $\boldsymbol{\rho}(\boldsymbol{x}_k)$ from a chained representation $\boldsymbol{y}$ with terminal partitions $\boldsymbol{a}_1$.

Step	Statement	Branch
1	$h \leftarrow \nu(\boldsymbol{x}) \,|_1\, (h + 1)$	
2	$f \leftarrow \boldsymbol{b} \perp ((f \downarrow \boldsymbol{\alpha}^g)/\boldsymbol{\pi})$	
3	$h : k$	$\neq$ → 1
4a	$j \leftarrow f + g$	
4b	$\boldsymbol{\pi}_j : \boldsymbol{a}_1$	$=$ → 4d
4c	$j \leftarrow j + 1$	→ 4b
4d	$d \leftarrow j - f$	
5	$\boldsymbol{z} \leftarrow (f \downarrow \boldsymbol{\alpha}^d)/\boldsymbol{\pi}$	
6	$\boldsymbol{\rho}(\boldsymbol{x}_k) \leftarrow \overline{\boldsymbol{\alpha}}^g/\boldsymbol{z}$	

0-origin indexing for $\boldsymbol{\pi}$ only	
h, f	f is the leading address of the hth component of the chained representation of $\boldsymbol{x}$.
$\boldsymbol{b}$	Base used for representation of the elements of the grid matrix.
g	Dimension in $\boldsymbol{\pi}$ of the elements of the grid matrix.
$\boldsymbol{a}_1$	Partition symbol.
$\boldsymbol{z}$	kth component of the chained representation of $\boldsymbol{x}$ exclusive of the terminal partition symbol.
d	Dimension of $\boldsymbol{z}$ in $\boldsymbol{\pi}$.

Legend

Program 3.6 Determination of $\boldsymbol{\rho}(\boldsymbol{x}_k)$ from a chained representation of $\boldsymbol{x}$ with terminal partitions $\boldsymbol{a}_1$

Program 3.6. The program is similar to Program 3.4 and the step numbering indicates the correspondences. The dimension d is so determined (steps 4a–d) as to exclude the terminal partition itself from the quantity $\boldsymbol{z}$ specified by step 5. Since only the first column of the grid matrix is incorporated in the partitioned representation, step 6 excises a prefix of dimension g rather than $2g$ as in Program 3.4.

Pools

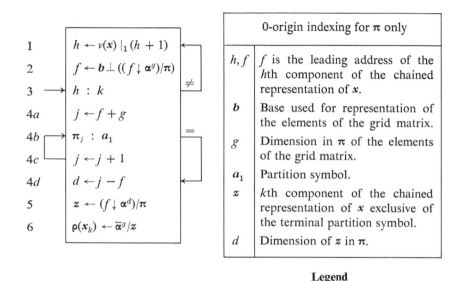

Components of the physical vector $\boldsymbol{\pi}$ in use for the representation of one quantity must not be allocated to the representation of some other quantity. The *construction* of a chained representation therefore poses one problem not encountered in its *use*, namely, the specification and observation of restrictions on the availability of components of $\boldsymbol{\pi}$. The restrictions can conveniently be specified as a *pool*, consisting of the available components of π. Each allocation made must then be reflected in a corresponding change in the pool. Moreover, as each piece of data is deleted, the components allocated to it are returned to the pool.

If, as in Program 3.5, a pool is treated as a stack, then the component next taken from the pool is the component last added to it. The queue of components in the pool thus obeys a so-called *last in first out*, or LIFO discipline. The dimension in π of the last component of a pool will not, in general, agree with the dimension required for the next quantity it is called on to represent. If it exceeds the requirements, the extra segment may be left in the pool, and the pool therefore tends to accrue more and more components of smaller and smaller dimension. Hence it may be wise, or even essential, to revise the pool occasionally so as to coalesce the segments into the smallest possible number of infixes. This process can even be extended to allow substitutions in other vectors in order to return to the pool short segments which may unite existing segments of the pool. This, however, will require a systematic scan of the chained vectors.

If the dimension of the last component (or perhaps of all components) of the pool falls short of the requirements for representing a new quantity, segments of the pool can be chained together. This requires the use of a special partition symbol or other indication to distinguish two types of links, one which marks the end of a given representation and one which does not. More generally, it may be convenient to use multilevel partition symbols to distinguish several levels of links, as was suggested for the representation of a matrix.

Queue disciplines other than LIFO may be used. Three other types of primary interest in allocation queues are the FIFO (first in first out), the *dimension-ordered*, and the *address-ordered* disciplines. FIFO uses a forward chain and may be preferred over LIFO because it uses the entire original pool before using any returned (and usually shorter) segments.

The components of a dimension-ordered pool are maintained in ascending (or descending) order on their dimensions in π. This arrangement is convenient in selecting a pool element according to the dimension required. The components of an address-ordered pool are arranged in ascending order on their leading addresses. This arrangement facilitates the fusion of components which together form an infix of π.

If each of the available components of π is set to a special value which is used for no other purpose, then the available components can be determined by a scan of π. Such a pool has no structure imposed by chaining and will be called a *marked pool.*

A marked pool requires little maintenance, since components returned to it are simply marked, but selection from it requires a scan of π and is therefore relatively slow. The use of marked and chained pools may also be combined—all returned components go to a marked pool which is left undisturbed until the chained pool is exhausted, at which time the entire marked pool is organized into a chained pool.

Summary

Since any structured operand can first be reduced to an equivalent vector, the problems of representation can be discussed in terms of vectors alone. The characteristics of the linear, chained, and partitioned representations of a vector may be summarized as follows. A linear representation permits the address of any component to be computed directly as a linear function of its indices and hence requires no scanning of the vector. However, the strict limitations which it imposes on allocation may engender: (1) conflicts with allocations for other operands, (2) waste of storage due to the imposition of a common dimension in $\boldsymbol{\pi}$ for all components, or (3) uneconomical execution due to the extensive reallocations occasioned by the insertion or deletion of other than terminal components.

The concept of the grid matrix is helpful even when the corresponding allocation is implicit in the program. The explicit use of a grid matrix which is itself in a linear representation removes the restrictions on the allocation of the vector itself while retaining the advantage of direct address computation. The address computation differs from the linear case only in the addition of a single reference to the grid matrix and hence requires no scanning. The difficulties enumerated for the direct linear representation are not eliminated but merely shifted to the linearly represented grid matrix itself, where they may, however, prove much less serious.

A chained representation allows virtually arbitrary allocation, relatively simple operations for the insertion and deletion of components, the direct representation of more complex structures such as trees, and economical joint representations of vectors which have one or more components in common. However, a chained representation requires extra storage for the grid matrix which it incorporates and occasions additional operations for scanning when the components are selected in other than serial order. The required scanning can be reduced by the retention of auxiliary information which allows the chained representation to be entered at several points.

A partitioned representation requires the allocation of a single infix of $\boldsymbol{\pi}$, and selection requires a fine scan, i.e., a component-by-component scan of $\boldsymbol{\pi}$ to detect partition symbols. Partitioning removes the need to incorporate the grid matrix explicitly and does not impose a common dimension in $\boldsymbol{\pi}$ for all components.

Mixed systems employing combinations of linear, chained, and partitioned representations are frequently advantageous. *Block chaining*, for example, involves the chaining of blocks, each consisting of an infix of $\boldsymbol{\pi}$ and each serving as a linear representation of some infix of the represented vector. Alternatively, each chained block may be a partitioned representation of some infix.

3.3 REPRESENTATION OF MATRICES

Structured operands other than vectors may be represented by first reducing them to equivalent vectors which can, by employing the techniques of the preceding section, be represented, in turn, in the physical vector $\boldsymbol{\pi}$. In the case of a matrix $\boldsymbol{A}$, two alternative reductions are of interest, the row list $\boldsymbol{r} = \mathsf{E}/\boldsymbol{A} = \boldsymbol{A}^1 \oplus \boldsymbol{A}^2 \oplus \cdots \oplus \boldsymbol{A}^\mu$ and the column list $\boldsymbol{c} = \mathsf{E}//\boldsymbol{A}$. If r_h, A_j^i, and c_k are corresponding elements of the three alternative representations, then in a 0-origin system:

$$h = \nu i + j,$$
$$k = i + \mu j.$$

Consequently,

$$i = \lfloor h \div \nu \rfloor = \mu \,|_0\, k,$$

and

$$j = \nu \,|_0\, h = \lfloor k \div \mu \rfloor.$$

The dependence of h on k can be obtained directly by substituting the foregoing expressions in the identity

$$h = \nu \times \lfloor h \div \nu \rfloor + \nu \,|_0\, h$$

to yield

$$h = \nu \times (\mu \,|_0\, k) + \lfloor k \div \mu \rfloor.$$

Similarly,

$$k = \mu \times (\nu \,|_0\, h) + \lfloor h \div \nu \rfloor.$$

The permutation $\boldsymbol{h}$ which carries the row list $\boldsymbol{r}$ into the column list $\boldsymbol{c}$ (that is, $\boldsymbol{c} = \boldsymbol{h} \int_0 \boldsymbol{r}$) can be obtained directly from the foregoing expression for h as follows:

$$\boldsymbol{h} = \nu \times (\mu\boldsymbol{\epsilon} \,|_0\, \boldsymbol{\iota}^0) + \lfloor \boldsymbol{\iota}^0 \div \mu\boldsymbol{\epsilon} \rfloor.$$

The expression for the kth component of $\boldsymbol{h}$ is identical with the expression for h above. Hence, if $\boldsymbol{c} = \boldsymbol{h} \int_0 \boldsymbol{r}$, then $c_k = r_{h_k} = r_h$ as required.

If the row list (or column list) is itself represented linearly, then the address of any component A_j^i is obtained as a linear function of the indices i and j. If either a file or a chained representation is to be used for the list vector, then the components are processed most efficiently in serial order, and the use of column list or row list is dictated by the particular processes to be effected.

If a large proportion of the elements of a matrix are null elements, it is called a *sparse* matrix. Sparse matrices occur frequently in numerical work (where zero serves as the null element), particularly in the treatment of partial difference equations. A sparse matrix $\boldsymbol{A}$ can be represented compactly by the row list $\boldsymbol{r} = \boldsymbol{U}/\boldsymbol{A}$, and the logical matrix $\boldsymbol{U}$, where $\boldsymbol{U} = (\boldsymbol{A} \neq 0)$. The matrix $\boldsymbol{A}$ may then be obtained by expansion: $\boldsymbol{A} = \boldsymbol{U}\backslash\boldsymbol{r}$.

Alternatively, the column list $\boldsymbol{c} = (\boldsymbol{A} \neq 0)//\boldsymbol{A}$ may be used. The transformation between the column list $\boldsymbol{c}$ and row list $\boldsymbol{r}$ must, in general, be performed as a sequential operation on the elements of $\boldsymbol{U}$. Since it is frequently necessary to scan a given matrix in both row and column order (e.g., as either pre- or post-multiplier in a matrix multiplication), neither the row list nor the column list alone is satisfactory. A chaining system can, however, be devised to provide both row and column scanning.

Let $\boldsymbol{L}$ be a matrix such that $\boldsymbol{L}_1$ is a list of the nonzero elements of a matrix $\boldsymbol{A}$ in arbitrary order, $\boldsymbol{L}_2{}^i$ is the column index in $\boldsymbol{A}$ of element $\boldsymbol{L}_1{}^i$, and $\boldsymbol{L}_3{}^i$ is the row index in $\boldsymbol{L}$ of the next nonzero element following $\boldsymbol{L}_1{}^i$ in its row of $\boldsymbol{A}$. If $\boldsymbol{L}_1{}^i$ is the last nonzero element in its row, $\boldsymbol{L}_3{}^i = \circ$. Let $\boldsymbol{f}_j$ be the row index in $\boldsymbol{L}$ of the first nonzero element of row $\boldsymbol{A}^j$, and let $\boldsymbol{f}_j = \circ$ if $\boldsymbol{A}^j = 0$. The following example shows corresponding values of $\boldsymbol{A}$, $\boldsymbol{L}$, and $\boldsymbol{f}$:

$$\boldsymbol{A} = \begin{pmatrix} 6 & 0 & 0 & 9 \\ 0 & 3 & 0 & 0 \\ 0 & 0 & 0 & 0 \\ 7 & 8 & 0 & 4 \\ 0 & 0 & 5 & 0 \end{pmatrix} \quad \boldsymbol{L} = \begin{pmatrix} 8 & 2 & 7 \\ 5 & 3 & \circ \\ 6 & 1 & 5 \\ 3 & 2 & \circ \\ 9 & 4 & \circ \\ 7 & 1 & 1 \\ 4 & 4 & \circ \end{pmatrix} \quad \boldsymbol{f} = \begin{pmatrix} 3 \\ 4 \\ \circ \\ 6 \\ 2 \end{pmatrix}.$$

The matrix $\boldsymbol{L}$ will be called a *row-chained* representation of $\boldsymbol{A}$ and may be used, together with the vector $\boldsymbol{f}$, for the efficient scanning of any row $\boldsymbol{A}^i$ as illustrated by Program 3.7. The vector $\boldsymbol{L}_3$ can be modified so as to give the address in $\boldsymbol{\pi}$ directly rather than the row index in $\boldsymbol{L}$ of the next element in the row, and Program 3.7 can then be easily re-expressed in terms of the physical vector $\boldsymbol{\pi}$.

Program 3.7. Step 2 yields the index in $\boldsymbol{L}$ of the first element of the ith row of $\boldsymbol{A}$. Step 4 determines its column index j, and step 6 determines the index of the succeeding component. The process terminates at step 3 when the scan of the row is completed.

If $\boldsymbol{L}_1$ is chosen as a row list, the vector $\boldsymbol{L}_3$ reduces to the form $\boldsymbol{L}_3{}^k = k + 1$ or $\boldsymbol{L}_3{}^k = \circ$. Its function can then be served instead by incrementation of

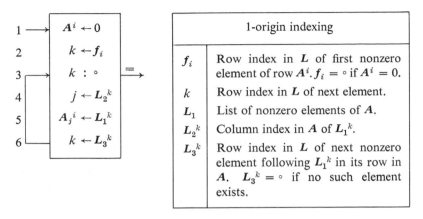

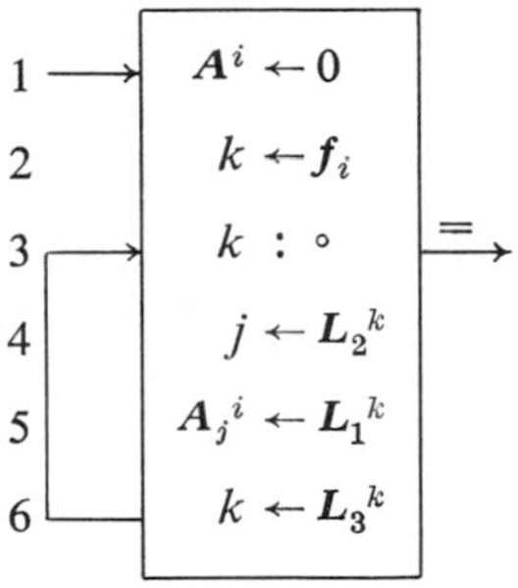

1-origin indexing	
f_i	Row index in L of first nonzero element of row A^i. $f_i = \circ$ if $A^i = 0$.
k	Row index in L of next element.
L_1	List of nonzero elements of A.
L_2^k	Column index in A of L_1^k.
L_3^k	Row index in L of next nonzero element following L_1^k in its row in A. $L_3^k = \circ$ if no such element exists.

Legend

Program 3.7 Determination of the row vector A^i from a row-chained representation of A

the index k and by the use of the logical vector $u = (L_3 = \circ\epsilon)$ for determining the end of each row.

The construction of a column-chained representation is analogous to that of a row-chained representation, and the two representations can be combined in a single matrix L which gives both row and column chaining employing but a single representation (that is, L_1) of the nonzero elements of A.

3.4 REPRESENTATION OF TREES*

A tree **T** may be represented by a matrix and hence, in turn, by a vector in a number of useful ways as follows:

1. by a full right list matrix]**T** or by any column permutation thereof (Sec. 1.23),
2. by a full left list matrix [**T** or by any column permutation thereof,
3. by a right list matrix $\boldsymbol{\alpha}^2$/]**T**,
4. by a left list matrix $\boldsymbol{\alpha}^2$/[**T**,
5. by various chain list matrices.

The full left and right lists seldom prove more convenient than the more concise left and right lists. Except for the special case of a homogeneous

* Johnson (1962) provides a comprehensive treatment of the representations of trees and discusses the suitability of each representation for a variety of search procedures.

tree, both the right list and the left list are awkward to use for path tracing. This function is better served by the chain list matrix, to be defined as a formalization of the chaining scheme suggested in Sec. 3.2.

Simplified list matrices

In certain important special cases, the various list representations of trees may be simplified. If the degree of each node is a known function δ of the value of the node, then for any list matrix $\boldsymbol{M}$, $\boldsymbol{M}_1{}^i = \delta(\boldsymbol{M}_2{}^i)$, and the degree vector $\boldsymbol{M}_1$ may be eliminated without loss. The node vector alone then represents the tree and may be referred to as a *right* or *left list vector* as the case may be.

For example, in the tree of Fig. 3.8 (which represents the compound logical statement $\bar{x} \wedge (y \vee z)$), a fixed degree is associated with each of the logical operators *and*, *or*, and *not* (namely, 2, 2, and 1), and the degree zero is associated with each of the variables. The statement can therefore be represented unambiguously by the left list vector

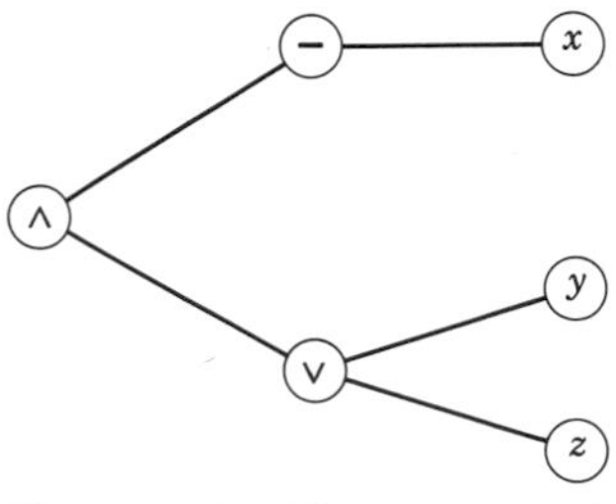

Figure 3.8 The compound logical statement $\bar{x} \wedge (y \vee z)$

$$\boldsymbol{v} = (\wedge, \overline{\ }, x, \vee, y, z).$$

This is the so-called *Lukasiewicz*, *Polish*, or *parenthesis-free* form of the compound statement [Lukasiewicz (1951) and Burks et al. (1954)]. Frequently, the only significant nodes of a tree **T** are its leaves (e.g., in Example 3.2 and in a certain key transformation of Fig. 4.7) and all other nodes may be considered as nulls. Hence if $\boldsymbol{M}$ is any list matrix, the significant portions of $\boldsymbol{M}_1$ and $\boldsymbol{M}_2$ are $(\boldsymbol{M}_1 \neq 0)/\boldsymbol{M}_1$ and $(\boldsymbol{M}_1 = 0)/\boldsymbol{M}_2$, respectively. These significant portions may then be coalesced to form the single vector

$$\boldsymbol{v} = /\boldsymbol{M}_1, (\boldsymbol{M}_1 = 0), \boldsymbol{M}_2/,$$

which, together with the logical vector $(\boldsymbol{M}_1 = 0)$, forms a *leaf list matrix* that describes the tree. Moreover, if the values of the leaves are distinguishable from the components of the degree vector, the logical vector $(\boldsymbol{M}_1 = 0)$ may also be dropped.

The use of left lists

The use of the right list matrix is illustrated by the repeated selection sort treated in Sec. 6.4. The use of left lists will be illustrated here by two examples, each of interest in its own right: the partitioning of the left list of an n-tuply rooted tree to yield the left lists of the component singular

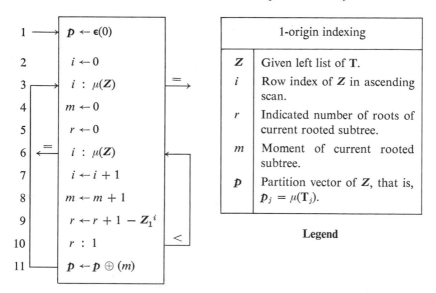

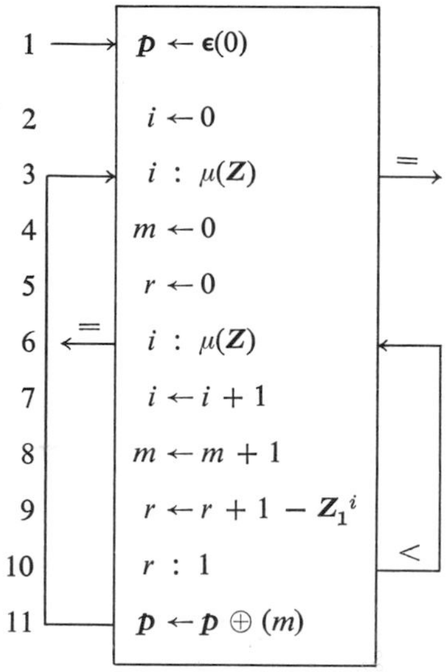

1-origin indexing	
Z	Given left list of **T**.
i	Row index of Z in ascending scan.
r	Indicated number of roots of current rooted subtree.
m	Moment of current rooted subtree.
p	Partition vector of Z, that is, $p_j = \mu(\mathbf{T}_j)$.

Legend

Program 3.9 Partitioning of the left list of an n-tuply rooted tree

subtrees and the construction of a Huffman minimum-redundancy prefix code.

Example 3.1. Partitioning of an *n*-tuply rooted tree. Program 3.9 shows a scheme for partitioning a left list Z of a tree $\mathbf{T}$ into component subtrees, i.e., for determining the vector p such that p_j is the moment of the singular subtree $\mathbf{T}_j$. Thus $\nu(p) = \mu_1(\mathbf{T})$, $p_j = \mu(\mathbf{T}_j)$, and the infix $((p \overset{+}{\underset{\times}{}} \alpha^{j-1}) \downarrow \alpha^{p_j})//Z$ is the left list of $\mathbf{T}_j$.

The loop 6–10 scans successive components of the degree vector Z_1 (in ascending order) and computes r, the indicated number of roots. The value of r increases by, at most, one per iteration, and when r becomes unity, the end of a singly rooted tree has been reached. Its moment m is then appended (step 11) as a new final component of the partition vector p, the parameters m and r are reset, and the scan of the next rooted tree is begun. Normal termination occurs at step 3; termination at step 6 indicates ill formation of Z.

Example 3.2. Huffman minimum redundancy prefix code. If b is any set such that $\nu(b) > 1$, then any other finite set a can be encoded in b, that is, represented by b. (The sets a and b may be called the "alphabet" and "basic alphabet," respectively.) If $\nu(a) \leq \nu(b)$, the encoding may be described by a mapping vector k such that $\rho(a_i) = b_{k_i}$. If $\nu(a) > \nu(b)$, then each a_i must be represented by a vector $x^i \subseteq b$. For example, if $a = \iota^0(10)$ and $b = \iota^0(2)$, then the decimal digits a may be encoded in the so-called 8421 system:

$$(2\,\epsilon\,(4)) \perp x^i = a_i.$$

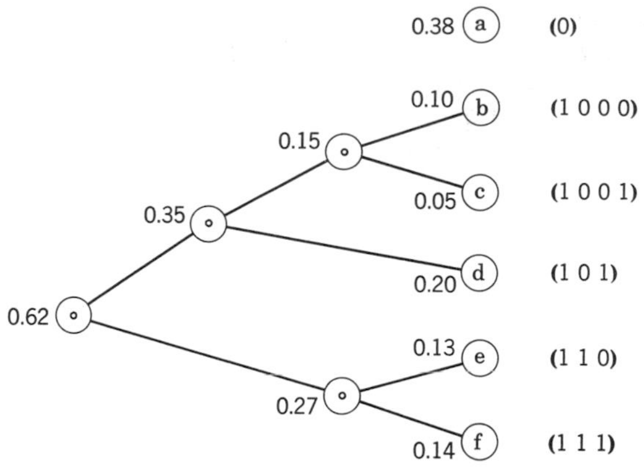

Figure 3.10 Construction of a Huffman prefix code

In so-called fixed length coding the vectors $\boldsymbol{x}^i$ have a common dimension d, and the decoding of a message $\boldsymbol{m}$ (consisting of the catenation of vectors $\boldsymbol{x}^i$) involves the selection of successive infixes of dimension d. If the probability distribution of the characters $\boldsymbol{a}_1$ occurring in messages is not uniform, more compact encoding may be achieved by using variable length codes and assigning the shorter codes to the more frequent characters. Decoding of a message in variable length coding can be performed only if the boundaries between the successive $\boldsymbol{x}_1$ are indicated in some way.

The boundaries between characters in a message in variable length code may be demarked by special partition symbols (which is inefficient) or by using a *prefix* code in which no legitimate *code point* $\boldsymbol{x}^i$ is the prefix of any other legitimate code point, including itself. The index vectors of the leaves of any tree possess this property; conversely, any set of prefix codes can be arrayed as the leaves of some tree. Hence if each character of the set to be encoded is assigned as the leaf of a common tree, and if each character is encoded by the associated index vector, a so-called prefix code is attained. Figure 3.10 furnishes an example of a binary code (i.e., the branching ratios do not exceed two) constructed in this manner. 0-origin indexing is used. The discussion will be limited to binary trees.

If $\boldsymbol{f}_i$ is the frequency of the ith character and $\boldsymbol{l}_i$ is the length of the assigned code (i.e., the length of path to the root), then the most efficient code is attained by minimizing the scalar product $\boldsymbol{f} \overset{+}{\underset{\times}{}} \boldsymbol{l}$. This may be achieved by the following construction, shown to be optimal by Huffman (1952). First, the characters to be encoded are all considered as roots, and the two roots of lowest frequency are rooted to an auxiliary node (shown as a null element in Fig. 3.10), which is then assigned their combined frequency. The process is repeated until only two roots remain. The tree of Fig. 3.10 is optimal with respect to the frequencies shown to the left of the leaves. The appropriate combined frequencies are shown to the left of each of the nonleaves.

Programs 3.11 and 3.12 show the construction of the tree **T** representing a

```
1  →  T ← c
2  →  μ₁(T) : 2                                   = →
3     T ← (θ/f)∫T
4     T ← \\(○) ⊕ α²//T, ᾱ¹, ᾱ²//T\\
5     f ← (θ/f)∫f
6     f ← \ + /α²/f, ᾱ¹, ᾱ²/f\
```

Program 3.11 Construction of the binary Huffman code **T** for characters ***c*** with frequency ***f***

Huffman code for a set of characters $\boldsymbol{c}_i$ with frequencies $\boldsymbol{f}_i$, the former in terms of the tree itself and the latter in terms of its left list.

Program 3.11. The frequency vector ***f*** is permuted (step 5) to bring it to ascending order, and the tree is subjected (step 3) to the same permutation. Step 4 replaces the first two rooted subtrees of **T** by the single subtree obtained by rooting them in a null, and step 6 makes the corresponding alterations in the frequency vector. The tree is initialized (step 1) as a one-level tree whose roots are the given characters, and the process terminates when the number of roots of **T** has been reduced to two.

Program 3.12. The tree **T** of Program 3.11 is represented by the left list node vector $\boldsymbol{z}$, in conjunction with the implicit degree vector $\boldsymbol{d} = 2 \times (\boldsymbol{z} = \circ\boldsymbol{\epsilon})$. The algorithm differs from Program 3.11 primarily in the reordering of the subtrees (steps 6–9). Step 7 appends to $\boldsymbol{x}$ the left list of the ith subtree (of the reordered tree) selected by the partition vector $\boldsymbol{p}$ according to the conventions of Program 3.9. Step 10 prefixes $\boldsymbol{x}$ by the new null root, and steps 11-12 redefine $\boldsymbol{p}$ appropriately.

Program 1.21 can be applied to the left list produced by Program 3.12 to determine the associated index matrix (in a 0-origin system), and hence the actual codes assigned.

It is not essential that the characters be assigned to leaves in precisely the order specified by Programs 3.11 and 3.12, and it is sufficient that the dimension of the leaf index increase monotonically with decreasing frequency of the character. It is therefore unnecessary to carry the characters themselves through the process; it suffices to determine the structure of the tree, sort the corresponding index matrix to right list order (which is ordered on dimension of the index vectors), and assign the characters (in decreasing order by frequency) to successive leaves. Since the structure of such a tree (whose nodes have a common irrelevant value and whose nonleaves all have a common branching ratio equal to the number of roots) is sufficiently determined by the moment vector $\mu(\mathbf{T})$, the process of Program 3.12 can be simplified.

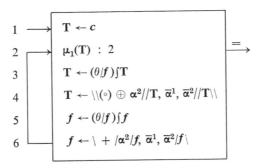

1	$\boldsymbol{z} \leftarrow \boldsymbol{c}$	
2	$\boldsymbol{p} \leftarrow \boldsymbol{\epsilon}(\nu(\boldsymbol{z}))$	
3	$\nu(\boldsymbol{f}) : 2$	$=$ → (exit)
4	$i \leftarrow 1$	
5	$\boldsymbol{x} \leftarrow \boldsymbol{\epsilon}(0)$	
6	$j \leftarrow (\theta/\boldsymbol{f})_i$	
7	$\boldsymbol{x} \leftarrow \boldsymbol{x} \oplus (((\boldsymbol{p} \overset{+}{\times} \boldsymbol{\alpha}^{j-1}) \downarrow \boldsymbol{\alpha}^{\boldsymbol{p}_j})/\boldsymbol{z})$	
8	$i \leftarrow i + 1$	
9	$i : \nu(\boldsymbol{f})$	$\leq$ → 6
10	$\boldsymbol{z} \leftarrow (\circ) \oplus \boldsymbol{x}$	
11	$\boldsymbol{p} \leftarrow (\theta/\boldsymbol{f}) \int \boldsymbol{p}$	
12	$\boldsymbol{p} \leftarrow (1 + (\boldsymbol{p} \overset{+}{\times} \boldsymbol{\alpha}^2)) \oplus \overline{\boldsymbol{\alpha}}^2/\boldsymbol{p}$	
13	$\boldsymbol{f} \leftarrow (\theta/\boldsymbol{f}) \int \boldsymbol{f}$	
14	$\boldsymbol{f} \leftarrow (+/\boldsymbol{\alpha}^2/\boldsymbol{f}) \oplus \overline{\boldsymbol{\alpha}}^2/\boldsymbol{f}$	→ 3

1-origin indexing	
$\boldsymbol{c}$	Given character set.
$\boldsymbol{z}$	Left list of Huffman tree.
$\boldsymbol{f}_i$	Frequency of ith subtree of $\boldsymbol{z}$.
$\boldsymbol{p}$	Partition vector $\boldsymbol{p}_i$ is the moment of the ith subtree of $\boldsymbol{z}$.
$\boldsymbol{x}$	Reordered left list with subtrees in ascending order on frequency.

Legend

Program 3.12 Construction of the left list $\boldsymbol{z}$ of the binary Huffman code for characters $\boldsymbol{c}$ with frequency $\boldsymbol{f}$

Chain list matrices

The full chain list matrix of a tree **T** is a matrix $\boldsymbol{P}$ of dimension $\mu(\mathbf{T}) \times (\delta(\mathbf{T}) + 2)$ defined as follows: $\boldsymbol{P}_2$ is some node vector of **T**, $\boldsymbol{P}_1$ is the associated degree vector, $\boldsymbol{P}^i_{j+2}$ is null if j exceeds the associated degree $\boldsymbol{P}_1{}^i$ and is otherwise the row index in $\boldsymbol{P}$ of the jth node emanating from node $\boldsymbol{P}_2{}^i$. Table 3.13 shows a full chain list matrix for the tree of Fig. 1.16. A full chain list matrix is called a full *right* (*left*) chain list matrix if the nodes occur in right (left) list order.

The full chain list matrix is a formalization of the scheme suggested in the discussion of chained representations (Sec. 3.2). Its convenience in forward path tracing is obvious. Since it does not identify the roots of the tree, an auxiliary vector must be provided for this purpose. However, if the ordering chosen for the nodes is that of a right list, the roots occur first in the list, their number $r = \nu(\boldsymbol{P}_1) - (+/\boldsymbol{P}_1)$ is specified by the degree vector $\boldsymbol{P}_1$, and the need for the auxiliary vector vanishes. Moreover, since a right list groups all nodes emanating from a given node, each row of $\overline{\boldsymbol{\alpha}}^2/\boldsymbol{P}$ is simply a sequence of integers followed by null elements, and the information necessary to path tracing is provided by the column $\boldsymbol{P}_3$ alone.

The *right chain list matrix* of a tree **T** is therefore defined as $\boldsymbol{\alpha}^3/\boldsymbol{P}$, where

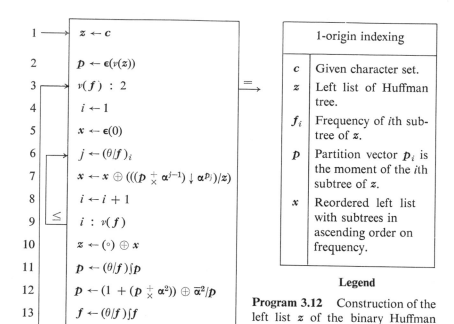

	d'	n'	Q				d''	n''	p	d'	n'	f	h	
1	1	n	18	∘	∘	∘	3	a	4	1	n	∘	18	1
2	2	g	16	26	∘	∘	2	b	7	2	g	∘	16	2
3	0	u	∘	∘	∘	∘	2	g	9	0	u	14	∘	3
4	0	t	∘	∘	∘	∘	4	c	11	0	t	19	∘	4
5	3	a	24	9	1	∘	0	z	∘	3	a	6	24	5
6	2	b	8	20	∘	∘	1	n	15	2	b	2	8	6
7	0	v	∘	∘	∘	∘	0	k	∘	0	v	∘	∘	7
8	0	k	∘	∘	∘	∘	3	h	16	0	k	20	∘	8
9	0	z	∘	∘	∘	∘	0	j	∘	0	z	1	∘	9
10	0	o	∘	∘	∘	∘	0	l	∘	0	o	17	∘	10
11	0	f	∘	∘	∘	∘	0	f	∘	0	f	15	∘	11
12	0	r	∘	∘	∘	∘	0	d	∘	0	r	21	∘	12
13	0	y	∘	∘	∘	∘	0	r	∘	0	y	∘	∘	13
14	2	s	4	19	∘	∘	0	e	∘	2	s	23	4	14
15	0	d	∘	∘	∘	∘	2	i	19	0	d	12	∘	15
16	0	j	∘	∘	∘	∘	0	o	∘	0	j	26	∘	16
17	3	m	3	14	23	∘	3	m	21	3	m	7	3	17
18	2	i	22	25	∘	∘	0	v	∘	2	i	∘	22	18
19	0	w	∘	∘	∘	∘	0	p	∘	0	w	∘	∘	19
20	3	h	10	17	7	∘	0	q	∘	3	h	∘	10	20
21	0	e	∘	∘	∘	∘	0	u	∘	0	e	∘	∘	21
22	0	p	∘	∘	∘	∘	2	s	24	0	p	25	∘	22
23	1	x	13	∘	∘	∘	1	x	26	1	x	∘	13	23
24	4	c	11	15	12	21	0	t	∘	4	c	9	11	24
25	0	q	∘	∘	∘	∘	0	w	∘	0	q	∘	∘	25
26	0	l	∘	∘	∘	∘	0	y	∘	0	l	∘	∘	26

A full chain list matrix (*a*) — The right chain list matrix (*b*) — Filial-heir chain list (*c*)

Table 3.13 Chain lists of the tree of Fig. 1.16

P is the full right chain list matrix of **T**. It is illustrated by Table 3.13*b* Program 3.14 shows its use in path tracing. Although the degree vector $\boldsymbol{P}_1$ is redundant (that is, $\boldsymbol{P}_1$ and $\boldsymbol{P}_3$ can be determined one from the other), it provides a direct check (step 6) on the legitimacy of the index vector ***r*** which would be difficult to obtain from $\boldsymbol{P}_3$ alone.

For a search of the type described by Program 3.14, it is necessary to scan down a level until agreement is reached and then across to the next level. For this type of scan, the *filial-heir chain list* is compact and convenient.

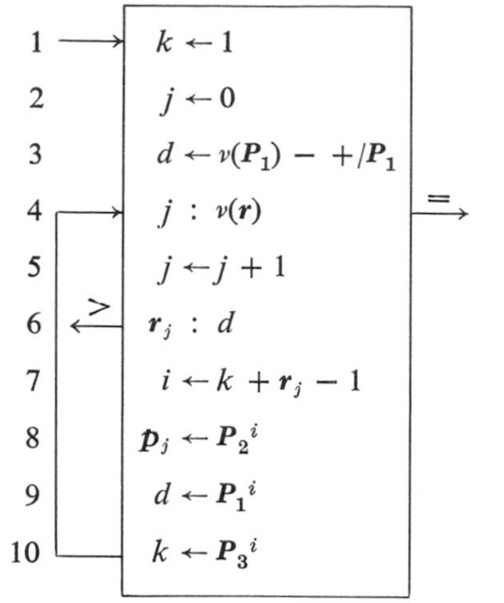
1 $k \leftarrow 1$
2 $j \leftarrow 0$
3 $d \leftarrow \nu(\boldsymbol{P}_1) - +/\boldsymbol{P}_1$
4 $j : \nu(\boldsymbol{r})$
=
5 $j \leftarrow j + 1$
6 $\boldsymbol{r}_j : d$
>
7 $i \leftarrow k + \boldsymbol{r}_j - 1$
8 $\boldsymbol{p}_j \leftarrow \boldsymbol{P}_2{}^i$
9 $d \leftarrow \boldsymbol{P}_1{}^i$
10 $k \leftarrow \boldsymbol{P}_3{}^i$

1-origin indexing	
$\boldsymbol{r}$	Given index vector.
$\boldsymbol{P}$	Right chain list matrix of **T**.
$\boldsymbol{P}_1$	Degree vector of **T**.
$\boldsymbol{P}_2$	Node vector of **T**.
$\boldsymbol{P}_3$	Chaining vector of **T**.
$\boldsymbol{p}$	Path vector $\mathbf{T}^{\boldsymbol{r}}$.
d	Degree of current node.
k	Base address of the infix containing the current node.
i	Index of succeeding node in the path $\mathbf{T}^{\boldsymbol{r}}$.
j	Current index of index vector $\boldsymbol{r}$.

Legend

Program 3.14 Determination of the path $\boldsymbol{p} = \boldsymbol{T}^{\boldsymbol{r}}$ from the right chain list matrix $\boldsymbol{P}$

The set of $(j + 1)$th level nodes of the subtree $\mathbf{T}_{\boldsymbol{i}}$ are collectively called the *jth filial vector* of node $\boldsymbol{i}$, and the first member of the first filial vector of node i is called the *heir* of node $\boldsymbol{i}$. (For brevity, the first filial vector of a node will also be called its filial vector.) If each node is chained only to its successor in the filial vector containing it and to its heir, the resulting representation is called a *filial-heir chain list*. Formally, the filial-heir representation of a tree **T** is a matrix $\boldsymbol{F}$ of dimension $\mu(\mathbf{T}) \times 4$ such that $\boldsymbol{F}_2$ is a node vector of **T**, $\boldsymbol{F}_1$ is the associated degree vector, $\boldsymbol{F}_3$ is a *filial chain* such that $\boldsymbol{F}_3{}^i = j$ if node $\boldsymbol{F}_2{}^j$ is the successor of node $\boldsymbol{F}_2{}^i$ in the smallest filial set containing it and $\boldsymbol{F}_3{}^i = \circ$ if node $\boldsymbol{F}_2{}^i$ has no such successor, and $\boldsymbol{F}_4$ is an *heir chain* such that $\boldsymbol{F}_4{}^i = h$ if node $\boldsymbol{F}_2{}^h$ is the heir of node $\boldsymbol{F}_2{}^i$ and $\boldsymbol{F}_4{}^i = \circ$ if $\boldsymbol{F}_2{}^i$ is a leaf. The filial-heir chain list is illustrated in Table 3.13*c*.

REFERENCES

Blaauw, G. A., (1959), "Indexing and Control-Word Techniques," *IBM Journal of Research and Development*, vol. 3, pp. 288–301.

Brooks, F. P., Jr., and K. E. Iverson, (1962), (in press) *Automatic Data Processing*, Wiley, New York.

Burks, A. W., D. W. Warren, and J. B. Wright, (1954), "An Analysis of a Logical Machine Using Parenthesis-free Notation," *Mathematical Tables and Other Aids to Computation*, vol. VIII, pp. 53–57.

Dewey, Godfrey, (1923), *Relativ Frequency of English Speech Sounds*, Cambridge University Press, p. 185.

Huffman, D. A., (1952), "A Method for the Construction of Minimum Redundancy Codes," *Proc. IRE*, vol. 40, pp. 1098–1101.

Iverson, K. E., (1955), "Report by the Staff of the Computation Laboratory to the American Gas Association and Edison Electric Institute," Section III, Report No. 1, Harvard Computation Laboratory.

Johnson, L. R., (1962), "On Operand Structure, Representation, Storage, and Search," Research Report # RC-603, IBM Corp.

Lukasiewicz, Jan, (1951), *Aristotle's Syllogistic from the Standpoint of Modern Formal Logic*, Clarendon Press, Oxford, England, p. 78.

Marimont, R. B., (1959), "A New Method of Checking the Consistency of Precedence Matrices," *J. ACM*, vol. 6, pp. 164–171.

Ross, I. C., and F. Harary, (1960), "The Square of a Tree," *Bell System Tech. J.*, vol. XXXIX, pp. 641–8.

Shaw, J. C., A. Newell, H. A. Simon, and T. O. Ellis, (1958), "A Command structure for complex information processing," *Proc. Western Joint Computer Conference*, pp. 119–128.

EXERCISES

The symbols $\boldsymbol{a}$ and $\boldsymbol{c}$ will be used exclusively to denote lower case and capital alphabets defined as follows:

$\boldsymbol{a} = (\circ, \text{a}, \text{b}, \text{c}, \ldots, \text{z}, ., ,, \#, *, +)$.

$\boldsymbol{c} = (\circ, \text{A}, \text{B}, \text{C}, \ldots, \text{Z}, ., ,, \#, *, +)$.

The expression $\boldsymbol{\pi} \subseteq \boldsymbol{x}$ will be used to specify the set $\boldsymbol{x}$ as the range of the components of $\boldsymbol{\pi}$.

3.1 For each of the following cases, specify a suitable encoding matrix and format vector and show the explicit value of the infix of $\boldsymbol{\pi}$ which (in a solid representation) represents the given example vector $\boldsymbol{x}$:

(a) the decimal digits $\boldsymbol{d} = \boldsymbol{\iota}^0(10)$ in a ranked fixed-length code for $\boldsymbol{\pi} \subseteq \boldsymbol{\iota}^0(2)$.
Example: $\boldsymbol{x} = (6, 8, 9)$.

(b) the set $\boldsymbol{a}$ in a ranked fixed-length code for $\boldsymbol{\pi} \subseteq \boldsymbol{\iota}^0(2)$.
Example: $\boldsymbol{x} = (\text{c}, \text{a}, \text{t})$.

(c) the set $\boldsymbol{a} \cup \boldsymbol{c} \cup \boldsymbol{\iota}^0(10)$ in a fixed-length code for $\boldsymbol{\pi} \subseteq \boldsymbol{\iota}^0(10)$.
Example: $\boldsymbol{x} = (\text{M}, \text{a}, \text{y}, \circ, 3, ,, 1, 9, 6, 0, .)$.

(d) the set $\boldsymbol{a} \cup \boldsymbol{c}$ in a two-case code (with single-character shift) for $\boldsymbol{\pi} \subseteq \boldsymbol{a}$. (See Brooks and Iverson, 1962.)
Example: $\boldsymbol{x} = (\text{T}, \text{r}, \text{o}, \text{y}, ,, \text{N}, ., \text{Y}, .)$.

(e) the set $\boldsymbol{a}$ in a Huffman prefix code for $\boldsymbol{\pi} \subseteq \boldsymbol{\iota}^0(2)$. Assume the frequency distribution given in Dewey (1923).
Example: $\boldsymbol{x} = (\text{t}, \text{r}, \text{e}, \text{e})$.

3.2 For each of the cases of Exercise 3.1 write a program which decodes the infix $(i \downarrow \boldsymbol{\alpha}^j)/\boldsymbol{\pi}$, that is, which produces the vector $\boldsymbol{z}$ represented by the infix. The auxiliary physical vector $\boldsymbol{\pi}^1 \subseteq \boldsymbol{s}$ may be employed to represent the first column of the encoding matrix, where $\boldsymbol{s}$ is the set encoded. Perform a partial trace of each program for the example value used in Exercise 3.1.

3.3 The ordered set of months $\boldsymbol{m} = $(JANUARY, FEBRUARY, . . . , DECEMBER) is to be represented by the physical vector $\boldsymbol{\pi} \subseteq \mathbf{c} \cup \iota^0(10)$. For each of the following types of representation, specify a particular representation and show the values of the relevant components of $\boldsymbol{\pi}$:

(a) a linear representation (employing null elements for filling to a common dimension in $\boldsymbol{\pi}$).

(b) a solid representation for each element of $\boldsymbol{m}$ and an appropriate grid matrix itself represented linearly.

(c) a chained representation.

(d) a double chained representation.

3.4 (a) For each of the cases of Exercise 3.3, write a program which selects month $\boldsymbol{m}_k$.

(b) Trace each program for the case $k = 2$.

(c) For case (d) of Exercise 3.3, write a program which selects $\boldsymbol{m}_k$ by forward chaining if $k \leq \nu(\boldsymbol{m}) \div 2$, and by backward chaining if $k > \nu(\boldsymbol{m}) \div 2$.

3.5 For each of the cases of Exercise 3.3, write a program which "prints out" the set of months in a minimum number of n-character lines, inserting a single null between successive months except where (i) further nulls must be added to prevent the continuation of a single word from one line to the next, or (ii) no null is needed between two successive words, the first of which is coterminous with the line. In other words, produce a matrix $\boldsymbol{Z}$ of row dimension n and of minimum column dimension such that $(\boldsymbol{Z} \neq {\circ}\mathbf{E})/\boldsymbol{Z} = (\rho(\boldsymbol{m}_1) \oplus \rho(\boldsymbol{m}_2) \oplus \cdots \oplus \rho(\boldsymbol{m}_{12})$, and such that each row $\boldsymbol{Z}^i$ may be partitioned into one or more vectors of the form $\rho(\boldsymbol{m}_k) \oplus {\circ}\boldsymbol{\epsilon}$, all but the last of which must be of dimension $\nu[\rho(\boldsymbol{m}_k)] + 1$.

3.6 Assuming a linear representation for each of the logical vectors involved, and a forward-chained representation for each of the remaining operands, write programs for the following operations. Assume in each case that the arguments $\boldsymbol{x}$ and $\boldsymbol{y}$ need not be retained, and assume the use of a backward-chained pool where necessary.

(a) $\boldsymbol{z} \leftarrow \backslash \boldsymbol{x}, \boldsymbol{u}, \boldsymbol{y} \backslash$

(b) $\boldsymbol{z} \leftarrow / \boldsymbol{x}, \boldsymbol{u}, \boldsymbol{y} /$

(c) $\boldsymbol{z} \leftarrow k \uparrow \boldsymbol{x}$

(d) $\boldsymbol{z} \leftarrow k \downarrow \boldsymbol{x}$

3.7 Repeat Exercise 3.6(a), using separate grid matrices for $\boldsymbol{x}$, $\boldsymbol{y}$, and $\boldsymbol{z}$ instead of chained representations. Specify a suitable linear representation for each of the grid matrices.

3.8 (a) If a chained representation is used for a vector $\boldsymbol{x}$, then the selection of a specified component can be made faster by providing a number of alternative starting points for the required scan. State precisely the quantities required in such a process and write a program showing its use.

(b) If provision is made for starting the scan at any component of $\boldsymbol{x}$, the chained representation may itself be simplified. Show precisely what the simplified form is and identify the type of representation to which it is equivalent.

3.9 Frequently a vector $\boldsymbol{x}$ kept in a partitioned representation (for efficient use of storage) must be "unpacked" to a linear or other more accessible form for efficient processing. The converse operation of "packing" is also required. Let the partitioned representation be a file Φ employing an intercomponent partition λ_1, and a terminal partition λ_2, and write both packing and unpacking programs for each of the following cases. Assume that the maximum dimension in π of any component is n.

(a) A solid linear representation employing null fill.

(b) An allocation prescribed by a grid matrix $\boldsymbol{G}$ with $\boldsymbol{G}_2 = n\boldsymbol{\epsilon}$.

3.10 Let $\pi \subseteq \iota^0(2)$, let the set $\boldsymbol{a}$ be encoded in a five-bit code such that $(2\boldsymbol{\epsilon}) \perp \rho(\boldsymbol{a}_i) = i$, and let each component of the vector $\boldsymbol{x}$ be an (uncapitalized) English word. Using 0-origin indexing throughout, specify a suitable partitioned representation in π for the vector $\boldsymbol{x}$, and repeat Exercises 3.9(a) and 3.9(b), using it in lieu of the files.

3.11 For each of the following pool organizations, write a program to convert a given marked pool into a backward-chained pool:

(a) dimension-ordered.

(b) address-ordered.

3.12 For each of the following queue disciplines, write programs which take from and return to the pool an infix of length n. Use secondary linking and relegate to a marked pool any infix which is too short for linking. In each case choose the type of chaining best suited to the particular queue discipline.

(a) LIFO (last-in-first-out).

(b) FIFO (first-in-first-out).

(c) Dimension ordered.

(d) Address-ordered (utilize the possibility of fusing adjacent infixes).

3.13 Give a complete specification of a scheme for representing a tree $\mathbf{T}$ by a full chain list matrix which is not in right list order. Write a program (expressed in terms of the physical vector π) which determines the path vector $\mathbf{T}^{\boldsymbol{i}}$ for a given index vector $\boldsymbol{i}$.

3.14 Give a complete specification of a scheme allowing joint representation of those components shared by two or more of a family of vectors $\boldsymbol{x}^1, \boldsymbol{x}^2, \ldots, \boldsymbol{x}^n$ as suggested in Sec. 3.2. Write programs to (i) select component $\boldsymbol{x}_j^i$, and (ii) delete component $\boldsymbol{x}_j^i$.

3.15 Let $\pi \subseteq \boldsymbol{a} \cup \iota^0(10)$, and let $\boldsymbol{x}^1, \boldsymbol{x}^2, \ldots, \boldsymbol{x}^n$ be a family of vectors whose components belong to the set $\bar{\boldsymbol{\alpha}}^1/[\boldsymbol{a} \cup \iota^0(10)]$. Let the average and the maximum dimensions of the vectors $\boldsymbol{x}^i$ be a and m, respectively. Assume that the chaining index is represented in decimal, with each digit represented by one component of π. Determine (as a function of m and n) the value of a below which a chained representation provides more compact storage than a linear representation with null fill.

3.16 Write a program which uses the minimization operation $\boldsymbol{u} \leftarrow \boldsymbol{v} \lfloor \boldsymbol{x}$ to determine the ordering permutation vector $\boldsymbol{p} \leftarrow \theta_1/(\boldsymbol{a} \, \iota_1 \, \boldsymbol{b})$.

3.17 Let $\boldsymbol{U} = (\boldsymbol{X} \neq 0)$ and $\boldsymbol{r} = \boldsymbol{U}/\boldsymbol{X}$ jointly represent the sparse matrix $\boldsymbol{X}$.

(a) Write a program which determines (as a function of $\boldsymbol{U}$ and $\boldsymbol{r}$) a suitable row-chained and column-chained representation of $\boldsymbol{X}$.

(b) Write a program defined on the representation produced in part (a) to compute the product $\boldsymbol{Y} = \boldsymbol{X} \overset{+}{\underset{\times}{}} \boldsymbol{X}$, itself represented in the form $\boldsymbol{V} = (\boldsymbol{Y} \neq 0)$ and $\boldsymbol{p} = \boldsymbol{V}/\boldsymbol{Y}$.

(c) Write a program to determine the trace (that is, $+/\boldsymbol{I}/\boldsymbol{X}$) of $\boldsymbol{X}$ from the representation produced in part (a).

3.18 The unique assignment of Huffman codes produced by Program 3.12 is, in general, only one of many equally efficient assignments, since the symbols to be coded need only be assigned, in decreasing order on frequency, to the leaves of the code tree in increasing order on their levels. Show that the structure of the tree produced can be sufficiently described by its moment vector alone, and write a program for the construction of a Huffman code based on this fact.

3.19 Following the notation and terminology used in Program 3.9 for the analogous case of a left list write a program which determines from the right list $\boldsymbol{R}$ of a tree $\mathbf{T}$, the partition vector $\boldsymbol{p}$ which partitions it by levels.

3.20 Write a program which determines the right list $\boldsymbol{R} = \boldsymbol{\alpha}^2/]\mathbf{T}$ as a function of the left list $\boldsymbol{L} = \boldsymbol{\alpha}^2/[\mathbf{T}$. Incorporate tests of well formation.

3.21 Let $[\boldsymbol{X} \overset{\odot_1}{\underset{\odot_2}{}}]^p$ denote the pth power of the square matrix $\boldsymbol{X}$ with respect to the operators $\odot_1$ and $\odot_2$, that is, $[\boldsymbol{X} \overset{\odot_1}{\underset{\odot_2}{}}]^p = \boldsymbol{X} \overset{\odot_1}{\underset{\odot_2}{}} \boldsymbol{X} \overset{\odot_1}{\underset{\odot_2}{}} \cdots \overset{\odot_1}{\underset{\odot_2}{}} \boldsymbol{X}$ to p factors.

(a) Show that $([\boldsymbol{C} \overset{\vee}{\underset{\wedge}{}}]^p)_j^i = 1$ if and only if there is a path of length p from node i to node j in the graph $(\boldsymbol{n}, \boldsymbol{C})$.

(b) Show that $[\boldsymbol{C} \overset{\vee}{\underset{\wedge}{}}]^p = 0$ for some $p < \nu(\boldsymbol{C})$ if and only if $(\boldsymbol{n}, \boldsymbol{C})$ contains no circuits.

(c) If $(\boldsymbol{n}, \boldsymbol{C})$ contains no circuits, the connection matrix $\boldsymbol{C}$ is said to be "consistent." The result of part (a) can be used to check consistency. Program the alternative method of Marimont (1959).

(d) If $\boldsymbol{H} = \boldsymbol{C} \vee \boldsymbol{I}$, then $([\boldsymbol{H} \overset{\vee}{\underset{\wedge}{}}]^p)_j^i = 1$ if and only if $i = j$ or there exists a path from node i to node j of length $n \leq p + 1$. Show that for any connection matrix $\boldsymbol{C}$, $[\boldsymbol{H} \overset{\vee}{\underset{\wedge}{}}]^p$ converges to a limit.

3.22 Devise programs to determine

(a) whether a given connection matrix $\boldsymbol{C}$ represents a tree.

(b) the left list of the tree $(\boldsymbol{n}, \boldsymbol{C})$.

(c) the right list of the tree $(\boldsymbol{n}, \boldsymbol{C})$.

(d) a node list $\boldsymbol{n}$ and connection matrix $\boldsymbol{C}$ as a function of

(i) a left list $\boldsymbol{L}$

(ii) a right list $\boldsymbol{R}$.

3.23 Show that $(\boldsymbol{n}, \boldsymbol{C})$ and $(\boldsymbol{n}_p, \boldsymbol{C}_p{}^p)$ represent the same graph for any permutation $\boldsymbol{p}$.

3.24 If $(\boldsymbol{n}, \boldsymbol{C})$ is a tree and if $\boldsymbol{K} = \boldsymbol{C} \overset{\vee}{\underset{\wedge}{}} \boldsymbol{C}$, then $\boldsymbol{C}$ can be determined as a function of $\boldsymbol{K}$ (see Ross and Harary, 1960). Write a program for determining $\boldsymbol{C}$ from $\boldsymbol{K}$.

chapter 4

SEARCH TECHNIQUES

In classical applied mathematics most functions of interest can be approximated by some algorithm which becomes, for practical purposes, the definition of the function. In other areas, however, many functions of practical, if not general, interest (such as the correspondence between employee name and salary) can be specified only by an exhaustive listing of each argument value and its corresponding function value. Such a function will be called *fortuitous*.

The basic algorithm applicable to the evaluation of a fortuitous function is a *search* of the list of arguments, i.e., a comparison of the given argument with the list of arguments to determine the correspondent to be selected. In such an algorithm it is convenient (as illustrated by Program 1.12*a*) to distinguish three phases which successively determine the following quantities:

(1) the index or rank $r = \boldsymbol{k} \iota k$ of the argument k in $\boldsymbol{k}$.
(2) the index $i = \boldsymbol{p}_r$ of the correspondent in $\boldsymbol{s}$.
(3) the correspondent $s = \boldsymbol{s}_i$.

Step (2) is a permutation defined by the permutation vector $\boldsymbol{p}$. Steps (2) and (3) are simple selections from structured operands (normally in linear representations) and require no further discussion. Step 1 is called *ranking*, and the methods for accomplishing it merit detailed treatment.

The argument k of a mapping (and hence of a ranking) operation will be called a *key*. The German-English dictionary mapping of Example 1.2 is typical of mappings from key to correspondent. Ranking is itself a special mapping from the key set $\boldsymbol{k}$ onto its own index set $\boldsymbol{\iota}^1(\nu(\boldsymbol{k}))$.

If the representation used for some or all of the data imposes certain restrictions (such as serial access), there may be some advantage in coalescing the three phases of the mapping operation so as not to determine the rank explicitly. It will, however, be convenient to limit the discussion almost exclusively to the problem of ranking.

There are two main types of ranking processes: scanning and key transformations. A *scanning* process compares the key k successively with selected elements of the key set $\boldsymbol{k}$ to determine the rank $r = \boldsymbol{k} \iota k$. A *key transformation* is any function or algorithm $t(k)$ which maps the set $\boldsymbol{k}$ into some subset of the integers. The set of *derived keys* is defined as the set $\boldsymbol{d}$ containing all derived keys arranged in ascending order. The set of all keys which map into $\boldsymbol{d}_j$ is called the *jth equivalence class* defined by the transformation t.

If $\nu(\boldsymbol{d}) = \nu(\boldsymbol{k})$, the key transformation is biunique and the ranking operation may therefore be completed by a permutation $\boldsymbol{p}$ such that $\boldsymbol{p}_j = i$ for $j = t(\boldsymbol{k}_i)$. If $\nu(\boldsymbol{d}) < \nu(\boldsymbol{k})$, then at least two distinct elements of $\boldsymbol{k}$ map into the same element of $\boldsymbol{d}$ and the ranking process must be completed by a scan of one of the equivalence classes defined by t.

If, for example, $\boldsymbol{k} =$ (m, tu, w, th, f) is the ordered set of working days encoded according to the encoding matrix

$$\begin{matrix}1\\2\\3\\4\\5\end{matrix} \quad C = \begin{pmatrix} \text{m} & 0 & 0 & 1 \\ \text{tu} & 0 & 1 & 0 \\ \text{w} & 0 & 1 & 1 \\ \text{th} & 1 & 0 & 0 \\ \text{f} & 1 & 1 & 1 \end{pmatrix}$$

and format vector $\boldsymbol{f} = (0, 1, 1, 1)$, then scanning can be accomplished by comparing $\rho(k)$, the encoded representation of the key k, with successive rows of $\boldsymbol{f}/C$ to determine the rank r of the row on which agreement occurs. Moreover, the key transformation

$$t(k) = (2\epsilon) \perp \rho(k)$$

is unique, but requires an associated mapping vector $\boldsymbol{m} = (1, 2, 3, 4, \circ, \circ, 5)$. Had $\rho(\text{f})$ (that is, $\boldsymbol{f}/C^5$) been chosen as (1, 0, 1), the mapping vector would not have been required. Finally, the key transformation

$$t'(k) = 1 + \rho_3(k)$$

has the range $\boldsymbol{d} = (1, 2)$, is not unique, and requires a subsequent scan of one or other of the equivalence classes $\boldsymbol{e}^1 =$ (tu, th), and $\boldsymbol{e}^2 =$ (m, w, f), represented by (010, 100) and (001, 011, 111), respectively.

Although a strict ranking operation maps element $\boldsymbol{k}_i$ into the integer i, any biunique mapping onto the index set $\iota^1(\nu(\boldsymbol{k}))$ will frequently serve as well. For, if $\boldsymbol{p}$ is the permutation required to complete the ranking process, and if a subsequent permutation $\boldsymbol{j}$ is required (as in step 4 of Program 1.12*a*), the two permutations can be combined in the single permutation $\boldsymbol{q} = \boldsymbol{j} \int \boldsymbol{p}$. Similarly, the ranking of a set $\boldsymbol{k}$ may be considered as equivalent to the ranking of any set obtained by permuting $\boldsymbol{k}$.

4.1 SCANNING METHODS FOR RANKING

The two main methods of scan are called *directed* and *controlled*. A *directed scan* is begun in one of two possible directions from a given initial point i, either *ascending* (that is, $i, i + 1, i + 2, \ldots$) or *descending*. The direction chosen may be determined by a comparison between the given argument and the set element $\boldsymbol{k}_i$ at the initial point i. A *controlled scan* is executed in a sequence which is determined by successive comparisons between the argument and each element scanned. In an effective controlled scan, each comparison must determine the choice of the next element for comparison so as to (approximately) minimize the expected number of elements scanned. The directed scan is clearly well suited to the use of a file or chained representation, which imposes serial access to the elements, whereas the controlled scan is not.

The *scan length* (i.e., the number of key elements scanned) will be used as a measure in analyzing and evaluating scanning methods. The same measure and the same analysis apply also to the converse situation, where the rank of an element is given and the element itself must be obtained from a chained or other representation which permits only serial access. An alternative related measure is the normalized scan length or *scan fraction*, defined as the scan length divided by the number of elements in the set of keys.

A scan is said to be *rooted* if each execution begins at the same point r. A rooted scan may be advantageous when the frequency distribution of the arguments is nonuniform and the most frequent keys can be grouped near the root. A scan is called *catenated* if each execution is begun at the end point of the preceding scan. A catenated scan may be employed in using a file when the intervals between successive scans are so short as to allow little or no time for return to a fixed root or when the arguments are arranged in the same relative order as the items in the file.

Directed scan

A directed scan is called *cyclic* if element $\boldsymbol{k}_1$ follows $\boldsymbol{k}_\nu$ in an ascending scan and if $\boldsymbol{k}_\nu$ follows $\boldsymbol{k}_1$ in a descending scan. It is called *noncyclic* if the direction of scan is reversed whenever either of the terminal elements $\boldsymbol{k}_1$ or $\boldsymbol{k}_\nu$ is encountered. A cyclic scan is appropriate to a chained representation with end-around chaining; a noncyclic scan is appropriate to a file or to a chained representation without end-around chaining.

The initial direction of scan may be chosen in several ways, the more important of which are enumerated and discussed below. For independently and uniformly distributed arguments, the expected scan fractions

Type of Scan				pr($f \leq b$) for Scan Fraction f					
No.	Initial Position	Initial Direction	Cyclic or Noncyclic	$0 \leq b \leq \frac{1}{2}$	$\frac{1}{2} \leq b \leq 1$	$1 \leq b \leq 1\frac{1}{2}$	$1\frac{1}{2} \leq b \leq 2$	Average	Maximum
1	Any	Fixed, continue or reverse	Cyclic	b	b	1	1	$\frac{1}{2}$	1
2	Any	To argument	Cyclic	$2b$	1	1	1	$\frac{1}{4}$	$\frac{1}{2}$
3	1	Fixed	Noncyclic	b	b	1	1	$\frac{1}{2}$	1
4	Catenated	Fixed	Noncyclic	$-b^2/4 + b$	$-b^2/4 + b$	$-b^2/4 + b$	$-b^2/4 + b$	$\frac{2}{3}$	2
5	$\lfloor(\nu(k)+1)\div 2\rfloor$	To argument	Noncyclic	$2b$	1	1	1	$\frac{1}{4}$	$\frac{1}{2}$
6	Catenated	To argument	Noncyclic	$-b^2 + 2b$	$-b^2 + 2b$	1	1	$\frac{1}{3}$	1
7	Catenated	To nearer terminal	Noncyclic	$-b^2/2 + b$	$b^2/2 + \frac{1}{4}$	$-b^2 + 3b - \frac{5}{4}$	1	$\frac{2}{3}$	$1\frac{1}{2}$
8	Catenated	To farther terminal	Noncyclic	b	$-b^2 + 2b - \frac{1}{4}$	$b^2/2 - b + \frac{5}{4}$	$-b^2/2 + 2b - 1$	$\frac{2}{3}$	2
9	Catenated	Continue previous	Noncyclic	$b^3/4 - b^2/2 + b$	$b^3/4 - b^2/2 + b$	$b^3/4 - 3b^2/2 + 3b - 1$	$b^3/4 - 3b^2/2 + 3b - 1$	$\frac{2}{3}$	2
10	Catenated	Reverse previous	Noncyclic	$-b^3/4 + b$	$-b^3/4 + b$	$-b^3/4 + b^2 - b + 1$	$-b^3/4 + b^2 - b + 1$	$\frac{2}{3}$	2

Table 4.1 Scan fraction of directed scans for uniform distribution of arguments (from Iverson, 1955)

are summarized in Table 4.1. Certain of the results are also plotted in Fig. 4.2.

Initial direction fixed (fixed scan). The ascending direction will be assumed. If the scan is rooted and cyclic, the root may, without loss of generality, be assumed to be *one*. The expected scan length for a set is then given by

$$e = \sum_{i=1}^{\nu(\boldsymbol{k})} f(\boldsymbol{k}_i) \times i = \boldsymbol{f} \overset{+}{\underset{\times}{}} \boldsymbol{\iota}^1$$

where $f(\boldsymbol{k}_i)$ is the normalized expected frequency of occurrence of the argument $\boldsymbol{k}_i$ and $\boldsymbol{f}$ is the corresponding frequency vector defined by $\boldsymbol{f}_i = f(\boldsymbol{k}_i)$.

The most efficient fixed rooted scan is therefore obtained by using the permuted set $\boldsymbol{a} = (\theta/(-\boldsymbol{f}))\int \boldsymbol{k}$ such that the components of $\boldsymbol{a}$ are arranged

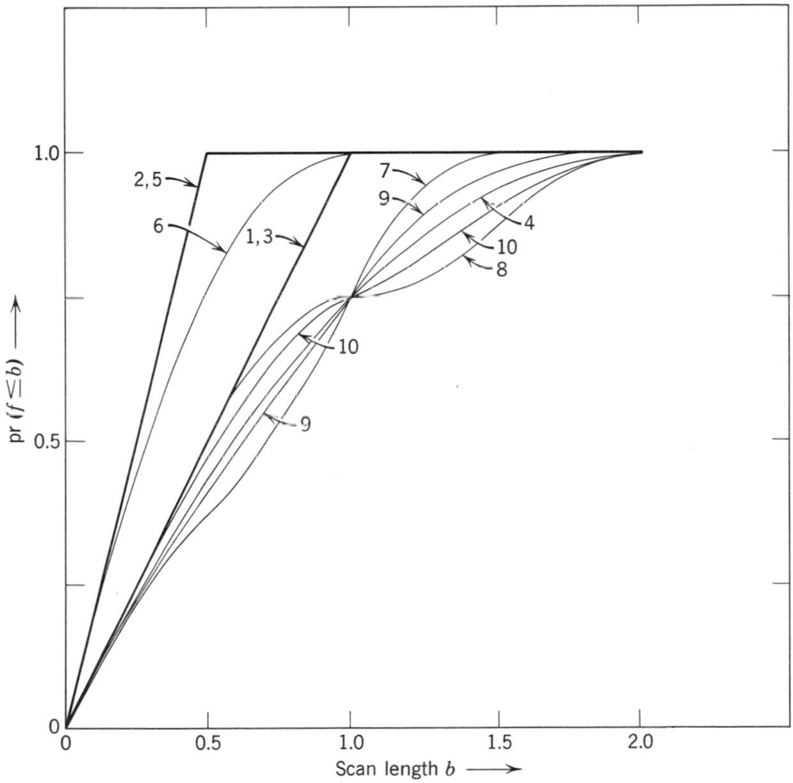

Figure 4.2 Plot of cumulative probabilities of Table 4.1 (Numbers refer to the entries in Table 4.1)

in decreasing order on frequency. If the distribution of arguments is uniform (that is, $f_i = 1/\nu(f)$), then the expected scan length is $(\nu(\boldsymbol{k}) + 1) \div 2$, and the expected scan fraction is approximately one half.

If a fixed scan is cyclic and catenated, the expected scan length depends on the distribution f, but if the arguments are independently distributed, then the expected scan length is independent of the ordering of the scanned set $\boldsymbol{k}$. This may be shown as follows. The expected length l_r of a scan rooted at r is given by $M^r \overset{+}{\times} f$, where M is the square matrix such that $M^r = (r - 1) \downarrow \iota^1$. The probability of beginning a catenated scan at r is the probability of ending the previous scan at r, that is, f_r. Consequently,

$$e = f \overset{+}{\times} l = f \overset{+}{\times} M \overset{+}{\times} f.$$

Since, in general, $f \overset{+}{\times} M \overset{+}{\times} f = f \overset{+}{\times} \tilde{M} \overset{+}{\times} f$, then $2e = (f \overset{+}{\times} N \overset{+}{\times} f)$, where $N = M + \tilde{M}$. If, for example, $\nu(\boldsymbol{k}) = 4$, then

$$M = \begin{pmatrix} 1 & 2 & 3 & 4 \\ 4 & 1 & 2 & 3 \\ 3 & 4 & 1 & 2 \\ 2 & 3 & 4 & 1 \end{pmatrix}, \quad \text{and} \quad N = \begin{pmatrix} 2 & 6 & 6 & 6 \\ 6 & 2 & 6 & 6 \\ 6 & 6 & 2 & 6 \\ 6 & 6 & 6 & 2 \end{pmatrix}.$$

It is easily shown that N is of the form

$$N = 2\mathbf{E} + \nu(\boldsymbol{k})\bar{\boldsymbol{I}}$$

and consequently $N_p^p = N$ for any permutation $\boldsymbol{p}$. But $f \overset{+}{\times} N \overset{+}{\times} f = (f_p) \overset{+}{\times} (N_p^p) \overset{+}{\times} (f_p)$ in general, and since $N_p^p = N$, then $f \overset{+}{\times} N \overset{+}{\times} f = (f_p) \overset{+}{\times} N \overset{+}{\times} (f_p)$. Hence the expected scan $e = (\frac{1}{2}) \times f \overset{+}{\times} N \overset{+}{\times} f$ remains the same for any permutation of f or, equivalently, for any permutation of the key set $\boldsymbol{k}$.

If the arguments are not independently distributed, the analysis is, in the general case, very complex. However, a simple but effective use of correlation is made in the method of *batching*. If $\boldsymbol{a}$ is a collection or *batch* of uncorrelated arguments, each of which is to be ranked in the set $\boldsymbol{k}$, then the total expected scan time for a fixed catenated scan will be $\nu(\boldsymbol{a})$ times the expected scan time for a single item. If, however, the set $\boldsymbol{a}$ is ordered on $\boldsymbol{k}$ (that is, $\boldsymbol{a} = \boldsymbol{k} \cap \boldsymbol{a}$), then the entire set $\boldsymbol{a}$ may be ranked in a fixed catenated scan whose normalized length does not exceed one.* If a given

* The length of the scan will be determined by the maximum rank (in $\boldsymbol{k}$) occurring in the set $\mathbf{a}$. The expected value of the scan fraction is approximately equal to the expected value of the maximum occurring in a sample of size $n = \nu(\mathbf{a})$ chosen from the continuous interval from zero to one. This value is known for various distributions [e.g., Cramèr (1951) p. 370]; for a uniform distribution it is $n \div (n + 1)$.

argument set $\boldsymbol{z}$ is not ordered on $\boldsymbol{k}$, it may first be permuted by some sorting process to yield the set $\boldsymbol{a} = \boldsymbol{p} \int \boldsymbol{z}$ which is ordered on $\boldsymbol{k}$. The set $\boldsymbol{a}$ may then be ranked in $\boldsymbol{k}$ and, if required, the set of ranks may then be subjected to the inverse permutation $\boldsymbol{q} = \boldsymbol{p}\, \iota_1\, \boldsymbol{\iota}^1$ to yield the ranks in the original set $\boldsymbol{z}$. The decrease in the total expected scan length may far outweigh the effect of the additional permutations required.

If a fixed scan is noncyclic and rooted at *one*, the expected scan length is the same as for the fixed cyclic rooted scan. The fixed noncyclic scan is generally unsuited to any initial points r other than *one* (e.g., to a catenated scan), since the first $(r - 1)$ elements of $\boldsymbol{k}$ are then reached only after a reversal of direction and a rescan of the set $\bar{\boldsymbol{\alpha}}^r / \boldsymbol{k}$.

For the case of a uniform distribution, the behavior of the fixed scan is summarized in entries 1, 3, and 4 of Table 4.1. The derivation will be illustrated in discussing entry 7.

Initial direction giving shortest scan. For a fixed root r, the minimum expected scan is achieved if the items are disposed on either side of the root so that the frequency $\boldsymbol{f}_i$ is a monotone decreasing function of $|i - r|$, the scan length in a direct scan to the argument. In a cyclic scan, the position of the root is immaterial; in a noncyclic scan it is best centered at the floor (or ceiling) of $(\nu(\boldsymbol{k}) + 1) \div 2$. In a 0-origin system this expression becomes $\nu(\boldsymbol{k}) \div 2$.

For an arbitrary frequency function, the expected scan length is given by the scalar product $\boldsymbol{f} \overset{+}{\underset{\times}{}} \boldsymbol{l}$, where $\boldsymbol{l} = |\boldsymbol{\iota}^1 - r\boldsymbol{\epsilon}|$. For a uniform distribution, the results are given in entries 2 and 5 of Table 4.1. For a catenated scan, the corresponding results appear in entries 2 and 6.

The possibility of choosing the initial direction so as to give the shortest scan to the argument depends on the information available. If the elements of $\boldsymbol{k}$ are strictly ranked on some function $g(\boldsymbol{k}_i)$, then the shortest direction from root r to argument x can, in the noncyclic case, be determined by a comparison of $g(x)$ and $g(\boldsymbol{k}_r)$. For the cyclic case this does not suffice, and it is necessary* to know the index in $\boldsymbol{k}$ of the argument x. This case is therefore of interest primarily in selecting a specified element from a serial-access representation and is of little interest in an actual ranking operation. However, any double-chained representation or reversible file can be used in a noncyclic as well as a cyclic manner and hence admits of a choice of direction which is best in the noncyclic sense.

Initial direction to nearer (farther) terminal. If the value of the root r is known for each individual scan in a catenated scan, the direction to the nearer terminal can be determined by comparing r with the midpoint

* Approximating functions may, however, be used for estimating the index and the probable best direction.

$(\nu(\mathbf{k}) + 1) \div 2$. A noncyclic scan starting toward the nearer end is clearly less efficient than one starting toward the argument, but it may be useful when the most direct route to the argument cannot be determined. The expected scan fraction is shown in entry 7 of Table 4.1; its analysis will illustrate the method used in constructing the entire table.

It is assumed that the number of elements $\nu(\mathbf{k})$ is sufficiently large that the scan fraction f may be considered as a continuous variable. Let $\text{pr}\,(f \leq b)$ be the probability that scan fraction f does not exceed b, and let the function be represented in three parts such that $\text{pr}\,(f \leq b) = \text{pr}_i\,(f \leq b)$ in the ith half-unit interval in b. Let x be the normalized initial position of a given scan. Then $0 \leq x \leq 1$, and, since the scan always begins toward the nearer terminal, the fraction of the set covered in a scan of length b is the same for the starting point $(1 - x)$ as for x. Using this symmetry, attention can be restricted to values of x in the range 0 to $\frac{1}{2}$. For the function $\text{pr}_1\,(f \leq b)$, the value of b is also restricted to the range 0 to $\frac{1}{2}$.

Consider fixed values of b and x with $b \leq \frac{1}{2}$. If $0 \leq x \leq b/2$, the fraction of the file covered by a scan of length b is given by $b - x$, for the scan begins at x, proceeds a distance x to the nearer terminal, and returns to the point $b - x$. If $b/2 \leq x \leq b$, the fraction covered is clearly x, for the scan will reach the nearer terminal but will not return past x. If $b \leq x \leq \frac{1}{2}$, the scan does not reach the nearer terminal, and the fraction scanned is therefore b. Since x is uniformly distributed, the function $\text{pr}_1\,(f \leq b)$ is obtained by integration as follows:

$$\text{pr}_1(f \leq b) = 2\left[\int_0^{b/2} (b - x)\,dx + \int_{b/2}^{b} x\,dx + \int_b^{1/2} b\,dx\right] = \frac{-b^2}{2} + b.$$

The factor of two arises from the symmetry in x and the restriction of x to the interval $0 \leq x \leq \frac{1}{2}$. Similarly,

$$\text{pr}_2(f \leq b) = 2\left[\int_0^{b/2} (b - x)\,dx + \int_{b/2}^{1/2} x\,dx\right] = \frac{b^2}{2} + \frac{1}{4},$$

and

$$\text{pr}_3(f \leq b) = 2\left[\int_0^{b-1} dx + \int_{b-1}^{1/2} (b - x)\,dx\right] = -b^2 + 3b - \frac{5}{4}.$$

Entry 8 shows the behavior of the scan starting toward the farther terminal. Although the distribution differs markedly from that obtained for starting toward the nearer terminal, it has the same expected value of $\frac{2}{3}$. As may be expected, the function obtained for a fixed scan (entry 4) is the average of the functions obtained for cases 7 and 8 and is linear in b. Case 7 (toward nearer terminal) yields the smallest maximum scan length of the three.

Initial direction reversed (continued) from previous scan. In the absence of any other basis of choice, the initial direction can be chosen as a reversal or continuation of the direction which terminated the preceding scan. The behavior is shown in entries 9 and 10 of Table 4.1. The relations between the functions for fixed scan (F), continuation (C), and reversal (R) are

$$F - R = -(F - C) \leq 0 \qquad \text{for } b \leq 1,$$

and

$$F - R = -(F - C) \geq 0 \qquad \text{for } b \geq 1.$$

Controlled scan

The sequence followed in a controlled scan is commonly determined by a comparison which determines the relative ranking of any pair of elements x and y in the set $\boldsymbol{k}$. It will therefore be assumed that comparison of the argument $x = \boldsymbol{k}_h$ with the element $\boldsymbol{k}_j$ determines whether $h < j$, $h = j$, or

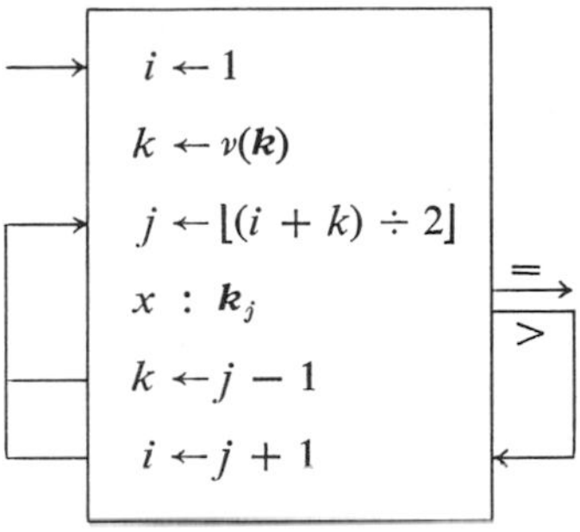

Program 4.3 Ranking of x in $\boldsymbol{k}$ by binary search

$h > j$. The subsequent scan may then be limited to one or other of the two subsets $\boldsymbol{\alpha}^{j-1}/\boldsymbol{k}$ and $\bar{\boldsymbol{\alpha}}^j/\boldsymbol{k}$. The maximum dimension of the subset remaining to be scanned is therefore minimized by choosing $j = \lfloor(\nu(\boldsymbol{k}) + 1) \div 2\rfloor$. If each subsequent element for comparison is chosen so as to (approximately) halve the dimension of the set remaining to be scanned, the process is called *binary search.* Program 4.3 shows the details of binary search; i and k are the indices of the terminal elements of the remaining subset, and j is the index of the element selected for comparison.

If $\nu(\boldsymbol{k}) = 2^k$, then any one of 2^{j-1} different arguments may be isolated on the jth comparison, for $j \in \iota^1(k)$, and the one remaining argument will be located on the $(k + 1)$th comparison. Hence for a uniform distribution of arguments, the expected number of comparisons required in a binary search is given by

$$e_b(2^k) = (1 \cdot 2^0 + 2 \cdot 2^1 + 3 \cdot 2^2 + \cdots + k \cdot 2^{k-1} + (k + 1)) \div 2^k.$$

It can be shown (e.g., by induction on k) that

$$e_b(2^k) = [(k - 1)2^k + k + 2] \div 2^k.$$

The expected number of comparisons is therefore approximately $(k - 1)$, and for a general value of $\nu(\boldsymbol{k})$, the number is approximately $\lceil \log_2 \nu(\boldsymbol{k}) \rceil - 1$. The expected value thus differs but slightly from the maximum value $\lceil \log_2 (\nu(\boldsymbol{k}) + 1) \rceil$.

If $e_s(\nu(\boldsymbol{k}))$ is the expected number of comparisons required in a fixed scan of $\boldsymbol{k}$ and if r is the ratio of the execution time for one step of binary search to the execution time for one step of fixed scan, binary search is (for a uniform distribution) the more or the less efficient according as e_s exceeds or is exceeded by re_b. Although the simplicity of Program 4.3 suggests that the ratio r is small, it will be large if the representation of the elements of $\boldsymbol{k}$ permits serial access only.

The methods may be combined by using k steps of binary search to select one of 2^k subsets, which is then subjected to a fixed scan. If the remaining subset contains m elements, the (approximate) reduction in the expected number of comparisons achieved by one further step of binary search is $e_s(m) - e_s(m/2)$, and binary search should therefore be discontinued when $e_s(m) - e_s(m/2) \leq r$. For a uniform distribution, this result yields the following approximate expression for the optimum number of steps of binary search:

$$s = \left\lceil \log_2 \left(\frac{\nu(\boldsymbol{k})}{4r} \right) \right\rceil.$$

The ranking type of comparison required in determining the sequence in a controlled scan is always attainable for any arbitrary set $\boldsymbol{k}$ or for some permutation thereof. For, if $\boldsymbol{\rho}(\boldsymbol{k}_i)$ is the representation of $\boldsymbol{k}_i$ in $\boldsymbol{\pi}$, if $\boldsymbol{\pi} \subseteq \boldsymbol{\iota}^0(b)$, if $\boldsymbol{t}_i = (b\boldsymbol{\epsilon}) \perp \boldsymbol{\rho}(\boldsymbol{k}_i)$, and if $\boldsymbol{a} = (\theta/\boldsymbol{t})\int \boldsymbol{k}$, then the relative ranking of any pair of elements of $\boldsymbol{a}$ can be determined by comparing the base b values of their representations. If, for example, $b = 10$, and the four successive elements of $\boldsymbol{k}$ are represented by (1, 0, 9), (0, 6, 4), (7, 1, 3) and (5, 0, 6), then $\boldsymbol{a}$ is represented by (0, 6, 4), (1, 0, 9), (5, 0, 6), and (7, 1, 3), and relative ranking in $\boldsymbol{a}$ is determined by comparing elements as decimal numbers.

In the execution of the binary search, the calculation of the index j (next element for comparison), and the explicit determination of the terminal indices i and k can be avoided by associating with each element $\boldsymbol{k}_j$ a pair of indices which indicate the two possible succeeding choices for j. More precisely, if $\boldsymbol{M}$ is a matrix of dimension $\nu(\boldsymbol{k}) \times 3$, whose first column is the set $\boldsymbol{k}$, and whose second and third columns are vectors of indices (or nulls) from the set $\boldsymbol{\iota}^1(\nu(\boldsymbol{k})) \cup (\circ)$, then Program 4.4 describes a directed scan of $\boldsymbol{k}$.

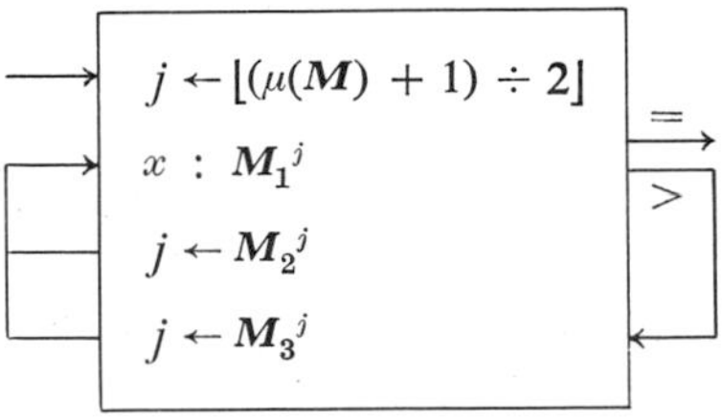

Program 4.4 Generalized binary search

The elements of $\boldsymbol{M}_2$ and $\boldsymbol{M}_3$ can be so chosen as to execute a binary search equivalent to that of Program 4.3. This is true, for example, for the matrix $\boldsymbol{M}$ of Fig. 4.5.

The ordering of the elements of $\boldsymbol{M}_1$ is clearly immaterial, i.e., if $\boldsymbol{M}_1$ were permuted, then columns $\boldsymbol{M}_2$ and $\boldsymbol{M}_3$ could be respecified so as to yield the original scanning order. One consequence of this is the fact that the rows can be reordered so that the scan conveniently begins with the first row rather than with row $\lfloor(\mu(\boldsymbol{M}) + 1) \div 2\rfloor$. A more important consequence is the possibility of applying the method to the problem of multiple keys, which will be raised in the treatment of key transformations.

As illustrated by Fig. 4.5, the matrix $\boldsymbol{M}$ specifies a tree whose nodes are the elements of $\boldsymbol{M}_1$, whose branching ratios are two, and whose paths are traced by Program 4.4. The columns $\boldsymbol{M}_2$ and $\boldsymbol{M}_3$ can clearly be chosen to specify a scan sequence other than that of binary search. In particular, the element $\boldsymbol{M}_1{}^j$ selected for comparison may be chosen so as to equalize (as far as possible) the total probability of the arguments in the two resulting

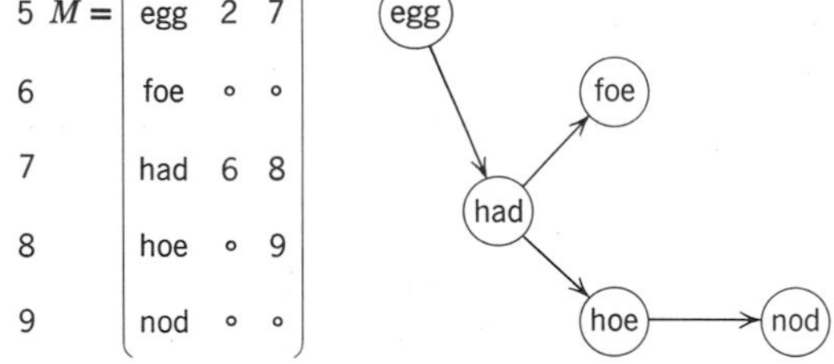

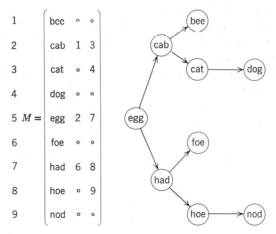

Figure 4.5 Tree traced by Program 4.4

subsets rather than to equalize the number of elements. This procedure yields the most efficient controlled scan. If the probability distribution is uniform, the method reduces to binary search. If the arguments are drawn from two or more sets having distinct probability distributions, the matrix $\boldsymbol{M}$ may be enlarged to include two index columns for each distinct set. Each such pair of columns may then be designed to provide an optimum scan for the associated distribution.

4.2 KEY TRANSFORMATIONS

Since a key transformation maps the set of keys $\boldsymbol{k}$ into a set of integers (the set of derived keys $\boldsymbol{d}$), any unique key transformation produces a derived key which can be used to select the component of a mapping vector directly and thus complete a ranking operation without the use of a scan. If the transformation is not unique, it may still be used to partition the original set $\boldsymbol{k}$ into $\nu(\boldsymbol{d})$ subsets for scanning and so reduce the expected scan time. Ideally a key transformation should be both simple and unique and should produce a derived set $\boldsymbol{d}$ having a narrow spread; in practice, compromises must be made.

Let $\boldsymbol{k}$ be the domain and $\boldsymbol{d}$ the range (in ascending order) of a key transformation $t(\boldsymbol{k}_i)$ and let $\boldsymbol{e}^j$ be the equivalence class in $\boldsymbol{k}$ which maps into $\boldsymbol{d}_j$, that is, $t(x) = \boldsymbol{d}_j$ for all $x \in \boldsymbol{e}^j$. The *coalescence of t in* $\boldsymbol{k}$ is then defined as the vector $\boldsymbol{c}$ such that $\boldsymbol{c}_j = \nu(\boldsymbol{e}^j)$, for $j \in \iota^1(\nu(\boldsymbol{d}))$. Since the equivalence classes are disjoint and collectively exhaust $\boldsymbol{k}$, then $+/\boldsymbol{c} = \nu(\boldsymbol{k})$. The *spread of t in* $\boldsymbol{k}$ is defined as $1 + \boldsymbol{d}_\nu - \boldsymbol{d}_1$. Thus if $\boldsymbol{k}$ is the set (Sunday, Monday, . . . , Saturday), and if t maps each day into the rank (in the alphabet) of its leading letter, then $\boldsymbol{d} = (6, 13, 19, 20, 23)$, the spread $s = 18$, $\boldsymbol{c} = (1, 1, 2, 2, 1)$, and $+/\boldsymbol{c} = \nu(\boldsymbol{k}) = 7$.

The key transformation is biunique if and only if $\boldsymbol{c} = \boldsymbol{\epsilon}$. Moreover, if the transformation t is biunique, the ranking operation (i.e., the determination of the index of the argument in $\boldsymbol{k}$) can be completed by a mapping vector whose components are selected by the index $j = t(\boldsymbol{k}_i) - \boldsymbol{d}_1 + 1$, and whose dimension is equal to the spread of t in $\boldsymbol{k}$. The key transformation of the preceding example is biunique when restricted to the set $\boldsymbol{x} =$ (Sunday, Monday, Tuesday), the set of derived keys is (13, 19, 20), and the mapping vector $\boldsymbol{m} = (2, \circ, \circ, \circ, \circ, \circ, 1, 3)$ of dimension eight serves to complete the mapping if its components are selected by the index $j = t(\boldsymbol{x}_i) - 12$.

A key transformation is called *j-origin* if $\boldsymbol{d}_1 = j$. Since the origin can be changed by subtraction of a constant, attention will be restricted to 1-origin transformations. The spread of a 1-origin transformation is clearly $\boldsymbol{d}_\nu$.

A biunique key transformation is always attainable since, as remarked in the treatment of directed scan, the base b value of the representation of the elements of the domain $\boldsymbol{k}$ can be used. The spread of such a transformation may, however, be impracticably large. If, for example, $\boldsymbol{x}$ were some small subset of the set of all ten-letter sequences, (e.g., all meaningful ten-letter words), then s would be 26^{10}, and the required dimension of the associated mapping vector would be impracticably large.

In general, if each element of $\boldsymbol{k}$ is of dimension h in $\boldsymbol{\pi}$ and if the (used) range of each element of $\boldsymbol{\pi}$ is the set $\iota^0(b)$, then the mapping vector required is of dimension b^h. The use of the base b value of the representation in selecting the component of the mapping vector is equivalent to selecting a path through a uniform b-way tree as illustrated (using 0-origin indexing) in Fig. 4.6, for $b = 3$ and $h = 3$. The branch to the jth level is selected according to the jth component of the representation.

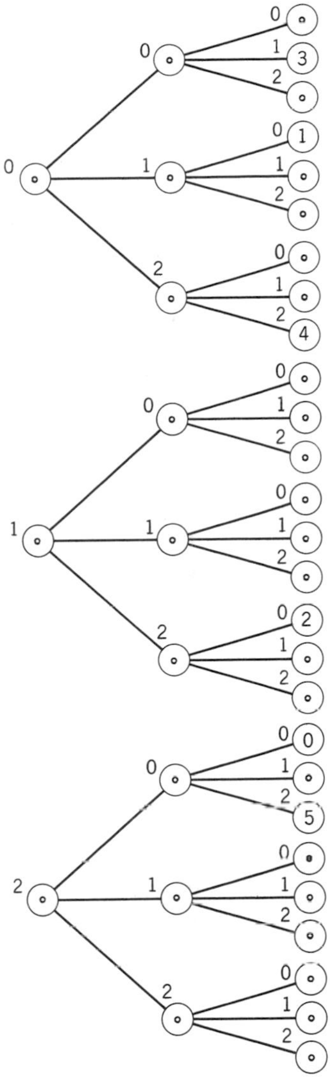

Figure 4.6 Uniform tree and mapping vector for the set $\boldsymbol{k}$ = (200, 010, 120, 001, 022, 202)

Sequential level-by-level selection in the tree is less convenient than the direct use of the base b value, except that the former frequently allows the full tree to be greatly contracted. If, for example, the tree of Fig. 4.6 is used for the set $\boldsymbol{k} = (200, 010, 120, 001, 022, 202)$ (as indicated by the numeric leaves whose values are the 0-origin ranks in $\boldsymbol{k}$), then the full tree can be contracted to the nonhomogeneous tree of Fig. 4.7. The contraction is defined formally as follows: if the subtree rooted in a given node contains no significant leaves, the subtree is replaced by a single null leaf; if the subtree contains exactly one significant leaf, the subtree is replaced by that leaf. The contracted tree can then be represented by a chain list matrix or, since all nodes save the leaves are null, by a leaf list matrix $\boldsymbol{M}$. For the example of Fig. 4.6,

$$\begin{array}{r} \mathbf{0}\\ \mathbf{1}\\ \mathbf{2}\\ \mathbf{3}\\ \mathbf{4}\\ \mathbf{5}\\ \mathbf{6}\\ \mathbf{7}\\ \mathbf{8}\\ \mathbf{9}\\ \mathbf{10}\\ \mathbf{11} \end{array} \quad M = \begin{pmatrix} 3 & 0\\ 2 & 1\\ 6 & 0\\ 3 & 1\\ 1 & 1\\ 4 & 1\\ 9 & 0\\ \circ & 0\\ \circ & 0\\ 0 & 1\\ \circ & 0\\ 5 & 1 \end{pmatrix}$$

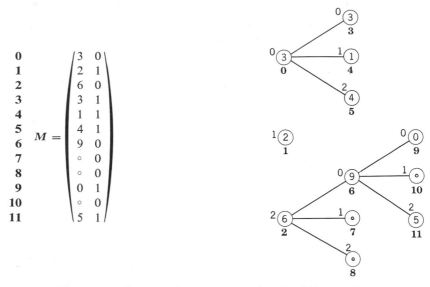

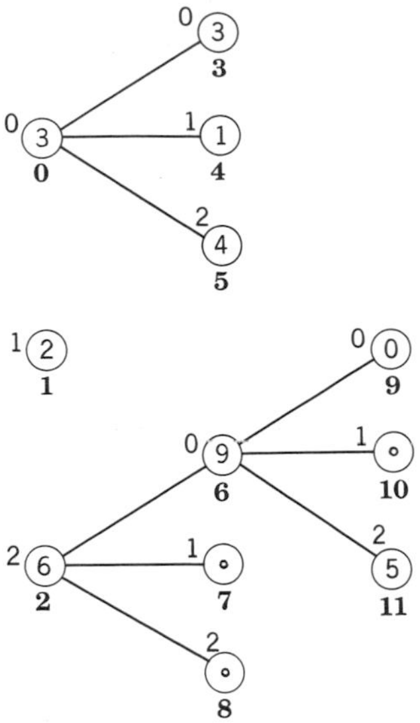

Figure 4.7 Contracted tree and associated leaf list matrix $\boldsymbol{M}$ for the set $\boldsymbol{k} = (200, 010, 120, 001, 022, 202)$

$\boldsymbol{M}$ is given in Fig. 4.7. The sequential biunique key transformation on the leaf list matrix of the contracted tree is described by Program 4.8.

Program 4.8. The components of the argument $\boldsymbol{x}$ are scanned by the index j, and step 5 determines i as the index of the current node in the path. If node i is not a leaf, then step 6 determines k as the index of the first node reachable from node i. If node i is a leaf, then k is specified as the value of the leaf, and the right-pointing exit is followed on step 8 unless the exit at step 7 is taken first. This exit occurs only if $\boldsymbol{x}$ is an illegitimate argument which leads to one of the null leaves (such as the last leaf of Fig. 4.7) remaining in the contracted tree. The contraction was performed in the specified manner so as to allow the incorporation of such a test. If it is not required, the tree can be further contracted by eliminating the null leaves. The left-pointing exit on step 4 also indicates an illegitimate argument $\boldsymbol{x}$, but one of insufficient dimension for the particular path specified.

The biunique key transformation provided by Program 4.8 is very effective when applied to a set whose dimension is small compared to the spread of the transformation produced by taking the base b value of the representation as, for example, in a glossary of English words.* A disadvantage of the process is the need to revise the entire leaf list matrix when additions to or changes in the argument set occur. The process can

* See, for example, Lamb and Jacobsen (1961).

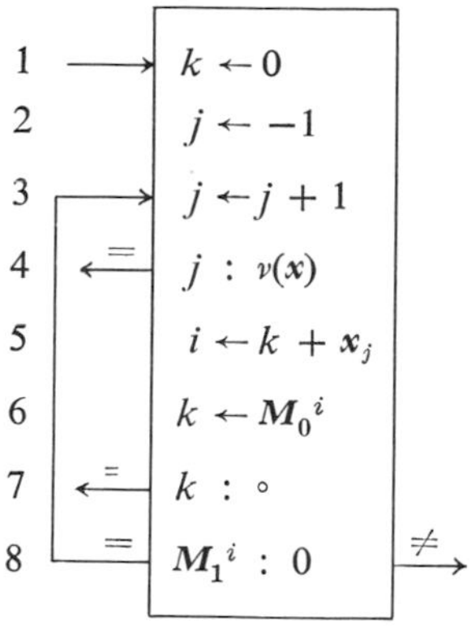

	0-origin indexing
$\boldsymbol{x}$	Argument.
i	Current node.
j	Current index of argument.
k	Index of first node reachable from node i and finally the rank of $\boldsymbol{x}$.
$\boldsymbol{M}$	Leaf list matrix.
$\boldsymbol{M}_1$	$\boldsymbol{M}_1^h = 1 \Leftrightarrow h$ is a leaf.
$\boldsymbol{M}_0$	Combined leaf and chaining vector.

Legend

Program 4.8 Biunique transformation on key represented by $\boldsymbol{x}$, using the leaf list of the contracted tree of key set $\boldsymbol{k}$.

be modified to produce a simpler but nonunique transformation by contracting the tree further so that some or all of the remaining leaves each represent two or more significant leaves of the original tree.

Nonunique key transformations

Although it is frequently impossible to obtain a sufficiently simple biunique transformation having a sufficiently small spread, it is always possible to produce a simple key transformation of arbitrarily small spread if the requirement of uniqueness is dropped. For example, the spread of the key transformation

$$j \leftarrow \lfloor((b\boldsymbol{\epsilon}) \perp \rho(x)) \div d\rfloor$$

varies inversely with d, but the transformation is usually nonunique for $d > 1$.

If a key transformation is not unique, the ranking must be completed by a scan of one of the equivalence classes which it defines. The scan of each of the equivalence classes $\boldsymbol{e}^j$ may, in general, be either directed or controlled, and the individual subsets may be ordered by frequency of occurrence, by the base b value of their representations, or by some externally imposed (e.g., chronological) order. If a chained representation or file is used for each subset, a directed scan is normally used.

The expected length of a directed scan of each of the equivalence classes $\boldsymbol{e}^j$ may be computed and weighted by the relative frequency of the class to yield an expected over-all scan length. If the distribution of arguments is uniform, the expected scan length for e^j is given by

$$(\nu(e^j) + 1) \div 2 = (c_j + 1) \div 2,$$

where c is the coalescence of the transformation. Moreover, the relative frequency of arguments from e^j is $c_j \div (+/c)$. Consequently, the over-all expected scan length l is given by

$$l = \frac{[(c + \epsilon) \overset{+}{\times} c]}{2(+/c)} = \left[1 + \frac{c \overset{+}{\times} c}{c \overset{+}{\times} \epsilon}\right] \div 2.$$

For a fixed dimension of the derived set d (and hence of c), and for a necessarily fixed value of $+/c = \nu(k)$, the value of l is clearly minimized if the coalescence vector c is uniform, i.e., if the components of c are all equal. Hence the expected scan length is minimized by a key transformation whose equivalence classes are of equal dimension.

A given key transformation is frequently employed to rank a variety of subsets of its domain k rather than k itself. For example, if k is the set of English words in a given dictionary, then one of the subsets to be ranked may be the set of distinct words in a particular sample of English text. If a particular subset of k is specified, then the coalescence of the key transformation in the specified subset x can be determined, and the transformation can be chosen accordingly. More generally (as in the case of samples of English text), the active domain x may be only partially specified. The transformation should then be chosen so that its coalescence is nearly uniform for the expected active domains. If, for example, k is the set of all five-letter sequences, and if each active domain is the set of five-letter sequences beginning with a specified letter, then the key transformation used should depend only on the last four letters. If the set of derived keys produced by a key transformation has a spread s and a random uniform distribution within that spread, then the expected length of a scan (of the equivalence classes) can be shown* to be $1 + \nu(k) \div 2s$.

Scanning of the equivalence classes. If an element x is to be ranked in k by a scan of k itself, no auxiliary information is required since the rank of component k_j is simply its index j. If some permutation of k is used instead, then an auxiliary ranking vector r (i.e., a permutation vector) must provide the rank in the given set k. Specifically, if $y = p \int k$ is used for ranking, then r is the permutation vector inverse to p, and the rank of element y_j is r_j. Finally, if the vector y is itself to be scanned in some prescribed order other than simple cyclic order, the order may be represented by a chaining vector q.

The vectors y and r or y, r, and q can be combined into a two-column

* See Johnson (1961) and Exercise 4.4.

matrix S or a three-column matrix C which contains all information requisite to the ranking operation. More generally, a collection of matrices F, V, etc., can be used, each representing some subset of the given key set k.

The method of scanning the equivalence classes defined by a given key transformation is largely determined by the type of matrix or matrices used to represent the key set k. The five major methods of practical interest are enumerated below. Each is illustrated in Fig. 4.9. A 1-origin key transformation t is assumed.

(a) *Overflow.* A two-column matrix F of column dimension $s = d_\nu$ represents the first elements of the equivalence classes (and their ranks), as follows:

$$F_1^{d_j} = e_1^{\,j},\ j \in \iota^1(\nu(d)),$$

$$F_1^{\,i} = \circ,\ i \notin d.$$

All remaining elements of the sets (i.e., $\bar{\alpha}^1/e^i$) are represented in arbitrary order in a two-column "overflow" matrix V.

The scan procedure is given by the Program of Fig. 4.9*a*. If the given argument x is not equal to $F_1^{t(x)}$, then the overflow matrix V is scanned in ascending order. The left-pointing exit indicates that $x \notin k$.

For a uniform distribution, the expected scan length is clearly given by

$$l = 1 + ((\mu(V) + 1) \times \mu(V)) \div 2\nu(k),$$

where $\mu(V) = \nu(k) - \nu(d)$. The expected scan length is therefore large unless the average dimension of the equivalence classes (that is, $\nu(k) \div \nu(d)$) is close to unity. For a known nonuniform distribution, the expected scan can be reduced by placing the most frequent element of each equivalence class in F and ordering the elements in V according to their frequency.

(b) *Overflow with chaining.* The two-column matrices F and V used in method (a) can each be augmented by a third column chaining vector which chains each equivalence class. Thus $F_3^{d_k}$ is the row index in V of element $e_2^{\,k}$ if it exists, and is otherwise null. Similarly, if $V_1^{\,h} = e_j^{\,i}$, then $V_3^{\,h}$ is the row index in V of e_{j+1}^{i} if it exists, and is otherwise null. The program is given in Fig. 4.9*b*. The expected scan length for a uniform distribution can, as shown earlier, be expressed in terms of the coalescence vector c as follows:

$$l = \left(1 + \frac{c \overset{+}{\times} c}{c \overset{+}{\times} \epsilon}\right) \div 2\,.$$

(c) *Single table with chaining.* In the overflow methods [(a) and (b)], certain rows of the matrix F go unused, and a saving in storage can be

$\boldsymbol{k}$ = (Sunday, Monday, Tuesday, Wednesday, Thursday, Friday, Saturday)

$t(\boldsymbol{k}_i) = 1 + (6 |_0\, \boldsymbol{n}_i)$, where

$\boldsymbol{n}$ = (19, 13, 20, 23, 20, 6, 19)

($\boldsymbol{n}_i$ is the rank in the alphabet of the first letter of $\boldsymbol{k}_i$)

$\boldsymbol{z}$ = (2, 2, 3, 6, 3, 1, 2), where $\boldsymbol{z}_i = t(\boldsymbol{k}_i)$,

$\boldsymbol{d}$ = (1, 2, 3, 6), and $s = 6$.

Data of examples

$\boldsymbol{F} =$

1	Friday	6
2	Sunday	1
3	Tuesday	3
4	∘	∘
5	∘	∘
6	Wednesday	4

$\boldsymbol{V} =$

1	Monday	2
2	Thursday	5
3	Saturday	7

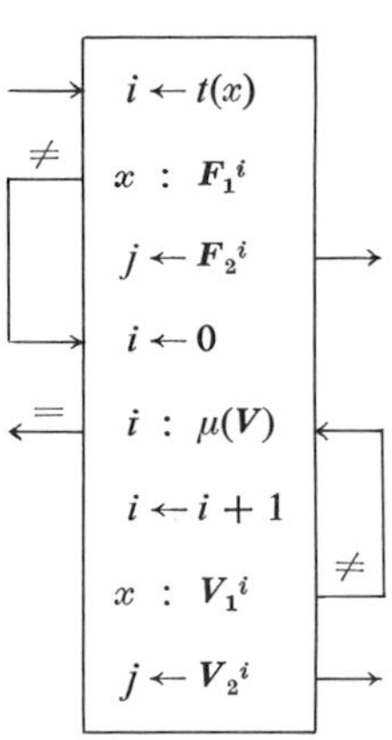

Overflow
(*a*)

$\boldsymbol{F} =$

1	Friday	6	∘
2	Sunday	1	1
3	Tuesday	3	2
4	∘	∘	∘
5	∘	∘	∘
6	Wednesday	4	∘

$\boldsymbol{V} =$

1	Monday	2	3
2	Thursday	5	∘
3	Saturday	7	∘

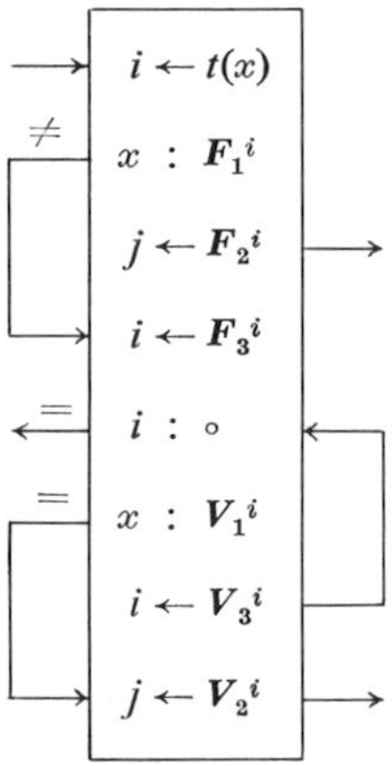

Overflow with chaining
(*b*)

$\boldsymbol{T} =$

1	Friday	6	∘
2	Sunday	1	4
3	Tuesday	3	5
4	Monday	2	7
5	Thursday	5	∘
6	Wednesday	4	∘
7	Saturday	7	∘

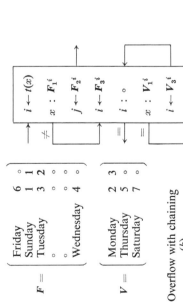

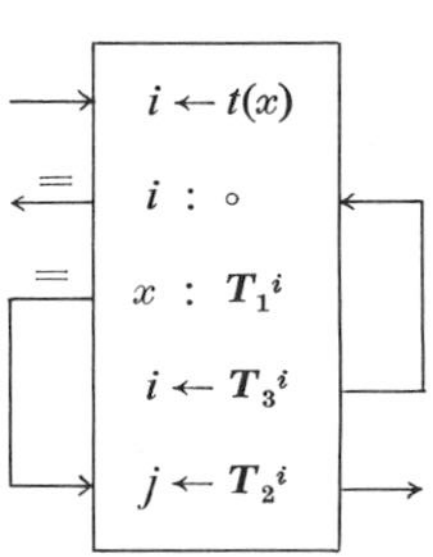

Single table with chaining
(*c*)

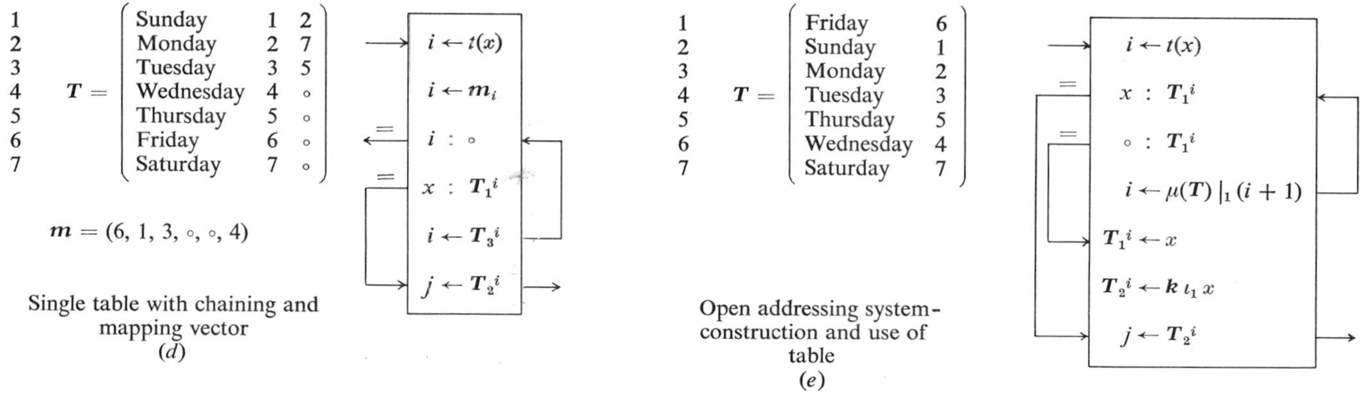

Figure 4.9 Programs and examples for methods of scanning equivalence classes defined by a 1-origin key transformation t

effected by combining the three-column matrices $\boldsymbol{F}$ and $\boldsymbol{V}$ in a single table $\boldsymbol{T}$ of column dimension

$$\mu(\boldsymbol{T}) = \max(s, \nu(\boldsymbol{k})), \qquad \text{where } s = \boldsymbol{d}_\nu = \mu(\boldsymbol{F}).$$

Let $\boldsymbol{u}$ be a logical vector such that $\boldsymbol{u}/\iota^1(\mu(\boldsymbol{F})) = \boldsymbol{d}$. Then $\overline{\boldsymbol{u}}//\boldsymbol{F}$ constitutes the unused and $\boldsymbol{u}//\boldsymbol{F}$ the used rows of $\boldsymbol{F}$. Let $\boldsymbol{v}$ be a vector of dimension $\mu(\boldsymbol{T})$ obtained by appending a zero suffix to $\boldsymbol{u}$. The first two columns of $\boldsymbol{T}$ are then defined as follows:

$$\boldsymbol{v}//(\boldsymbol{\alpha}^2/\boldsymbol{T}) = \boldsymbol{u}//(\boldsymbol{\alpha}^2/\boldsymbol{F}),$$
$$\overline{\boldsymbol{v}}//(\boldsymbol{\alpha}^2/\boldsymbol{T}) = \boldsymbol{\alpha}^2/(\boldsymbol{V}^{\boldsymbol{p}}),$$

where $\boldsymbol{p} \supseteq \iota^1(\mu(\boldsymbol{V}))$ and $\nu(\boldsymbol{p}) = +/\overline{\boldsymbol{v}}$. (The vector $\boldsymbol{p}$ permits an arbitrary reordering of the rows of $\boldsymbol{V}$). The third column of $\boldsymbol{T}$ is a chaining vector which chains each of the equivalence classes $\boldsymbol{e}^i$.

The appropriate scan program (Fig. 4.9*c*) is similar to that of method (b), and the expected scan length is identical. The serious disadvantage of the method lies in the construction of the matrix $\boldsymbol{T}$—all of the rows (specified by $\boldsymbol{v}$) required for the leading elements of the equivalence classes must be known before any of the nonleading elements can be allocated. The table $\boldsymbol{T}$ is therefore usually constructed in two passes over the given key set. Moreover, any addition to, or change in, the active key set $\boldsymbol{k}$ which introduces a new equivalence class may occasion reallocation of some row of $\boldsymbol{T}$.

(d) *Single table with chaining and mapping vector.* The main deficiency remarked in method (c) is occasioned by the fixed vector $\boldsymbol{v}$ and the fixed order of the rows of $\boldsymbol{v}//\boldsymbol{T}$, both imposed by the given key transformation t. The difficulty can be shifted from the matrix $\boldsymbol{T}$ to a mapping vector $\boldsymbol{m}$ which is used (as indicated in the program of Fig. 4.9*d*) to effect a further transformation of the index $i = t(x)$. The rows of $\boldsymbol{T}$ may then be arranged in any desired order, provided only that for each $h \in \iota^1(\nu(\boldsymbol{d}))$, $\boldsymbol{m}_i = j$, where $\boldsymbol{e}_1{}^h = \boldsymbol{k}_k = \boldsymbol{T}_1{}^j$, and $t(\boldsymbol{e}_1{}^h) = i$. Moreover, if $\boldsymbol{T}_1 = \boldsymbol{k}$, then the ranking vector $\boldsymbol{T}_2$ may be omitted.

Except for the extra step occasioned by the operation $j \leftarrow \boldsymbol{m}_i$, the expected scan length is again the same as for method (b). However, the requirement that $\mu(\boldsymbol{T}) \geq \max(s, \nu(\boldsymbol{k}))$ may now be relaxed to the form $\mu(\boldsymbol{T}) \geq \nu(\boldsymbol{k})$, whereas $\nu(\boldsymbol{m})$ must equal or exceed s. Since the squared length of the coalescence vector (that is, $\boldsymbol{c} \overset{+}{\underset{\times}{}} \boldsymbol{c}$) can, in general, be reduced by increasing the spread s of the transformation t, the expected scan length can now be reduced at the cost of increasing the dimension of the mapping vector $\boldsymbol{m}$ rather than at the (usually much higher) cost of increasing the column dimension of T. A similar advantage can be gained by employing the mapping vector m in methods (a), (b), and (c).

(e) *Open addressing system.** The open addressing system employs a single table T but requires neither the chaining vector T_3 nor the mapping vector m. As shown by the program of Fig. 4.9*e*, each argument x is obtained by a forward scan of T_1, beginning at component $T_1^{t(x)}$. Since the scan is cyclic, it is necessarily successful. It can also be made fairly efficient by constructing T as follows. The matrix is first specified as a matrix of nulls. The elements of k are then assigned in order, element k_j being assigned to the first unassigned row following row $t(k_j) - 1$.

The program of Fig. 4.9*e* describes both the construction and the use of the table T. The branch on step 3 can occur only if the element x has not yet been entered in the matrix T, and steps 5 and 6 then complete its entry and the specification of the corresponding component of the ranking vector T_2. The use of T can, in fact, proceed concurrently with its construction, i.e., each argument x presented to the program defines a new entry in T if it has not previously occurred, the k index of x being determined by some algorithm independent of T.

If the active argument set k is not fixed, it may be desired either to add new elements or to respecify the rank of some element already defined in T. Respecification may be incorporated by allowing the scan used in defining an entry in T to terminate on encountering either the null element or the argument itself. Although respecification of an entry may be allowed, *deletion* of an entry and its replacement by the null element cannot, for the occurrence of such an inserted null element between the beginning point $i = t(k_j)$ and the point at which k_j is entered in T would later cause an erroneous indication that k_j was not defined in T. Replacement of a deleted entry by a special "deletion character" distinct from the null element could, however, be used.

The expected scan length in the open addressing system exceeds that for method (d), since the expected length of scan of each equivalence class is increased by the potential interleaving of elements from different equivalence classes. Thus, in the example of Fig. 4.9*e*, the expected scan lengths for each of the equivalence classes (Sunday, Monday, Saturday), (Tuesday, Thursday), (Wednesday), and (Friday) are $(1 + 2 + 6)/3$, $(2 + 3)/2$, 1, and 1, respectively, yielding an over-all expected scan length of 16/7. The corresponding scan lengths for a chained scan (e.g., method (d)) are $(1 + 2 + 3)/3$, $(1 + 2)/2$, 1 and 1, with an over-all expected scan length of 11/7. However, since it uses a fixed scan, the open addressing system is better suited to a serial store than is the chained system.

* The open addressing system appears to have been first used by A. L. Samuel, G. M. Amdahl, and E. Boehm in constructing address tables for an assembly program.

If the derived keys are uniformly distributed in the range 1 to $\mu(\boldsymbol{T})$ then, as shown by Schay and Spruth (1961), the expected scan length is $1 + \rho \div 2(1 - \rho)$, where $\rho = \nu(\boldsymbol{k}) \div \mu(\boldsymbol{T})$. For a nonuniform distribution, the expected scan length can be reduced by allocating the most frequent elements first, i.e., by defining $\boldsymbol{T}$ from the set $\boldsymbol{k}$ reordered in descending order on frequency.

Bucket files. In certain files the locations divide naturally into blocks or *buckets* of n successive locations each, such that the entire contents of any bucket can be scanned in virtually the same time required to scan any one location in the bucket. Such a file is called a *bucket file* (Peterson, 1957). In a magnetic disc file, for example, each track forms a bucket. Each of the foregoing methods of scanning equivalence classes can be adapted to suit the characteristics of a bucket file. The equivalence classes can be grouped in buckets, with chaining provided only from bucket to bucket.

*Clustering.** The active argument sets of interest may be relatively small subsets of the complete set $\boldsymbol{k}$. Moreover, their elements commonly share some characteristic so that a key transformation which gives uniform coalescence and uniform spacing of the derived keys with respect to $\boldsymbol{k}$ may yield highly nonuniform coalescence or nonuniform spacing, or both, with respect to a given active domain $\boldsymbol{x}$. This effect is called *clustering*. If, for example, each element of $\boldsymbol{k}$ is represented by a vector of decimal digits of dimension ten, then the key transformation

$$t(x) = \lfloor((10\boldsymbol{\epsilon}) \perp \boldsymbol{\rho}(x)) \div 10^7\rfloor$$

yields a mapping onto the range $\boldsymbol{\iota}^0(10^3)$ which has both uniform coalescence and uniform spacing. On the active domain $\boldsymbol{x}$, whose elements are all represented by vectors $\boldsymbol{\rho}(x)$ such that $\boldsymbol{\alpha}^3/\boldsymbol{\rho}(x) = (2, 4, 7)$, however, all elements "cluster" in the single derived key 247.

The deleterious effects of such correlations among elements of the active domain can be reduced by employing key transformations which depend on all components of the representation and do so in a manner which shows no systematic relationship to the structure of the representation. The *mid-square method*, for example, consists in squaring the given key and extracting the middle digits of the resulting product. A commonly used transformation is the taking of residues modulo some number m such that $m \geq \nu(\boldsymbol{x})$ and is either prime or contains few factors.

* *Note added in proof:* M. Hanan and F. P. Palermo offer an important solution to clustering by the application of Bose-Chaudhuri codes. R. T. Chien and C. V. Freiman have remarked a similar application of Fire codes (private communications).

4.3 MULTIPLE KEYS*

If in some mapping operation the access to both the key set and the set of correspondents is serial (or partially serial), considerable advantage can be gained by replacing the vector $\boldsymbol{T}_2$ of ranks by the suitably reordered set of correspondents, that is, $\boldsymbol{T}_2{}^i$ becomes the correspondent of the key $\boldsymbol{T}_1{}^i$. For, the ranking operation on the argument $\boldsymbol{k}_j$ which gives access to the element $\boldsymbol{T}_1{}^i = \boldsymbol{k}_j$ also gives immediate access to the correspondent $\boldsymbol{T}_2{}^i$ in the same row $\boldsymbol{T}^i$. This is equivalent to eliminating the permutation operation (through reordering of the set of correspondents) and coalescing the ranking and selection phases so that together they require a single access to the (partially) serial memory.

For a single functional correspondence, the coalescing of the ranking and selection phases can (by a suitable ordering of $\boldsymbol{T}$) be accomplished by the single-table process (Fig. 4.9*c*) without introducing the mapping vector $\boldsymbol{m}$ of process (d). Frequently, however, a number of related functional correspondences must be provided between pairs of a family of vectors $\boldsymbol{Q}_j$ so ordered that $\boldsymbol{Q}_i{}^k$ corresponds to $\boldsymbol{Q}_j{}^k$ for all i, j, and k. In an accounting system, for example, $\boldsymbol{Q}_1$, $\boldsymbol{Q}_2$, $\boldsymbol{Q}_3$, and $\boldsymbol{Q}_4$ might be, respectively, the vector of account numbers, names, addresses, and balances in a given ledger. Those vectors which may occur as arguments in a mapping process are called key vectors; those which never occur as arguments are called *satellite vectors*.

$\boldsymbol{Q}$ may be reordered (and augmented by a suitable chaining vector) so as to permit the use of the program of Fig. 4.9*c* for some selected key set $\boldsymbol{Q}_i$. However, for any other key set $\boldsymbol{Q}_j$, the order will, in general, be unsuitable. The program of Fig. 4.9*d* may, however, be used together with an appropriate mapping vector $\boldsymbol{m}^j$ and chaining vector $\boldsymbol{q}^j$. For the sake of uniformity and the advantage of allowing an arbitrary ordering for $\boldsymbol{Q}$, the distinguished key set $\boldsymbol{Q}_i$ may also be provided with a mapping vector $\boldsymbol{m}^i$ and treated like the rest.

The generalized binary search of Program 4.4 can be applied to the case of multiple keys by providing a pair of chaining vectors ($\boldsymbol{M}_2$ and $\boldsymbol{M}_3$) for each key. The open addressing system is clearly unsuited to multiple keys.

REFERENCES

Burks, A. W., D. W. Warren, and J. B. Wright, (1954) "An Analysis of a Logical Machine Using Parenthesis-free Notation," *Mathematical Tables and Other Aids to Computation*, vol. VIII, pp. 53–57.

Cramèr, Harald, (1951), *Mathematical Methods of Statistics*, Princeton University Press.

* See Johnson (1961).

Johnson, L. R., (1961), "An Indirect Chaining Method for Addressing on Secondary Keys," *Communications of the Association for Computing Machinery*, vol. 4, No. 5, pp. 218–222.

Lamb, S. M. and W. H. Jacobsen, Jr., (1961), "A High-Speed Large Capacity Dictionary System," *Mechanical Translation*, vol. 6, pp. 76–107.

Lukasiewicz, Jan, (1951), *Aristotle's Syllogistic from the Standpoint of Modern Formal Logic*, Clarendon Press, Oxford, England, p. 78.

Peterson, W. W., (1957), "Addressing for Random-Access Storage," *IBM Journal of Research and Development*, vol. I, pp. 130–146.

Schay, G., Jr., and W. G. Spruth, (1961) "Analysis of a File Addressing Method," Technical Memorandum 17–051, Advanced Systems Development Division, IBM Corporation, New York.

EXERCISES

4.1 Give a formal proof of the fact that the binary search of Program 4.3 will not work properly if steps 5 and 6 are replaced by the statements $k \leftarrow j$ and $i \leftarrow j$, respectively.

4.2 (a) The argument $\boldsymbol{k}_i$ in the set of keys $\boldsymbol{k} = (\boldsymbol{k}_1, \boldsymbol{k}_2, \ldots, \boldsymbol{k}_\nu)$ occurs with the relative unnormalized frequency i. For the case $\nu(\boldsymbol{k}) = 10$, design the matrix $\boldsymbol{M}$ which will minimize the expected scan length when applying Program 4.4.

(b) Show how additional keys may be incorporated in the system of part (a) without revising the entire matrix $\boldsymbol{M}$. Discuss the effects on the expected scan length.

4.3 Consider the ledger $\boldsymbol{L}$ defined as

$\boldsymbol{L} =$

3125	ADAMS, S. H.○○	435○ASH○○○○○○○
0168	BAKER, J. C.○○	76○ELM○○○○○○○○
7926	FOX, R. L.○○○○	435○LAUREL○○○○
3420	FOX, R. L.○○○○	435○LAUREL○○○○
1925	HILL, K.○○○○○	118○LINDEN○○○○
2486	JONES, J. C.○○	61○MAPLE○○○○○○
9127	JONES, J. C.○○	736○LINDEN○○○○
6135	KING, K. M.○○○	76○ELM○○○○○○○○

and the argument domains $\boldsymbol{k}^1$, $\boldsymbol{k}^2$, and $\boldsymbol{k}^3$, consisting of all 4-digit decimal numbers (account numbers), all 12-letter names (in capitals, with null fill), and all 14-character addresses (alphanumeric with null fill), respectively, and let the rows of $\boldsymbol{\alpha}^4/\boldsymbol{L}$, $(4 \downarrow \boldsymbol{\alpha}^{12})/\boldsymbol{L}$, and $\boldsymbol{\omega}^{14}/\boldsymbol{L}$ represent the corresponding active domains $\boldsymbol{x}^1$, $\boldsymbol{x}^2$, and $\boldsymbol{x}^3$.

(a) Specify a simple key transformation on the set $\boldsymbol{k}^1$ whose range lies in the set $\boldsymbol{\iota}^1(\mu(\boldsymbol{L}))$, which, when applied to the active key set $\boldsymbol{x}^1$, yields a derived key set of dimension three or greater.

(b) Reorder the ledger $\boldsymbol{L}$ and add a chaining vector to chain the equivalence classes so that the resulting matrix $\boldsymbol{M}$ may be used with the key transformation of part (a) and a program of the type of Program 4.9*c*. Show the resulting matrix $\boldsymbol{M}$ and the specific program used for selecting the row $\boldsymbol{M}^i$ determined by an argument $a \in \boldsymbol{x}^1$.

(c) Specify simple key transformations on each of the sets $\boldsymbol{k}^2$ and $\boldsymbol{k}^3$ which yield derived sets of dimension not less than three when applied to the active domains $\boldsymbol{x}^2$ and $\boldsymbol{x}^3$, respectively.

(d) Augment the matrix $\boldsymbol{M}$ of part (b) by a permutation vector and a chaining vector suited to each of the key transformations of part (c).

(e) Write a program which selects, as a function of a and j, the row of $\boldsymbol{M}$ corresponding to the argument $a \in \boldsymbol{x}^j$, for $j = 1, 2,$ or 3.

4.4 Let $\boldsymbol{t}_i = t(\boldsymbol{k}_i)$, where t is a key transformation such that $\boldsymbol{t} \subseteq \iota^1(\nu(\boldsymbol{k}))$. The vector $\boldsymbol{t}$ takes on n^n distinct values (where $n = \nu(\boldsymbol{k})$), which are assumed to be equiprobable. For $n = 2$, the cases are (1, 1), (1, 2), (2, 1), and (2, 2), with expected scan lengths 1, $\frac{3}{2}$, 1, and $\frac{3}{2}$.

(a) Show that the over-all expected scan length is 1.25 for $n = 2$.

(b) Calculate the expected scan lengths for $n = 3$ and for $n = 4$.

(c) Generalize the result of part (b) to show that the expected scan length rapidly approaches 1.5. [See Johnson (1961) for an alternative derivation.]

4.5 Design an open addressing system for the ledger $\boldsymbol{L}$ of Exercise 4.3 and the key transformation of part (a).

4.6 Program and discuss the extension of binary search to m-way search.

4.7 Let $\boldsymbol{l}_i$ be the time required to scan over the ith element of a vector $\boldsymbol{x}$ which is represented in a chained (or other serially-scanned) representation, and let $\boldsymbol{f}_i$ be the frequency of occurrence of the argument $\boldsymbol{x}_i$. Discuss the role of the "standardized frequency" $\boldsymbol{s} = \boldsymbol{f} \div \boldsymbol{l}$ in determining the optimum ordering of the vector $\boldsymbol{x}$.

4.8 The *neighbors* problem requires that the near neighbors of an object in n-dimensional space be found. The technique used depends on the dimensionality and the particular criteria of adjacency.

(a) The position of a vehicle on a turnpike is represented by the distance in miles of the vehicle from the south end, and $\boldsymbol{p}_i$ is the coordinate of the ith patrol car. Write programs to:

(i) identify the patrol car nearest an accident at position a,

(ii) identify the two cars nearest to each other.

(b) A three-column matrix $\boldsymbol{V}$ specifies the locations and radio call-signs of a fleet of merchant vessels on a flat lake, where $\boldsymbol{V}_1{}^i$ is the call-sign of the ith vessel, $\boldsymbol{V}_2{}^i$ is its distance in miles from the meridian tangent to the lake on the west, $\boldsymbol{V}_3{}^i$ is its distance in miles from the perpendicular tangent to the lake on the south. Write a program to determine the call-sign of the neighbor nearest to a distressed vessel whose call-sign c is given.

(c) The matrix of part (b) is used to specify call-signs and locations at time t of a fleet of bombers over a flat territory. When each bomb is released, neighboring planes must be at a safe distance. Construct a program which will find the call-signs of all pairs of planes within r miles of each other at time t.

(d) In a certain hydrodynamic calculation, the motion of each elementary volume of fluid is traced. The ith elementary volume is described by row $\boldsymbol{L}^i$ of a matrix: $(4 \downarrow \boldsymbol{\alpha}^3)/\boldsymbol{L}$ represents the three space coordinates (in a rectilinear system), and $\overline{\boldsymbol{\alpha}}^7/\boldsymbol{L}$ represents the remaining parameters. At each time step the parameters of volume i are redetermined by those of the four elements nearest it. Write a program to determine $\boldsymbol{\alpha}^4/\boldsymbol{L}^i$ as the set of indices of the four nearest neighbors of element i. *Hint.* Attach an explicit index vector before sorting.

chapter 5

METAPROGRAMS

It is frequently necessary to treat a program as an argument of some process, as in the systematic analysis of a faulty program or in the translation of a program expressed in one language to an equivalent program expressed in a second language. Such a process defined on programs may itself be formalized as a *meta*program.

Formally, a *metaprogram* is defined as a program whose domain is a set of programs, each element of the domain being called an *argument program*. If the range of a metaprogram is also a set of programs, the metaprogram is called a *translator*. An element of the range of a translator is called a *function program*; i.e., a translator operates on argument programs to produce function programs. A metaprogram whose range is not a set of programs is called an *analyzer*. Thus an analyzer produces, not a function program, but data useful in the analysis or application of the argument program. If, for example, the instructions of a computer program are sorted on the data address and listed, the list brings together all data references to each register used and therefore facilitates analysis of the (possibly conflicting) uses of registers in the program. A metaprogram which schedules and directs the execution of other programs (and metaprograms) is called a *director* or *supervisor*.

Four main types of translator are distinguished: compilers, assemblers, generators, and interpreters. A *compiler* accepts programs expressed in a given language (the *argument language*) and produces corresponding programs expressed in a second language (the *function language*).

An *assembler* is a special case of a compiler which is limited as follows: (1) the statements of the argument program are virtually independent and may therefore be treated one at a time, and (2) the statements of the argument program are *simple* (not compound) and need not be analyzed into component statements. There usually exists a fixed correspondence between the operations of the argument program and those of the function program; the translation thus consists essentially of a substitution of symbols for the operations and/or operands.

A *generator* produces, by specialization, any one of a family of function programs. Thus a single generator might, for each specified value of n, produce a specialized program for evaluating the function x^n. The argument of a generator is usually viewed as two distinct parts; the *skeleton program*, which determines the family of potential function programs, and the *specification*, which determines the particular member of the family produced. Generators are frequently incorporated in compilers.

A translator is called an *interpreter* if it (1) executes the segment of function program corresponding to a statement of the argument program immediately after it is produced, and (2) selects the statements of the argument program in a sequence determined by the execution of the function program. The function program itself is normally treated as an intermediate result, and only the outputs of the executed argument program are retained. The execution of an interpreter can therefore be viewed as follows: each statement of the argument program is first "interpreted" in the function language and is then executed.

The *trace program* and the *utility program* are special cases of the interpreter. The former executes the argument program without modification but produces, in addition to the normal outputs of the argument program, a *trace* of the argument program listing each instruction executed and the intermediate results produced. In a narrow sense, a utility program is an interpreter whose argument program is supplied directly by a computer operator via the control console. More broadly, the term is used to denote any program frequently used by the computer operator.

The present discussion of metaprograms will be limited to one important aspect of compilers, the analysis of compound statements occurring in the argument program. The treatment embraces the translation between the common parenthesis notation and the Lukasiewicz (1951) notation which proves most convenient in the analysis of compound statements.

5.1 COMPOUND STATEMENTS

Each statement of a program can be considered as an *operator* which maps the given operands into the specified result. If the operator corresponding to a given statement belongs to a given set of operators $\boldsymbol{p}$, the statement is said to be *elementary* in $\boldsymbol{p}$. A finite program whose operators all belong to a set $\boldsymbol{p}$ is called a *program in* $\boldsymbol{p}$. A statement which is not elementary in $\boldsymbol{p}$ but which can be expressed as a finite program in $\boldsymbol{p}$ is said to be *compound in* $\boldsymbol{p}$. The *analysis in* $\boldsymbol{p}$ of a compound statement is the specification of a corresponding finite program in $\boldsymbol{p}$.

For example, the statement

$$z \leftarrow (x + y) \times r + (s - t)^n$$

is compound in the operator set

$$\boldsymbol{p} = (\text{addition, subtraction, multiplication, exponentiation}),$$

and Program 5.1*a* shows one possible analysis in $\boldsymbol{p}$. Program 5.1*b* shows a similar analysis in the set

$$\boldsymbol{q} = (\text{addition, subtraction, multiplication, branch}).$$

A metaprogram that translates all statements which are elementary in a set of operations $\boldsymbol{p}$ can be extended to translate statements which are

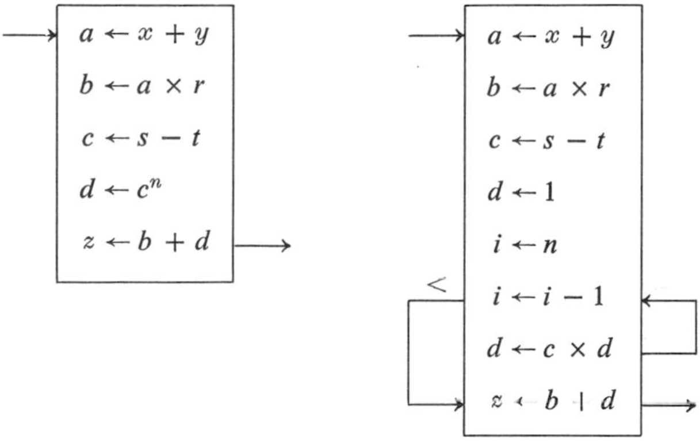

Analysis in $\boldsymbol{p}$
(*a*)

Analysis in $\boldsymbol{q}$
(*b*)

Program 5.1 Analysis of the compound statement $z \leftarrow (x + y) \times r + (s - t)^n$

compound in $\boldsymbol{p}$ by the addition of a metaprogram for analyzing compound statements. The conventions adopted for the representation of compound statements must, of course, be complete and precise so that interpretation is unequivocal. These conventions should be familiar and convenient to the programmer and should also permit easy analysis by a metaprogram. The common parenthesis notation of elementary algebra is congenial to programmers, whereas statements in Lukasiewicz notation are easier to translate and evaluate, easier to transform to an optimum form which minimizes the amount of intermediate data storage and execution time required in their evaluation or translation, and possess the simple criterion for well formation developed for the left list matrix of a tree in Sec. 1.23. The analysis of compound statements will therefore be discussed in terms of Lukasiewicz notation, and algorithms for translating between the parenthesis and Lukasiewicz notations will be presented.

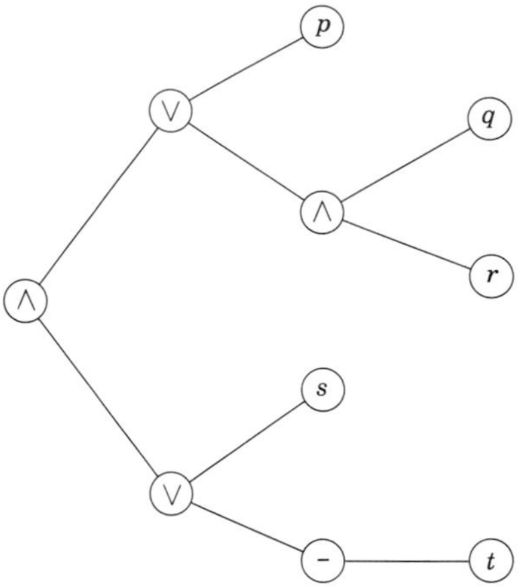

Tree

(*a*)

2	$\wedge$	1	∘	∘	∘
2	$\vee$	1	1	∘	∘
0	p	1	1	1	∘
2	$\wedge$	1	1	2	∘
0	q	1	1	2	1
0	r	1	1	2	2
2	$\vee$	1	2	∘	∘
0	s	1	2	1	∘
1	-	1	2	2	∘
0	t	1	2	2	1

Full left list matrix

(*b*)

2	$\wedge$
2	$\vee$
0	p
2	$\wedge$
0	q
0	r
2	$\vee$
0	s
1	-
0	t

Left list matrix

(*c*)

$(\wedge, \vee, p, \wedge, q, r, \vee, s, -, t)$

Left list vector or Lukasiewicz form

(*d*)

$((q \wedge r) \vee p) \wedge (s \vee \bar{t})$

Parenthesis form

(*e*)

Figure 5.2 Representations of a compound statement

Figure 5.2 shows several alternative representations of a compound statement. The tree representation (5.2*a*) is perhaps the most graphic, and the other forms may be viewed as alternative representations of the tree. The common parenthesis form of Fig. 5.2*e*, for example, specifies the requisite structure primarily by grouping the nodes of each subtree within parentheses with the root in the middle of the group. As shown in Sec. 3.4, the left list matrix of Fig. 5.2*c* can be supplanted by the simpler left list vector of Fig. 5.2*d*, providing that the degree of each operator p is a known function $\delta(p)$.

The left list vector notation for a compound statement is also called *Lukasiewicz,* Polish*, or *parenthesis-free* notation. The Lukasiewicz and the parenthesis notations will hereafter be referred to as $\mathscr{L}$-notation and $\mathscr{P}$-notation, respectively.

5.2 LUKASIEWICZ NOTATION

Although $\mathscr{L}$-notation can be viewed as the left list vector of a tree representing a compound statement, it is helpful to develop an alternative equivalent formulation as follows. Let $\boldsymbol{l}$ and $\boldsymbol{p}$ be two disjoint sets whose elements are literals and operators, respectively, and whose union $\boldsymbol{v} = \boldsymbol{l} \oplus \boldsymbol{p}$ is called a *vocabulary*. A strictly positive integral degree function $\delta(p)$ is defined on each element of $\boldsymbol{p}$, and each operator p of degree d accepts d elements of $\boldsymbol{l}$ as operands to define a result or value in $\boldsymbol{l}$. In symbolic logic, for example, $\boldsymbol{l} = (0, 1)$, $\boldsymbol{p} = (\wedge, \vee, \overline{\ \ })$, $\delta(\wedge) = \delta(\vee) = 2$, and $\delta(\overline{\ \ }) = 1$. Consistent with these notions, the degree of each literal is defined to be zero.†

Each operator p of degree $\nu(q)$ defines a function (i.e., a mapping) from each vector $\boldsymbol{q} \subseteq \boldsymbol{l}$ into an element $y \in \boldsymbol{l}$. This function is denoted by the vector $\boldsymbol{f} = (p) \oplus \boldsymbol{q}$. The vector $\boldsymbol{f}$ is called an *$\mathscr{L}$-phrase of length $\nu(\boldsymbol{f})$*, and the element y is called its *value*. Table 5.3 shows, for example, the $\mathscr{L}$-phrases in the system for symbolic logic based on *and*, *or*, and *not*. The vector $\boldsymbol{f}$ is clearly contained in the vocabulary $\boldsymbol{v}$, that is, $\boldsymbol{f} \subseteq \boldsymbol{v}$. Where its omission raises no ambiguity, the prefix will be dropped from the term "$\mathscr{L}$-phrase" and from similar terms to be defined.

A vector $\boldsymbol{z} \subseteq \boldsymbol{v}$ is called an *$\mathscr{L}$-formula of length $\nu(\boldsymbol{z})$*. In particular, every phrase is a formula. The *degree vector* of a formula $\boldsymbol{z}$ will be denoted by $\delta(\boldsymbol{z})$ and defined by the relation $(\delta(\boldsymbol{z}))_i = \delta(\boldsymbol{z}_i)$.

* First proposed by Lukasiewicz (1951) and first analyzed by Burks et al. (1954).

† The system is extended to include variables as well as literals by considering the vocabulary $\boldsymbol{v} = \boldsymbol{x} \oplus \boldsymbol{l} \oplus \boldsymbol{p}$, where $\boldsymbol{x}$ is the set of variables, and $\boldsymbol{x} \cap (\boldsymbol{l} \oplus \boldsymbol{p}) = \boldsymbol{\epsilon}(0)$. The degree of each variable is, like that of a literal, defined as zero. The domain of the operators is still confined to the set $\boldsymbol{l}$, and in any legitimate algorithm each variable is specified as a literal by some statement before it enters as an argument.

Phrase	Value
$(\vee, 0, 0)$	0
$(\vee, 0, 1)$	1
$(\vee, 1, 0)$	1
$(\vee, 1, 1)$	1
$(\wedge, 0, 0)$	0
$(\wedge, 0, 1)$	0
$(\wedge, 1, 0)$	0
$(\wedge, 1, 1)$	1
$(^{-}, 0)$	1
$(^{-}, 1)$	0

Table 5.3 Phrases in $\mathscr{L}$-system for symbolic logic based on operators *and*, *or*, *not*

If some infix of $\boldsymbol{z}$ is a phrase, and if the infix is replaced by its value, then the resulting vector $\boldsymbol{y}$ is called an $\mathscr{L}$-reduction of $\boldsymbol{z}$. If $\boldsymbol{y}$ is any $\mathscr{L}$-reduction of $\boldsymbol{z}$ which cannot be further reduced, it is called a *complete reduction* of $\boldsymbol{z}$ or, since it can be shown to be unique, *the* complete reduction of $\boldsymbol{z}$. Complete reduction of $\boldsymbol{z}$ will be denoted by $\mathscr{L}(\boldsymbol{z})$. A formula $\boldsymbol{z}$ is said to be *singular** if its complete reduction is a single literal, i.e., if $\nu(\mathscr{L}(\boldsymbol{z})) = 1$ and $\mathscr{L}(\boldsymbol{z}) \in \boldsymbol{l}$. Thus $\boldsymbol{q} = (\wedge, 1, \vee, 0, 1)$ and $\boldsymbol{r} = (1)$ are singular, but $\boldsymbol{s} = (\wedge, 1, 1, 0)$ and $\boldsymbol{t} = (\wedge)$ are not.

For example, complete reduction of the singular formula $\boldsymbol{z} = (\wedge, \vee, 1, \wedge, 0, 1, \vee, 1, {}^{-}, 1)$ may be performed as follows:

$$\begin{aligned}
\boldsymbol{z} &= (\wedge, \vee, 1, \wedge, 0, 1, \vee, 1, \underbrace{{}^{-}, 1})\\
\boldsymbol{z}^1 &= (\wedge, \vee, 1, \wedge, 0, 1, \underbrace{\vee, 1, 0})\\
\boldsymbol{z}^2 &= (\wedge, \vee, 1, \underbrace{\wedge, 0, 1}, 1)\\
\boldsymbol{z}^3 &= (\wedge, \underbrace{\vee, 1, 0}, 1)\\
\boldsymbol{z}^4 &= \underbrace{(\wedge, 1, 1)}\\
\boldsymbol{z}^5 &= 1
\end{aligned}$$

Program 5.4 shows the complete reduction of a formula $\boldsymbol{z}$, including tests of singularity.

Program 5.4. The components of the given formula $\boldsymbol{z}$ are examined in reverse order and assembled into a stack vector $\boldsymbol{y} = (\boldsymbol{z}_i, \boldsymbol{z}_{i+1}, \ldots, \boldsymbol{z}_\nu)$, where $\boldsymbol{z}_i$ is the

* The term *well formed* used by Burks et al. (1954) and others is avoided here because singularity implies not only that the formula represents a well formed tree but also that the tree is singular.

```
1    s ← (ν(y) = 1)
2    s ← 0
3    y ← ε(0)
4    i ← ν(z) + 1
5    i ← i − 1            = → 1
6    y ← (z_i) ⊕ y
7    δ(y_1) : 0           = → 5
8    j ← δ(y_1) + 1
9    j : ν(y)             > → exit
10   x ← 𝓛(α^j/y)
11   y ← (x) ⊕ ᾱ^j/y      → 5
```

1-origin indexing	
z	Given formula.
y	Reduced suffix of z.
i	Index of z in descending scan.
j	Dimension of phrase to be reduced.
s	Singularity indicator.

Legend

Program 5.4 Evaluation of the formula z

component currently examined. When an operator (i.e., a node of nonzero degree) is first encountered, the prefix of y forms a phrase of dimension $j = \delta(y_1) + 1$, which is immediately reduced (i.e., evaluated) on step 10 and is then replaced by its reduced value on step 11. Singularity of the vector z is indicated by a nonzero value of s, which is set to one only if the exit occurs from step 1 with $\nu(y) = 1$. The case $\nu(y) > 1$ can occur if the formula represents a well formed but nonsingular tree, i.e., if the formula contains two or more singular formulas. The exit from step 9 occurs if the indicated dimension of any phrase exceeds the current dimension of y and leaves the indicator s at its initial zero value.

The singular formulas are clearly the meaningful compound statements in the system. Moreover, if L_2 is a singular formula and if $L_1 = \delta(L_2)$, then L is the left list of a singular tree. The singularity of a given formula z can therefore be determined from its associated degree vector $d = \delta(z)$. The necessary and sufficient condition for singularity of the associated tree is simply $\nu(d) - (+/d) = 1$. As shown in Sec. 1.23, the necessary and sufficient condition for well formation is that all components of the suffix dispersion vector s defined by*

$$s = (I + \boxdot) \overset{+}{\underset{\times}{}} (\epsilon - d)$$

must be strictly positive. The maximum over the components of s will be called the *maximum suffix dispersion of* z.

* The suffix dispersion vector describes the dispersion (number of roots) of all suffixes of z, as may be more easily seen from the alternative expression

$$s_{j+1} = \nu(\bar{\alpha}^j/d) - (+/\bar{\alpha}^j/d).$$

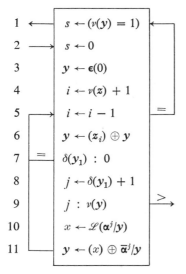

5.3 THE MINIMAX FORM OF AN $\mathscr{L}$-FORMULA

Two formulas are said to be *equivalent* if they have the same value for each possible specification of their variables. If $\mathbf{z}$ is any formula whose operators are all symmetric (i.e., whose operands commute), then any reordering of the component singular formulas of $\mathbf{z}$ which leaves the span of each operator unchanged leads to an equivalent formula. For example, since the operators $\wedge$ and $\vee$ are symmetric, the formulas

$$\mathbf{z} = (\wedge, \vee, \wedge, \vee, w, \wedge, u, v, r, q, p)$$

and

$$\mathbf{q} = (\wedge, p, \vee, q, \wedge, r, \vee, w, \wedge, u, v)$$

are equivalent, as may be easily verified. In the tree representation this reordering appears as a reordering of the group of subtrees rooted in a common node.

A formula whose maximum suffix dispersion is minimal with respect to the set of all equivalent formulas is said to be in *minimax form*.

The dimension of the stack vector $\mathbf{y}$ employed in the evaluation of a formula $\mathbf{z}$ (cf. Program 5.4) takes on successive values equal to the number of roots in the tree represented by the suffix of $\mathbf{z}$ currently scanned. It therefore assumes the values (in reverse order) of the components of the associated suffix dispersion vector $\mathbf{s}$. The maximum dimension of the stack vector determines, in turn, the amount of auxiliary storage required in the evaluation of the formula or in the compilation of a function program for its evaluation. It also determines, in part, the number of transfers of intermediate results to and from storage in evaluating the formula in a computer having a limited number of central registers. A formula in minimax form minimizes the maximum dimension of the stack vector and is therefore to be preferred.

The transformation of a singular formula $\mathbf{z}$ to equivalent minimax form is based on the following theorem: if each of the $\delta(\mathbf{z}_1)$ component singular formulas of $\bar{\alpha}^1/\mathbf{z}$ is in minimax form, then the entire formula can be brought to minimax form by arranging the component singular formulas in ascending order on their maximum suffix dispersion.

For example, if $\mathbf{z} = (\wedge, \vee, \wedge, a, b, \wedge, c, d, \vee, e, f)$, then $\delta(\mathbf{z}_1) = 2$, and $\bar{\alpha}^1/\mathbf{z}$ contains two singular formulas, $\mathbf{y}^1 = (\vee, \wedge, a, b, \wedge, c, d)$, and $\mathbf{y}^2 = (\vee, e, f)$, each in minimax form and possessing maximum suffix dispersions of 3 and 2, respectively. Moreover,

$$\mathbf{q} = (\mathbf{z}_1) \oplus \mathbf{y}^2 \oplus \mathbf{y}^1 = (\wedge, \vee, e, f, \vee, \wedge, a, b, \wedge, c, d)$$

is an equivalent formula in minimax form, with a maximum suffix dispersion of 3 as compared with a value of 4 for the same function of $\mathbf{z}$.

To establish the theorem, let z be any singular formula, let $r(z)$ be its dispersion (that is, the number of roots), let $s(z)$ be the maximum suffix dispersion of z, let $d = \delta(z_1)$, and let

$$\overline{\alpha}^1/z = y^1 \oplus y^2 \oplus \cdots \oplus y^d$$

be the unique (cf. Program 3.9) partitioning of $\overline{\alpha}^1/z$ into its component singular formulas. Then $y^i \oplus y^{i+1} \oplus \cdots \oplus y^{i+k-1}$ represents a k-tuply rooted tree and $r(y^i \oplus y^{i+1} \oplus \cdots \oplus y^{i+k-1}) = k$. Moreover,

$$\begin{aligned} s(\overline{\alpha}^1/z) &= \max\,[s(y^1) + r(y^2 \oplus y^3 \oplus \cdots \oplus y^d),\quad s(y^2 \oplus y^3 \oplus \cdots \oplus y^d)] \\ &= \max\,[s(y^1) + d - 1,\quad s(y^2 \oplus y^3 \oplus \cdots \oplus y^d)] \\ &= \max\,[s(y^1) + d - 1,\quad s(y^2) + d - 2,\quad s(y^3 \oplus \cdots \oplus y^d)] \\ &= \max_{j=1}^{d}\,[s(y^j) + d - j] \\ &= d + \max_{j=1}^{d}\,[s(y^j) - j]. \end{aligned}$$

Since the component formulas are in minimax form, the $s(y^j)$ are individually minimal, and the maximum over $s(y^j) - j$ is clearly minimized by arranging the $s(y^j)$ in ascending order. This concludes the proof.

To ensure that each component formula is itself optimal, it suffices to apply this reordering procedure in turn to the successive singular formulas encountered in scanning the given formula from right to left, as shown in Program 5.5.

Program 5.5. The vector y is the suffix $\overline{\alpha}^i/z$ permuted to optimal form, p is its partition vector* (that is, $((p \overset{+}{\times} \alpha^{j-1}) \downarrow \alpha^{p_j})/y$ is the jth singular formula of y), and g is its maximum suffix dispersion vector (that is, g_j is the maximum suffix dispersion of the jth singular formula of y). The main control parameter i is decremented on step 11, and, if it is not zero, the degree $d = \delta(z_i)$ of the next component to be added to y is examined. If z_i is not an operator, the branch to step 8 occurs with $h = 1$. The component z_i is then a formula of length 1 and steps 8–10 add it to y and make the appropriate changes in p and g.

If z_i is an operator (of degree d), the loop 15–22 scans the vector g and reorders the first d component formulas of y so that their maximum suffix dispersions are brought to ascending order. This is accomplished by the simple, but not necessarily efficient, sorting process of comparing successive pairs of adjacent components of g and interchanging the corresponding component formulas of y (by rotation

* The conventions used for p are those established in the subtree partitioning of Program 3.9.

1	$s \leftarrow 0$
2	$y \leftarrow \epsilon(0)$
3	$g \leftarrow \epsilon(0)$
4	$p \leftarrow \epsilon(0)$
5	$i \leftarrow \nu(z) + 1$
6	$f \leftarrow \alpha^d/g - \iota^1(d)$
7	$h \leftarrow d + ((\epsilon\lceil f)/f)_1$
8	$g \leftarrow (h) \oplus \bar{\alpha}^d/g$
9	$p \leftarrow ((p \overset{+}{\underset{\times}{}} \alpha^d) + 1) \oplus \bar{\alpha}^d/p$
10	$y \leftarrow (z_i) \oplus y$
11	$i \leftarrow i - 1$
12	$s \leftarrow (\nu(p) = 1)$
13	$d \leftarrow \delta(z_i)$
14	$d : \nu(p)$
15	$h \leftarrow 0$
16	$h \leftarrow h + 1$
17	$h : d$
18	$g_h : g_{h+1}$
19	$u \leftarrow (p \overset{+}{\underset{\times}{}} \alpha^{h-1}) \downarrow \alpha^{p_h + p_{h+1}}$
20	$y \leftarrow \backslash \bar{u}/y, u, p_h \uparrow (u/y)\backslash$
21	$g_h \leftrightarrow g_{h+1}$
22	$p_h \leftrightarrow p_{h+1}$

1-origin indexing	
z	Given formula.
y	The transformed suffix $\bar{\alpha}^i/z$.
p	Partition vector of y; p_j is the dimension of the jth singular formula of y.
g_j	Maximum suffix dispersion of the jth singular formula of y.
d	Degree of z_i.
s	Singularity indicator.

Legend

Program 5.5 Transformation of the formula z to minimax form

of the infix representing the pair) if an interchange is required. Steps 21 and 22 effect the corresponding interchanges in the vectors p and g. The loop is terminated by the branch from step 17 to step 6, the first d formulas of y (forming the prefix α^n/y, where $n = (+/\alpha^d/p)$) are then in ascending order on their maximum suffix dispersions, and the new formula $(z_i) \oplus \alpha^n/y$ is therefore in optimal form. Its maximum suffix dispersion is computed by steps 6 and 7 and replaces the prefix α^d/g (step 8) so that g becomes the maximum suffix dispersion vector of

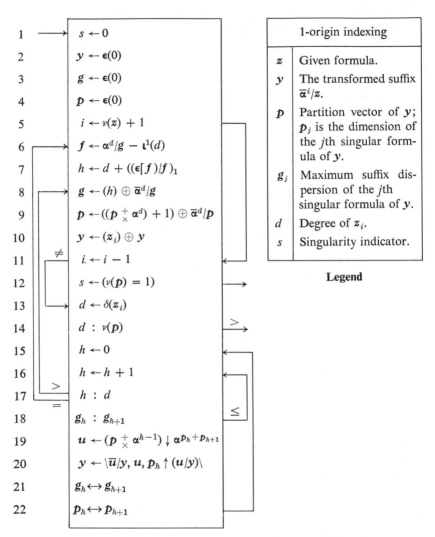

$(\mathbf{z}_i) \oplus \mathbf{y}$. The partition vector $\mathbf{p}$ is respecified by step 9. The one component of $\mathbf{g}$ remaining at the conclusion is the maximum suffix dispersion of the optimized statement $\mathbf{y}$.

The minimax form of a formula is, in general, not unique. It can be made unique, however, by using some assigned orderings of the operators, literals, and variables (e.g., the ordering specified by the vocabulary $\mathbf{v} = \mathbf{x} \oplus \mathbf{l} \oplus \mathbf{p}$) as a minor category in the reordering of component formulas. Such a unique form is helpful in detecting the occurrence of equivalent compound statements within a formula, with the aim of obviating repeated segments in a corresponding function program.

5.4 TRANSLATION FROM COMPLETE PARENTHESIS TO LUKASIEWICZ NOTATION

Ordinary parenthesis notation is complicated by the occasional or consistent use of certain conventions for eliding parentheses. For example, the expression

$$(x + (y \times z))$$

may also be written as

$$(x + y \times z)$$

by the convention that multiplication takes precedence over addition, or as

$$x + y \times z,$$

with the understanding that the entire expression need not be enclosed in parentheses.

The problem posed by the use of such conventions can be segregated by considering a *complete parenthesis notation* in which all implied parentheses are included, i.e., in which each operator and its associated operands are enclosed in parentheses. The analysis of a statement in parenthesis notation can therefore be performed in two steps, a translation to complete parenthesis notation according to the prescribed conventions, followed by the analysis of the resulting statement. The present discussion will be limited to expressions in complete parenthesis form.

The complete parenthesis notation will be referred to as $\mathscr{P}$-notation and the terminology adopted for $\mathscr{L}$-notation will be extended analogously. Thus, $\mathbf{z} = ([, [, x, +, y,], \times, r,])$ is a $\mathscr{P}$-formula more commonly denoted by $(x + y) \times r$. To avoid confusion with the normal use of parentheses (e.g., in enclosing vectors), brackets will be used (as in the foregoing vector $\mathbf{z}$) to represent the $\mathscr{P}$-notation.

The discussion will be limited to a system of unary and binary operations only (i.e., $\delta(p) = 1$ or 2) and will again be illustrated by the system of logical operations. Assuming a vocabulary of the form $\boldsymbol{v} = \boldsymbol{x} \oplus \boldsymbol{l} \oplus \boldsymbol{p} \oplus$ ([,]), the rules of composition for $\mathscr{P}$-notation may be formulated as follows:

1. If $v \in \boldsymbol{x} \oplus \boldsymbol{l}$, then v is a singular $\mathscr{P}$-formula.
2. If $\boldsymbol{z}$ is any singular formula, if $u \in \boldsymbol{p}$, and if $\delta(u) = 1$, then $([) \oplus (u) \oplus \boldsymbol{z} \oplus (])$ is a singular $\mathscr{P}$-formula.
3. If $\boldsymbol{y}$ and $\boldsymbol{z}$ are both singular formulas, if $b \in \boldsymbol{p}$, and if $\delta(b) = 2$, then $([) \oplus \boldsymbol{y} \oplus (b) \oplus \boldsymbol{z} \oplus (])$ is a singular $\mathscr{P}$-formula.

In particular, ([, y, $\wedge$, z,]) is singular but (y, $\wedge$, z) is not; (y) is singular but ([, y,]) is not, and ([, $\overline{\ }$, y,]) is singular but ($\overline{\ }$, y) is not.

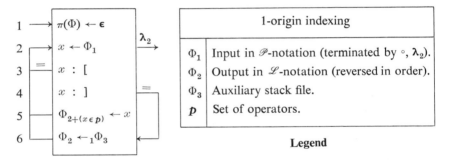

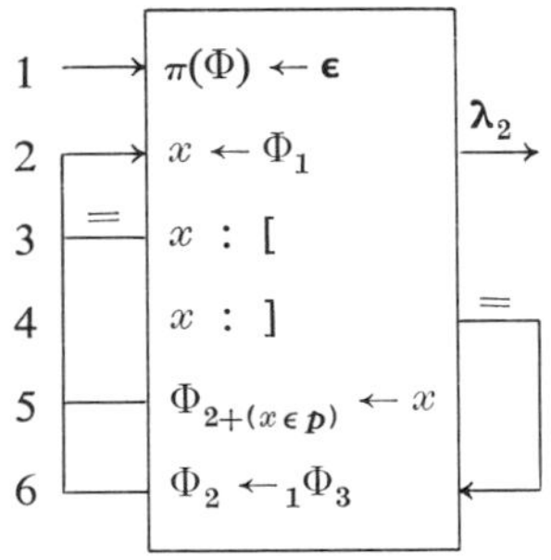

1-origin indexing	
Φ_1	Input in $\mathscr{P}$-notation (terminated by $\circ$, λ_2).
Φ_2	Output in $\mathscr{L}$-notation (reversed in order).
Φ_3	Auxiliary stack file.
$\boldsymbol{p}$	Set of operators.

Legend

Program 5.6 Translation from complete parenthesis to Lukasiewicz notation

The translation from $\mathscr{P}$- to $\mathscr{L}$-notation can be performed with the aid of one auxiliary file or stack vector. Program 5.6 shows a suitable process which will correctly translate any singular formula, but which includes no tests for singularity. It is noteworthy that all left parentheses are simply ignored. A similar process can, of course, be designed to use only the left parentheses and to ignore all right parentheses.* Any translation which tests for singularity clearly must use all parentheses. If the $\mathscr{L}$- and $\mathscr{P}$-notations employ different sets of operator symbols (e.g., $\wedge$, $\vee$, $\overline{\ }$, and $\times$, $+$, $\sim$), the appropriate translation can easily be incorporated in the program.

Program 5.6. The original statement is assumed to be recorded on a file $\Phi_{\mathfrak{f}}$, with partitions λ_1 following each symbol and with a null item and partition λ_2 at

* Oettinger (1960) analyzes three types of parenthesis notation: *left*, *right*, and *complete*.

the end. File Φ_2 receives the resulting $\mathscr{L}$-formula in reverse order, i.e., from right to left. The stack file Φ_3 receives each operator symbol as it is read from Φ_1 and transfers them one at a time in reverse order (i.e., by a backward read) to Φ_2 at each occurrence of a right parenthesis. A trace of the program shows, for example, that the $\mathscr{P}$-formula ([, [, x, $\vee$, y,], $\wedge$, [, $^-$, z,],]) translates correctly into the $\mathscr{L}$-formula (x, y, $\vee$, z, $^-$, $\wedge$) reversed from normal order.

A partial test of singularity can be provided by testing each component for compatibility with its predecessor, the ordered pair being declared compatible if and only if it can occur in some singular formula. For example, an operator may be followed by either a left parenthesis or a variable, but not by a right parenthesis or another operator. These first-order compatibility constraints can be expressed in terms of the following classes: left parenthesis, unary operator, binary operator, variable or literal, and right parenthesis. These classes will be denoted by [, u, b, v, and], or alternatively by 1, 2, 3, 4, and 5. The constraints are summarized in the matrix $\boldsymbol{M}$ of Program 5.7.

The test of singularity provided by the first-order constraints is not complete,* but can be completed by the following expedient.† The auxiliary file which receives the operators (file Φ_3 of Program 5.7) also receives the left parentheses in their turn. The following tests are then added:

1. Each operator is accepted and *replaces* the previous entry in the auxiliary file if and only if the previous entry is a left parenthesis.
2. The transfer of one component from the auxiliary file to the output file normally occasioned by the appearance of a right parenthesis is accepted by the right parenthesis if and only if the component transferred is an operator.
3. The possible exhaustion of the auxiliary file is tested each time it is read.

The first test prevents the acceptance of two successive operators without an intervening left parenthesis. At each application of the test, the corresponding left parenthesis is removed from the file. Since the auxiliary file may now contain left parentheses as well as operators, the second test is required to prevent their acceptance as operators. The complete testing and translation process is described by Program 5.7.

Program 5.7. The current component x is read from the input file on step 8 and its class k is determined before the repetition of the main loop at step 5. Step 5

* The tests provided in compilers have frequently been limited to essentially this type. See, for example, Carr (1959).

† This procedure is due to Oettinger (1960).

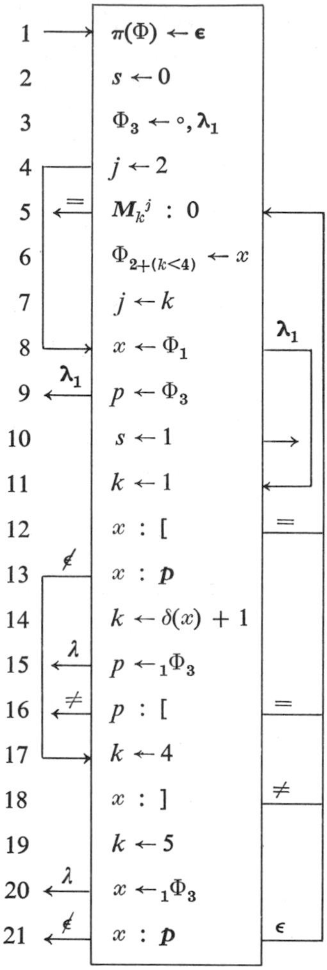

1-origin indexing		
$\boldsymbol{M}$	[u b v] 1 2 3 4 5 [1 1 1 0 1 0 u2 1 0 0 1 0 b3 1 0 0 1 0 v4 0 0 1 0 1]5 0 0 1 0 1	First-order compatibility constraints.
$\boldsymbol{M}_k^j$	j accepts $k \Leftrightarrow \boldsymbol{M}_k^j = 1$.	
Φ_3	Auxiliary stack file.	
Φ_2	Output in $\mathscr{L}$-notation (reversed order).	
Φ_1	Input in $\mathscr{P}$-notation (terminated by $\circ$, λ_1).	
j	Class of previous component.	
k	Class of current component.	
$\boldsymbol{p}$	Set of operations.	
$\delta(x)$	Degree of operator x.	
s	Singularity indicator.	

Legend

Program 5.7 Translation from complete parenthesis to Lukasiewicz notation with full checking of singularity

determines the first-order compatibility of k with its preceding value j. (The singularity indicator s is set to unity only at the exit on step 10.) Each component occasions the recording (step 6) of one item on one file—the auxiliary file Φ_3 if $k < 4$, or the output file Φ_2 if $k \geq 4$. The item recorded is the current component unless it is a right parenthesis. In the latter event, the variable x is first respecified (step 20) by a backward read from the stack file. The test on step 21 assures that the item read is an operator.

If the current component is an operator, the previous item recorded on the auxiliary file must first be read, compared with "[," and discarded. This occurs on steps 15 and 16. The exits on steps 15 and 20 indicate nonsingularity due to the exhaustion of the stack file. Step 9 provides a final test to ensure that the stack file is exhausted when the input file becomes exhausted. Since the first component of any singular formula must be either a variable, literal, or left parenthesis, the initial setting of j to 2 on step 4 provides the appropriate initial compatibility condition.

Each of the translation programs considered produces the resulting $\mathscr{L}$-formula in reverse order. This is the order in which it is most easily evaluated and, consequently, the order in which the synthesis of a corresponding function program is most easily performed. Synthesis may therefore proceed concurrently with analysis. The analysis may, on the other hand, be completed first, and the output file Φ_2 rewound before beginning the synthesis. The latter alternative allows the use of separate metaprograms for analysis and synthesis, and hence makes lesser demands for metaprogram storage. It also allows the application of an intervening transformation of the $\mathscr{L}$-formula to some preferred equivalent form. However, as shown by Program 5.4, the transformation to minimax form also treats the $\mathscr{L}$-formula in reverse order. It can therefore be performed concurrently with the translation from parenthesis notation.

5.5 TRANSLATION FROM LUKASIEWICZ TO COMPLETE PARENTHESIS NOTATION

The inverse translation from Lukasiewicz to complete parenthesis notation is, unlike the evaluation of the Lukasiewicz formula, best performed by a forward scan. The suffix dispersion criterion of singularity must then be applied in the following way. The dispersion of the entire statement is assumed to be one, and the dispersions of successively shorter suffixes are obtained by subtracting $(1 - \delta(x))$ for each succeeding component x. The suffix dispersion thus computed must reach zero when and only when the remaining suffix is null; if not, the statement is nonsingular. The translation of Program 5.8 provides complete checking of singularity.

Program 5.8. The resulting $\mathscr{P}$-formula is produced on file Φ_2 in reverse order. Each operator encountered is recorded in the auxiliary file together with a preceding left parenthesis, and it also causes a right parenthesis to be recorded in the output (steps 9–11). Each variable encountered is recorded (step 12) in the output file and initiates a transfer from the auxiliary file to the output file which terminates (step 19) only when an operator of degree two is encountered or (step 13) when the file becomes exhausted. In the latter event, steps 14 and 15 are executed as a final check on singularity—exhaustion of the stack file, exhaustion of the input file, and the first zero value of the suffix dispersion m must occur together.

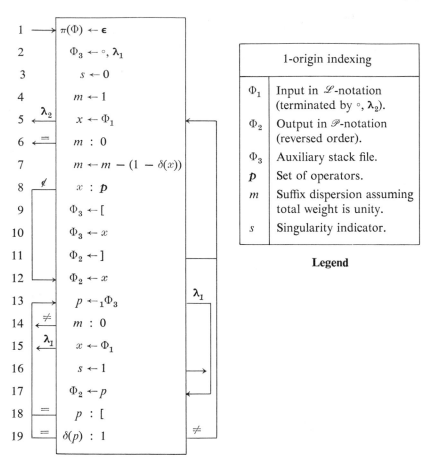

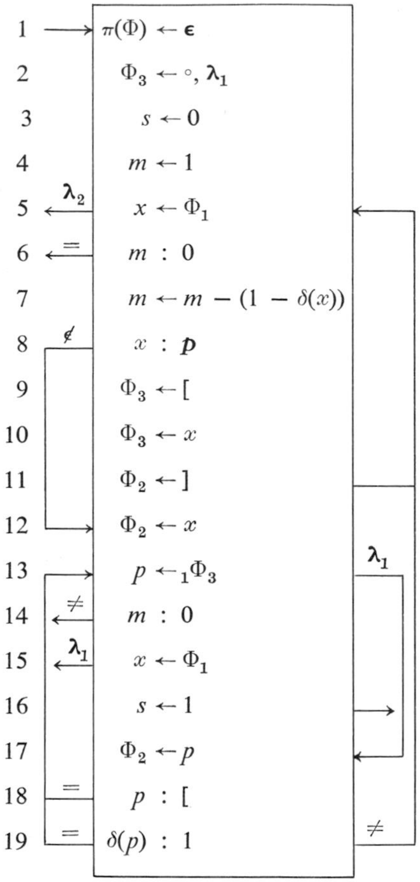

1-origin indexing	
Φ_1	Input in $\mathscr{L}$-notation (terminated by $\circ$, λ_2).
Φ_2	Output in $\mathscr{P}$-notation (reversed order).
Φ_3	Auxiliary stack file.
$\mathbf{p}$	Set of operators.
m	Suffix dispersion assuming total weight is unity.
s	Singularity indicator.

Legend

Program 5.8 Translation from Lukasiewicz to complete parenthesis notation with complete test of singularity

REFERENCES

Burks, A. W., D. W. Warren, and J. B. Wright, (1954), "An Analysis of a Logical Machine Using Parenthesis-free Notation," *Mathematical Tables and Other Aids to Computation*, vol. VIII, pp. 53–57.

Carr, J. W., III, (1959), "Digital Computer Programming," Chapter 2 of Grabbe, Ramo, and Wooldridge (Eds.), *Handbook of Automation, Computation, and Control*, vol. 2, Wiley, New York.

Lukasiewicz, Jan, (1951), *Aristotle's Syllogistic from the Standpoint of Modern Formal Logic*, Clarendon Press, Oxford, England, p. 78.

Oettinger, A. G., (1961), "Automatic Syntactic Analysis and the Pushdown Store," *Proc. Twelfth Symposium in Appl. Math.*, April 1960, published by American Mathematical Society.

EXERCISES

5.1 For each of the following logical functions, exhibit an equivalent (i) tree, (ii) $\mathscr{P}$-formula, and (iii) $\mathscr{L}$-formula:

(a) $f(x, y, z) = x \wedge (y \vee z)$.

(b) $g(w, x, y, z) = (w \vee (y \neq z)) \wedge \overline{(x \vee (w = y))}$.

(c) the function of part (b), limiting the operators employed to *and*, *or*, and *not*.

5.2 Let $f(x, y, z)$ be a logical function of three variables, let $\boldsymbol{q}$ be an equivalent formula in $\mathscr{P}$-notation, and let $\boldsymbol{r}$ be an equivalent formula in $\mathscr{L}$-notation. Write programs to determine the intrinsic vector $\boldsymbol{i}(f)$ (cf. Sec. 7.2) as a function of

(a) the $\mathscr{P}$-formula $\boldsymbol{q}$.

(b) the $\mathscr{L}$-formula $\boldsymbol{r}$.

5.3 Let
$$\begin{aligned}
\boldsymbol{a} &= (\wedge, \bar{\ }, 0, \vee, 1, 0)\\
\boldsymbol{b} &= (\bar{\ }, 0, \vee, 1, 0)\\
\boldsymbol{c} &= (\wedge, \vee, 0, \vee, 1, 0)\\
\boldsymbol{d} &= (\wedge, \vee, q, r, \bar{\ }, t)\\
\boldsymbol{e} &= (\vee, q, r, \bar{\ }, t)\\
\boldsymbol{q} &= ([, [, q, \vee, r,], \wedge, [, \bar{\ }, t,],])\\
\boldsymbol{r} &= ([, q, \vee, r,], \wedge, [, \bar{\ }, t,],])
\end{aligned}$$
Trace the operation of

(a) Program 5.4 for each of the cases $\boldsymbol{z} = \boldsymbol{a}$, $\boldsymbol{z} = \boldsymbol{b}$, and $\boldsymbol{z} = \boldsymbol{c}$.

(b) Program 5.5 for $\boldsymbol{z} = \boldsymbol{d}$.

(c) Program 5.6 for Φ_1 containing $\boldsymbol{q}$.

(d) Program 5.7 for Φ_1 containing $\boldsymbol{q}$ and for Φ_1 containing $\boldsymbol{r}$.

(e) Program 5.8 for Φ_1 containing $\boldsymbol{d}$ and for Φ_1 containing $\boldsymbol{e}$.

5.4 Write a program for translating from $\mathscr{P}$-notation to $\mathscr{L}$-notation which is analogous to Program 5.6 except that it ignores right rather than left parentheses.

5.5 Write a program to extend the minimax transformation of Program 5.5 to the case of an operator set of the form $\boldsymbol{p} = \boldsymbol{p}^1 \oplus \boldsymbol{p}^2$, where $\boldsymbol{p}^1$ and $\boldsymbol{p}^2$ are a set of symmetric and asymmetric operators, respectively.

5.6 Write a program which extends the minimax transformation of Program 5.5 to include ordering on the variables and operators so as to bring the formula to unique canonical form, as suggested in Sec. 5.3.

5.7 Write a program which will recognize all identical singular subformulas occurring in a singular $\mathscr{L}$-formula $\boldsymbol{z}$ and which will produce a record of the associations in some convenient form.

chapter 6

SORTING

The order in which a set of items is arranged in a large-capacity store often has a marked effect on the simplicity and speed of execution of algorithms defined on them, and it therefore becomes necessary to *sort* or rearrange groups of items.

The problem of sorting may be described as follows: given a vector $\boldsymbol{a}$, determine the ordering vector $\boldsymbol{p} = \theta/(\boldsymbol{k}(\boldsymbol{a}))$ and the permuted vector $\boldsymbol{c} = \boldsymbol{p} \int \boldsymbol{a}$, where $k(\boldsymbol{a}_i)$ is a numeric function defined on the components of $\boldsymbol{a}$, and $\boldsymbol{k}(\boldsymbol{a})$ is the vector defined by $(\boldsymbol{k}(\boldsymbol{a}))_j = k(\boldsymbol{a}_j)$. The function k is called the *key* of the sorting process, and $\boldsymbol{k}(\boldsymbol{a})$ is called the *key vector* associated with $\boldsymbol{a}$. The key function is frequently an index in some set $\boldsymbol{b}$, that is, $\boldsymbol{k}(\boldsymbol{a}) = \boldsymbol{b} \iota \boldsymbol{a}$. The components of $\boldsymbol{a}$ will also be called *items*; since the vector $\boldsymbol{a}$ is commonly represented in a file, it will also be called a *file*.

Most sorting processes determine the ordered vector $\boldsymbol{c} = \boldsymbol{p} \int \boldsymbol{a}$ without explicitly determining the permutation vector $\boldsymbol{p}$. A sorting process which explicitly determines and uses the permutation $\boldsymbol{p}$ is called an *address table sort*.

Sorting processes fall into two major classes, called *serial-* or *random-access*, according to whether the files used to represent the original and the intermediate vectors produced are serial-access or not. Random-access processes are also called *internal*, for they are normally performed in the "internal" storage of a computer. Combinations of serial processes and internal processes are used, but the two types can and will be described, analyzed, and evaluated independently.

Input	Output	Name of Process
Single	Single	Duplication
Single	Multiple	Classification
Multiple	Single	Merging (or Merge)
Multiple	Multiple	Revision

Table 6.1 Types of file operations

Four types of operations on files are distinguished, according to whether one file or several files are used in input and in output. They are shown in Table 6.1. A classification (merge) involving m output (input) files is called an m-way classification (merge).

6.1 SERIAL SORTING METHODS

Copy operations

A serial sorting process is executed as a sequence of *copy operations*. A copy operation is defined as follows: all items from a given set of input files are transferred to a given set of output files, and each item read from any input file must be transferred to some output file before a further item is read from the same input.

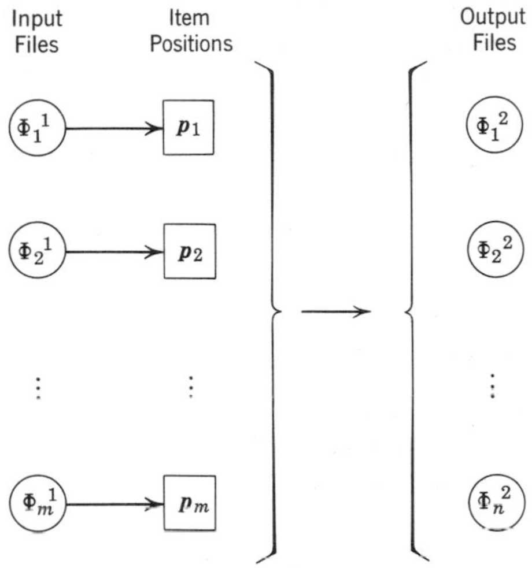

Figure 6.2 Copy operation

Figure 6.2 provides a graphic description of the copy operation. The m components $p_1, p_2, \ldots, p_m$ denote storage for m items, the kth input file may be read to the kth item position only, and the occupant of any item position may be transferred to any one of the output files. Once an item is so transferred, the evacuated position may be refilled by the next item from the corresponding input file. Any copy operation can clearly be performed by serial input files and serial output files, with each item being read and recorded but once, and with no auxiliary repositioning of the files.

A copy operation is also called *rank-preserving*, since it satisfies the following definition of that term. [The concept of rank preservation and its use in the analysis of sorting processes were first introduced by Ashenhurst (1953).] Any item may be specified by a pair of coordinates (f, r), the *file coordinate* f designating the file to which it belongs, and the *rank coordinate* r designating its rank (i.e., its index) in the file. Two items with initial coordinates (f_1, r_1) and (f_2, r_2) and with final coordinates (f_1', r_1') and (f_2', r_2'), respectively, are said to be *relatable* if and only if $f_1 = f_2$ and $f_1' = f_2'$. An operation is called rank-preserving if precedence relations are maintained for all relatable items, i.e.,

$$r_1 < r_2 \Leftrightarrow r_1' < r_2'.$$

Henceforth the terms *merge* and *classification* will, unless otherwise specified, refer to *rank-preserving* merge and *rank-preserving* classification, respectively. A merge in which each input file forms an infix of the output file is called a *simple merge*, and a classification in which each output file is formed from an infix of the input is called a *simple classification*.

An m-way classification and a subsequent m-way merge together effect a rearrangement from a single file to a single file. If the classification and merge are both rank-preserving, the possible rearrangement effected is restricted. However, a sequence of such orderings using alternate classification and merge can effect an arbitrary reordering. In particular, the following two important subclasses of such orderings will each be shown to suffice:

1. simple classification and merge,
2. classification and simple merge.

A sequence of copy operations of the first type used to effect complete ordering on some key is also referred to as a *merge sort*. A sequence of the second type is called a *column sort*.

Simple classification and merge

An infix in a file vector for which the key is a monotone increasing (decreasing) function of the rank is called an *increasing* (*decreasing*) *string*. The *length* of a string is the number of items it contains, and a *maximal* string is a string contained in no longer string. A file containing a single maximal string is ordered on the key.

For example, the sequence of keys

$$1, 3, 5, 8, 4, 7, 9$$

contains several increasing strings including 1, 3; 1, 3, 5, 8; and 7, 9, but it contains only two maximal increasing strings, 1, 3, 5, 8 and 4, 7, 9 and six maximal decreasing strings. Henceforth the term *string* will normally refer to a maximal string.

Two files, each containing one string, may be merged to produce a single string by selecting at each step the item with the smaller key of the two next available from the input files. More generally, if the inputs each contain n strings, and if the foregoing process is generalized to produce the longest possible output strings, each output string will contain precisely one string from each input. If the inputs contain n_1 and n_2 strings, respectively, then $n = \max(n_1, n_2)$ strings are produced in the output. A subsequent simple two-way classification which assigns $\lceil n \div 2 \rceil$ strings to the first file and the remaining strings to the second, yields the greatest possible reduction in the maximum number of strings in any one file. Repetition of the merge and classification phases eventually produces an ordered file.

The generalization of the process to an m-way merge and m-way classification is immediate,* the optimum number of strings assigned to each output file by the classification process being limited to $\lceil n \div m \rceil$. Referring to Fig. 6.2, the m-way merge may be described as follows: those item positions containing keys which equal or exceed the key last recorded on the single output file are said to be *eligible*, and the next item chosen for recording is the eligible item with the minimum key. When no eligible items remain, all positions are again made eligible and the process continues, initiating another string in the output file. The number of output strings produced is clearly the maximum of the number occurring in an input file. Figure 6.3 illustrates the process for $m = 3$. The vertical strokes in the figure indicate the division into maximal strings and do not denote information represented directly within the files.

In any sorting procedure, the smallest subprocess which treats the entire set of items once is called a *phase*. The smallest subprocess which by simple iteration produces the sorting process is called a *stage*. A stage may comprise one or more phases. In the merge sort described above, for example, the classification phase and the subsequent merge phase together constitute a stage which is iterated until order is achieved; the process is therefore called a *two-phase merge*. The use of a revision operation (Table 6.1) permits the classification and the merge to be coalesced into a single phase, and the resulting process is called a *single-phase merge*. The single-phase merge requires m input files and m output files, whereas the two-phase merge requires only $(m + 1)$ files—one input and m outputs in the classification phase, and m inputs and one output in the merge phase.

The following format will be assumed for the original files in all programs in this chapter: the terminal item is a dummy (null) which is not to be

* This method, commonly credited to Goldstine and von Neumann (1948), was presented by J. W. Mauchly in July 1946 in the Moore School lectures (1948).

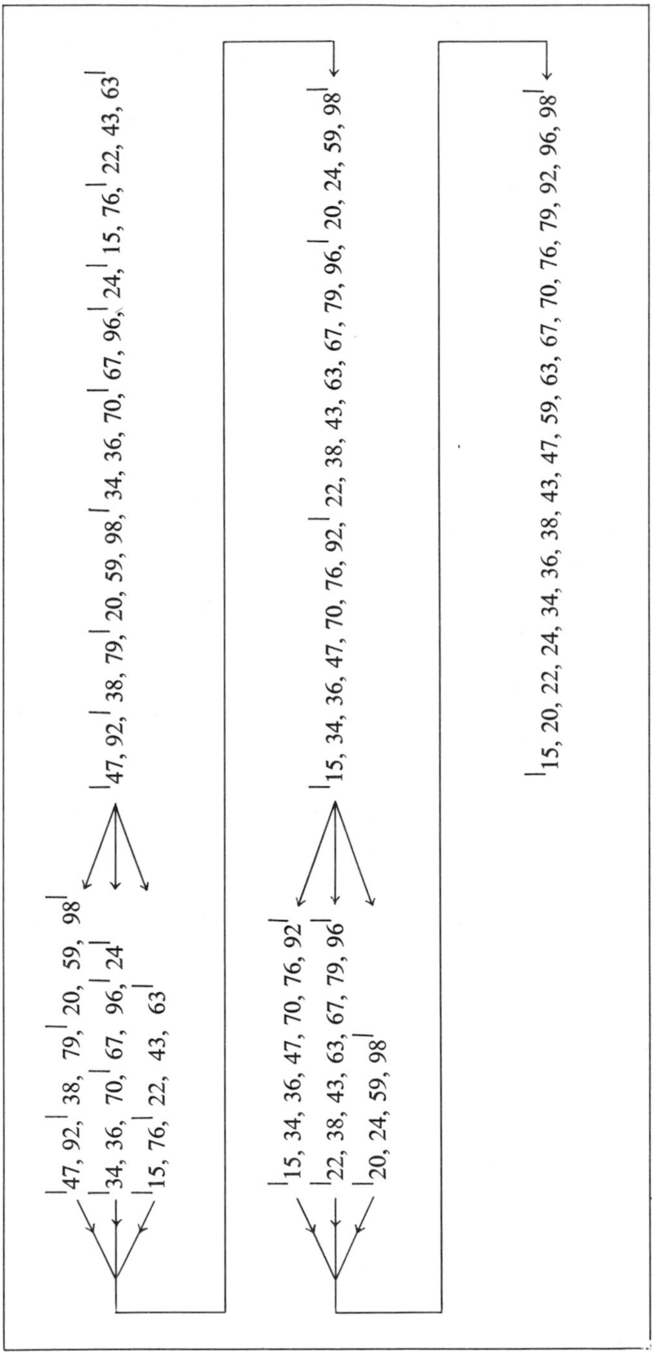

Figure 6.3 Simple classification and merge

sorted and which is accompanied by a terminal partition $\boldsymbol{\lambda}_{j+1}$, where j is the index origin in use; all other items are separated by the partition $\boldsymbol{\lambda}_j$. The final dummy item facilitates the use of the immediate branching convention introduced in Sec. 1.22.

Two-phase merge. The $(m + 1)$ files used will be labeled $\Phi_1^1, \Phi_2^1, \ldots, \Phi_m^1$, and Φ_1^2, the last serving as initial input and as input during each classification phase. Program 6.4 describes the entire merge.

Program 6.4. The merge phase is shown on the left and the classification phase on the right. The heart of the former is the loop 7–17. Its operation is controlled by the logical vectors $\boldsymbol{v}$ and $\boldsymbol{z}$ (of dimension m), which specify the set of exhausted files and the set of ineligible items, respectively. An *eligible* item is one which has been read to one of the m item positions $\boldsymbol{p}_i$, is not a dummy, (i.e., null), and possesses a key which equals or exceeds r, the key of the item last recorded.

The merge phase terminates on step 7, when all files are exhausted. Step 8 initializes the vector $\boldsymbol{z}$ (ineligible item positions) to the value $\boldsymbol{v}$ (exhausted files), and step 9 increments the output string count s. Each execution of the subloop 10–14 records on Φ_1^2 the item $\boldsymbol{p}_j$ having the smallest key of all eligible items. Steps 10–12 select and record the item $\boldsymbol{p}_j$ and preserve its key as the variable r. Step 13 reads the next item from file j. If this exhausts the file, the branch to step 15 is followed. Step 15 adds j to the set of exhausted files and step 16 adds it (since the new item $\boldsymbol{p}_j$ is a final dummy) to the set of ineligible items. Step 17 then repeats the subloop if any eligible items remain and otherwise re-enters the major loop at step 7. If the files are all exhausted, step 7 branches to step 18 to begin the classification. If not, the production of a new maximal string is begun on step 8.

If step 13 does not exhaust the file, it is followed by the decision on step 14, which repeats the subloop if r does not exceed the new key, and otherwise adds j to the set of ineligible items on step 16.

The necessary initialization is performed by steps 3–6. Step 3 rewinds all input and output files. Steps 4 and 5 perform the initial read from each unexhausted file to the corresponding item position and respecify $\boldsymbol{v}$ to indicate any file which may be exhausted by the initial read itself. The vector $\boldsymbol{v}$ is itself specified external to the process, so that the initial set of input files may be restricted at will. On subsequent repetitions of the merge, all files are made available by step 2.

The classification phase begins by terminating the output file with a dummy item and final partition $\boldsymbol{\lambda}_2$, and rewinding it. The m input files are also rewound to serve as output files in the subsequent m-way classification, and the process is terminated by step 20 if the output string count is equal to *one*. Step 21 redefines s as the maximum number of strings to be allotted to the output files in turn, and step 22 reads the first item from the input file Φ_1^2.

The output files are selected in ascending order by the index i. The variable j, which counts the strings, is initialized on step 25 and decremented on step 30 each time a break is indicated by the preceding comparison on step 29. When s strings

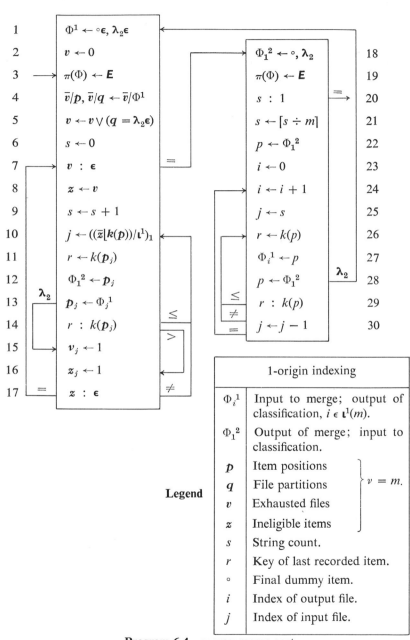

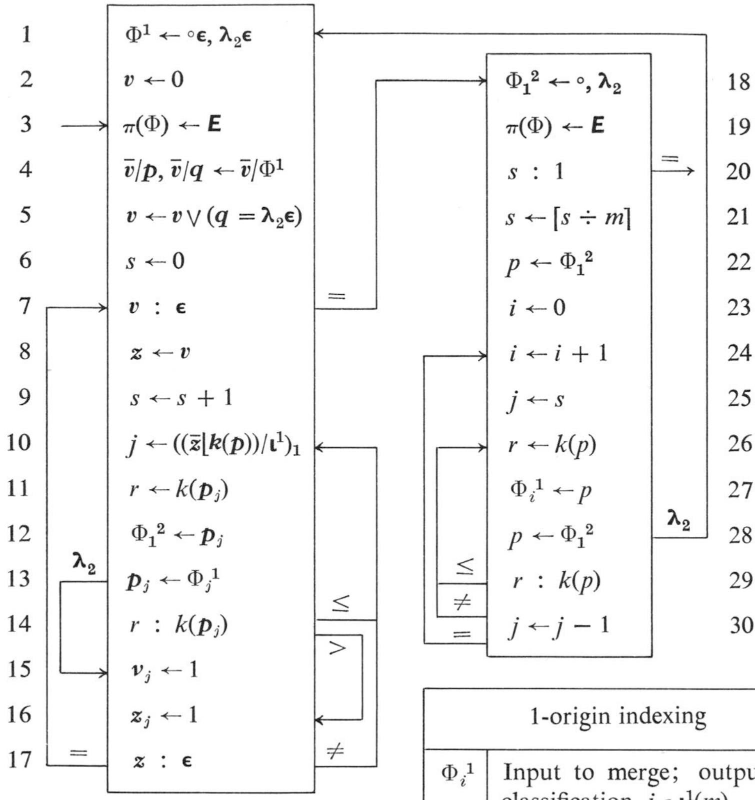

Legend

1-origin indexing	
Φ_i^1	Input to merge; output of classification, $i \epsilon \iota^1(m)$.
Φ_1^2	Output of merge; input to classification.
$\boldsymbol{p}$	Item positions } $\nu = m$.
$\boldsymbol{q}$	File partitions } $\nu = m$.
$\boldsymbol{v}$	Exhausted files } $\nu = m$.
$\boldsymbol{z}$	Ineligible items } $\nu = m$.
s	String count.
r	Key of last recorded item.
$\circ$	Final dummy item.
i	Index of output file.
j	Index of input file.

Program 6.4 *m*-way merge sort

have been recorded, the branch from step 30 to step 24 is followed to repeat the process for the next output file.

The classification phase is terminated by the occurrence of the partition $\boldsymbol{\lambda}_2$ on step 28. Step 1 then records a dummy and a final partition on each output file (including any which may have received no items), and step 2 resets the vector $\boldsymbol{v}$ to zero.

The merge phase with which Program 6.4 begins is essential, even though the original data are contained in a single file, since it also serves to determine the string count s needed in the subsequent classification. The need for the string count can be avoided by using a classification process which merely assigns successive strings to successive files in cyclic sequence. This process does not satisfy the definition of a simple classification, and it will be given the name *string classification.* String classification is frequently more convenient to use than simple classification, particularly in processes such as the single-phase merge to be described next. Two successive strings assigned to a given file in string classification can coalesce to form a single string, but the probability of such an occurrence is small, especially in later stages.

Single-phase merge. The two phases of the merge sort can be coalesced in a single revision operation employing m input and m output files. The two rows of files Φ^1 and Φ^2 serve alternately as input and output on successive stages.

Program 6.5. The main subprocess (15–22) differs from the corresponding segment (10–17) of Program 6.4 only in the control of file selection, the alternation of input and output being controlled by the alternator u, which alternates between 1 and 2 (step 2) on successive stages. The classification is controlled by the variable i, which selects the particular output file on step 17 and which is itself cycled through the integers 1 to m by step 14. When all files are exhausted, the branch to step 2 is followed, resetting the vector $\boldsymbol{v}$ to zero, terminating the output files, and rewinding all files. The final output is contained in file $\Phi_1{}^a$.

Elimination of file rewind. Each of the sorting processes described requires a rewind of all files between successive stages. If the files employed are capable of backward read, the processes can be modified so as to eliminate the need for rewind. Since each file is alternately read and recorded in successive stages, each will always be read in a fixed direction and recorded in the other. Since the space needed for recording is not known in advance, it is necessary to do all recording in the forward direction and therefore to read in the backward direction. The changes required will be illustrated by modifying the single-phase merge of Program 6.5.

Program 6.6. Since the alternate forward record and backward read effectively reverse the order of all files on successive stages, alternate stages must assemble

1	$(a, s) \leftarrow (1, 0)$
2	$a \leftarrow 2 \mid_1 (a + 1)$
3	$v \leftarrow 0$
4	$\Phi^a \leftarrow {}^\circ\epsilon, \lambda_2\epsilon$
5	$\pi(\Phi) \leftarrow \mathbf{E}$
6	$s : 1$
7	$s \leftarrow 0$
8	$\bar{v}/p, \bar{v}/q \leftarrow \bar{v}/\Phi^a$
9	$v \leftarrow v \vee (q = \lambda_2\epsilon)$
10	$i \leftarrow 0$
11	$v : \epsilon$
12	$z \leftarrow v$
13	$s \leftarrow s + 1$
14	$i \leftarrow m \mid_1 (i + 1)$
15	$j \leftarrow ((\bar{z}\lfloor k(p))/\iota^1)_1$
16	$r \leftarrow k(p_j)$
17	$\Phi_i^{3-a} \leftarrow p_j$
18	$p_j \leftarrow \Phi_j{}^a$
19	$r : k(p_j)$
20	$v_j \leftarrow 1$
21	$z_j \leftarrow 1$
22	$z : \epsilon$

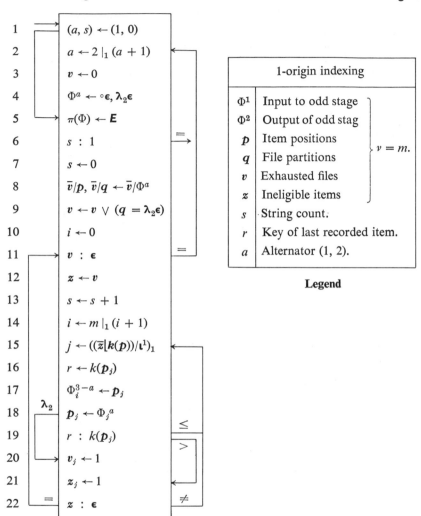

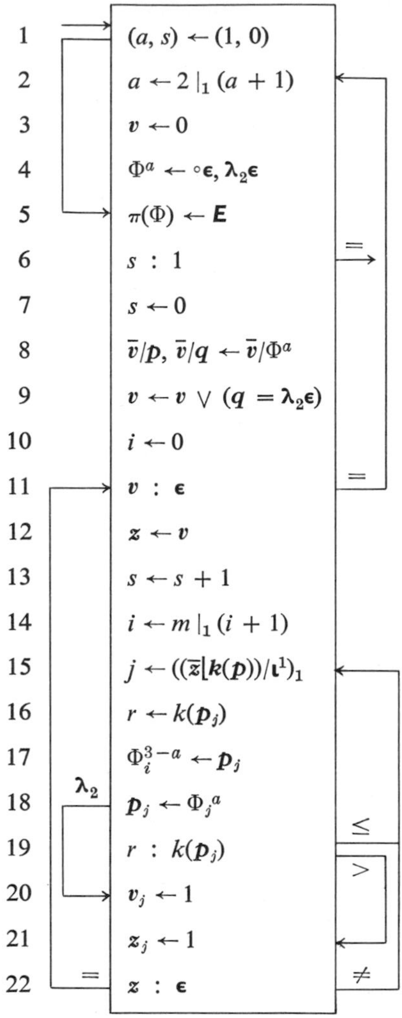

1-origin indexing

Φ^1	Input to odd stage	
Φ^2	Output of odd stag	
p	Item positions	
q	File partitions	$v = m.$
v	Exhausted files	
z	Ineligible items	
s	String count.	
r	Key of last recorded item.	
a	Alternator (1, 2).	

Legend

Program 6.5   *m*-way single phase merge sort

ascending strings and descending strings, respectively. This is achieved by reversing the algebraic sign of the key in statements 20 and 24 (by use of the alternator *a*) on even-numbered stages.

Except when the entire process is terminated by failure to follow the branch from step 8 to step 11, the output files are never terminated by a partition, nor rewound, but are simply read backward as in statements 13 and 23. To ensure that the backward read of a file terminates properly, each is provided with an initial dummy item (step 11), and the branch on step 23 occurs on either the

Line	Statement	Branch
1	$(c, a) \leftarrow (0, 1)$	
2	$\pi(\Phi) \leftarrow \mathbf{E}$	
3	$v \leftarrow 0$	
4	$c : 1$	$=$
5	$c \leftarrow 1$	
6	$\pi(\Phi^a) \leftarrow \boldsymbol{\epsilon}$	
7	$a \leftarrow 2 \vert_1 (a + 1)$	
8	$s : a - 1$	$\neq$
9	$\Phi_1{}^2 \leftarrow \circ, \boldsymbol{\lambda}_2$	
10	$\pi(\Phi_1{}^2) \leftarrow 1$	$\rightarrow$
11	$\Phi^{3-a} \leftarrow \circ\boldsymbol{\epsilon}$	
12	$s \leftarrow 0$	
13	$\bar{v}/p, \bar{v}/q \leftarrow \bar{v}/_c\Phi^a$	
14	$v \leftarrow v \vee (q = \boldsymbol{\lambda}_2\boldsymbol{\epsilon})$	
15	$i \leftarrow 0$	
16	$v : \boldsymbol{\epsilon}$	$=$
17	$z \leftarrow v$	
18	$s \leftarrow s + 1$	
19	$i \leftarrow m \vert_1 (i + 1)$	
20	$j \leftarrow ((\bar{z} \lfloor (3 - 2a) k(p))/\iota^1)_1$	
21	$r \leftarrow k(p_j)$	
22	$\Phi_i^{3-a} \leftarrow p_j$	
23	$p_j \leftarrow {}_c\Phi_j{}^a$	$\lambda, \boldsymbol{\lambda}_2$
24	$(3 - 2a)r : (3 - 2a)k(p_j)$	$\leq$, $>$
25	$v_j \leftarrow 1$	
26	$z_j \leftarrow 1$	
27	$z : \boldsymbol{\epsilon}$	$=$, $\neq$

Program 6.6 Single-phase merge without rewind

	1-origin indexing	
Φ^1	Input to odd stage	$v = m$.
Φ^2	Output of odd stage	$v = m$.
p	Item positions	$v = m$.
q	Partitions	$v = m$.
v	Exhausted files	$v = m$.
z	Ineligible items	$v = m$.
s	String count.	
r	Key of last recorded item.	
a	Alternator (1, 2).	
c	Direction of read.	

Legend

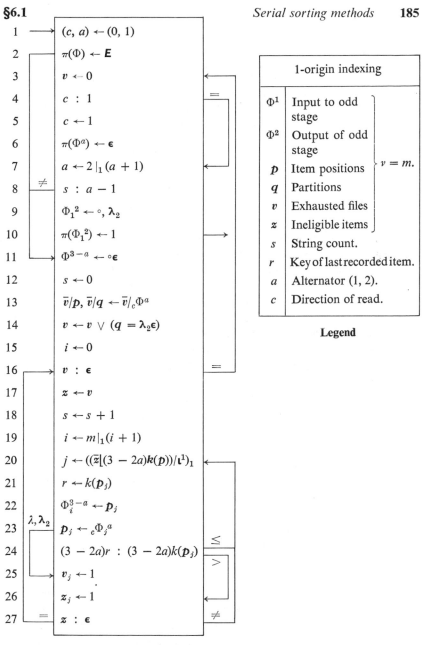

terminal partition λ_2 or the permanent initial partition λ. The entire process is terminated by equality of s and $a - 1$ on step 8, which can occur only if $s = 1$ and $a = 2$. This pair of conditions ensures not only that the number of strings is unity but also that an odd number of stages has been executed, and hence that the final output (on $\Phi_1{}^2$) is in ascending order.

Since the initial input file must normally be read forward, an exception is made through the agency of the variable c. On the first pass only, $c = 0$, and the reads on steps 13 and 23 are therefore forward. The forward read on the first pass necessitates a subsequent rewind of the input files, which is provided by step 6.

A commonly used variant of the m-way merge sort (called *string-doubling* from its behavior in the case $m = 2$) treats the initial input as if the maximal strings contained were each of length one, and therefore produces strings of uniform length m in the output. These uniform strings may not be maximal but are treated on the next stage as if they were, i.e., output strings of length m^2 are produced. In general, the kth stage produces strings of uniform length m^k, and $\lceil \log_m n \rceil$ stages are required to order n items. The number of stages does not depend on the initial number of maximal strings, and no use is made of possible inherent order in the original array. The comparison operations may, however, be somewhat simplified, since the need to test eligibility is replaced by counts of the items read from each file or by recording partitions between successive strings. If n is not an integral power of m, some of the strings will be shorter than the normal length. They can be expanded by dummy items, although the use of partitions renders this unnecessary.

Classification and simple merge

The classification and simple merge sort is also referred to as a column or digital sort, for the successive classification phases are controlled by successive columns (digit positions) of a positional representation of the key. The behavior of the process is not so obvious as the behavior of the merge of the previous section, and a formal proof of its ability to produce ordering will be given at the end of this section. Since the process is based on a positional representation of the key, it will be convenient to use 0-origin indexing for all operands.

Let k be the (nonnegative) sorting key, let $\boldsymbol{d}$ be its digital representation in a base b number system (that is, $(b\boldsymbol{\epsilon}) \perp \boldsymbol{d} = k$), and let $q = \nu(\boldsymbol{d})$, where b^q exceeds the largest existing key. The complete column sort comprises q stages, each stage consisting of a b-way classification followed by a b-way simple merge. The classification on stage j is based on $\boldsymbol{d}_{\nu-j}$ (the jth digit of the key counting from the low-order end), and each item is assigned to file Φ_i, where $i = \boldsymbol{d}_{\nu-j}$. The simple merge is defined such that the output file has the form $\Phi_0, \Phi_1, \ldots, \Phi_{b-1}$, where the Φ_i are the b output files of the preceding classification.

Two-phase column sort. Like the merge sort, the base b column sort may either be two-phase (classification followed by simple merge and using $b + 1$ files) or single-phase (using $2b$ files); the two methods are described by Programs 6.7 and 6.8, respectively.

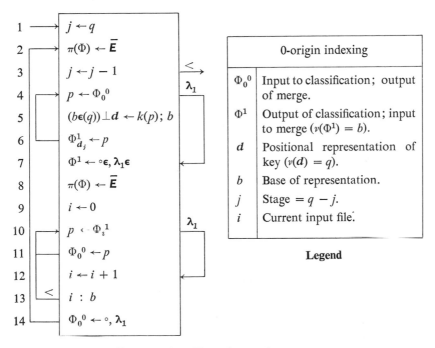

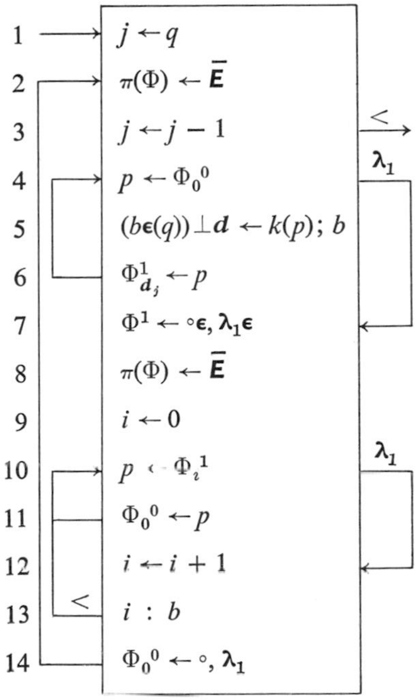

0-origin indexing	
$\Phi_0{}^0$	Input to classification; output of merge.
Φ^1	Output of classification; input to merge ($\nu(\Phi^1) = b$).
$\boldsymbol{d}$	Positional representation of key ($\nu(\boldsymbol{d}) = q$).
b	Base of representation.
j	Stage $= q - j$.
i	Current input file.

Legend

Program 6.7 Two-phase column sort

Program 6.7. Steps 1–7 constitute the classification and steps 8–14 the merge phase. File $\Phi_0{}^0$ is the single input to the classification and the single output of the simple merge. The remaining b files are denoted by $\Phi_i{}^1$, $i \in \iota^0(b)$.

The component of $\boldsymbol{d}$ which controls the current classification (step 6) is selected by j, which scans $\boldsymbol{d}$ from right to left. In the (implicit) specification of $\boldsymbol{d}$ on step 5, b serves as an auxiliary variable (cf. Sec. 1.19). When the classification phase ends with the exhaustion of $\Phi_0{}^0$ (step 4), the output files are terminated, all files are rewound, and the simple merge is performed (steps 10–13) to re-collect on $\Phi_0{}^0$ the results of the preceding classification. This file is then terminated by step 14, and the entire process is repeated from step 2 for the next lower value of j. The dimension of $\boldsymbol{d}$ is specified (by compatibility with $\epsilon(q)$ on step 5) as q, and q is, of course, specified externally.

Program 6.8. The alternator a again determines the roles of the two sets of files (input or output) on successive stages, but because of the use of 0-origin indexing, it alternates between the values 0 and 1. The classification process (steps 7–11) differs from that of Program 6.7 only in the control exercised by the alternator a, and in the specification of a sequence of input files $\Phi_0^a, \Phi_1^a, \ldots, \Phi_{b-1}^a$ instead of the single file Φ_0^0.

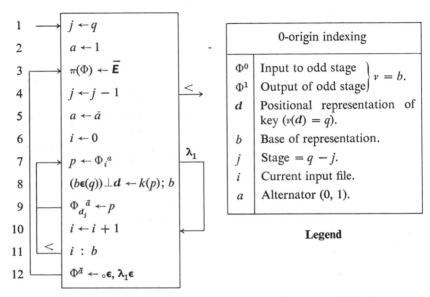

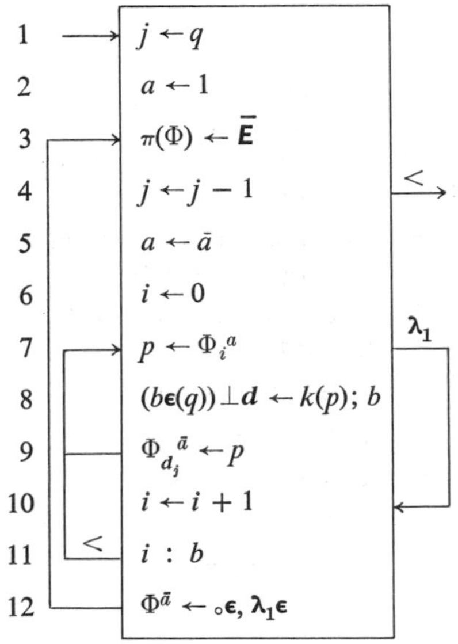

0-origin indexing	
Φ^0	Input to odd stage } $\nu = b$.
Φ^1	Output of odd stage }
$\boldsymbol{d}$	Positional representation of key ($\nu(\boldsymbol{d}) = q$).
b	Base of representation.
j	Stage $= q - j$.
i	Current input file.
a	Alternator (0, 1).

Legend

Program 6.8 Single-phase column sort (output on b files)

The program is deficient in two respects: it requires that the original input be on a full set of b files, and it produces a final output on b files rather than one. The first defect may be remedied by the use of an externally specified logical vector $\boldsymbol{v}$ to designate the input files which are unused in the original stage. The second may be remedied by a final simple merge following the qth stage. This could be added as a separate program, but it can be effected more simply by replacing q with $q + 1$ to ensure that the high order digit $\boldsymbol{d}_0$ is identically zero and so restricts the final output to a single file.

*Validity of the column sort.** If $\boldsymbol{d}$ is the q-digit, base b representation of the key k of an item p, then the $(q - j)$th pass of the base b column sort assigns the item to file Φ_i^a, where $i = \boldsymbol{d}_j$. The subsequent simple merge collects the files in the order $\Phi_0^a, \Phi_1^a, \ldots, \Phi_{b-1}^a$. Consider any two items p_1 and p_2 with distinct keys k_1 and k_2 represented by $\boldsymbol{d}^1$ and $\boldsymbol{d}^2$, respectively. It may

* This proof is due to Ashenhurst (1953).

be assumed, without loss of generality, that $k_1 < k_2$. Since the keys are distinct, there exists an integer r such that $\boldsymbol{d}_r^{\,1} < \boldsymbol{d}_r^{\,2}$ and that $\boldsymbol{\alpha}^r/\boldsymbol{d}^1 = \boldsymbol{\alpha}^r/\boldsymbol{d}^2$. Thus r is the (0-origin) index of the highest order column in which the keys differ.

In the $(n - r)$th pass, the items p_1 and p_2 are therefore assigned to files $\Phi_h{}^a$ and $\Phi_i{}^a$ such that $h < i$. Hence at the conclusion of the subsequent merge, item p_1 precedes item p_2. In each subsequent stage the two items are always assigned to the same file (since $\boldsymbol{d}_s^{\,1} = \boldsymbol{d}_s^{\,2}$, $s < r$), and the two items are therefore always relatable with respect to these operations. Since each stage is a copy operation, and therefore rank-preserving, the relative ordering of all relatable items is preserved, and p_1 thus precedes p_2 at the conclusion of the process. Thus for any pair of items p_1 and p_2 with keys k_1 and k_2, such that $k_1 < k_2$, item p_1 precedes p_2 in the final arrangement.

Vector keys and categories. The column sort is actually based on the components of the vector $\boldsymbol{d}$ and only indirectly on the numerical key it represents. The process can therefore be generalized to any numerical vector key $\boldsymbol{y}$ defined on each item $\boldsymbol{a}_i$. It can be further extended to an arbitrary key vector $\boldsymbol{b}$ belonging to the product set

$$\boldsymbol{C} = \boldsymbol{c}^0 \otimes \boldsymbol{c}^1 \otimes \cdots \otimes \boldsymbol{c}^{\nu(\boldsymbol{b})-1}$$

as follows: on the classification stage based on component $\boldsymbol{b}_j$, the item is assigned to file $\boldsymbol{c}^j \,\iota\, \boldsymbol{b}_j$. An obvious generalization of the foregoing proof of validity shows that the resulting ordering is that of the product set $\boldsymbol{C}$.

The component set $\boldsymbol{c}^j$ is called the *jth category*, $\boldsymbol{c}^0$ is called the *major category*, $\boldsymbol{c}^{\nu(\boldsymbol{b})-1}$ the *minor category*, and the ordering is said to be defined on category $\boldsymbol{c}^{\nu(\boldsymbol{b})-1}$ within $\boldsymbol{c}^{\nu(\boldsymbol{b})-2} \ldots$ within $\boldsymbol{c}^0$. For example, a nine-column employee number $\boldsymbol{b} = (\boldsymbol{b}_0, \boldsymbol{b}_1, \boldsymbol{b}_2, \boldsymbol{b}_3)$ may be based on four categories, the first component $\boldsymbol{b}_0$ representing the employee's one-bit payroll classification (hourly or salaried), the second his two-decimal-digit department number, the third his two-alphabetic-character job code, and the fourth his four-decimal-digit identification number. The column sort on the base b representation of a numerical key is clearly a special case of a vector key in which each of the categories is the set $\boldsymbol{\iota}^0(b)$.

It is frequently necessary to order a set of items on certain subsets of the given categories, and on different rankings of the categories. In general, if $\boldsymbol{b}$ is a vector key and $\boldsymbol{m}$ is any compatible mapping vector, then a *related ordering* may be defined on the vector $\boldsymbol{d} = \boldsymbol{b}_{\boldsymbol{m}}$. If—continuing the previous example—it is required to produce a list ordered by employee's department within job classification, then $\boldsymbol{m} = (2, 1)$ and $\boldsymbol{d} = (\boldsymbol{b}_2, \boldsymbol{b}_1)$.

Any infix of $\boldsymbol{b}$ defines a related ordering which is actually achieved at some stage of the column sort on $\boldsymbol{b}$, and the ordering defined by it is therefore said to be *contained in* the ordering $\boldsymbol{b}$. If the orderings $\boldsymbol{d}^0, \boldsymbol{d}^1, \ldots, \boldsymbol{d}^{r-1}$ are all contained in $\boldsymbol{b}$, they can all be achieved at some stage in the ordering $\boldsymbol{b}$, and the total number of passes required may be less than that required to achieve the r different orders independently. For example, $\boldsymbol{d}^0 = (b_2, b_1)$, $\boldsymbol{d}^1 = (b_0, b_2, b_1)$, and $\boldsymbol{d}^2 = (b_2, b_1, b_0, b_3, b_4)$ are all contained in $\boldsymbol{f} = (b_0, b_2, b_1, b_0, b_3, b_4)$ and can be achieved jointly by sorting on the six components of $\boldsymbol{f}$ rather than on the ten components of $\boldsymbol{d}^0$, $\boldsymbol{d}^1$, and $\boldsymbol{d}^2$.

The usefulness of this result is further extended [Ashenhurst (1953)] by the following fact: if a given component recurs in an ordering vector, its later occurrences may be ignored. For example, the second occurrence of b_0 in the vector $\boldsymbol{f}$ (as f_3) may be ignored, and $\boldsymbol{f}$ therefore contains the ordering $\boldsymbol{d}^3 = (b_0, b_2, b_1, b_3, b_4)$ as well.

The propriety of suppressing later recurrences of a component of an ordering vector is easily established. Let $\boldsymbol{b}$ be a given ordering vector and let $\boldsymbol{d} = \boldsymbol{b}_{\boldsymbol{m}}$ and $\boldsymbol{c} = \boldsymbol{b}_{\boldsymbol{n}}$ be two related orderings. Moreover, let $\boldsymbol{d}$ be obtainable from $\boldsymbol{c}$ by suppressing all later recurrences of components of $\boldsymbol{b}$. This implies that the mapping vector $\boldsymbol{m}$ is obtained from the mapping vector $\boldsymbol{n}$ by the same process, i.e., $\boldsymbol{m} = (\sigma/\boldsymbol{n})/\boldsymbol{n}$. If p_1 and p_2 are two items whose (distinct) keys $\boldsymbol{c}^1$ and $\boldsymbol{c}^2$ agree in all components up to but not including the jth, then their relative order is determined by the component $c_j = b_{n_j}$. In the corresponding keys $\boldsymbol{d}^1$ and $\boldsymbol{d}^2$ it is clear that the first component in which the items differ is again b_n and that the same relative order is therefore determined by $\boldsymbol{d}$. Since a third ordering $\boldsymbol{v} = \boldsymbol{b}_{\boldsymbol{p}}$ is also equivalent to the ordering $\boldsymbol{c} = \boldsymbol{b}_{\boldsymbol{n}}$ if $\boldsymbol{p}$ is also reducible to $\boldsymbol{m}$, the result concerning equivalent orderings can be extended as follows: two orderings $\boldsymbol{y} = \boldsymbol{z}_{\boldsymbol{m}}$ and $\boldsymbol{w} = \boldsymbol{z}_{\boldsymbol{n}}$ are equivalent if $(\sigma/\boldsymbol{m})/\boldsymbol{m} = (\sigma/\boldsymbol{n})/\boldsymbol{n}$.

Choice of number base. In the merge process of Program 6.4, the value of m may be chosen to suit the number n of files available, that is, $m = n - 1$. In the column sort, on the other hand, the number of files required is determined directly by b, the base of the number system representing the key. If the choice of b is otherwise arbitrary, it can be chosen as $n - 1$ for any $n > 2$. However, explicit execution of the base conversion indicated by the statement

$$(b\boldsymbol{\epsilon}) \perp \boldsymbol{d} \leftarrow k(p)$$

is usually avoided by using the base in which the key is represented in the original files. If a base conversion is required, it can be performed once on the first stage and the resulting vector $\boldsymbol{d}$ incorporated with the item for use on subsequent stages.

Base conversion may sometimes be inconvenient or impossible as, for example, in the case of special purpose sorting equipment devoid of arithmetic units. In this event the stage required for each digit (b-way classification and subsequent merge) may be executed as a series of copy operations each utilizing fewer than $(b + 1)$ files. If, for instance, the digits are represented in a ranked binary n-bit code, a series of n two-way classifications and two-way simple merges will effect the desired ordering on one digit of the key. More generally, a group of p successive binary digits can be treated at each pass, providing that $2^p + 1$ does not exceed the number of files available.

Repeated block sort. If a set of items is classified on the high-order column of an associated vector key, each of the resulting subvectors can be separately ordered and then merged in a final simple merge. Thus each of the subvectors forms an infix or *block* in the final arrangement. Such *block sorting* can be used to distribute the labor among a number of independent sorters.

Block sorting can also be repeated by further classifying each block on the next lower-order column of the key. For a key vector of dimension q, q repetitions of the block sort yield a complete classification, and ordering can then be achieved by a subsequent simple merge. However, since the number of blocks produced is (except for duplicate keys) equal to the original number of items, the use of repeated block sorting is unattractive unless simplified by special schemes for keeping record of and controlling the numerous blocks. Two such schemes will be discussed. The *radix exchange sort* (Sec. 6.4) is appropriate to random-access storage only; the *amphisbaenic sort* is appropriate to serial files.

Partial pass methods

Each of the sorting schemes discussed thus far is constrained to treat the entire collection of items at each stage. *Partial pass* methods obtained by relaxing this requirement normally achieve a reduction in the total number of items handled, but at the cost of some increase in complexity. The partial pass methods gain their advantage by largely obviating explicit merge phases.

The basic column sort gives rise to two partial pass methods of interest, the *amphisbaenic sort* and the *partial pass column* sort. The *cascade sort* arises from the use of partial passes in a merge sort.

*Partial pass column sort.** This method achieves the effect of one stage of a column sort on a base b key with fewer than $(b + 1)$ files by using a sequence of partial passes. The method will be illustrated by an example [taken from Ashenhurst (1953)] involving four files and a decimal key.

* Presented by John Mauchly in the Moore School lectures (1948) and treated more fully by Ashenhurst (1953).

Table 6.9. This table describes the partial pass column sort for reordering on a single column of the decimal key (the *j*th). The parenthetical expression following each file Φ_i indicates that it contains all items whose *j*th key digit equals one of the enclosed integers. A second pair of parentheses indicates a second set of items in the file following, and grouped separately from, the first set. Thus the original input file Φ_0 is described by $\Phi_0(0, 1, 2, 3, \ldots, 9)$ or by any permutation of the decimal digits enclosed in a single pair of parentheses.

Step	Input File	Output Files: Remaining from previous steps	Output Files: Copied	Pass Fraction
1	Φ_0: (0, 1, 2, 3, 4, 5, 6, 7, 8, 9)	Φ_1: Φ_2: Φ_3:	(0, 2, 4, 7) (1, 5, 6) (3, 8, 9)	1.0
2	Φ_1: (0, 2, 4, 7)	Φ_2: (1, 5, 6) Φ_3: (3, 8, 9) Φ_0:	(2, 7) (4) (0)	0.4
3	Φ_2: (1, 5, 6)(2, 7)	Φ_3: (3, 8, 9)(4) Φ_0: (0) Φ_1:	(5) (1)(2) (6)(7)	0.5
4	Φ_3: (3, 8, 9)(4)(5)	Φ_0: (0)(1)(2) Φ_1: (6)(7) Φ_2:	(3)(4)(5) (8) (9)	0.5
5	Φ_1: (6)(7)(8)	Φ_0: (0)(1)(2)(3)(4)(5) Φ_2: (9) Φ_3:	(6)(7)(8)	0.3
6	Φ_2: (9)	Φ_0: (0)(1)(2)(3)(4)(5)(6)(7)(8) Φ_3: Φ_1:	(9)	0.1
			Total	2.8

Table 6.9 The partial pass column sort

The first step copies each item whose *j*th key digit is (0, 2, 4, 7) to file Φ_1, items (1, 5, 6) to file Φ_2, and items (3, 8, 9) to file Φ_3. After each step, only the previous input file and the next input file are rewound, in this case Φ_0 and Φ_1. In step two, items (2, 7) are copied to Φ_2, and therefore *follow* the group (1, 5, 6), as indicated by the separate parentheses. Similarly, items (4) and (0) are copied to Φ_3 and Φ_0, respectively.

Step three is preceded by a rewind of Φ_2 and Φ_1. Since items (1) and (2) occur in separate groups in the new input file Φ_2, they can be copied to Φ_0 in separate groups (1) (2) as indicated. Similar remarks apply to items (6) and (7) copied to Φ_1. The three subsequent steps complete the required ordering, producing in the original input file Φ_0 the ordered array (0) (1) . . . (9). The rightmost column shows that fraction of the original file (assuming a uniform distribution of the key digits) copied on each pass. The total at the bottom indicates that the expected execution time is equivalent to 2.8 full passes.

The partial pass process of Table 6.9 is described more concisely by the 0-origin matrix $\boldsymbol{M}$ of Table 6.10. Element M_r^s specifies the file to which

Digit 0	1	0				
Digit 1	2		0			
Digit 2	1	2	0			
Digit 3	3			0		
Digit 4	1	3		0		
Digit 5	2		3	0		
Digit 6	2		1		0	
Digit 7	1	2	1		0	
Digit 8	3			1	0	
Digit 9	3			2		0
Input	0	1	2	3	1	2

Table 6.10 Matrix $\boldsymbol{M}$ describing the partial pass column sort of Table 6.9

items with key digit s are to be assigned in the rth step of the process, for $r \in \iota^0(6)$ and $s \in \iota^0(10)$. The eleventh and last row of $\boldsymbol{M}$ specifies the input files, i.e., $\boldsymbol{M}_r^{\mu}$ is the index of the input file in the rth step. An algorithm based upon the matrix $\boldsymbol{M}$ is described by Program 6.11.

Program 6.11. The subloop 14–18 performs the classification according to the element $\boldsymbol{M}_r^s$, using file i (specified by $\boldsymbol{M}_r^b$ on step 9) as input. When the file is exhausted, the branch to step 6 increments r and repeats the process unless $r = \nu(\boldsymbol{M})$. Equality indicates completion of the jth column and causes a branch to step 4 to decrement j and reset r. The comparison on j is deferred to line 13 so as to follow the termination and rewind of the new input file. The branch on step 10 prevents the recording of a dummy item on the original input file. The previous input file is rewound by step 8.

Program 6.11 includes the two-phase column sort as a special case, for if $(b + 1)$ files $\Phi_0, \Phi_1, \ldots, \Phi_b$ are available, the matrix shown on p. 194 specifies a process essentially identical with that of Program 6.7. File Φ_b corresponds to file $\Phi_0{}^0$, the first column of $\boldsymbol{M}$ determines the b-way classification, and each of the b succeeding columns specifies the copying of one file in the b-way simple merge onto file Φ_b.

The method of partial passes is frequently used in the sorting of alphabetic data. Variants include the $1\frac{2}{3}$ pass-per-character method of sorting

$$
M = \begin{array}{|c|c|c|c|c|}
\hline
0 & & & \cdots & \\
\hline
1 & b & & \cdots & \\
\hline
2 & & b & \cdots & \\
\hline
\vdots & \vdots & \vdots & & \vdots \\
\hline
b-1 & & & \cdots & b \\
\hline
b & 0 & 1 & \cdots & b-1 \\
\hline
\end{array}
$$

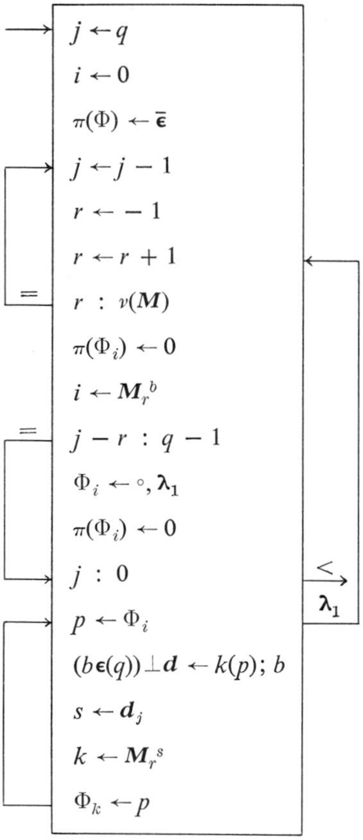

0-origin indexing	
Φ_i	Files ($i = 0$ for initial data).
$\boldsymbol{M}$	As in Table 6.10.
$\boldsymbol{d}$	Positional representation of key ($\nu(\boldsymbol{d}) = q$).
b	Base of representation.
j	Column stage $= q - j$.
r	Partial pass stage.
i	Current input file.

Legend

Program 6.11 Method of partial passes for m files

punched cards* and the procedure described by McCracken et al. (1959), p. 312.

Amphisbaenic sort. The amphisbaenic sort (Nagler, 1959) is a particular arrangement of the repeated block sort employing partial passes. For a base b key it requires $b + 1$ files and proceeds as a sequence of classifications, with a simple merge of the last b subblocks produced occurring immediately after each classification on the low-order column. Each classification allots digits to the available output files according to the rank of the file index, e.g., if file Φ_0 is the input, the digits $0, 1, 2, \ldots, b - 1$ are allotted to files $1, 2, 3, \ldots, b$, and if file Φ_3 is the input, they are allotted to files $0, 1, 2, 4, 5, \ldots, b$. The files are recorded forward and (except for the initial input) are read backward without intervening rewind. The subblocks are designated by the key digits on which they have been classified, e.g., by $0, 1, 2, \ldots, b - 1$, 00, 01, 02, etc. The block chosen for classification at each step is the one with the smallest designation among those not yet merged, the designations being ranked according to their values as decimal (b-ary) fractions. Thus block 213 precedes block 214, which precedes block 22.

Table 6.12 shows the steps of an amphisbaenic sort on a three-digit, base three key using files Φ_0, Φ_1, Φ_2, and Φ_3, with the initial and final data on file Φ_0. The input files are designated by asterisks. Thus file Φ_0 is the input to step 1, and blocks 0, 1, 2, are classified to files Φ_1, Φ_2, and Φ_3 as indicated. Step 2 classifies the smallest block (0) from file Φ_1 to files Φ_0, Φ_2, and Φ_3. Step 3 classifies blocks 000, 001, and 002 to files Φ_1, Φ_2, and Φ_3. The next step merges these blocks to file Φ_0, and the following step begins classification of the next smallest block (01) on file Φ_2. It is clear that if the files are read backward, the next block to be classified is always immediately available. The general process for a q-digit, base b key is described by Program 6.13.

Program 6.13. 0-origin indexing is used throughout. Each classification is controlled by the "current" vector $\boldsymbol{c}$ (of dimension b), whose components are the successive indices of the available output files. Thus $\boldsymbol{c}_k$ is the index of the file to which digit k is classified (steps 16–19). The current vector is determined by step 10 so as to omit the index i of the current input file. The selection of the block to be classified is determined by the vector $\boldsymbol{h}$ (of dimension q), the next block to be classified on digit j being determined by the prefix $\boldsymbol{\alpha}^{j+1}/\boldsymbol{h}$. Because the classifications proceed for increasing values of j and the blocks just produced appear last on the files, the selection can be determined by the last component of the prefix alone, i.e., by $\boldsymbol{h}_j$. This is done on step 7, where the index i of the input

* Described in IBM Form 22-3177-2 *Sorter Manual*, p. 12.

Step	1	2	3	4 (merge)	5	6 (merge)	7	8 (merge)	9	10	11 (merge)
Φ_0	*	00	*	000–002	000–002, 010	000–012	00–012, 020	000–022	000–022, 10	000–022*	000–102
Φ_1	0	*	000	*	011	*	021	*	11	11, 100	11*
Φ_2	1	1, 01	1, 01, 001	1, 01*	1*	1	1, 022	1*	*	101	*
Φ_3	2	2, 02	2, 02, 002	2, 02*	2, 02, 012	2, 02*	2*	2	2, 12	2, 12, 102	2, 12*
h	(0, 0, 0)	(0, 0, 0)	(0, 0, 0)	(0, 1, 0)	(0, 1, 0)	(0, 2, 0)	(0, 2, 0)	(1, 0, 0)	(1, 0, 0)	(1, 0, 0)	(1, 1, 0)
i	0	1	0	1	2	1	3	0	2	0	2
j	0	1	2	1	2	1	2	0	1	2	1
s	(0, 0, 0)	(0, 1, 0)	(0, 1, 0)		(0, 1, 2)		(0, 1, 3)		(0, 2, 3)	(0, 2, 0)	
c	(1, 2, 3)	(0, 2, 3)	(1, 2, 3)		(0, 1, 3)		(0, 1, 2)		(0, 1, 3)	(1, 2, 3)	

Step	12	13 (merge)	14	15 (merge)	16	17	18 (merge)	19	20 (merge)	21	22 (merge)
Φ_0	000–102, 110	000–112	000–112, 120	000–122	000–122, 20	000–122*	000–202	000–202, 210	000–212	000–212, 220	000–222
Φ_1	*		121	*	21	21, 200	21*	*		221	*
Φ_2	111	*	122	*	22	22, 201	22*	22, 211	22*	*	
Φ_3	2, 12, 112	2, 12*	2*	2	*	202	*	212	*	222	*
h	(1, 1, 0)	(1, 2, 0)	(1, 2, 0)	(2, 0, 0)	(2, 0, 0)	(2, 0, 0)	(2, 1, 0)	(2, 1, 0)	(2, 2, 0)	(2, 2, 0)	(0, 0, 0)
i	1	2	3	0	3	0	3	1	3	2	
j	2	1	2	0	1	2	1	2	1	2	−1
s	(0, 2, 1)		(0, 2, 3)		(0, 3, 3)	(0, 3, 0)		(0, 3, 1)		(0, 3, 2)	
c	(0, 2, 3)		(0, 1, 2)		(0, 1, 2)	(1, 2, 3)		(0, 2, 3)		(0, 1, 3)	

Table 6.12 Amphisbaenic sort on 3-digit base 3 key

Φ_i	Files ($i = 0$ for initial and final data); $i \in \iota^0(b + 1)$.	c	Indices of current output files. $\nu(c) = b$.
b	Base of representation.	h	α^{j+1}/h specifies input block to classification on digit j.
j	d_j controls current classification.		
i	Index of current input.	s	s_j is index of input file to classification on digit j.
f	Controls forward read and rewind of initial input.	d	Positional representation of key.

$\left. \begin{array}{c} \\ \\ \end{array} \right\} \nu = q$

Legend

```
1  →  π(Φ) ← ε̄(b)
2     f ← 0
3     h ← ε̄(q)                        ≠ ┌ f : 0                    ← 20
4     s ← ε̄(q)                           │ f ← 1                      21
5     i ← 0                              │ π(Φ₀) ← 0                  22
6  ┌  j ← 0                          └→  p ← ₁Φᵢ                     23
7  │  i ← (ε̄ⁱ/ι⁰(b))ₕⱼ        ←       <  j : q − 1               ←  24
8  │  j ← j + 1                          k ← (c₀ = 0)                25
9  │  sⱼ ← i                       ┌→   p ← ₁Φ_{cₖ}          λ₁    26
10 └→ c ← ε̄ⁱ/ι⁰(b)                   │   Φ₀ ← p                     27
11    k ← (j = q − 1) ∧ (c₀ = 0)      │   p ← ₁Φ_{cₖ}            ←  28
12 ┌  Φ_{cₖ} ← °, λ₁                   │   k ← k + 1                29
13 │  Φ_{cₖ} ← °, λ₀               <   └ k : b                      30
14 │  k ← k + 1                     ┌→  j ← j − 1               <  31
15 └< k : b                         │ = hⱼ ← b |₀ (hⱼ + 1)        32
16 ┌  p ← ₍f₎Φᵢ              λ₁      │   i ← sⱼ                     33
17 │  (bε(q)) ⊥ d ← k(p) ; b        │   Φ₀ ← °, λ₁             ←  34
18 │  k ← dⱼ                         │   π(Φ₀) ← 0              →  35
19 └  Φ_{cₖ} ← p
```

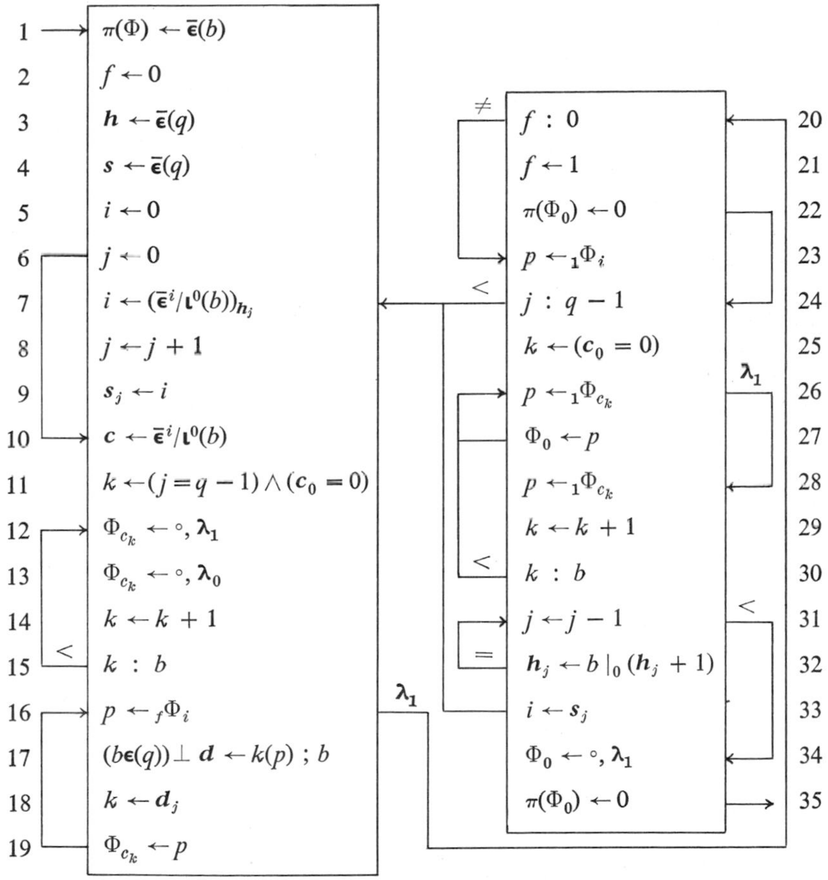

Program 6.13 Amphisbaenic sort

to the preceding stage determines the vector $\bar{\boldsymbol{\epsilon}}^i/\boldsymbol{\iota}^0(b)$ of output indices, from which the new input index is selected as the $\boldsymbol{h}_j$th component. The successive values of $\boldsymbol{h}$, i, j, $\boldsymbol{s}$, and $\boldsymbol{c}$ listed in the example of Table 6.12 may be helpful in tracing the operation of the program.

When classification on the last digit is completed, the last subblocks are merged (steps 25–30) onto the output file Φ_0. The variable j must then be decremented and the component $\boldsymbol{h}_j$ incremented modulo b (steps 31–32). When $\boldsymbol{h}_j$ completes a cycle (becomes zero), the corresponding subblocks are exhausted and j must be decremented repeatedly until the corresponding $\boldsymbol{h}_j$ does not become zero. The main process through increasing values of j is then repeated.

Although $\boldsymbol{h}_j$ determines the input subblock for the classification on digit j, it determines the index of the input file only indirectly (step 7) through the vector of output files, itself determined by the input file i used in the classification on the preceding digit. When j is increasing, the value of i is simply the value from the preceding stage. However, when j is decremented (steps 31–32), it is necessary to determine the input i used in an earlier classification. A record of the value of i corresponding to each classification j is therefore kept (step 9) in the vector $\boldsymbol{s}$, and is used to redefine i on step 33.

Each file to be used as output (except possibly file Φ_0) is first closed with a partition (steps 12–15) to demark the beginning of each of the subblocks to be recorded. Since backward read is to be used, two dummy items are provided so that the branch on $\boldsymbol{\lambda}_1$ coincides with the read of a dummy item. An extra read then disposes of the extra dummy. Any partition recorded on the final output file Φ_0 before a fully classified subblock (when $j = q - 1$) would remain in the final output. Step 11 prevents this by initializing the index k to 1 if $j = q - 1$ and the index of the first output file (that is, $\boldsymbol{c}_0$) is zero. In a similar manner, step 25 prevents the attempt to copy file Φ_0 to itself during the merge phase (steps 25–30). Step 28 reads the extra dummy item recorded in the partitioning operation of steps 12–15.

All files are read backward except the initial input in the first stage. This behavior is controlled by the logical variable f (steps 16 and 20–21). The branch on step 20 fails the first time only, allowing f to be respecified as 1 and rewinding file Φ_0. On subsequent stages, the branch to step 23 causes the read of the extra dummy partition.

*Cascade sort.** The cascade sort is a partial pass merge sort, with each stage proceeding as follows. The strings are initially distributed (unequally) among m of the $m + 1$ available files; an m-way merge to the empty file is performed until some input is exhausted; an $m - 1$ way merge to the newly emptied file is then performed from the remaining inputs, and so on to a final two-way merge. The effectiveness of the process depends on a particular initial distribution of the input strings.

Table 6.14 illustrates the process for 190 strings distributed among five of six available files as shown in the first row. Succeeding rows show the

* Due to Betz and Carter (1959). See also Gilstad (1960) and Carter (1962).

Stage	Distribution of strings				
0	15	29	41	50	55
1	5	9	12	14	15
2	1	2	3	4	5
3	1	1	1	1	1
4	0	0	0	0	1

Table 6.14 Cascade merge sort

distribution of strings at the end of the succeeding stages.* The process requires but four passes, only the last of which is a complete pass (e.g., the last five strings need not be copied in stage 1).

The power of a merge process may be defined as the (average) factor by which the number of strings decreases per pass, i.e., as $\sqrt[p]{s}$, where s is the number of strings whose ordering can be completed in p passes. For the given example, the power is approximately 3.7. This surpasses the power of 3.0 attainable in a three-way single phase merge sort using the same number of files.

Gilstad (1960) has proposed a variant of the cascade sort (called *polyphase*) in which every phase is an m-way merge, i.e., each newly recorded output enters immediately as input in the following phase. Its power is slightly greater than that of the cascade sort.

6.2 EVALUATION OF SERIAL SORTING METHODS

Three major factors enter the evaluation of a serial sorting process: the amount of program storage required, the number of serial-access files used, and the execution time. The first two factors require little analysis, and attention will be limited primarily to the third.

Because the execution time of a serial sorting process is normally determined almost completely by the time required to transfer information to and from the serial files, the execution time is assumed to be directly proportional to the number of passes of the files required. Each phase corresponds to a pass or (as in partial pass methods) to some fraction of a pass, and the number of passes per stage is determined by summation over the component phases.

The constant of proportionality relating actual execution time and number of passes depends on such factors as the average length of the items, the reading and recording rate of the serial files, and (in processes

* The jth column of the table refers not to a specific file but to that file which ranks jth in number of strings.

requiring rewinding after each phase) the rewinding speed. Since these factors are specific to particular equipment and particular tasks, and since the nature of the dependence is obvious, the present analysis is limited to consideration of the number of passes.

Consideration is also given to related orderings (cf. vector keys and categories), which may, in the use of column sorting, be achieved more efficiently jointly than separately.

Simple classification and merge

The number of stages required in the m-way merge sorting methods depends on s_0, the number of maximal strings in the original file, and on m. For, if s_j is the number of (maximal) strings at the conclusion of the jth stage, then $s_{j+1} \doteq \lceil s_j \div m \rceil$. Since the eventual string length must be one, the number of stages required is given by

$$r = \lceil \log_m s_0 \rceil,$$

for which the approximation $r \doteq \log_m s_0$ will be used. The number of passes is then $2r$ for a two-phase merge and r for a single-phase merge. If the "cost" of the process is assumed to be of the form

$$c = (a + m)r = (a + m) \log_m s_0,$$

for some constant a, then the optimum choice of m is obtained as the solution of the equation

$$\log_e m = 1 + a \div m.$$

The two-phase and single-phase methods may be compared for a fixed number of files as follows. Let $n = 2k$ be the number of files,* let s be the number of strings, and let t_1 and t_2 be the execution times for the single-phase and two-phase methods, respectively. Then

$$\frac{t_2}{t_1} = \frac{2 \log_{m_2} s}{\log_{m_1} s} = \frac{2 \log_{(2k-1)} s}{\log_k s}$$
$$= \frac{2 \log_s k}{\log_s (2k - 1)} = \frac{2 \log_{10} k}{\log_{10} (2k - 1)} = \frac{2 \log_e k}{\log_e (2k - 1)}.$$

This ratio increases monotonically from 1.26 at $k = 2$ to an asymptotic value of two. Since it exceeds unity, the single-phase process is to be preferred.

Expected number of strings. Since the original file is frequently specified in terms of the number of items n rather than the number of maximal strings

* An odd number n would prejudice the result against the single-phase method, since one file would necessarily be left idle.

s, it is desirable to determine the relation between n and the expected value of s for a random distribution of the keys.

Let $\boldsymbol{k}$ be a vector of dimension $n + 1$ whose first n components are the successive keys of the file and whose last component is infinite, and let $\boldsymbol{f} = (\boldsymbol{k} < \downarrow\boldsymbol{k})$, $\boldsymbol{d} = (\boldsymbol{k} = \downarrow\boldsymbol{k})$, and $\boldsymbol{b} = (\boldsymbol{k} > \downarrow\boldsymbol{k})$.
If, for example,

$$\boldsymbol{k} = 7\ \ 9\ 3\ 5\ 5\ 8\ 2\ 1\ 4\ \infty,$$

then

$$\begin{aligned} \downarrow\boldsymbol{k} &= \infty\ 7\ 9\ 3\ 5\ 5\ 8\ 2\ 1\ 4 \\ \boldsymbol{f} &= \ \ 1\ 0\ 1\ 0\ 0\ 0\ 1\ 1\ 0\ 0 \\ \boldsymbol{d} &= \ \ 0\ 0\ 0\ 0\ 1\ 0\ 0\ 0\ 0\ 0 \\ \boldsymbol{b} &= \ \ 0\ 1\ 0\ 1\ 0\ 1\ 0\ 0\ 1\ 1. \end{aligned}$$

Each unit component of $\boldsymbol{f}$ marks the beginning of each maximal ascending string in the forward direction (left to right), each unit component of $\uparrow\boldsymbol{b}$ marks the beginning of each maximal string in the backward direction, and a unit component of $\boldsymbol{d}$ marks each key which duplicates its predecessor. Consequently, $+/\boldsymbol{f}$, $+/\boldsymbol{b}$, and $+/\boldsymbol{d}$ are the number of forward strings, backward strings, and duplicates, respectively. Since the relations $<$, $=$, and $>$ are exhaustive and mutually disjoint, the three logical vectors are exhaustive and mutually disjoint, i.e., $\boldsymbol{f} \vee \boldsymbol{d} \vee \boldsymbol{b} = \boldsymbol{\epsilon}$, and $\boldsymbol{f} \wedge \boldsymbol{d} = \boldsymbol{f} \wedge \boldsymbol{b} = \boldsymbol{d} \wedge \boldsymbol{b} = 0$.
Consequently

$$(+/\boldsymbol{f}) + (+/\boldsymbol{b}) + (+/\boldsymbol{d}) = \nu(\boldsymbol{k}) = n + 1.$$

Denoting the expected value of x by $e(x)$, it follows that

$$e\,(+/\boldsymbol{f}) + e(+/\boldsymbol{b}) + e(+/\boldsymbol{d}) = n + 1.$$

Symmetry and the assumed random distribution together imply that $e(+/\boldsymbol{f}) = e(+/\boldsymbol{b})$. Consequently, the expected number of strings $e(s)$ is given by

$$e(s) = e(+/\boldsymbol{f}) = (n + 1 - e(+/\boldsymbol{d})) \div 2.$$

If there are no duplicates, the expected number of strings is approximately $n/2$, and the expected string length is therefore approximately two. Assuming a uniform distribution of keys in a range of g values, the probability that $\boldsymbol{d}_i = 1$ is clearly $1/g$ for all $i \in \iota^2(n - 1)$. Therefore $e(+/\boldsymbol{d}) = (n - 1) \div g$.

Classification and simple merge

The number of stages required in the column sort is equal to q, the number of significant digits in the representation of the key. To facilitate comparison between different number bases, it is convenient to use the variable g denoting the range of the key. Thus in any base b, the number of significant digits q required in the key is given by $q = \lceil \log_b g \rceil$, or approximately by $q = \log_b g$. For any pair of bases b_1 and b_2, the corresponding number of stages q_1 and q_2 are related as follows:

$$\frac{q_1}{q_2} = \frac{\log_{b_1} g}{\log_{b_2} g} = \frac{\log_g b_2}{\log_g b_1} = \frac{\log_{b_1} b_2}{\log_{b_1} b_1} = \log_{b_1} b_2.$$

A more practical form for calculation is

$$\frac{q_1}{q_2} = \frac{\log_{10} b_2}{\log_{10} b_1}.$$

The foregoing expressions are identical in form to those obtained for the number of stages required in the merge sort, but with the range g replacing the initial number of strings s_0, and with b replacing m. Moreover, the number of files required depends on b in the same way that the corresponding merge processes depend on m. This holds for both the two-phase column sort ($b + 1$ files) and the single-phase column sort ($2b$ files). The analysis concerning the optimal value of m therefore carries over directly to the choice of the base b, the only additional consideration being the possible need for base conversions on the key. The comparison between two-phase and single-phase processes also applies directly to the column sort, with the conclusion that the single-phase method is superior.

Of the methods discussed, the column sort is the only one which shows significant advantages in the joint treatment of two or more related orderings. If $\mathbf{x} = \mathbf{z}_p$ and $\mathbf{y} = \mathbf{z}_q$ are two vector keys, and if $\boldsymbol{\omega}^i/\mathbf{p} = \boldsymbol{\alpha}^i/\mathbf{q}$, then the ordering defined by the key $\mathbf{z}_r$, for $\mathbf{r} = \overline{\boldsymbol{\omega}}^i/\mathbf{p}$ will, when applied to the set of items ordered on $\mathbf{y}$, suffice to produce ordering on $\mathbf{x}$. The total number of columns sorted to achieve the two orderings jointly is then reduced by i.

More generally, if $\boldsymbol{\omega}^i/\mathbf{p}$ agrees with a selected subvector of the prefix $\boldsymbol{\alpha}^j/\mathbf{q}$ and if the remaining elements of the prefix occur in $\overline{\boldsymbol{\omega}}^i/\mathbf{p}$ (in any order), then sorting on the columns corresponding to $\boldsymbol{\omega}^i/\mathbf{p}$ may again be elided. More precisely, if there exist integers i and j, and a logical vector $\mathbf{u}$ such that

$$\boldsymbol{\omega}^i/\mathbf{p} = \mathbf{u}/(\boldsymbol{\alpha}^j/\mathbf{q}),$$

and

$$(\overline{\boldsymbol{\omega}}^i/\mathbf{p}) \supseteq (\overline{\mathbf{u}}/(\boldsymbol{\alpha}^j/\mathbf{q})),$$

then the ordering $\mathbf{x}$ can be achieved by applying the ordering $\overline{\boldsymbol{\omega}}^i/\mathbf{p}$ to the ordering $\mathbf{y}$, and the total number of columns sorted is reduced by i. It is assumed that neither $\mathbf{p}$ nor $\mathbf{q}$ contains any repeated components, for if they do, each of the later occurrences may be suppressed.

Since the ordering on x can be performed before rather than after the ordering on y, the roles of p and q may also be reversed, and the case showing the larger reduction may be chosen. If three or more orderings are prescribed, the foregoing method may be applied to evaluate each of the possible sequences of ordering.

Partial pass methods

In the absence of a general method for designing a partial pass column sort, its efficiency will be indicated only by an analysis of the four-file decimal key example of Table 6.9. If g is the range of the key, the number of passes is given by $p_1 = 2.8q = 2.8 \log_{10} g$. This may be compared with the value $p_3 = 2 \log_3 g$ obtained for the straightforward base three column sort, which can also be performed with four files. The ratio

$$\frac{p_1}{p_3} = (2.8 \log_{10} g) \div (2 \log_3 g) = 1.4 \log_{10} 3 = 0.668,$$

indicates the superior efficiency of the partial pass column sort for this case. The four files can also be used for a single-phase column sort in a base two number system, yielding the value $p_2 = \log_2 g$ for the number of passes. Hence $p_1/p_2 = 0.843$, and the method of partial passes is again the more efficient.

In the amphisbaenic sort on n items with a q-digit base b key, $b + 1$ files are required, and the total number of items handled in the classification phases is nq. In the merge phases, however, each item is handled at most* once, and the total number of passes is therefore less than $(q + 1)$. This may be compared with the $2q$ passes required in a two-phase column sort using the same number of files. Alternatively, conversion of the key to a base $\lfloor (b + 1) \div 2 \rfloor$ representation could permit the use of a more efficient single-phase merge requiring approximately $q \log_{(b+1)/2} b$ passes.

The disadvantages of the amphisbaenic sort reside in the more complex program required and in the need for frequent reversal of the direction of the files, i.e., from forward record to backward read. The time lost in such reversal may be considerable for certain files.

The power of the cascade sort is, as indicated by the example of Table 6.14, somewhat greater than that of the corresponding merge sort. Its behavior is most conveniently analyzed [in the manner developed by Carter (1962)] in terms of the difference equation satisfied by the number of strings occurring in successive states. The formulation of these equations is indicated in Exercise 6.19. Carter provides asymptotic solutions for cases of practical interest.

* If the final output file Φ_0 is among the set of output files in the classification on the low-order digit, the subblock assigned to it need not be recopied in the merge phase.

In addition to its greater complexity, the cascade sort suffers from the need for a particular initial distribution of the strings, and from the dispersal of the file rewinds (which can be performed concurrently by most computers) throughout the process. Moreover, in the event of a computer error, a rerun from the last correct input files is much more difficult to program than is a corresponding rerun for a straightforward merge.

6.3 AIDS TO SERIAL SORTING PROCESSES

Internal sorting normally enjoys a much higher basic execution rate than does serial sorting, but for large volume files the limited size of internal storage may make serial sorting necessary. The amount of serial sorting may, however, be reduced by some use of internal sorting. For example, a preliminary internal sort can produce maximal strings whose lengths are limited only by the size of the internal store and thus reduce the number of strings presented for subsequent serial merge sorting.

The present section is devoted to methods of reducing serial sorting by the auxiliary use of internal sorting. For this discussion, the only knowledge assumed concerning the internal sorting process is its capacity to order a specified number of items.

Two classes of processes arise, one for aiding merge sorting and one for aiding column sorting. The aid to merge sorting is the simpler, since it consists merely in assembling long strings by internal sorting before beginning the serial merge sort. A serial column sort, on the other hand, may be aided by a final internal sort performed *after* the column sort.

If $\boldsymbol{k} = \boldsymbol{k}(\boldsymbol{x})$ is a key vector associated with $\boldsymbol{x}$, and if m is any positive integer, then a serial column sort performed on the key vector

$$\boldsymbol{k}^1 = \lfloor \boldsymbol{k} \div m\boldsymbol{\epsilon} \rfloor$$

produces the vector $\boldsymbol{x}^0 \oplus \boldsymbol{x}^1 \oplus \cdots \oplus \boldsymbol{x}^p$, where the vector $\boldsymbol{x}^i$ contains all items such that $\boldsymbol{k}_j^1 = i$. If the infix vectors $\boldsymbol{x}^i$ are then copied in turn from the file, individually reordered on the key

$$\boldsymbol{k}^2 = (m\boldsymbol{\epsilon})|_0\boldsymbol{k}$$

and recorded, the resulting file will be ordered on $\boldsymbol{k}$. Table 6.15 shows an example for $m = 4$.

If internal storage allows the internal ordering of as many as n items, then the reordering of the infixes $\boldsymbol{x}^i$ can be accomplished by an internal sort provided that m is so chosen that $\nu(\boldsymbol{x}^i) \leq n$ for all i. If the original keys are all distinct, m may be chosen equal to n.

If the sort on $\boldsymbol{k}^1$ is performed as a base b serial column sort, the number of stages required is reduced by approximately $\log_b m$ from the number

Original Order x	k	k^1	k^2	Ordered on k^1 x	k	k^1	k^2	Sets of Duplicates in k^1	Final Order x	k	k^1	k^2
x_1	7	1	3	x_3	2	0	2	x^0	x_3	2	0	2
x_2	9	2	1	x_7	3	0	3		x_7	3	0	3
x_3	2	0	2	x_1	7	1	3		x_6	4	1	0
x_4	11	2	3	x_5	6	1	2	x^1	x_5	6	1	2
x_5	6	1	2	x_6	4	1	0		x_1	7	1	3
x_6	4	1	0	x_2	9	2	1	x^2	x_2	9	2	1
x_7	3	0	3	x_4	11	2	3		x_4	11	2	3

Table 6.15 Internal aid to column sort ($m = 4$)

required for a corresponding sort on the original key. The subsequent internal sort on $\mathbf{k}^2$ therefore serves as an aid to the serial column sort.

The arithmetic operations indicated in the definition of keys $\mathbf{k}^1$ and $\mathbf{k}^2$ may be simplified if m is chosen as an integral power of the base b of the original key. For, if the vector $\mathbf{d}$ is the q-digit base b representation of $\mathbf{k}_i$, and if $m = b^t$, then $\overline{\boldsymbol{\omega}}^t/\mathbf{d}$, and $\boldsymbol{\omega}^t/\mathbf{d}$ are the base b representations of $\mathbf{k}_i^1$ and $\mathbf{k}_i^2$, respectively. The keys are therefore obtained from $\mathbf{k}$ by extracting the specified columns, and the serial sorting is reduced by exactly t stages.

6.4 INTERNAL SORTING METHODS

Since the range of practical sorting methods is clearly broadened by the use of random-access storage, internal sorting methods include all of the serial processes treated in Sec. 6.1. However, since the use of random-access storage introduces certain new problems in the execution of these processes, they will be reconsidered before proceeding to methods suited to random-access storage only.

If the available random-access storage is divided into a number of areas or *fields*, these fields can be used in lieu of the serial files. The serial sorting methods then carry over unchanged except that the automatic self-indexing property of the serial files must be replaced by an explicitly programmed indexing of the corresponding fields.

The efficacy of an internal sorting process depends not only on the speed of execution but also on the number n of items which can be ordered, using a given storage capacity c (measured in number of items). Since n is nearly linear in c, this property is measured in terms of the *storage ratio* $r = c \div n$.

In using random-access storage, the effect of a simple merge or a simple classification can be achieved rather easily through address modification. Hence there is little advantage in splitting either the merge or the column sort into two separate phases, and attention will be limited to the single-phase processes. The two-phase processes can prove superior if efficient block transfer of data is available in the execution of the program, but their behavior should, in any event, be clear from the treatment of the analogous single-phase processes.

Simple classification and merge

An internal single-phase merge analogous to the serial single-phase merge of Program 6.5 can be based on the assignment of two matrices ${}^1\boldsymbol{X}$ and ${}^2\boldsymbol{X}$ to correspond to the sets of input and output files. The rows ${}^a\boldsymbol{X}^i$ of the matrices ${}^a\boldsymbol{X}$ correspond to the files Φ_i^a of the serial process, each item being represented by a single matrix element. Items are read sequentially from and to fields; for each input field ${}^a\boldsymbol{X}^j$, an index $\boldsymbol{r}_j$ indicates the element ${}^a\boldsymbol{X}_{\boldsymbol{r}_j}^j$ to be read next; for each output field ${}^{(3-a)}\boldsymbol{X}^i$, an index $\boldsymbol{s}_i$ indicates the element next to be specified. The items in each field occupy the leading positions in the field, and the index of the first unoccupied element in the input field ${}^a\boldsymbol{X}^j$ is indicated by the parameter $\boldsymbol{t}_j$. The process is described by Program 6.16.

Program 6.16. As in Program 6.5, the vectors $\boldsymbol{v}$ and $\boldsymbol{z}$ specify exhausted fields (files) and ineligible fields (positions), respectively. The parameters a and $\boldsymbol{t}$ are initially specified external to the process. At the beginning of each stage the vector $\boldsymbol{v}$ (exhausted fields) is specified (step 3) according to the unit components of $\boldsymbol{t}$. At each stage except the first, $\boldsymbol{t}$ is respecified (step 2) by the final value of $\boldsymbol{s}$ from the previous stage. When only one string remains, each component of $\boldsymbol{s}$, save the first, will remain at its initial value of unity, and this condition is used to terminate the process at step 1. The vector $\boldsymbol{k}$ represents the keys of the current items in the m input fields and is initially specified (step 7) by the keys of the column vector ${}^a\boldsymbol{X}_1$ of initial items of the input fields. The remainder of the process is closely analogous to Program 6.5.

If the total number of items to be sorted is n, then each of the $2m$ fields ${}^a\boldsymbol{X}^j$ must accommodate n items, and the total storage allocated must be $2nm$. The storage ratio is therefore $2m$. It can be reduced to two by putting the output in a single field and keeping a record of the beginning location of each successive set of $s' = \lceil s \div m \rceil$ strings, where s is the maximum number of strings in any one input field.

Let the input be represented by the single field $\boldsymbol{X}^a$, let $\boldsymbol{b}$ be a vector of dimension $m + 1$, whose kth component specifies the beginning location of the kth set of maximal strings, for $k = 1, 2, \ldots, j$, the jth set numbering possibly less than s', and let $\boldsymbol{b}_{j+1}$ be the location of the first unused position of the field. Obviously $j \leq m$, and if $j < m$, the remaining undefined components of $\boldsymbol{b}$ are immaterial. If the j sets are to serve as inputs to an m-way merge, then the prefix $\boldsymbol{\alpha}^m/\boldsymbol{b}$ serves to initialize the vector $\boldsymbol{r}$ of

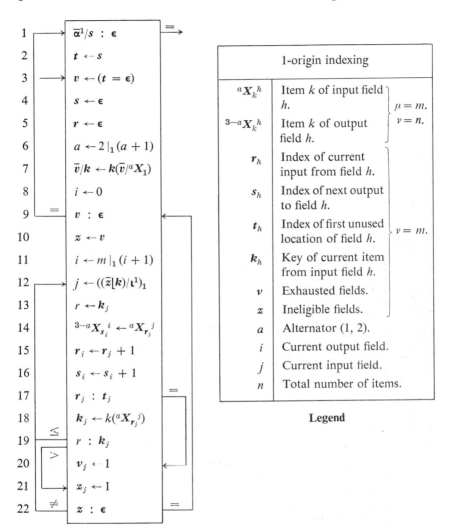

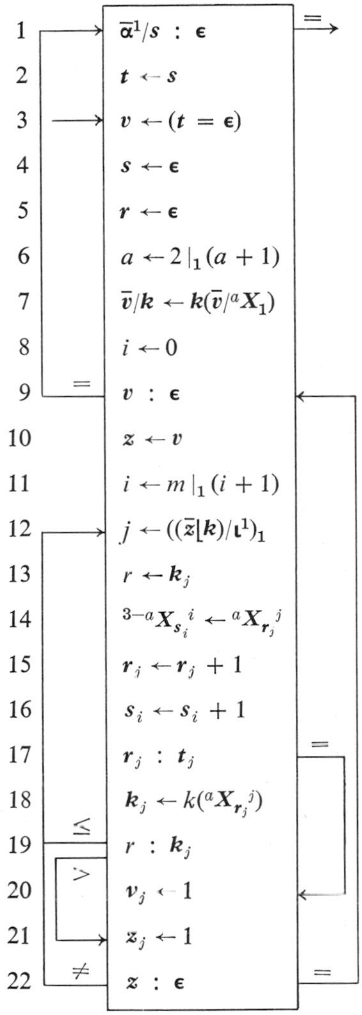

	1-origin indexing	
$^{a}X_k^h$	Item k of input field h.	$\mu = m$.
$^{3-a}X_k^h$	Item k of output field h.	$\nu = n$.
r_h	Index of current input from field h.	
s_h	Index of next output to field h.	
t_h	Index of first unused location of field h.	$\nu = m$.
k_h	Key of current item from input field h.	
v	Exhausted fields.	
z	Ineligible fields.	
a	Alternator (1, 2).	
i	Current output field.	
j	Current input field.	
n	Total number of items.	

Legend

Program 6.16 Internal single-phase m-way merge using $2m$ fields

current input indices, and the suffix $\boldsymbol{\omega}^m/\boldsymbol{b}$ defines the terminating locations $\boldsymbol{t}$.

The strings produced by the merge from the sets of maximal strings in X^a can be transferred without classification to the single output field X^{3-a}. If the vector $\boldsymbol{b}$ is redefined by the beginning locations in the output field of successive sets of $\lceil s' \div m \rceil$ items, it can be used to define the input fields in a subsequent merge from the field X^{3-a}. Program 6.17 shows a convenient arrangement of the process.

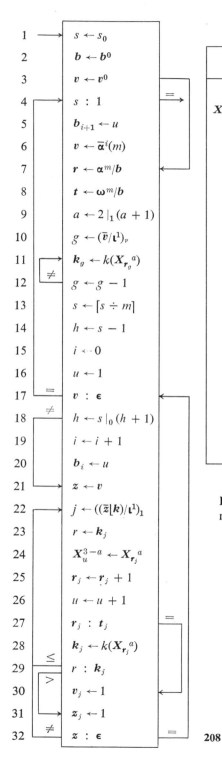

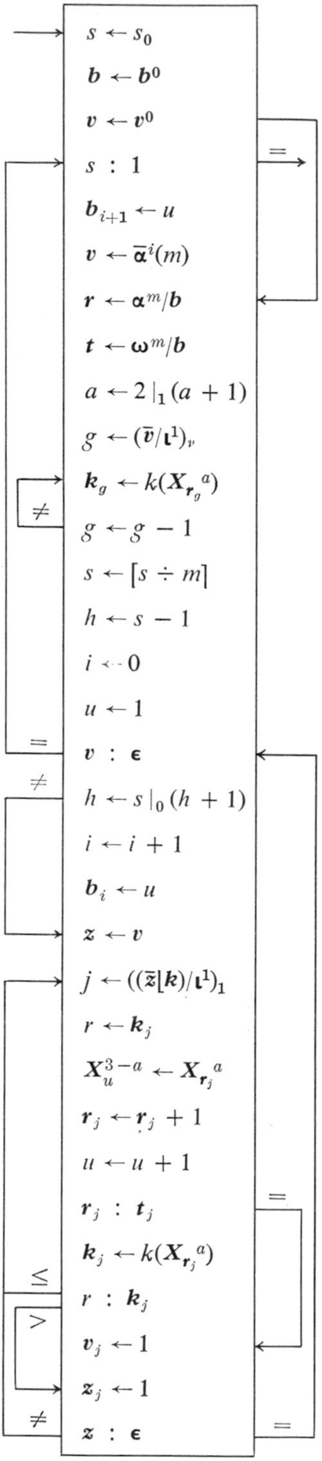

1	$s \leftarrow s_0$
2	$b \leftarrow b^0$
3	$v \leftarrow v^0$
4	$s : 1$
5	$b_{i+1} \leftarrow u$
6	$v \leftarrow \bar{\alpha}^i(m)$
7	$r \leftarrow \alpha^m/b$
8	$t \leftarrow \omega^m/b$
9	$a \leftarrow 2 \mid_1 (a + 1)$
10	$g \leftarrow (\bar{v}/\iota^1)_v$
11	$k_g \leftarrow k(X_{r_g}{}^a)$
12	$g \leftarrow g - 1$
13	$s \leftarrow \lceil s \div m \rceil$
14	$h \leftarrow s - 1$
15	$i \leftarrow 0$
16	$u \leftarrow 1$
17	$v : \epsilon$
18	$h \leftarrow s \mid_0 (h + 1)$
19	$i \leftarrow i + 1$
20	$b_i \leftarrow u$
21	$z \leftarrow v$
22	$j \leftarrow ((\bar{z}|k)/\iota^1)_1$
23	$r \leftarrow k_j$
24	$X_u^{3-a} \leftarrow X_{r_j}{}^a$
25	$r_j \leftarrow r_j + 1$
26	$u \leftarrow u + 1$
27	$r_j : t_j$
28	$k_j \leftarrow k(X_{r_j}{}^a)$
29	$r : k_j$
30	$v_j \leftarrow 1$
31	$z_j \leftarrow 1$
32	$z : \epsilon$

1-origin indexing	
X^a	Input field. $\left.\vphantom{\begin{matrix}a\\b\end{matrix}}\right\}$ $v = n$
X^{3-a}	Output field.
b_d	Beginning of subfield d in output. $\left.\vphantom{\begin{matrix}a\\b\\c\end{matrix}}\right\}$ $v = m + 1$
r_d	Index of current input for subfield d.
t_d	Index of first location following subfield d.
k_d	Key of current item from subfield d.
v	Exhausted subfields.
z	Ineligible subfields.
u	Index of next output.
a	Alternator (1, 2).
h	Output string counter.
i	Index of current output subfield.
j	Index of current input subfield.
n	Total number of items.

(the bracket from r_d through z labelled $v = m$)

Legend

Program 6.17 Internal single-phase merge using two fields

Program 6.17. As in Program 6.16, the vector $\boldsymbol{r}$ determines the current set of items being examined, and $\boldsymbol{t}$ determines the terminal value of $\boldsymbol{r}$. The first m components of $\boldsymbol{b}$ initialize $\boldsymbol{r}$ (step 7), and the last m components initialize $\boldsymbol{t}$ (step 8). The index u determines the component of the output vector $\boldsymbol{X}^{3-a}$, which is next to be specified (step 24).

The remainder of the process differs from Program 6.16 primarily in the determination of $\boldsymbol{b}$. The counter h allows i and $\boldsymbol{b}_i$ to be respecified (steps 19–20) at the end of each group of s strings. The last specified component of $\boldsymbol{b}$ is determined separately by step 5. Step 6 redetermines $\boldsymbol{v}$ for the next stage.

Since some of the initial values s_0, $\boldsymbol{v}^0$, and $\boldsymbol{b}^0$ may be unknown, the initialization of the process (steps 1–3) merits some attention. If s_0 alone is known, $\boldsymbol{v}^0$ and $\boldsymbol{b}^0$ may be chosen as follows: $\boldsymbol{v}^0 = \bar{\boldsymbol{\alpha}}^1$; $\boldsymbol{b}_1{}^0 = 1, \boldsymbol{b}_2{}^0 = \nu(\boldsymbol{X})$. The effect is to perform the first merge from a single input area. Consequently, the first stage performs no rearrangement but does determine the vectors $\boldsymbol{v}$ and $\boldsymbol{b}$.

If s_0 is unknown, s may be determined by a preliminary string count. Alternatively, it may be set to any integer value $y \geq s_0$. The process remains valid, but the required number of stages is increased by $\lceil \log_m y \rceil - \lceil \log_m s_0 \rceil$.

Since s_0 cannot exceed the number of items, the initial value $s = \nu(\boldsymbol{X})$ is always valid, and for an assumed random distribution it exceeds the expected value by a factor of two only. If greater initial order is expected, it may be desirable to modify Program 6.17 to allow a small initial choice of s, accompanied by automatic respecification in the event that it proves too small. The modification may be simply made by inserting a branch on equality of i and m, following step 18. The branch would succeed only in the event that the initial specification of s were too small and should lead to a process for increasing (e.g., doubling) s and repeating the process.

The case $m = 2$ is of especial interest, partly because it leads to significant simplification in the storage allocation, and partly because the advantages which large values of m enjoy in serial sorting largely disappear in internal sorting. These advantages arise from the reduction in the number of stages with increasing m, with a nearly constant time per stage due to the fixed reading and recording time for the serial files. In internal sorting, the time required for key comparisons and address calculations in choosing the minimum key becomes relatively more important and, since the key comparison time is an increasing function (frequently linear) of m, the advantage may lie with small values of m.

The simplification of storage allocation arises in the following way. A two-way string classification on n items may be used in conjunction with a single output field with a total capacity of n items by assigning the odd-numbered strings from the beginning of the field in normal order and the

Step	Statement
1	$s_2 : \nu(\boldsymbol{X})$
2	$a \leftarrow 2 \vert_1 (a + 1)$
3	$\boldsymbol{r} \leftarrow (1, \nu(\boldsymbol{X}))$
4	$\boldsymbol{s} \leftarrow \boldsymbol{r}$
5	$i \leftarrow 1$
6	$r \leftarrow -\infty$
7	$r_1 : r_2$
8	$j \leftarrow 1 + (k(\boldsymbol{X}_{r_1}{}^a) > k(\boldsymbol{X}_{r_2}{}^a))$
9	$r : k(\boldsymbol{X}_{r_j}{}^a)$
10	$j \leftarrow 2 \vert_1 (j + 1)$
11	$r : k(\boldsymbol{X}_{r_j}{}^a)$
12	$j \leftarrow 2 \vert_1 (j + 1)$
13	$i \leftarrow 2 \vert_1 (i + 1)$
14	$r \leftarrow k(\boldsymbol{X}_{r_j}{}^a)$
15	$\boldsymbol{X}_{s_i}^{3-a} \leftarrow \boldsymbol{X}_{r_j}{}^a$
16	$\boldsymbol{r} \leftarrow \boldsymbol{r} + \boldsymbol{Q}^j$
17	$\boldsymbol{s} \leftarrow \boldsymbol{s} + \boldsymbol{Q}^i$

	1-origin indexing
$\boldsymbol{Q}$	$\begin{pmatrix} 1 & 0 \\ 0 & -1 \end{pmatrix}$.
$\boldsymbol{X}^a$	Input field.
$\boldsymbol{X}^{3-a}$	Output field.
r_k	Index of kth input subfield, $k \in (1, 2)$.
s_k	Index of output subfield, $k \in (1, 2)$.
j	Index of current input subfield.
i	Index of current output subfield.
r	Key of last recorded item.
a	Alternator (1, 2).

Legend

Program 6.18 Two-way internal single-phase merge

even-numbered strings from the end of the field in reverse order. Thus if $\boldsymbol{s}^j$ is the jth string of $2k$ strings so classified, the output field would contain the array

$$\underrightarrow{\boldsymbol{s}^1 \oplus \boldsymbol{s}^3 \oplus \boldsymbol{s}^5 \oplus \cdots \oplus \boldsymbol{s}^{2k-1}} \oplus \underleftarrow{\boldsymbol{s}^{2k} \oplus \cdots \oplus \boldsymbol{s}^6 \oplus \boldsymbol{s}^4 \oplus \boldsymbol{s}^2},$$

where the arrows indicate the increasing directions of the associated strings. The restriction to an even number of strings in the foregoing example is clearly not essential. The corresponding two-way internal single-phase merge is described by Program 6.18.

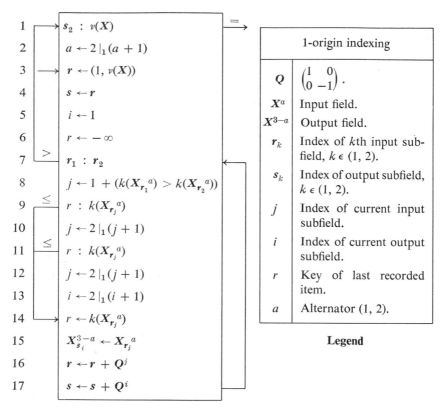

Program 6.18. Since the current index vectors $\boldsymbol{r}$ (for input) and $\boldsymbol{s}$ (for output) may always be initialized as shown in steps 3 and 4, and since termination of a phase occurs when r_1 exceeds r_2 (step 7), explicit use of the vectors $\boldsymbol{b}$ and $\boldsymbol{t}$ of Program 6.17 is obviated. The only added complication lies in the different treatment of indices r_1 and s_1, which must be *incremented* whenever used, and of

indices r_2 and s_2, which must be *decremented*. This treatment is effected by addition (steps 16–17) of the rows Q^j and Q^i of the matrix

$$Q = \begin{pmatrix} 1 & 0 \\ 0 & -1 \end{pmatrix}.$$

It is interesting to note that the use of indexed variables to allow comparisons with the larger (or smaller) of two keys (steps 9 and 11) reduces the requisite number of comparisons from four to three.

The method of string-doubling also permits some simplification in storage allocation and address calculations.

Classification and simple merge

As in the case of the internal merge sort, the internal column sort differs from the corresponding serial sort primarily in the problem of storage allocation. Again, the straightforward solution lies in the allocation of $2b$ fields of n item positions each, and the use of b-dimensional indexing vectors $\boldsymbol{r}$, $\boldsymbol{s}$, and $\boldsymbol{t}$ to control the input and output fields. The sorting process used is identical with that of Program 6.8 (serial single-phase column sort), and the indexing problems are analogous to those of Program 6.16 (internal single-phase merge using $2m$ fields).

As in the corresponding merge sort using $2m$ fields, the foregoing process has a high storage ratio which can be reduced to two by a two-field process. Unlike the corresponding case for the internal merge of Program 6.17, the explicit classification process cannot be avoided. Consequently, it is necessary to determine in advance the size of field required for each of the b classes corresponding to digits $0, 1, \ldots, (b-1)$. This leads to the so-called *pre-count column sort* of Program 6.19, in which each stage incorporates an examination of the next higher order position of the key and a count of each of the digits occurring.

Program 6.19. 0-origin indexing is used, and the vectors $\mathbf{X}^a$ and $\mathbf{X}^{\bar{a}}$ (for $a = 0$ or 1) serve as input and output fields. The classification on the key digit $\boldsymbol{d}_j$ is performed so that all items which agree in the jth column of the key form an infix in the output $\boldsymbol{X}^{\bar{a}}$, and so that the value of $\boldsymbol{d}_j$ associated with successive infixes increases monotonically. The output indexing is determined by the vector $\boldsymbol{s}$, which is, in turn, initialized by the vector $\boldsymbol{b}$. The value of $\boldsymbol{b}$ for the succeeding stage is determined by steps 13 and 14*, according to the value of the next higher key digit $\boldsymbol{d}_{j-1}$. The initial value of $\boldsymbol{b}$ is assumed to be defined externally. It must

* Statement 14 is, for most computers, an inefficient procedure for determining $\boldsymbol{b}$. Normally it is preferable to make a simple count of each of the digits and to sum the counts to determine $\boldsymbol{s}$ at the beginning of the next stage.

Step	Statement
1	$j \leftarrow q + 1$
2	$j \leftarrow j - 1$ (exit on $=$)
3	$a \leftarrow \bar{a}$
4	$s \leftarrow \boldsymbol{b}$
5	$\boldsymbol{b} \leftarrow \bar{\boldsymbol{\epsilon}}(b)$
6	$i \leftarrow -1$
7	$i \leftarrow i + 1$
8	$i : \nu(\boldsymbol{X})$ (on $=$, go to 2)
9	$(b\boldsymbol{\epsilon}(q + 1)) \perp \boldsymbol{d} \leftarrow k(\boldsymbol{X}_i^a);\ b$
10	$h \leftarrow \boldsymbol{d}_j$
11	$\boldsymbol{X}_{s_h}^a \leftarrow \boldsymbol{X}_i^a$
12	$s_h \leftarrow s_h + 1$
13	$k \leftarrow \boldsymbol{d}_{j-1}$
14	$\boldsymbol{b} \leftarrow \boldsymbol{b} + \bar{\boldsymbol{\alpha}}^{k+1}$ (go to 7)

0-origin indexing		
$\boldsymbol{X}^a$	Input field.	$\nu = b$
$\boldsymbol{X}^{\bar{a}}$	Output field.	$\nu = b$
s_h	Index of output subfield h.	$\nu = b$
$\boldsymbol{b}_k$	Beginning of output subfield k for next stage, $k \in \iota^0(b)$.	$\nu = b$
$\boldsymbol{d}$	Positional representation of key.	$\nu = q + 1$
b	Base of representation.	
j	Current column of key.	
i	Index of currrent input.	
h	Current output subfield.	
a	Alternator (0, 1).	

Legend

Program 6.19 Pre-count column sort

be determined by a preliminary count, perhaps performed when reading the items into the initial field. The use of $q + 1$ instead of q in steps 1 and 9 ensures that the pre-count quantity $\boldsymbol{d}_{j-1}$ is properly defined even for the final stage.

Special internal sorting methods

The present section is devoted to internal sorting methods which are specifically unsuited to serial files. The storage ratio provides a major categorization of methods; a method either possesses unity storage ratio or it does not.

Unity storage ratio is achieved by methods which proceed by the interchange of item pairs. The type of interchange may be limited to the transposition of adjacent items, to "insertion" of an item accompanied by a movement of all intervening items toward the evacuated position, or to the exchange of an arbitrary pair. The corresponding methods are characterized as *transposition*, *insertion*, and *exchange methods*, respectively.

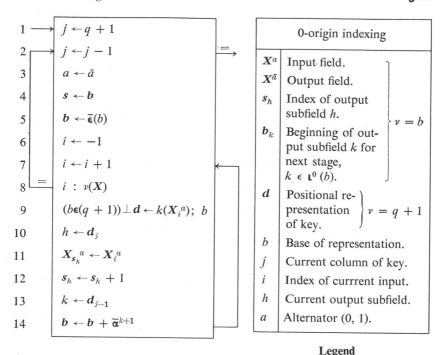

Exchange methods include the *radix exchange sort*. This is an arrangement of the repeated block sort for a base two key, for which the *operation*

count (number of elementary operations required to order n items) is of the order of $n \log_2 n$.

Transposition methods include the *bubble sort*, *odd-even transposition*, and the *ranking sort*. They are characterized by relatively simple programs, an operation count of the order of n^2 for random initial order, and the capacity to utilize existing order to reduce the operation count.

The only insertion method treated is *ranking by insertion*. The operation count (counting comparisons only and not counting the individual item transfers of the block movements associated with each insertion) is of the order of $n \log_2 n$ for random order, and is reduced by existing order. It is most attractive in a computer providing efficient block movement of items.

Methods having a storage ratio greater than unity include the merge and column sorts previously discussed. One additional method of this type is treated—the *pth-degree repeated selection sort*. The operation count is of the order pn^q, where $q = (p + 1) \div p$.

Any internal sorting method can be broken into two distinct phases, the first utilizing only the keys to determine the permutation required on the items, and the second effecting the permutation of the items. Since the permutation vector is, in effect, a table of addresses of the items, the process is called an *address table sort*. Address table sorting is particularly advantageous if the volume of data in the item is large compared to the data in its key.

Any sorting method in which each stage isolates the item with the smallest key (among the items remaining from previous stages) can be modified to produce longer strings by the use of one auxiliary serial input file and one auxiliary serial output file. The modification is called *sorting with replacement*. It consists in recording the selected minimum item in the output file and reading from the input file a replacement item which enters in the subsequent stages only if it is eligible for continuation of the string already recorded.

The internal methods are evaluated and compared in Sec. 6.5, and the results are summarized in Table 6.37.

Radix exchange. Radix exchange is a form of the repeated block sort for a base two key. The high-order column of the key is scanned first. The first zero item (item with key digit zero) is exchanged with the last unit item, the second zero item is exchanged with the second last unit item, and so on, until the first stage of the block sort is completed. The zero items now form a prefix in the vector of items, and the unit items form a suffix. The process is then repeated on the next column of the key, first on the prefix obtained from the first stage, and then independently on the suffix. Each column of the key is treated in turn, the exchange process being performed independently on each of the disjoint infix vectors defined by the preceding stage. 0-origin indexing will be used throughout the discussion.

Primary control of the process is exercised by the vector $\boldsymbol{b}$, whose successive components specify the beginning index of successive subblocks (infixes). In particular, $b_0 = 0$, and $b_{\nu-1} = \nu(\boldsymbol{x})$, and at the beginning of the kth stage, $\nu(\boldsymbol{b}) = 2^{k-1} + 1$. The storage required for $\boldsymbol{b}$ is therefore significant but may be reduced by either of two expedients. The vector $\boldsymbol{b}$ may be replaced by a logical vector $\boldsymbol{u}$ such that $\boldsymbol{u}/\iota^0 = \boldsymbol{b}$. Determination of the next component of $\boldsymbol{b}$ then requires a scan of the components of $\boldsymbol{u}$. The use of $\boldsymbol{u}$ is thus normally unattractive except in a computer equipped for the efficient determination of the location of the leading nonzero component of a logical vector. The second expedient leads to a more complex but more practicable process. The straightforward use of $\boldsymbol{b}$ will be treated first.

Program 6.20. Steps 10–21 perform the exchange on the subblock with indices k in the interval $b_i \leq k < b_{i+1}$. The indices r_0 and r_1 designate the pair last exchanged, k is the index of the current item examined, j is the current column of the key, and a is an alternator which is zero during the forward scan of the zero section and unity during the backward scan of the unit section. The alternator a determines which of the indices r_0 and r_1 will initialize k (step 13), the direction of the scan (step 14), the type of key digit (0 or 1) sought in the next item to be exchanged (step 18), and which of the indices r_0 and r_1 is to be redefined by k (step 19) when the search terminates through failure of the branch at step 18. If a does not become zero from negation on step 20, the process is repeated from step 13 with $a = 1$, producing a backward search for a unit digit in the key. If a becomes zero, both the forward and backward scans have been completed, and the required item exchange is performed on step 21. The final exit from the entire loop 13–21 occurs when $k = r_{\bar{a}}$, that is, when $k = r_0$ on a backward scan or $k = r_1$ on a forward scan. In either event, the final value of k is the beginning index of the new subblock defined by the exchange, and it is used immediately to specify c_i on step 16. The vector $\boldsymbol{c}$ is eventually meshed with $\boldsymbol{b}$ (step 6) to re-specify $\boldsymbol{b}$ as $(b_0, c_0, b_1, c_1, \ldots)$. The initial specification of $\boldsymbol{b}$ on step 1 ensures that the first subblock treated is the entire vector $\boldsymbol{x}$.

The number of subblocks which must be distinguished at any one time can be reduced to the dimension of the key by a method due to Hildebrandt and Isbitz (1959). The process is controlled by a partition vector $\boldsymbol{p}$ of dimension $q + 1$, whose successive nonzero components specify the beginning indices of the subblocks of $\boldsymbol{x}$ remaining to be ordered. At each stage, the first remaining subblock is exchanged on the appropriate key digit $\boldsymbol{d}_j$, i.e., for j increased by one over the value used in generating the particular subblock. When the exchange occurs for $j = q - 1$, the ordering of the two leading subblocks is complete, and they are removed from

Legend

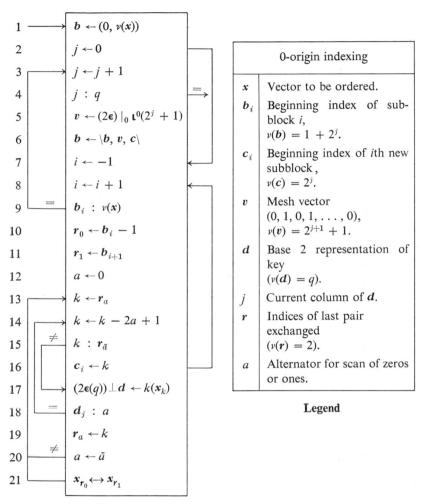

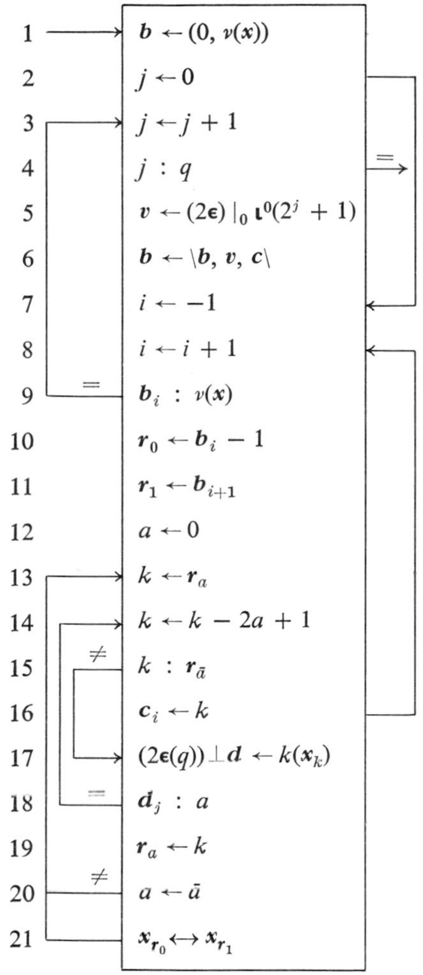

	0-origin indexing
x	Vector to be ordered.
b_i	Beginning index of subblock i, $\nu(b) = 1 + 2^j$.
c_i	Beginning index of ith new subblock, $\nu(c) = 2^j$.
v	Mesh vector $(0, 1, 0, 1, \ldots, 0)$, $\nu(v) = 2^{j+1} + 1$.
d	Base 2 representation of key $(\nu(d) = q)$.
j	Current column of d.
r	Indices of last pair exchanged $(\nu(r) = 2)$.
a	Alternator for scan of zeros or ones.

Program lines:

1. $b \leftarrow (0, \nu(x))$
2. $j \leftarrow 0$
3. $j \leftarrow j + 1$
4. $j : q$
5. $v \leftarrow (2\epsilon) \mid_0 \iota^0(2^j + 1)$
6. $b \leftarrow \backslash b, v, c \backslash$
7. $i \leftarrow -1$
8. $i \leftarrow i + 1$
9. $b_i : \nu(x)$
10. $r_0 \leftarrow b_i - 1$
11. $r_1 \leftarrow b_{i+1}$
12. $a \leftarrow 0$
13. $k \leftarrow r_a$
14. $k \leftarrow k - 2a + 1$
15. $k : r_{\bar{a}}$
16. $c_i \leftarrow k$
17. $(2\epsilon(q)) \perp d \leftarrow k(x_k)$
18. $d_j : a$
19. $r_a \leftarrow k$
20. $a \leftarrow \bar{a}$
21. $x_{r_0} \leftrightarrow x_{r_1}$

Program 6.20   Radix exchange with $\nu(b) < 2^{\nu(d)}$

further consideration by respecifying p_0 by p_u and resetting p_u and p_v to zero, where p_u and p_v are the first nonzero components of $\bar{\alpha}^1/p$. The end of the new leading subblock is now determined by p_w, the new leading nonzero component of $\bar{\alpha}^1/p$, and the exchange is executed on the appropriate column j.

Record of the value of j appropriate to a given subblock is kept by recording its terminal partition as p_{q-j}. This is achieved, first, by recording each new partition generated by exchange on column $j - 1$ in component p_{q-j}, and, second, by advancing the component p_w (determined in the

0	$p \leftarrow \bar{\epsilon}(q + 1)$
1	$k \leftarrow v(x)$
2	$j \leftarrow 0$
3	$j \leftarrow j - 1$
4	$p_0 \leftarrow p_1$
5	$j \leftarrow j - 1$
6	$p_{q-j} : 0$
7	$k \leftarrow p_{q-j}$
8	$p_{q-j} \leftarrow 0$
9	$j : q - 1$
10	$j \leftarrow j + 1$
11	$r_0 \leftarrow p_0 - 1$
12	$p_{q-j} \leftarrow k$
13	$r_1 \leftarrow k$
14	$a \leftarrow 0$
15	$k \leftarrow r_a$
16	$k \leftarrow k - 2a + 1$
17	$k : r_{\bar{a}}$
18	$(2\epsilon(q))\perp d \leftarrow k(x_k)$
19	$d_j : a$
20	$r_a \leftarrow k$
21	$a \leftarrow \bar{a}$
22	$x_{r_0} \leftrightarrow x_{r_1}$

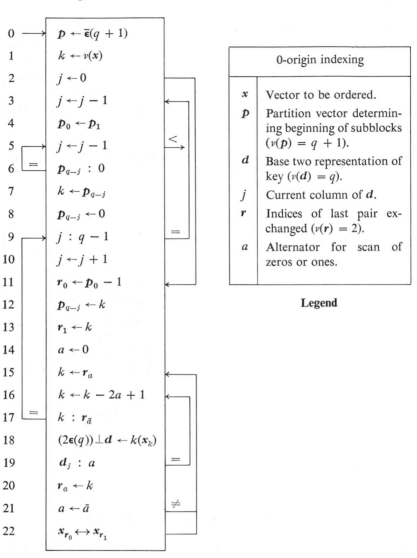

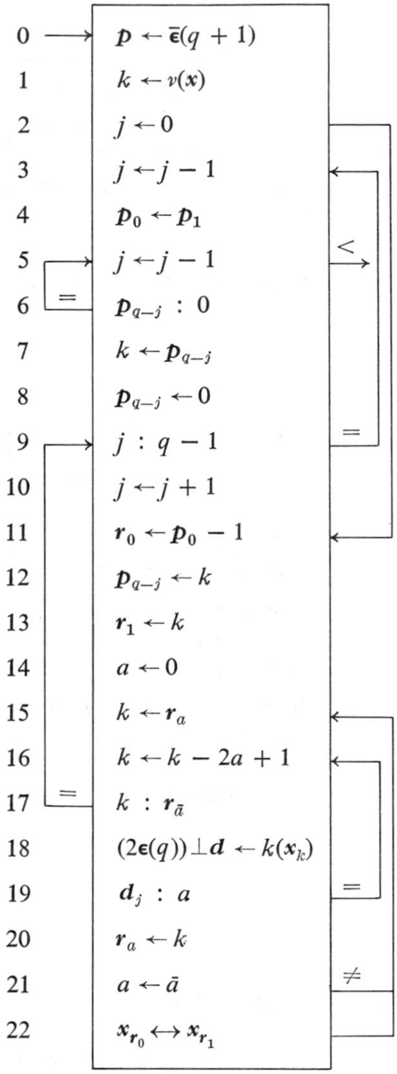

0-origin indexing	
x	Vector to be ordered.
p	Partition vector determining beginning of subblocks ($v(p) = q + 1$).
d	Base two representation of key ($v(d) = q$).
j	Current column of d.
r	Indices of last pair exchanged ($v(r) = 2$).
a	Alternator for scan of zeros or ones.

Legend

Program 6.21   Radix exchange with $v(p) = v(d) + 1$

prefix removal phase) to p_{w-1} and resetting p_w to zero. Incidentally, this procedure ensures that p_u and p_v always occur as p_1 and p_2. In practice, these two components need not be reset if the scan for p_w is begun with p_3.

Program 6.21. The reader may find it helpful to trace the program (i.e., record successive values of all parameters in tabular form) for a simple case of a few keys of small dimension. The exchange phase (15–22) is identical with that of Program 6.20 except that the specification of $\mathbf{c}_i$ is omitted. If $j \neq q - 1$ at the conclusion of the exchange, j is incremented (step 10), $\mathbf{r}_0$ is reset to $\mathbf{p}_0 - 1$, and the new partition k specifies both $\mathbf{p}_{q-j}$ and $\mathbf{r}_1$. If $j = q - 1$, the prefix removal is executed by steps 4–8. Step 4 respecifies $\mathbf{p}_0$, and the scan of steps 5–6 (which begins with $\mathbf{p}_3$) locates a nonzero component $\mathbf{p}_{q-j}$ which is advanced to $\mathbf{p}_{q-(j+1)}$ (indirectly by steps 7, 10, and 12) and is reset to zero by step 8. Steps 0–1 provide the initial specification of $\mathbf{p}_0$ and (via step 12) of $\mathbf{p}_q$.

Bubble sort. The basic operation of the bubble sort is the comparison and possible transposition of a pair of adjacent items so as to place the smaller of the two keys earlier in the sequence. The first stage consists of such operations performed in sequence on the item pairs $(\mathbf{x}_{\nu-1}, \mathbf{x}_\nu)$, $(\mathbf{x}_{\nu-2}, \mathbf{x}_{\nu-1})$,

Original Items	Original Keys	Stage 1	Stage 2	Stage 3	Stage 4	Final Items
$\mathbf{x}_1$	8	3	3	3	3	$\mathbf{x}_5$
$\mathbf{x}_2$	6	8	4	4	4	$\mathbf{x}_6$
$\mathbf{x}_3$	11	6	8	6	6	$\mathbf{x}_2$
$\mathbf{x}_4$	9	11	6	8	8	$\mathbf{x}_1$
$\mathbf{x}_5$	3	9	11	9	9	$\mathbf{x}_4$
$\mathbf{x}_6$	4	4	9	11	11	$\mathbf{x}_3$

Table 6.22 Bubble sort example

$\ldots, (\mathbf{x}_1, \mathbf{x}_2)$. The result is to bubble each item upward in the sequence until it encounters an item with a smaller (or equal) key and then to leave it and continue bubbling the new smaller item. In particular, the smallest item is bubbled to the top. Successive stages repeat the process, but since the jth stage brings the jth smallest item to the jth position, the $(j + 1)$th stage need not treat the first j positions. It is clear that $\nu(\mathbf{x}) - 1$ stages suffice, but it is advantageous to allow termination at the end of the first stage during which no transpositions occur.

Table 6.22 shows the arrangements prevailing at the end of each stage of a bubble sort. The items above the staircase line are not re-examined. Although the items are in correct order at the end of stage three, there is no available indication of the fact until stage four is executed without the occurrence of a transposition.

Program 6.23. The detailed behavior of the bubble sort process described by this program should be clear from the foregoing discussion. It may, however, be remarked that at most $r = \nu(\mathbf{x}) - 1$ stages are executed, even though the final order is achieved only at the rth stage.

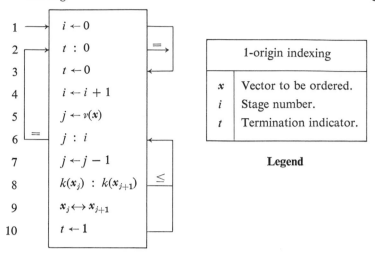

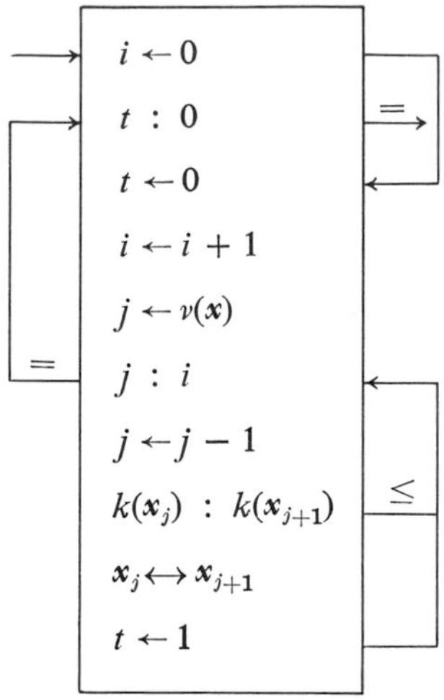

1-origin indexing	
$\boldsymbol{x}$	Vector to be ordered.
i	Stage number.
t	Termination indicator.

Legend

Program 6.23 Bubble sort

If a given set of items is completely ordered except for a single item which is displaced upward from its proper position by j places, j stages of the bubble sort will be required to complete the ordering. On the other hand, a single stage of the bubble sort performed in the alternate direction (i.e., scanning from $\boldsymbol{x}_1$ to $\boldsymbol{x}_\nu$ and bubbling the large items downward) would suffice. In general, there is some advantage in performing successive stages of the bubble sort in alternate directions.

If on a backward scan (from $\boldsymbol{x}_\nu$ to $\boldsymbol{x}_1$) no transposition occurs between items $\boldsymbol{x}_j$ and $\boldsymbol{x}_{j-1}$, then $\boldsymbol{x}_j$ and $\boldsymbol{x}_{j+1}$ are in correct relative order. Consequently, if $\boldsymbol{x}_j$ and (the possibly new) $\boldsymbol{x}_{j-1}$ are not transposed on the succeeding forward scan, then $\boldsymbol{x}_j$ and $\boldsymbol{x}_{j+1}$ will suffer no transposition. This result may be extended to strings of items which suffer no transpositions, and a record of this existing order can be used to obviate the corresponding comparisons.

More precisely, if $\boldsymbol{s}$ is a logical vector such that $\boldsymbol{s}_j = 1$ if and only if no transposition occurred between items $\boldsymbol{x}_j$ and $\boldsymbol{x}_{j-1}$ in a backward scan, then no transposition between items $\boldsymbol{x}_{j-1}$ and $\boldsymbol{x}_j$ on the succeeding forward scan will also imply no transposition (i.e., no need for comparison) between $\boldsymbol{x}_j$ and $\boldsymbol{x}_{j+1}$ if $\boldsymbol{s}_j = 1$. More generally, if $a = \pm 1$ is an alternator such that $a = 1$ on the forward scan, then $\boldsymbol{s}_j$ may be defined as unity if and only if no transposition occurs between $\boldsymbol{x}_j$ and $\boldsymbol{x}_{j+a}$. Program 6.24 shows the entire process. This variant of the bubble sort is attractive only for computers in which the indicated scan of the logical vector can be performed efficiently.

Program 6.24. Multiplication of each key by the alternator a provides the required alternation in the behavior of the branch on step 10. The behavior is best appreciated by tracing a simple case.

Legend (1-origin indexing):

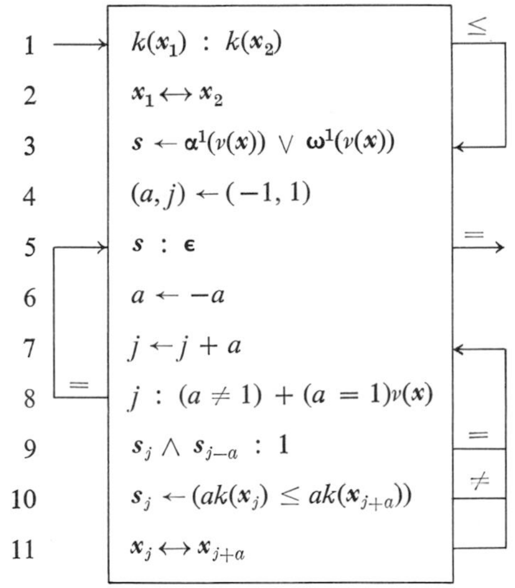

1-origin indexing	
x	Vector to be ordered.
s	String indicator $(v(s) = v(x))$.
j	Scan index.
a	Alternator (± 1).

Steps:

1. $k(x_1) : k(x_2)$
2. $x_1 \leftrightarrow x_2$
3. $s \leftarrow \alpha^1(v(x)) \vee \omega^1(v(x))$
4. $(a, j) \leftarrow (-1, 1)$
5. $s : \epsilon$
6. $a \leftarrow -a$
7. $j \leftarrow j + a$
8. $j : (a \neq 1) + (a = 1)v(x)$
9. $s_j \wedge s_{j-a} : 1$
10. $s_j \leftarrow (ak(x_j) \leq ak(x_{j+a}))$
11. $x_j \leftrightarrow x_{j+a}$

Program 6.24   Forward and backward bubble sort with string indicator

Odd-even transposition sort.   Like the bubble sort, the transposition sort has unity storage ratio and involves the comparison and possible transposition of adjacent items.   Each stage consists of two phases or *half-stages*. In the first half-stage, each item with an odd index (except the last if it is odd) is compared with its successor; in the second, each item with an odd index (except the first) is compared with its predecessor.   Table 6.25 provides an example.

Original Items	Original Keys	Stage 1		Stage 2		Stage 3		Stage 4	Final Items
x_1	8	6	6	6	6	3	3	3	x_5
x_2	6	8	8	8	3	6	4	4	x_6
x_3	11	9	9	3	8	4	6	6	x_2
x_4	9	11	3	9	4	8	8	8	x_1
x_5	3	3	11	4	9	9	9	9	x_4
x_6	4	4	4	11	11	11	11	11	x_3

Table 6.25   Odd-even transposition sort example

Program 6.26. The subloop 6–10 performs the first or the second half-stage of the transposition sort according as the alternator a is 0 or 1. Final termination occurs on step 3 as soon as one half-stage is completed without a transposition occurring, except that a minimum of two half-stages must be executed. The minimum of two half-stages is assured by the initialization of t on step 1.

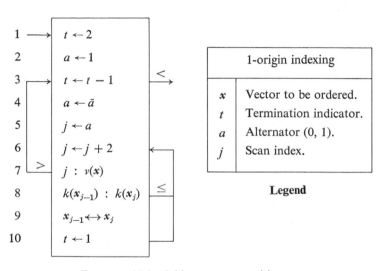

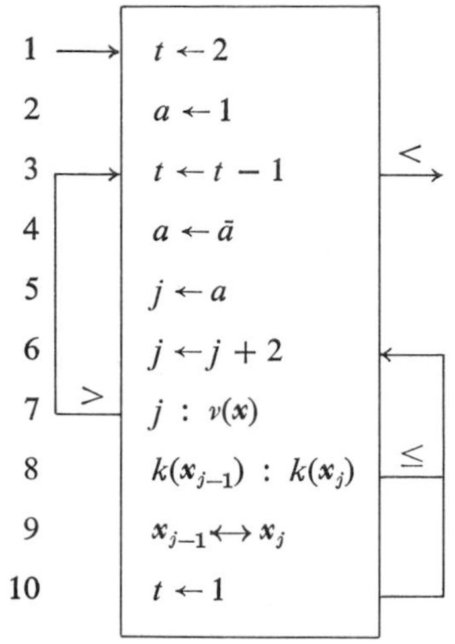

1-origin indexing	
$\boldsymbol{x}$	Vector to be ordered.
t	Termination indicator.
a	Alternator (0, 1).
j	Scan index.

Legend

Program 6.26 Odd-even transposition sort

The validity of the termination conditions of Program 6.26 follows from the following proposition: if any half-stage except the first effects no transpositions, the items are completely ordered. If the half-stage is odd, then

$$k(\boldsymbol{x}_1) \leq k(\boldsymbol{x}_2); \quad k(\boldsymbol{x}_3) \leq k(\boldsymbol{x}_4); \quad \ldots .$$

Since no transpositions occur, the conditions of the previous stage (which exists by hypothesis) also remain valid, i.e.,

$$k(\boldsymbol{x}_2) \leq k(\boldsymbol{x}_3); \quad k(\boldsymbol{x}_4) \leq k(\boldsymbol{x}_5); \quad \ldots .$$

The two sets of inequalities together imply ordering.* A similar argument applies for the case of an even half-stage.

In Sec. 6.5 the transposition sort is shown to be less efficient than the bubble sort. However, it enjoys the unique advantage that all comparisons

* This result may be combined with the fact (established in Sec. 6.5) that the number of transpositions required is finite to establish convergence of the transposition sort. For, if the set is not ordered, each half-stage must effect at least one transposition.

and transpositions in a given half-stage are independent and may therefore be executed in parallel.

Ranking sort. If one new item is added to a vector of items already ordered on a given key, the resulting vector can be ordered by *ranking* the new item, i.e., by comparing it with the items of the original vector in succession until the appropriate rank of the added item is determined. Moreover, n repetitions of this process, which draw the new items from a given vector of n items, will order the entire vector. Table 6.27 shows an example in

Original Items	Original Keys	Initial Set	Stage 1	Stage 2	Stage 3	Stage 4	Stage 5	Final Items
x_1	8	8	6	6	6	3	3	x_5
x_2	6		8	8	8	6	4	x_6
x_3	11			11	9	8	6	x_2
x_4	9				11	9	8	x_1
x_5	3					11	9	x_4
x_6	4						11	x_3

Table 6.27 Ranking sort example

which the individual ranking operations are each performed by comparing the added item with the ranked items in turn (starting with the largest), moving forward by one place each item whose key exceeds that of the added item.

Program 6.28. The index i controls the selection of successive items to define the item z (step 4) which is to be added to the ranked set by steps 6–9. The index j controls the selection of successive items of the ranked set for comparison with z, and each execution of the subloop terminates if either j becomes zero or if $k(z) \geq k(x_j)$. In either event, step 9 inserts the new item z into the position x_{j+1}, which was last evacuated. From the initialization of the index i it is clear that the process is actually completed in $\nu(\boldsymbol{x}) - 1$ rather than $\nu(\boldsymbol{x})$ stages.

Ranking by insertion. Since each stage of the ranking sort ranks one new item in an already ranked set, the determination of its position can be accomplished by a binary search. This sharply reduces the required number of comparisons. However, once the new position is determined, each of the succeeding items in the ranked set must be moved down one place to make way for the new item to be inserted. This method is particularly good where (due either to suitable facilities in the computer or to the use of a chained representation for the vector of items $\boldsymbol{x}$) such block transfer is easy to perform.

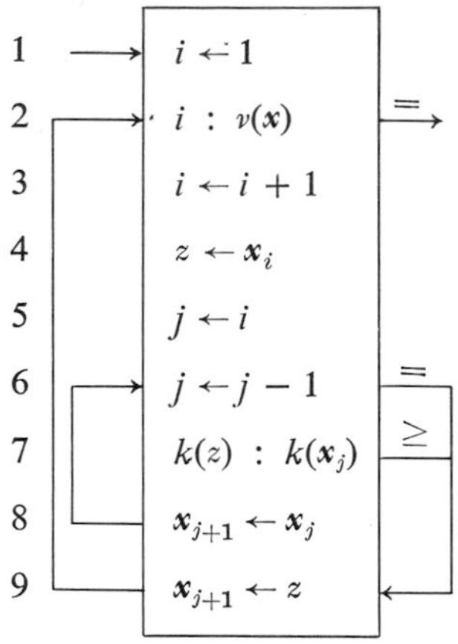

1-origin indexing	
$\boldsymbol{x}$	Vector to be ordered.
i	Index of current item to be ranked.
j	Scan index.
z	Current item to be ranked.

Legend

Program 6.28 Ranking sort

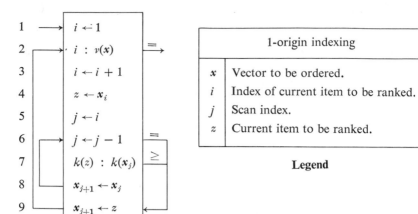

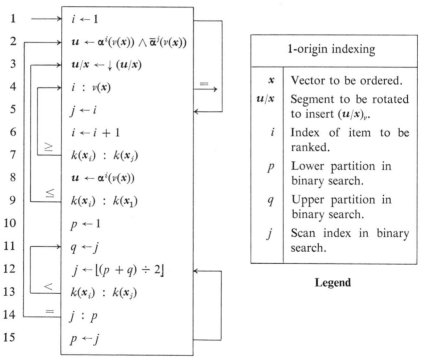

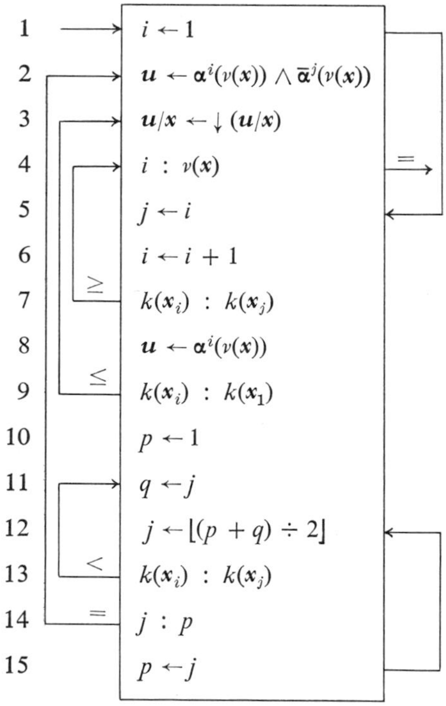

1-origin indexing	
$\boldsymbol{x}$	Vector to be ordered.
$\boldsymbol{u}/\boldsymbol{x}$	Segment to be rotated to insert $(\boldsymbol{u}/\boldsymbol{x})_\nu$.
i	Index of item to be ranked.
p	Lower partition in binary search.
q	Upper partition in binary search.
j	Scan index in binary search.

Legend

Program 6.29 Ranking by insertion

Program 6.29. The binary search is performed by the loop 11–15, which so determines j that the new item $\boldsymbol{x}_i$ is to be inserted after $\boldsymbol{x}_j$. Since the floor operation is used on step 12, j will eventually reach the value p, and step 14 therefore terminates the loop in a finite number of steps. Step 3 performs the required insertion by a right rotation of the infix of $\boldsymbol{x}$ bounded by $\boldsymbol{x}_j$ and $\boldsymbol{x}_i$. The cases where $\boldsymbol{x}_i$ lies outside the previously ranked set are treated by the comparisons on steps 7 and 9. Incidentally, step 7 takes full advantage of any initial order in the items, e.g., if the set is initially ordered, steps 8–15 are never executed.

Repeated selection sort. The process of scanning all items of a vector for the smallest key and transferring the selected item to a separate output area (in a serial or random access file) will be called *selection.* Repeated selection on the successive remaining (unselected) items will serve to transfer the items in the order determined by the specified key. This method of ordering is called a *(first-degree) selection sort.*

If the given vector of n items is divided into m subvectors of at most $\lceil n \div m \rceil$ items each, then a selection from each subvector will produce a vector of m items, the jth of which is the smallest of the jth subvector. A selection performed on the m items of the resulting vector will then select the smallest item of the entire original set. If the selected item came from the kth subvector, it is then replaced by a further selection on the remaining items of the kth subvector. Repetition of the process n times serves to order the items. Because selection is performed on two levels, the process is called *second-degree selection.*

In general, the smallest (first-level) item may be selected from a set of ν_2 *second-level items*, each of which is selected as the smallest of ν_3 *third-level items.* The process can clearly be extended to any desired number of levels. If p levels of selection are used, the process is termed pth-*degree selection* or *repeated* selection. It may be represented as a singular homogeneous tree $\mathbf{T}$ of height $p + 1$, as illustrated by Fig. 6.30.

Figure 6.30 shows the initial filling of the lower levels in a third-degree selection sort performed on the sixteen items at the top of the tree $\mathbf{T}$, with $\nu(\mathbf{T}) = (1, 2, 2, 4)$. The keys are indicated in parentheses. The positions of the third level are the nodes (1, 1, 1), (1, 1, 2), (1, 2, 1), and (1, 2, 2). They are first filled by items $\boldsymbol{x}_3(6)$, $\boldsymbol{x}_6(2)$, $\boldsymbol{x}_9(1)$, and $\boldsymbol{x}_{14}(4)$, respectively, each selected as the smallest among the second-level nodes of the corresponding subtrees $\mathbf{T}_{(1,1,1)}$, $\mathbf{T}_{(1,1,2)}$, $\mathbf{T}_{(1,2,1)}$, and $\mathbf{T}_{(1,2,2)}$, respectively. The first position of level two is then filled by $\boldsymbol{x}_6(2)$, selected as the smallest among the second-level nodes in its subtree, and so forth. Figure 6.31 shows the continuation of the process through the selection of the first two output items.

If e is some value which exceeds the absolute value of all keys, then the selection process may be made more uniform by assuming either that the entire top level of the tree is occupied by the items to be sorted or that

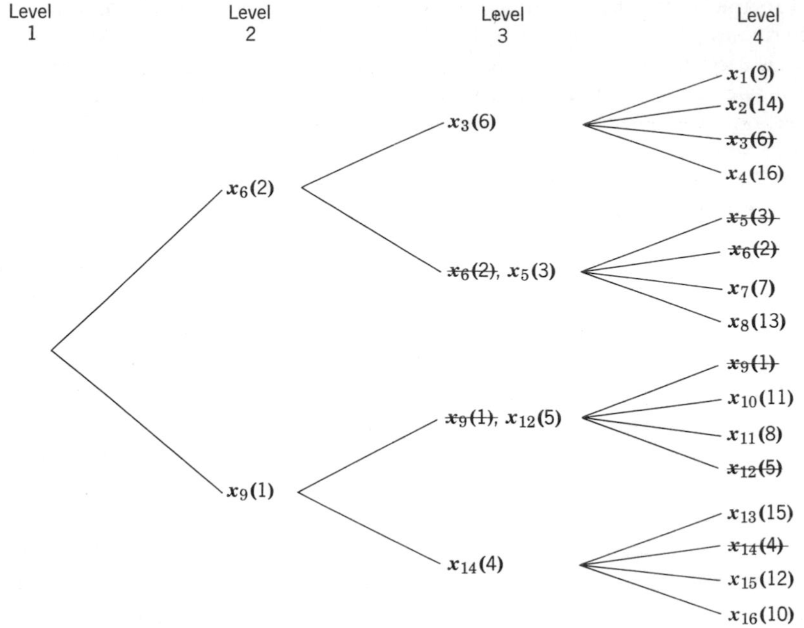

Figure 6.30 The tree **T** representing the third-degree selection sort for $\nu(\mathbf{T}) = (1, 2, 2, 4)$

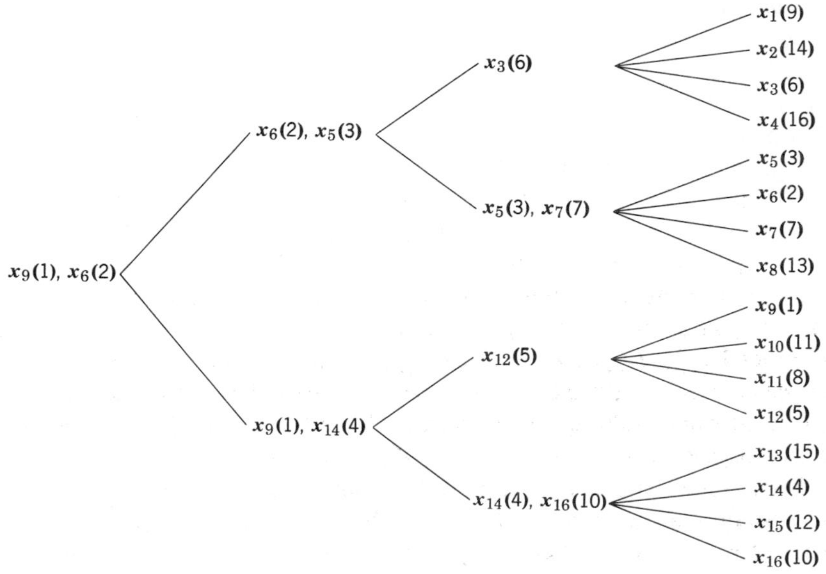

Figure 6.31 Continuation of the third-degree selection sort

unoccupied positions are filled with items having the key value e, and by replacing each item selected from the top level by an item with a similar key value. Termination of the process may then be determined by the appearance of such a key value at the output. Moreover, the initial filling may be simplified by filling all lower levels with dummy items having key values of $(-e)$. These may be recognized and discarded at the output. The normal process will remove all the dummy items first, leaving all levels in the state which would be produced by a special initial fill.

Program 6.32. The top level of the tree $\mathbf{T}$ initially contains the items to be sorted (completed if necessary by dummy items having the key value of e), and the remaining levels contain items with the key value $(-e)$. The index vector $\mathbf{s}$ scans the second-level nodes of the subtree $\mathbf{T}_{\bar{\omega}^1/\mathbf{s}}$ (steps 14–18) to determine the index $\mathbf{m}$ of the node having the minimum key z. If $z \neq e$, step 10 replaces the root of the subtree by the selected node value and step 11 respecifies $\mathbf{s}$ to begin the scan of the subtree rooted in $\mathbf{m}$. If $z = e$, then all second-level nodes contain dummy items with "infinite keys," and step 9 branches to step 1 to replace the root of the subtree by a dummy item as well. The branch from step 12 occurs when the scan of the top level has been completed; it also results in the insertion of a dummy item.

Since each complete scan (over all levels) begins with $\mathbf{s} = (1, 1)$ (steps 3, 11, 15), the resulting minimum item is brought to the root of the tree. Step 2 specifies z as its key, and steps 4 and 7 determine its disposal. If $z = e$, all legitimate items have been flushed from the tree, and the branch to step 5 terminates the output file, rewinds it, and ends the process. If $z = -e$, the item is a dummy initial fill and is discarded by skipping the recording of the output file on step 8.

Since the selection process proceeds by levels in the tree, a corresponding computer program can best be based on a right list—specifically, on the right list node vector $\boldsymbol{\epsilon}^2/]\mathbf{T}$ and the dispersion vector $\boldsymbol{\nu}(\mathbf{T})$. The computation of the list index $r(\mathbf{s})$ required in the path tracing is described (for 0-origin indexing) by the recursion on the functions f and g developed in Sec. 1.23. This recursion yields a relatively simple computer program for a general homogeneous tree. It will be shown, however, that a b-way rooted tree (i.e., a rooted tree with a common branching ratio b) is the case of greatest practical interest, and in this case the simpler recursion

$$r(\mathbf{s}) = b \times r(\bar{\boldsymbol{\omega}}^1/\mathbf{s}) + 1 + s_\nu$$

(also developed in Sec. 1.23) can be used. Program 6.33 shows the repeated selection sort of Program 6.32 executed on the right node list vector $\mathbf{r}$ of a b-way rooted tree.

Program 6.33. The initial conditions are as assumed for Program 6.32, and the steps of the two programs correspond very closely. The simple index modification required from stage to stage is shown in step 11.

1	$k((\mathbf{T}_{\overline{\omega}^1/s})^1) \leftarrow e$
2	$z \leftarrow k(\mathbf{T}^1)$
3	$m \leftarrow (1)$
4	$z \;:\; e$
5	$\Phi_2{}^1 \leftarrow \circ, \lambda_2$
6	$\pi(\Phi_2{}^1) \leftarrow 1$
7	$z \;:\; -e$
8	$\Phi_2{}^1 \leftarrow \mathbf{T}^1, \lambda_1$
9	$z \;:\; e$
10	$(\mathbf{T}_{\overline{\omega}^1/m})^1 \leftarrow (\mathbf{T}_m)^1$
11	$s \leftarrow m \oplus (0)$
12	$\nu(s) \;:\; \nu(\mathbf{T})$
13	$z \leftarrow e$
14	$s_\nu \;:\; \nu_{\nu(s)}(\mathbf{T})$
15	$s \leftarrow s + \omega^1$
16	$z \;:\; k((\mathbf{T}_s)^1)$
17	$z \leftarrow k((\mathbf{T}_s)^1)$
18	$m \leftarrow s$

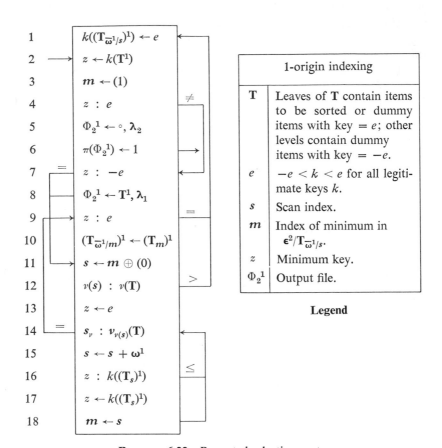

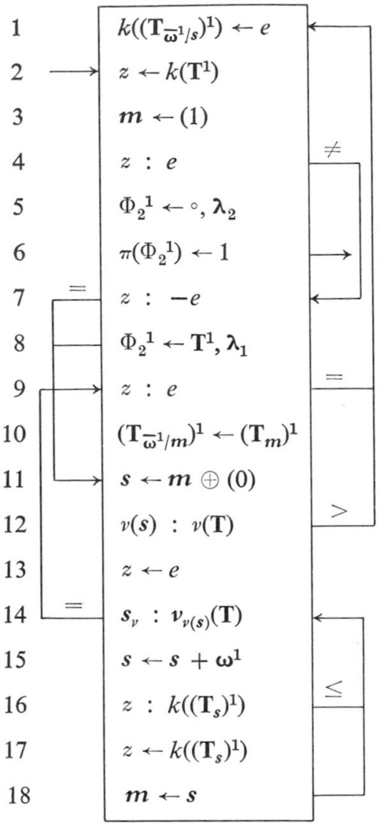

1-origin indexing	
$\mathbf{T}$	Leaves of $\mathbf{T}$ contain items to be sorted or dummy items with key $= e$; other levels contain dummy items with key $= -e$.
e	$-e < k < e$ for all legitimate keys k.
s	Scan index.
m	Index of minimum in $\epsilon^2/\mathbf{T}_{\overline{\omega}^1/s}$.
z	Minimum key.
$\Phi_2{}^1$	Output file.

Legend

Program 6.32   Repeated selection sort

The superiority of a common branching ratio is demonstrated as follows. The number of items scanned per item selected (ignoring initial fill and termination) is clearly the sum of the branching ratios, whereas the maximum number of items accommodated in the top level is equal to their product. It is therefore easily shown (e.g., by induction or by the use of Lagrange multipliers[*]) that for a fixed number of items, optimum execution is furnished by a common branching ratio.

Sorting with replacement.   Certain of the internal sorting processes discussed (bubble and repeated selection) proceed in a succession of stages, each of which results in the selection of the smallest remaining

---
[*] See, for example, Margenau and Murphy (1943), p. 205.

item. Since this item can be transferred immediately to an output area or serial output file, the evacuated position can be refilled by an item from a serial input file. Each output item can therefore be replaced by a new item from a serial input, and the resulting process is called *sorting with replacement.*

If the key of the newly introduced item exceeds or equals the key of the last output item of a group, the new item may be treated as a member of

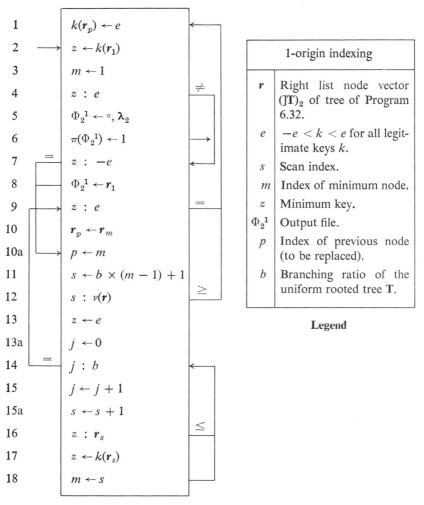

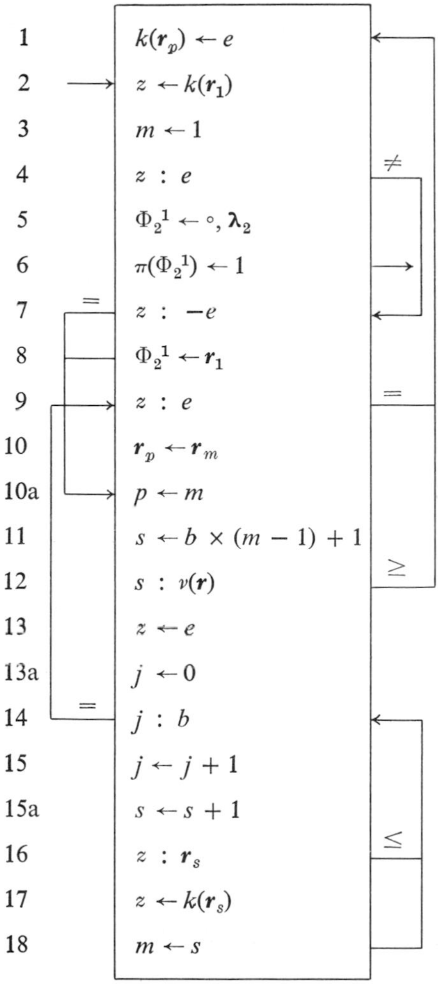

1-origin indexing	
$\mathbf{r}$	Right list node vector $(\rfloor\mathbf{T})_2$ of tree of Program 6.32.
e	$-e < k < e$ for all legitimate keys k.
s	Scan index.
m	Index of minimum node.
z	Minimum key.
Φ_2^1	Output file.
p	Index of previous node (to be replaced).
b	Branching ratio of the uniform rooted tree $\mathbf{T}$.

Legend

Program 6.33 Repeated selection sort of Program 6.32 executed on the right list node vector $\mathbf{r}$ of a uniform rooted b-way tree

1	$k((\mathbf{T}_{\overline{\boldsymbol{\omega}}^1/\mathbf{s}})^1) \leftarrow -(e+1)$
2	$\mathbf{p}_3 \leftarrow \mathbf{p}_1$
3	$(\mathbf{T}_{\overline{\boldsymbol{\omega}}^1/\mathbf{s}})^1 \leftarrow \Phi_1^1$
4	$z \leftarrow k(\mathbf{T}^1)$
5	$\mathbf{m} \leftarrow (1)$
6	$z : -e$
7	$\Phi_2^1 \leftarrow \circ, \boldsymbol{\lambda}_2$
8	$\pi(\Phi^1) \leftarrow \boldsymbol{\epsilon}$
9	$\Phi_2^1 \leftarrow \mathbf{T}^1, \boldsymbol{\lambda}_1$
10	$(\mathbf{T}_{\overline{\boldsymbol{\omega}}^1/\mathbf{m}})^1 \leftarrow (\mathbf{T}_{\mathbf{m}})^1$
11	$\mathbf{s} \leftarrow \mathbf{m} \oplus (0)$
12	$\nu(\mathbf{s}) : \nu(\mathbf{T})$
13	$w \leftarrow z$
14	$z \leftarrow e$
15	$s_\nu : \boldsymbol{\nu}_{\nu(\mathbf{s})}(\mathbf{T})$
16	$\mathbf{s} \leftarrow \mathbf{s} + \boldsymbol{\omega}^1$
17	$w : k((\mathbf{T}_\mathbf{s})^1)$
18	$z : k((\mathbf{T}_\mathbf{s})^1)$
19	$z \leftarrow k((\mathbf{T}_\mathbf{s})^1)$
20	$\mathbf{m} \leftarrow \mathbf{s}$
21	$z : e$
22	$w : -e$
23	$w \leftarrow -e$
24	$s_\nu \leftarrow 0$

1-origin indexing	
$\mathbf{T}$	Tree as in Program 6.32.
e	$-e < k < e$ for all legitimate keys k.
$\mathbf{s}$	Scan index.
$\mathbf{m}$	Index of minimum eligible node in $\boldsymbol{\epsilon}^2/\mathbf{T}_{\overline{\boldsymbol{\omega}}^1/\mathbf{s}}$.
z	Minimum key.
w	Minimum eligible key.
Φ_1^1	Input file terminated by dummy item with final partition $\boldsymbol{\lambda}_2$.
Φ_2^1	Output file.
$\mathbf{p}$	The program vector ($\mathbf{p}_i$ is statement i of this program).

Legend

Program 6.34 Repeated selection sort with replacement

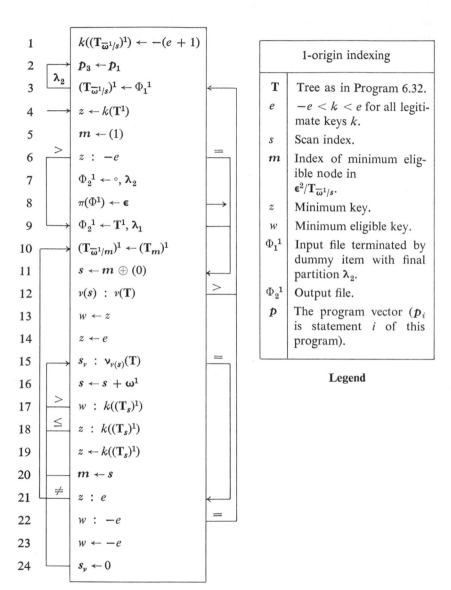

the original group. If not, the item must be allowed to retain its position but must be excluded from consideration in the sorting process. In general, sorting with replacement allows the production of longer output strings than would be otherwise possible with the same internal storage capacity. The expected increase is discussed in Sec. 6.5. Since the process terminates with the original positions completely occupied by ineligible items, the production of a further string can be begun simply by declaring all items eligible.

Repeated selection sort with replacement. In the repeated selection sort it is advantageous to apply the eligibility criterion at each level, i.e., to limit selection to keys which equal or exceed the key of the item being replaced. The item being replaced is, of course, the last one transferred (either to the output file or to the preceding level). The top level items are replaced from the input file or, when the file becomes exhausted, by dummy items. However, the use of the "infinite" dummy key value e as in Program 6.32 raises serious difficulties, which are avoided by the use of the value $-(e + 1)$. This is done in Program 6.34.

Program 6.34. This program is very similar to Program 6.32, and only the essential differences will be remarked. The main scan loop (15–20) differs only in the added comparison with w to prevent the selection of ineligible items. The variable w is normally specified (step 13) as the key of the item just transferred out of the position being filled. However, if all items are ineligible, then z remains unchanged from its initial value established by step 14, and the branch from step 21 to 22 occurs. The variable w is then set to $-e$ to make eligible all items except the dummy fills [with key value $(-(e + 1))$], which enter on exhaustion of the input file. If only these dummies remain in the level scanned, the process returns again to step 22. This time, however, the branch to step 3 occurs.

Step 3 is the file read (which replaces step 1 of Program 6.32). When the file becomes exhausted, the branch to step 2 replaces program statement $\mathbf{p}_3$ by $\mathbf{p}_1$, so that step 3 thereafter provides the requisite dummy keys.

Bubble sort with replacement. A straightforward bubble sort with replacement produces the same length strings as a first-order selection sort with replacement, and, indeed, differs from it mainly in the additional performance of item interchanges. Bubble sorting with replacement is therefore of interest only if the order induced in the remaining items by the interchanges can be used to reduce the number of items scanned. This can be achieved by accumulating the ineligible items in a growing suffix of the vector of items and restricting successive scans to the prefix of eligible items. This method is shown in Program 6.35.

Program 6.35. In the loop 11–13, w denotes the current item with the smallest key, and it is interchanged with $\mathbf{x}_i$ if $k(w)$ exceeds $k(\mathbf{x}_i)$. At step 14, w is therefore

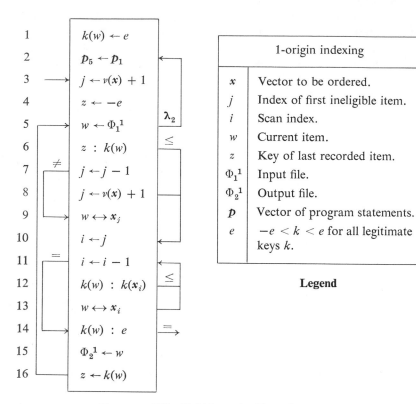

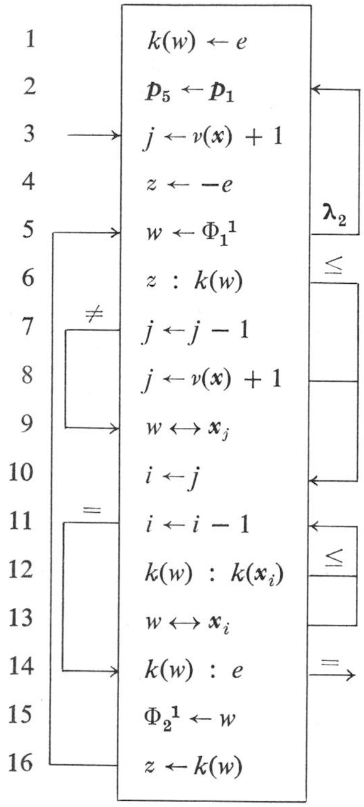

1	$k(w) \leftarrow e$
2	$p_5 \leftarrow p_1$
3	$j \leftarrow v(x) + 1$
4	$z \leftarrow -e$
5	$w \leftarrow \Phi_1^{1}$
6	$z \;:\; k(w)$
7	$j \leftarrow j - 1$
8	$j \leftarrow v(x) + 1$
9	$w \leftrightarrow x_j$
10	$i \leftarrow j$
11	$i \leftarrow i - 1$
12	$k(w) \;:\; k(x_i)$
13	$w \leftrightarrow x_i$
14	$k(w) \;:\; e$
15	$\Phi_2^{1} \leftarrow w$
16	$z \leftarrow k(w)$

1-origin indexing	
x	Vector to be ordered.
j	Index of first ineligible item.
i	Scan index.
w	Current item.
z	Key of last recorded item.
Φ_1^{1}	Input file.
Φ_2^{1}	Output file.
p	Vector of program statements.
e	$-e < k < e$ for all legitimate keys k.

Legend

Program 6.35   Bubble sort with replacement

the item with the smallest key among those scanned and (unless $k(w) = e$) is then recorded in the output file and used to define z, the key of the last recorded item. The main loop is then repeated from step 5, where w is respecified by reading an item from the input file. If the new item is eligible, the branch from step 6 to step 10 is followed; if not, the parameter j (denoting the index of the first ineligible item x_j) is decremented and w is interchanged with the last eligible item x_j before continuing to step 10. Since step 10 initializes i to the value j, the subsequent scan is limited to eligible items.

If j becomes zero on step 7, the entire set of items including w is ineligible. Step 8 then restores j so as to make all items eligible and hence to start a new string.

The branch from step 5 and the subsequent redefinition of step 5 on step 2 serve to introduce "infinite" keys after the input file is exhausted. The immediate redefinition of j and z (steps 3 and 4) to make all items eligible may appear redundant. It may be verified that this procedure (1) does not increase the number of strings produced, and (2) avoids the potential error of omitting the last string.

Address table sort. A sorting process can, in principle, be accomplished in two distinct phases, a determination of the permutation required and the execution of the permutation. In serial sorting, however, the process cannot be effectively divided in this way. For, because of the limitation to rank-preserving operations, the items could not be transferred directly to their final positions even if they were known. In internal sorting this limitation does not apply. A sorting process embodying these two separate phases is called an *address table sort.* The method offers advantages when the time required to transfer a complete item is large compared to the time required to transfer its key.

The permutation $\boldsymbol{p}$ must be so determined that the permuted vector $\boldsymbol{y} = \boldsymbol{x}_{\boldsymbol{p}}$ is ordered on the key. Let $\boldsymbol{K}^1$ be the vector of keys associated with the given vector $\boldsymbol{x}$, i.e., $\boldsymbol{K}_i^1 = k(\boldsymbol{x}_i)$, and let $\boldsymbol{K}^2$ be the identity permutation ι^1. For example, if the successive keys of the vector $\boldsymbol{x}$ are 17, 9, 6, 11, 4, 8, and 3, then

$$\boldsymbol{K} = \begin{pmatrix} 17 & 9 & 6 & 11 & 4 & 8 & 3 \\ 1 & 2 & 3 & 4 & 5 & 6 & 7 \end{pmatrix}.$$

If the columns of $\boldsymbol{K}$ are reordered (by any desired sorting process), to produce the matrix $\boldsymbol{P}$ such that $\boldsymbol{P}_i^1$ is monotone increasing in i, then $\boldsymbol{p} = \boldsymbol{P}^2$ is the desired permutation vector. In terms of the foregoing example,

$$\boldsymbol{P} = \begin{pmatrix} 3 & 4 & 6 & 8 & 9 & 11 & 17 \\ 7 & 5 & 3 & 6 & 2 & 4 & 1 \end{pmatrix},$$

and $$\boldsymbol{p} = (7, 5, 3, 6, 2, 4, 1).$$

6.5 EVALUATION OF INTERNAL SORTING METHODS

In evaluating internal sorting methods, both the execution time and the internal storage requirements must be considered. For the execution times of the internal merge sort and the internal column sort, the analysis of the corresponding serial sorting process applies directly. Since their storage requirements have also been discussed in Sec. 6.4, the present section will be limited to the special internal sorting methods.

The measures of interest in the evaluation of these methods are four:

1. the scan length
2. the number of stages required
3. the number of transpositions required
4. the storage ratio.

The number of comparisons executed is frequently used as a measure of execution time of a sorting process. However, since the selection of the keys to be compared (involving instruction modification and possibly extraction of key digits) usually accounts for the largest share of the time required in a comparison, the *scan length* (number of items scanned) is a more suitable measure. In a process which scans m items serially (as in each individual stage of a bubble or a ranking sort), the number of comparisons is $(m - 1)$ and differs but little from m. However, for m small (as in the successive selections in a repeated selection sort), the ratio $m \div (m - 1)$ is significant, and the scan length is the better measure. Moreover, in a process which does not use a serial scan, the number of comparisons may differ markedly from the scan length. For example, each half-stage of the interchange sort requires approximately $m/2$ comparisons for a scan of m items.

The storage ratio is defined as the ratio of the number of item storage locations required to the number of items entering the sorting process (without replacement). The four measures will be determined for each method in turn and then compared. Table 6.37 summarizes the main results for an assumed random initial distribution of keys. The entire analysis is based on the assumption of distinct keys.

Expected number of transpositions

Let $y(n)$ be the total number of transpositions required to order all of the $n!$ possible arrangements of n items. Since the $(n + 1)$th item added in the last position may rank first, second, . . . , or last, requiring n, $(n - 1)$, . . . , or 0 additional transpositions, respectively, for each of the $n!$ arrangements of the n items, then

$$\begin{aligned} y(n + 1) &= (n + 1)y(n) + n! \sum_{k=0}^{n} k \\ &= (n + 1)y(n) + \binom{n}{2}(n + 1)!. \end{aligned}$$

The function

$$y(n) = \frac{n!\,(n^2 - n)}{4}$$

satisfies this difference equation as well as the obvious boundary condition $y(0) = 0$, and the expected number of transpositions is therefore given by

$$\frac{y(n)}{n!} = \frac{(n^2 - n)}{4}.$$

The maximum and minimum number of transpositions are $(n^2 - n)/2$ and zero, respectively.

A pair of items whose relative order differs from the final arrangement will be called a *disordered pair*. Thus in the set (2, 4, 3, 1), the disordered pairs are (2, 1), (4, 3), (4, 1), and (3, 1). To establish order it is clearly necessary that each disordered pair be transposed. The sequential transposition of disordered pairs of adjacent items is also sufficient to produce ordering. Any transposition method which transposes only disordered pairs therefore achieves order with a minimum number of transpositions and hence with an expected number of $(n^2 - n)/4$. The ranking sort, bubble sort, and interchange sort all fall into this category. The sequence in which the transpositions occur will, however, normally vary for different methods. Thus the sequence of arrangements realized in reordering the set (2, 4, 3, 1) is (2, 4, 1, 3), (2, 1, 4, 3), (1, 2, 4, 3), and (1, 2, 3, 4) for the bubble sort, and (2, 3, 4, 1), (2, 3, 1, 4), (2, 1, 3, 4), and (1, 2, 3, 4) for the ranking sort.

Bubble sort

In the bubble sort, both the number of stages and the scan length depend on the initial order. The minimum and maximum number of stages required are one and $(n - 1)$, respectively. The minimum and maximum scan lengths are n and $(n^2 + n - 2)/2$, respectively.

The expected number of stages required for a random initial order is determined* as follows. If, at any stage, all items are ordered except for one which occupies a position below (later in the sequence than) its proper position, then one further stage will complete the ordering. On the other hand, each item which appears above its terminal position at a given stage will be moved down by exactly one position in the next stage. Consequently, the number of stages required will be determined by d, the maximum upward displacement from its final position of any item in the original array. More precisely, if $\boldsymbol{x}$ is the given vector of items, $\boldsymbol{y}$ the corresponding vector of ordered items, $\boldsymbol{p}$ is a permutation such that $\boldsymbol{y} = \boldsymbol{x}_{\boldsymbol{p}}$, and $\boldsymbol{d} = \boldsymbol{\iota}^1 - \boldsymbol{p}$, then $d = ((\boldsymbol{\epsilon}\lceil \boldsymbol{d})/\boldsymbol{d})_1$.

If the maximum upward displacement is d, then (assuming that all keys are distinct and that the final order is consequently unique) the last item in the final order (i.e., y_n) can initially occupy any one of the $(d + 1)$ components of the suffix $\boldsymbol{\omega}^{d+1}/\boldsymbol{x}$. Similarly, y_{n-1} may initially occupy any one of the remaining $(d + 1)$ positions of the suffix $\boldsymbol{\omega}^{d+2}/\boldsymbol{x}$, and so on for each of the $(n - d)$ items of the suffix $\boldsymbol{\omega}^{n-d}/\boldsymbol{y}$. The number of possible initial arrangements of the items of $\boldsymbol{\omega}^{n-d}/\boldsymbol{y}$ is therefore $(d + 1)^{(n-d)}$. Since the d leading items (i.e., $\boldsymbol{\alpha}^d/\boldsymbol{y}$) can occupy any one of the d remaining positions without restriction, the number of possible initial arrangements with a

* The exact expression for the number of stages is due to Friend (1956).

n	$c(n)$
1	0.798
5	0.853
10	0.877
15	0.893
20	0.904
30	0.918
40	0.927
50	0.934

Table 6.36 Coefficients for $z(n) \doteq c(n)\sqrt{\pi n/2}$

displacement not exceeding d is clearly $d!\,(d+1)^{(n-d)}$. The probability that the maximum displacement r does not exceed d is therefore given by

$$\text{pr}(r \le d) = \frac{(d+1)^{(n-d)}\,d!}{n!}.$$

Similarly,

$$\text{pr}(r \le d-1) = \frac{d^{(n-d+1)}(d-1)!}{n!},$$

and hence

$$\begin{aligned}\text{pr}(r = d) &= \text{pr}(r \le d) - \text{pr}(r \le d-1)\\ &= \frac{(d+1)^{(n-d)}\,d! - d^{(n-d+1)}(d-1)!}{n!}.\end{aligned}$$

The expected value of r is given by

$$\begin{aligned}e_r &= \sum_{d=0}^{n-1} d \times \text{pr}(r=d) = \sum_{d=1}^{n-1} d \times \text{pr}(r=d)\\ &= \frac{1}{n!}\left(\sum_{d=1}^{n-1} d(d+1)^{(n-d)}\,d! - \sum_{d=1}^{n-1} d \times d^{(n-d+1)}(d-1)!\right).\end{aligned}$$

A change of dummy variable in the second summand ($d = t + 1$) brings the two summands to similar form and yields the result

$$e_r = n - z(n),$$

where

$$z(n) = \frac{1}{n!}\sum_{s=1}^{n} s^{n-s}s!.$$

It is shown in the appendix to this chapter that $z(n)$ approaches the value $\sqrt{\pi n/2}$ for large n, and Table 6.36 gives coefficients $c(n)$ for the approximation

$$z(n) = c(n)\sqrt{\pi n/2}.$$

Since one extra stage is needed to determine that the ordering has been completed, the expected number of stages is given by

$$e_q = n + 1 - z(n).$$

Since the scan length in the jth stage of the bubble sort is known to be $n - j + 1$, a similar analysis can be used to determine the expected total scan length e_s. The result is

$$e_s = \frac{n^2 - n - 2}{2} + (n + 1)z(n + 1) - nz(n),$$

or approximately,

$$e_s \doteq \frac{n^2 - n - 2}{2} + \sqrt{\frac{3\pi n}{4}}.$$

Ranking sort

The number of stages in the ranking sort is clearly $(n - 1)$. The expected scan length on the kth stage is determined as follows. The item may rank in any one of $(k + 1)$ positions; first, second, . . . , last, with equal probability. There are therefore $(k + 1)$ cases requiring scan lengths of $2, 3, \ldots, k, (k + 1), (k + 1)$. The last case requires a scan length of $(k + 1)$ rather than $(k + 2)$, since the process terminates on comparison with the last item regardless of the outcome of the comparison. The total scan length for the $(k + 1)$ cases is therefore

$$\left(\sum_{r=2}^{k+2} r\right) - 1 = \frac{k^2 + 5k + 2}{2},$$

and the expected scan length is consequently $2 + k/2 - 1/(k + 1)$. Summing over the $(n - 1)$ stages and denoting the expected total scan length by e yields the relation

$$e = 2(n - 1) + \frac{1}{2}\sum_{k=1}^{n-1} k - \sum_{k=1}^{n-1} \frac{1}{k + 1}$$

$$= \frac{n^2 + 7n - 4}{4} - \sum_{k=1}^{n} \frac{1}{k}.$$

But

$$\sum_{k=1}^{n} \frac{1}{k} = \gamma + \log_e n + \frac{1}{2n} - \frac{1}{12n^2}$$

approximately,* where $\gamma = 0.5772 \cdots$ is *Euler's constant*. Hence

$$e = \frac{n^2 + 7n}{4} - 1.577 - \log_e n - \frac{1}{2n} + \frac{1}{12n^2},$$

* See, for example, Cramèr (1951) p. 125, or Woods (1926) p. 171.

correct to two decimal places for all $n > 1$. The maximum and minimum scan lengths are $(n^2 + n - 2)/2$ and $2(n - 1)$, respectively.

The ranking sort takes advantage of initial order and the minimum scan length of $2(n - 1)$ is achieved for an initially ordered set of items. Ranking by insertion with binary search, as described by Program 6.29, requires approximately $2 + \lceil \log_2 j \rceil$ comparisons on the jth stage. Hence if $n = 2^k$, the number of comparisons required is given by

$$\begin{aligned} e &= (2 + k)2^k - (2 + 2^2 + 2^3 + \cdots + 2^{k-1}) \\ &\doteq (2 + k)2^k - 2^k = (k + 1)2^k. \end{aligned}$$

In general, then,

$$e \doteq n(\log_2 n + 1).$$

For a random distribution, ranking by insertion with binary search requires fewer comparisons than any other method, and, in the form described by Program 6.29, also takes advantage of initial order. The insertion operation requires, of course, a number of rotations of relatively lengthy vectors.

Odd-even transposition sort

Estimates of the efficiency of the transposition sort may be obtained as follows. Each half-stage requires the scanning of (approximately) n items in $n/2$ comparisons, and results in reducing the displacement (either up or down) of each item by at most one. The fact that the reduction in the displacement may be zero for certain items can be illustrated with the initial arrangement (5, 6, 1, 2, 3, 4). The number of half-stages must therefore equal or exceed the maximum displacement, which, in turn, equals or exceeds the maximum upward displacement d used in the analysis of the bubble sort. Moreover, one final half-stage is required to determine that order has been achieved, and the expected number of half-stages will necessarily exceed the corresponding value obtained for the bubble sort, namely, $n + 1 - z(n)$. Since the number of items scanned per stage in the transposition sort exceeds the corresponding number in the bubble sort, it follows that the transposition sort is much less efficient. Moreover, the transposition sort does not allow sorting with replacement. Its sole advantage resides in the possibility of executing all operations in a given half-stage in parallel.

Repeated selection sort

The number of items scanned per item selected in a pth-degree selection sort is equal to the sum of the branching ratios of the associated tree, and, as already demonstrated, a minimum scan length is provided by a tree with a common branching ratio m. Since $m^p \geq n$, the number of items scanned per output item is given approximately by

$$s = mp \doteq m \log_m n.$$

The resulting expression for the total number of items scanned ($nm \log_m n$) is similar in form to the corresponding result for the m-way merge sort. The indicated optimum choice of m is Napier's number e.

The optimum integral value of m is three, and its efficiency differs from the theoretical optimum by less than 1%. The value $m = 2$ simplifies the required program and increases the expected amount of scan by only about 5%. This case ($m = 2$) is referred to as a *tournament sort*. Larger values of m may prove advantageous where the groups of items to be scanned are contained in a serial store whose scan time is not significantly reduced by reducing m.

Since p item transfers are required per item selected, a more realistic cost function for determining the optimum value of m may be given by the function

$$c = (m + a)p = (m + a) \log_m n,$$

where a is the ratio of the time required for an item transfer to the time required for the scan of a single key. As remarked in Sec. 6.2, the optimum value of m is obtained as a solution of the equation

$$\log_e m = 1 + \frac{a}{m}.$$

The amount of item storage required for a pth-degree selection sort is given by

$$x = 1 + m + m^2 + \cdots + m^p = \frac{m^{p+1} - 1}{m - 1}$$
$$\doteq \frac{mn}{m - 1},$$

since $n = m^p$. The storage ratio $r(m)$ is therefore given by $r(m) = m/(m - 1)$, a function which decreases with m, rapidly approaching unity. This ratio also represents the increase in execution time entailed in the initialization of the lower level positions. If sorting with replacement is used, initialization is required for the first string only.

The ratio $r(m)$ changes significantly for the first few values; thus

$$r(2) = 2.00; \quad r(3) = 1.50; \quad r(4) = 1.33.$$

If the expected scan time $s(m)$ is taken as a second criterion, then (since $s(2) = s(4) > s(3)$), the value $m = 2$ will be eclipsed by both 3 and 4.

Sorting Method	Stages			Scan Length			Item Transfers or Transpositions			Storage Ratio
	Expected	Max.	Min.	Expected	Max.	Min.	Expected	Max.	Min.	
Merge (m-way)	$\log_m\left(\frac{n}{2}\right)$	$\log_m n$	1	$n \log_m\left(\frac{n}{2}\right)$	$n \log_m n$	n	$n \log_m\left(\frac{n}{2}\right)$	$n \log_m n$	n	2*
Column (q digits base b)	q	q	q	nq	nq	nq	nq	nq	nq	2*
Bubble†	$n + 1 - z(n)$	$n - 1$	1	$\frac{n^2 - n - 2}{2} + (n+1)z(n+1) - nz(n)$	$\frac{n^2 + n - 2}{2}$	n	$\frac{n^2 - n}{4}$	$\frac{n^2 - n}{2}$	0	1
Interchange‡	$n + 1 - z(n)$	n	2	$\frac{n^2 - n - 2}{2} + (n+1)z(n+1) - nz(n)$	n^2	$2n$	$\frac{n^2 - n}{4}$	$\frac{n^2 - n}{2}$	0	1
Ranking	$n - 1$	$n - 1$	$n - 1$	$\frac{n^2 + 7n}{4} - 1.6 - \log_e n - \frac{1}{2n}$	$\frac{n^2 + n - 2}{2}$	$2n - 2$	$\frac{n^2 - n}{4}$	$\frac{n^2 - n}{2}$	0	1
Ranking by insertion (binary search)	$n - 1$	$n - 1$	$n - 1$	$n(\log_2 n + 2)$	$n(\log_2 n + 2)$	$2n - 2$	$\frac{n^2 - n}{4}$	$\frac{n^2 - n}{2}$	0	1
p-th degree selection† § (branching ratio m)	n	n	n	$nmp = nm \log_m n$	nmp	nmp	np	np	np	$\frac{m}{m-1}$

* With optimum allocation (2 fields).
† Replacement possible.

$$z(n) = \frac{1}{n!} \sum_{s=1}^{n} s^{n-s} s! \doteq \sqrt{\pi n/2}$$

‡ Parallel operation possible; estimates are lower bounds.
§ All values exclusive of initial fill.

Table 6.37 Characteristics of internal sorting methods (for random distribution of distinct keys)

Sorting with replacement

The use of replacement with any internal sorting method offers the advantage of increasing the expected length of the strings produced. Gassner (1958) has shown that for n item positions and random keys, the expected length of the first string is $(e - 1) \times n \doteq 1.718n$, and that for later strings the expected length rapidly approaches $2n$.

Comparison of internal sorting methods

The results of the preceding sections are summarized in Table 6.37. The ranking, bubble, and transposition processes show the most favorable storage ratio, exactly one half of the best attainable in the merge and the column sort processes. In the case of repeated selection, the storage ratio depends on m and ranges from two to a limit of one.

The execution time is approximately proportional to the function

$$f(n) = s + ct,$$

where s is the scan length, t the number of item transfers or transpositions, and c the ratio of the cost (in time) of one item transfer to the cost of a scan of one key. For any given method with variable parameters (such as the repeated selection sort), these parameters may be chosen so as to minimize $f(n)$. The choice between various methods may then be made (subject to storage considerations) so as to minimize $f(n)$.

Since the ranking, bubble, and odd-even transposition methods share the same number of transpositions, the choice between them depends on the scan length and auxiliary factors. The odd-even transposition sort is inferior to the bubble sort in this regard, and the bubble sort is, in turn, inferior (by a factor of two for large n) to the ranking sort for $n > 8$. The bubble sort retains the advantage that sorting with replacement may be used, and the transposition method allows parallel operation.

APPENDIX TO CHAPTER 6

The following derivation of the limit of the function

$$z(n) = \frac{1}{n!} \sum_{s=1}^{n} s!\, s^{n-s}$$

arising in the evaluation of the bubble sort was suggested by Robert Church. Clearly

$$L(n) = \int_0^n g(s)\, ds \leq z(n) \leq U(n) = \int_0^n g(s+1)\, ds,$$

where $g(s) = \frac{s!}{n!} s^{n-s}$. Moreover,

$$U(n) = \int_0^n \left(\frac{s+1}{s}\right)^{n-s} g(s)\, ds,$$

and since $g(s)$ is monotone increasing with a large positive derivative for large values of s, only the upper end of the integral is significant. It can therefore be shown that

$$\lim_{n\to\infty} U(n) = \lim_{n\to\infty} L(n).$$

Consequently,

$$\lim_{n\to\infty} L(n) = \lim_{n\to\infty} z(n).$$

Applying Stirling's formula,

$$\lim_{n\to\infty} L(n) \doteq \int_0^n \frac{\sqrt{2\pi} s^{s+½} e^{-s} s^{n-s}\, ds}{\sqrt{2\pi} n^{n+½} e^{-n}} = e^n n^{-(n+½)} \int_0^n s^{n+½} e^{-s}\, ds.$$

Setting $t = 1 - s/n$ yields

$$\lim_{n\to\infty} L(n) = e^n n^{-(n+½)} \int_0^1 n^{n+½}(1-t)^{n+½} e^{-n} e^{nt} n\, dt$$

$$= n \int_0^1 (1-t)^{n+½} e^{nt}\, dt,$$

$$= n \int_0^1 e^{nt+(n+½)\log_e(1-t)}\, dt.$$

Expanding $\log_e (1-t)$ yields

$$\lim_{n\to\infty} L(n) = n \int_0^1 e^{-t/2-(n+½)(t^2/2+t^3/3+\cdots)}\, dt.$$

For n large, only small values of t will be significant, and all terms in the exponent may be dropped except $-(n + 1/2)t^2/2$. Similarly, the upper limit of integration may be extended to infinity. Hence,

$$\lim_{n\to\infty} L(n) = n \int_0^\infty e^{-(n+½)t^2/2} dt = n(\pi/(2n+1))^{½}$$

$$\doteq (\pi n/2)^{½}.$$

REFERENCES

Ashenhurst, R. L., (1953), "Sorting and Arranging," *Theory of Switching*, Report No. BL-7, Harvard Computation Laboratory, Section I.

Betz, B. K., and W. C. Carter, (1959) "New Methods of Merge Sorting," 14th A.C.M. Conference, Cambridge, Mass.

Carter, W. C., (1962), "Mathematical Analysis of Merge Sorting Techniques," Congress of International Federation of Information Processing Societies, Munich.

Cramèr, H., (1951), *Mathematical Methods of Statistics*, Princeton University Press.

Friend, E. H., (1956), "Sorting on Electronic Computer Systems," *J.AC.M.*, vol. 3, pp. 134–168

Gassner, Betty Jane, (1958), "Proof of a Conjecture Concerning Sorting by Replacement Selecting," unpublished.

Gilstad, R. L., (1960), "Polyphase Merge Sorting—An Advanced Technique," *Proc. Eastern Joint Computer Conference.*

Goldstine, H. H., and J. von Neumann, (1948), "Planning and Coding Problems for an Electronic Computing Instrument," Part 2, vol. 2, Institute for Advanced Study, Princeton University Press.

Hildebrandt, P., and H. Isbitz, (1959), "Radix Exchange—An Internal Sorting Method for Digital Computers," *J.A.C.M.*, vol. 6, pp. 156–163.

Margenau, H., and G. M. Murphy, (1943), *The Mathematics of Physics and Chemistry*, Van Nostrand, New York.

Mauchly, J. W., (1948), "Sorting and Collating," *Theory and Techniques for Design of Electronic Digital Computers.* Lectures given at the Moore School, July 8–August 31, 1946, vol. III, University of Pennsylvania.

McCracken, D. D., H. Weiss, and Tsai-Hwa Lee, (1959), *Programming Business Computers*, Wiley, New York.

Nagler, H., (1959), "Amphisbaenic Sorting," *J.A.C.M.*, vol. 6, pp. 459–468.

Woods, F. S., (1926), *Advanced Calculus*, Ginn & Company, Boston, Mass.

EXERCISES

6.1 A given file contains a set of 15 items $x_1, \ldots, x_{15}$ with associated decimal keys 68, 9, 60, 14, 60, 73, 79, 15, 67, 5, 9, 41, 57, 9, 41. For each of the serial files used, show the contents at the conclusion of each stage of the following processes:

(a) a two-phase classification and merge using
  (i) four files.
  (ii) three files.
  (iii) six files.
(b) a string classification and merge using four files.
(c) a single-phase merge using
  (i) four files.
  (ii) six files.
(d) a single-phase merge without rewind.
(e) a base ten column sort using eleven files.
(f) a base ten column sort using twenty files.
(g) a base ten column sort using four files and the partial pass column sort.
(h) a column sort using four files and a base three representation of the keys.

6.2 Modify Program 6.4 so that it will work properly without dummy terminal items (i.e., each terminal partition λ_2 is to be associated with a legitimate item).

6.3 Write a program for the string-doubling merge sort.

6.4 (a) Write a program for a base b column sort which uses backward read to eliminate rewinding.

(b) Program a variant of the two-phase column sort ($b + 1$ files) so as to eliminate the copying of the "zero items" in each merge phase. Determine the relative efficiency of the method.

(c) Program an analogous variant of the m-way two-phase merge sort so as to eliminate the copying of part of the items in the classification phase.

6.5 Construct the matrix $\boldsymbol{M}$ (cf. Table 6.10) specifying an efficient partial pass column sort for the following cases:

(a) base ten and three files.
(b) base ten and five files.
(c) base eight and three files.
(d) base ten and four files using no rewind, i.e., files are to be read backward.
(e) base ten and three files using no rewind.

6.6 Using a set of matrices $^1\boldsymbol{M}, {}^2\boldsymbol{M}, \ldots, {}^p\boldsymbol{M}$, of the form of Table 6.10, write a program to generalize the partial pass sort to the case of a mixed radix key.

6.7 (a) Reprogram the amphisbaenic sort (Program 6.13) so as to reverse the order of the final output. (This is the form used in Nagler, 1959.)

(b) Program a generalization of the amphisbaenic sort which makes use of partial passes within columns of the key.

6.8 (a) Program a modification of the bubble sort process which on odd-numbered stages bubbles the smallest item to the leading end and on even-numbered stages bubbles the largest item to the tail end.

(b) By examining all 4! cases show that for four items the expected number of stages is slightly less for the method of part (a) than for the unmodified bubble sort.

(c) Program a bubble sort using a string indicator $\boldsymbol{s}$ as in Program 6.24 but using backward scan only.

6.9 (a) Program a modification of Program 6.17 to specify $s_0 = 2$ and to automatically double s_0 and restart if necessary.

(b) Compare the efficiency of the program of part (a) with that of the straightforward program in which the number s of strings is assumed equal to the number of items.

6.10 (a) Derive the relation $\log_e m = 1 + a/m$ which must be satisfied by an optimal value of m in order to minimize the cost function $c = (m + a) \log_m n$ (cf. Sec. 6.2).

(b) Determine the optimal integral value of m for each of the cases $a = 0$, 1, e^2.

6.11 For the amphisbaenic sort on a set of b^t items with distinct keys belonging to the set $\iota^0(b^t)$, determine

(a) the number of item transfers required.
(b) the number of file reversals (change of direction of read and record) required.

6.12 Write a program describing the odd-even transposition sort in terms of vector operations so as to show clearly the parallel nature of the process. Treat all items with odd indices (plus a dummy item) as a vector and all even items (plus a dummy item) as a second vector.

6.13 (a) For each of the following sorting methods, determine whether initial order of the items is preserved, i.e., whether the relative initial order of all item pairs with duplicate keys is preserved.
(i) simple classification and merge.
(ii) classification and simple merge.
(iii) ranking sort.
(iv) bubble sort.
(v) odd-even transposition.
(vi) radix exchange sort.
(b) Prescribe a simple modification of the key which will ensure the preservation of initial order.

6.14 For the sequence of keys given in Exercise 6.1, show the explicit execution of the following internal sorting processes:
(a) bubble sort with replacement (six item positions).
(b) pth-degree selection sort with replacement, with $p = 3$ and $m = 2$.
(c) ranking by insertion.

6.15 If the key is represented in a base b number system, with each digit represented in turn in a ranked binary code, then ordering can be achieved by a base two column sort on successive columns of the underlying binary representation.
(a) Show more generally that ordering can be achieved by a base 2^k column sort on (the base two value of) successive groups of k binary digits.
(b) Program the process suggested in part (a), including the determination of an optimum value of k for a given number n of available files. Assume an original key of q digits, each represented by r binary components. Do not neglect the problem of terminal conditions.
(c) If $b = 10$, $r = 4$, and if the successive decimal digits are coded alternately in a (ranked) bi-quinary and qui-binary system, the binary digits can be grouped in twos and threes so as to allow column sorting with a maximum of five output files. Program a suitable process.

6.16 Program a sequence of rotations of infixes of the vector $\boldsymbol{x}$ which will reverse the order of its components. (See the Ranking by insertion program (6.29) for the case when the key defines a complete reversal of order.)

6.17 Assuming that an item transfer takes c times as long as a comparison of two keys, determine a criterion for the choice of m in an m-way internal revision merge for the following cases
(a) assuming $2m$ comparisons per item (m comparisons for eligibility and m for minimization).
(b) assuming that a ranking sort is used on the m item positions.

6.18 (a) Let $\boldsymbol{z}$ be a vector key of dimension three whose successive components represent department number, job number, and name, respectively. Two lists are to be produced, one ordered by name within department within job and the other by department within job within name. Determine a mapping vector $\boldsymbol{p}$ such that $\boldsymbol{y} = \boldsymbol{z}_{\boldsymbol{p}}$ is the vector key of least dimension which contains the two required orderings.
(b) Let $\boldsymbol{y}^i = \boldsymbol{z}_{\boldsymbol{p}^i}$ be a set of vector keys defining a set of related orderings.

Determine a vector key of minimum dimension which contains all of the related orderings for the case $\boldsymbol{p}^1 = (3, 4, 1, 5)$, $\boldsymbol{p}^2 = (3, 1, 5, 6)$, and $\boldsymbol{p}^3 = (1, 4, 3, 5)$.

(c) Analyze the effect of related orderings on the expected execution time of a merge sort. (Consider the effects of duplicate keys on expected string lengths.)

6.19 Let $\boldsymbol{D}$ be a 0-origin matrix of the form of Table 6.14 which describes the cascade sort, i.e., row $\boldsymbol{D}^j$ describes the distribution of strings at the completion of stage j. Using the special matrices of Sec. 1.13, write concise expressions for the matrices $\boldsymbol{F}$ and $\boldsymbol{B}$ such that

(a) $\boldsymbol{D}^{j-1} = \boldsymbol{B} \overset{+}{\times} \boldsymbol{D}^j$

(b) $\boldsymbol{D}^j = \boldsymbol{F} \overset{+}{\times} \boldsymbol{D}^{j-1}$

(c) Show that $\boldsymbol{F}$ and $\boldsymbol{B}$ are inverse.

(d) Determine the dominant eigenvalue of $\boldsymbol{B}$ when $\nu(\boldsymbol{B}) = 3$, and show its relation to the power of the cascade sort for four files. (cf. Sec. 6.1 and Carter (1962).)

6.20 Determine the relative efficiencies of serial column sorting and serial merge sorting for the following conditions. Internal sorting, with a maximum of 100 item positions, is to be used as an aid to each of the processes, and the time for the internal sorting is assumed fixed. There are 10,000 items with 4-digit decimal keys, and each key value is associated with at most four items. The initial arrangement contains 3500 maximal (increasing) strings.

6.21 Program an address table sort.

6.22 (a) The determination of the permutation vector required in the address table sort can be considered as a mapping from each item onto its rank in the set. Show that for distinct keys this mapping can be performed by counting for each item the number of items having a smaller key.

(b) Program the method of part (a). (This is known as a *counting sort.*)

6.23 (a) Program a two-phase internal merge sort.

(b) Program a two-phase internal column sort.

6.24 Program an extension of Program 6.33 (pth-degree selection executed on the right list node vector $\boldsymbol{\epsilon}^2/]\mathbf{T}$) to

(a) sorting with replacement.

(b) the case of a singular homogeneous tree with dispersion vector $\boldsymbol{\nu}(\mathbf{T})$.

(c) cover both cases (a) and (b).

6.25 If the transfer from a serial file can proceed concurrently with other operations, it is frequently advantageous to associate two fields of internal storage (called *buffers*) with each file and to transfer the next group of items to one of the fields while executing necessary operations on the items of the other. Buffers may be used similarly for output files.

(a) Program an m-way single-phase merge using two buffers for each of the $2m$ serial files.

(b) Program a base b single-phase column sort using two buffers for each of the $2b$ serial files.

6.26 If the number of input buffers serving m files is reduced to $m + 1$ some advantage may still be gained by "predicting" the file whose (currently) associated buffer will next be exhausted, and initiating a transfer from it to the idle buffer. Repeat parts (a) and (b) of Exercise 6.25 for $(m + 1)$ and $(b + 1)$ input buffers, respectively. (See Friend, 1956.)

6.27 Repeat parts (a) and (b) of Exercise 6.25 with the number of output buffers also reduced as in Exercise 6.26.

6.28 Since a given initial arrangement may be easier to bring to descending than to ascending order on the keys, and since a final reversal of order may be easy to achieve (by backward read in the case of serial files or by address modification in the case of internal storage), it may be advantageous to choose ascending or descending order according to some estimate based on the initial arrangement. Write a program which first counts the number of ascending strings and then executes a ranking sort by insertion to produce either ascending or descending order according to which appears to be the easier to achieve.

6.29 For the first few values of n, compute and compare the following alternative evaluations of the expected number of stages in a bubble sort

(a) $n + 1 - z(n)$, where $z(n) = \sum_{s=1}^{n} \frac{s^{n-s} s!}{n!}$.

(b) $n + 1 - \sqrt{\pi n/2}$.

(c) $c/n!$, where c is the total count of all stages required for the $n!$ possible initial arrangements of n distinct keys.

chapter 7

THE LOGICAL CALCULUS

The present chapter develops two fundamental areas of symbolic logic: canonical forms and the basic procedures of decomposition. 0-origin indexing is used throughout.

7.1 ELEMENTARY IDENTITIES

Certain elementary identities will first be summarized for reference. The first of them (equation 7.1) merely defines a matrix of operators employed in equation 7.4.

$$\odot = \begin{pmatrix} \vee & \wedge \\ \neq & = \end{pmatrix} \tag{7.1}$$

De Morgan's laws

$$\wedge/\boldsymbol{x} = \overline{\vee/\overline{\boldsymbol{x}}} \tag{7.2}$$

$$\neq/\boldsymbol{x} = \overline{=/\overline{\boldsymbol{x}}} \tag{7.3}$$

$$\boldsymbol{X} \mathop{}\limits^{\odot_i^{\,h}}_{\odot_k^{\,j}} \boldsymbol{Y} = \overline{\overline{\boldsymbol{X}} \mathop{}\limits^{\odot_{\bar{i}}^{\,h}}_{\odot_{\bar{k}}^{\,j}} \overline{\boldsymbol{Y}}} \tag{7.4}$$

$$\neq/\boldsymbol{x} = 2 \mid +/\boldsymbol{x} \tag{7.5}$$

$$\neq/\boldsymbol{x} = ((\boldsymbol{x} \overset{\neq}{\wedge} \overline{\boldsymbol{y}}) \neq (\boldsymbol{x} \overset{\neq}{\wedge} \boldsymbol{y})) \tag{7.6}$$

$$\neq/\boldsymbol{X} = ((\boldsymbol{X} \overset{\neq}{\wedge} \overline{\boldsymbol{y}}) \neq (\boldsymbol{X} \overset{\neq}{\wedge} \boldsymbol{y})) \tag{7.7}$$

$$\boldsymbol{Z} = (\boldsymbol{a} \overset{\circ}{\wedge} \boldsymbol{c}) \wedge (\boldsymbol{q} \overset{\circ}{\wedge} \boldsymbol{r}) = (\boldsymbol{a} \wedge \boldsymbol{q}) \overset{\circ}{\wedge} (\boldsymbol{c} \wedge \boldsymbol{r}) \tag{7.8}$$

$$\vee/\vee//(\boldsymbol{x} \overset{\circ}{\wedge} \boldsymbol{y}) = (\vee/\boldsymbol{x}) \wedge (\vee/\boldsymbol{y}) \tag{7.9}$$

$$\neq/\neq//(\boldsymbol{x} \overset{\circ}{\wedge} \boldsymbol{y}) = (\neq/\boldsymbol{x}) \wedge (\neq/\boldsymbol{y}) \tag{7.10}$$

Identities 7.2, 7.3, and 7.5 may be established by induction on the dimension of $\boldsymbol{x}$. Equation 7.4 summarizes the sixteen identities obtained by extending equations 7.2 and 7.3 to arrays. For example, if $\odot_i^{\,h}$ and $\odot_k^{\,j}$ are the operators $\neq$ and $\wedge$, respectively, then equation 7.4 becomes

$$\boldsymbol{X} \overset{\neq}{\wedge} \boldsymbol{Y} = \overline{\overline{\boldsymbol{X}} \overset{=}{\vee} \overline{\boldsymbol{Y}}}.$$

The foregoing relation may be verified as follows:

$$
\begin{aligned}
(\boldsymbol{X} \overset{\neq}{\wedge} \boldsymbol{Y})_j^i &= \neq/(\boldsymbol{X}^i \wedge \boldsymbol{Y}_j) \\
&= \overline{=/(\overline{\boldsymbol{X}^i \wedge \boldsymbol{Y}_j})} && \text{(by equation 7.3)} \\
&= \overline{=/(\overline{\boldsymbol{X}}^i \vee \overline{\boldsymbol{Y}}_j)} && \text{(by equation 7.2)} \\
&= \overline{(\overline{\boldsymbol{X}} \overset{=}{\vee} \overline{\boldsymbol{Y}})_j^i}.
\end{aligned}
$$

Equation 7.7 is a direct extension of equation 7.6, which is itself derived as follows. Since the operator $\neq$ is associative and commutative, then

$$\neq/\boldsymbol{x} = ((\neq/(\overline{\boldsymbol{y}}/\boldsymbol{x})) \neq (\neq/(\boldsymbol{y}/\boldsymbol{x})).$$

Moreover,

$$\neq/\overline{\boldsymbol{y}}/\boldsymbol{x} = 2\,|(+/\overline{\boldsymbol{y}}/\boldsymbol{x}) = 2\,|(+/(\boldsymbol{x} \wedge \overline{\boldsymbol{y}})) = \neq/(\boldsymbol{x} \wedge \overline{\boldsymbol{y}}),$$

the first and second and the third and fourth limbs being related by equation 7.5. Consequently,

$$
\begin{aligned}
\neq/\boldsymbol{x} &= ((\neq/(\boldsymbol{x} \wedge \overline{\boldsymbol{y}})) \neq (\neq/(\boldsymbol{x} \wedge \boldsymbol{y}))) \\
&= ((\boldsymbol{x} \overset{\neq}{\wedge} \overline{\boldsymbol{y}}) \neq (\boldsymbol{x} \overset{\neq}{\wedge} \boldsymbol{y})).
\end{aligned}
$$

The following argument establishes equation 7.8. By definition,

$$
\begin{aligned}
\boldsymbol{Z}_j^i &= (\boldsymbol{a}_i \wedge \boldsymbol{c}_j) \wedge (\boldsymbol{q}_i \wedge \boldsymbol{r}_j) \\
&= (\boldsymbol{a}_i \wedge \boldsymbol{q}_i) \wedge (\boldsymbol{c}_j \wedge \boldsymbol{r}_j) \\
&= (\boldsymbol{a} \wedge \boldsymbol{q})_i \wedge (\boldsymbol{c} \wedge \boldsymbol{r})_j.
\end{aligned}
$$

Consequently, $\quad \boldsymbol{Z} = (\boldsymbol{a} \wedge \boldsymbol{q}) \overset{\circ}{\wedge} (\boldsymbol{c} \wedge \boldsymbol{r}).$

Equation 7.9 is obtained by noting that if $\boldsymbol{M} = \boldsymbol{x} \overset{\circ}{\wedge} \boldsymbol{y}$, then $\boldsymbol{M}_j = \boldsymbol{x} \wedge \boldsymbol{y}_j\boldsymbol{\epsilon}$. Then

$$(\vee//\boldsymbol{M})_j = \vee//\boldsymbol{M}_j = (\vee/\boldsymbol{x}) \wedge \boldsymbol{y}_j,$$

and $\quad (\vee//\boldsymbol{M}) = (\vee/\boldsymbol{x})\boldsymbol{\epsilon} \wedge \boldsymbol{y}.$

Finally, $\quad \vee/\vee//\boldsymbol{M} = (\vee/\boldsymbol{x}) \wedge (\vee/\boldsymbol{y}).$

The derivation of equation 7.10 is similar.

7.2 CANONICAL FORMS

Intrinsic vector

Any function defined on a finite domain can be specified by listing each possible value of the argument together with the corresponding function value. For a logical function of n variables, the n arguments may be considered as the components of a logical vector $\boldsymbol{x}$ of dimension n, and the domain of the function is then represented by the (rows of the) matrix $T(n)$ of dimension $2^n \times n$ defined as follows:

$$\perp T^k = k.$$

For $n = 3$, for example, T has the form shown in Table 7.1.

T	$i(f)$	$p = T \overset{\wedge}{=} x$
0 0 0	1	$\bar{x}_0 \wedge \bar{x}_1 \wedge \bar{x}_2$
0 0 1	0	$\bar{x}_0 \wedge \bar{x}_1 \wedge x_2$
0 1 0	1	$\bar{x}_0 \wedge x_1 \wedge \bar{x}_2$
0 1 1	0	$\bar{x}_0 \wedge x_1 \wedge x_2$
1 0 0	1	$x_0 \wedge \bar{x}_1 \wedge \bar{x}_2$
1 0 1	0	$x_0 \wedge \bar{x}_1 \wedge x_2$
1 1 0	0	$x_0 \wedge x_1 \wedge \bar{x}_2$
1 1 1	0	$x_0 \wedge x_1 \wedge x_2$

$$\begin{aligned} f(x) &= i(f) \overset{\vee}{\underset{\wedge}{}} p \\ &= (\bar{x}_0 \wedge \bar{x}_1 \wedge \bar{x}_2) \vee (\bar{x}_0 \wedge x_1 \wedge \bar{x}_2) \vee (x_0 \wedge \bar{x}_1 \wedge \bar{x}_2) \end{aligned}$$

Table 7.1 The disjunctive canonical form

A logical function f can therefore be specified by its *intrinsic vector* $i(f)$ defined by:

$$i_k(f) = f(T^k).$$

Table 7.1 shows $i(f)$ for the function

$$\begin{aligned} f(x) &= (\bar{x}_0 \wedge \bar{x}_1 \wedge \bar{x}_2) \vee (\bar{x}_0 \wedge x_1 \wedge \bar{x}_2) \vee (x_0 \wedge \bar{x}_1 \wedge \bar{x}_2) \\ &= (\bar{x}_0 \vee \bar{x}_1) \wedge \bar{x}_2. \end{aligned}$$

Applying the usual notation for operations on variables to operations on functions as well (e.g., $\bar{f}$ denotes the function inverse to f, and $f \wedge g$ denotes the conjunction of the functions f and g) permits the expression of certain easily derived identities concerning intrinsic vectors:

$$\begin{aligned} i(\bar{f}) &= \bar{i}(f) \\ i(f \vee g) &= i(f) \vee i(g). \end{aligned}$$

More generally, the intrinsic vector of any function of functions is the same function of their intrinsic vectors.

The two *trivial* functions *identically one* and *identically zero* will be called, respectively, the *unit* function and *zero* function, and will be denoted by 1 and 0. Thus $i(1) = \epsilon$, and $i(0) = \bar{\epsilon}$.

Characteristic vectors

A vector which represents a function f is called a *characteristic vector* of f. The intrinsic vector $\boldsymbol{i}(f)$ is but one of several useful characteristic vectors.

The expression $\boldsymbol{y} \underset{=}{\overset{\wedge}{}} \boldsymbol{x}$ denotes the function obtained by first negating each $\boldsymbol{x}_i$ for which $\boldsymbol{y}_i = 0$ and then taking the *conjunction* (that is, *and* function) over the resulting vector. Such a function is called a *minterm in* $\boldsymbol{x}$, and the components of the *minterm vector*

$$\boldsymbol{p} = \boldsymbol{T} \underset{=}{\overset{\wedge}{}} \boldsymbol{x}$$

comprise all possible minterms in $\boldsymbol{x}$ with no repetitions.

The component $\boldsymbol{p}_i$ is a function of $\boldsymbol{x}$ which assumes the value *one* if and only if $\boldsymbol{x} = \boldsymbol{T}^i$. Consequently, for any function f,

$$\begin{aligned} f(\boldsymbol{x}) &= \vee/(\boldsymbol{i}(f)/\boldsymbol{p}) \\ &= \vee/(\boldsymbol{i}(f) \wedge \boldsymbol{p}) \\ &= \boldsymbol{i}(f) \overset{\vee}{\underset{\wedge}{}} \boldsymbol{p}. \end{aligned}$$

This relation is illustrated by Table 7.1.

The expression

$$f(\boldsymbol{x}) = \boldsymbol{i}(f) \overset{\vee}{\underset{\wedge}{}} \boldsymbol{p} = \boldsymbol{i}(f) \overset{\vee}{\underset{\wedge}{}} (\boldsymbol{T} \underset{=}{\overset{\wedge}{}} \boldsymbol{x})$$

is called the *disjunctive canonical form* of the function f since it displays f as a (unique) disjunctive (that is, *or*) function of minterms, each of which involves all variables and conjunction and negation only. The disjunctive is one of several canonical forms of interest, each of which assumes the form

$$f(\boldsymbol{x}) = \boldsymbol{\gamma}(f) \overset{\odot_1}{\underset{\odot_2}{}} \boldsymbol{s}(\boldsymbol{x}),$$

where the characteristic vector $\boldsymbol{\gamma}(f)$ is a function of f only, and the *specific vector* $\boldsymbol{s}(\boldsymbol{x})$ is a function of the argument $\boldsymbol{x}$ only. Each of the four forms of interest is characterized by the particular over-all operator $\odot_1$ occurring in it and is therefore called the *disjunctive, conjunctive, exclusive disjunctive*, or *equivalence* canonical form* according to whether $\odot_1$ is the operator $\vee$, $\wedge$, $\neq$, or $=$.

The characteristic vector and the specific vector appropriate to each form will be characterized by its over-all operator $\odot_1$. Thus

$$f(\boldsymbol{x}) = \boldsymbol{\gamma}(f, \odot_1) \overset{\odot_1}{\underset{\odot_2}{}} \boldsymbol{s}(\boldsymbol{x}, \odot_1).$$

* The functions $x \vee y$, $x \wedge y$, $(x \neq y)$, and $(x = y)$ are, except for the trivial functions, the only associative commutative functions of two variables.

T	$i(f)$	$\gamma(f,\vee)$	$\overline{T} \overset{\wedge}{\underset{\neq}{}} x$	$\gamma(f,\wedge)$	$T \overset{\vee}{\underset{=}{}} \overline{x}$	$\gamma(f,\neq)$	$\overline{T} \overset{\wedge}{\underset{\vee}{}} x$	$\gamma(f,=)$	$T \overset{\vee}{\underset{\wedge}{}} \overline{x}$	$i(\overline{f})$	$\gamma(\overline{f},\vee)$	$\gamma(\overline{f},\wedge)$	$\gamma(\overline{f},\neq)$	$\gamma(\overline{f},=)$
0 0 0	1	1	$\overline{x}_0 \wedge \overline{x}_1 \wedge \overline{x}_2$	1	$x_0 \vee x_1 \vee x_2$	1	$1 \wedge 1 \wedge 1$	1	$0 \vee 0 \vee 0$	0	0	0	0	0
0 0 1	0	0	$\overline{x}_0 \wedge \overline{x}_1 \wedge x_2$	0	$x_0 \vee x_1 \vee \overline{x}_2$	1	$1 \wedge 1 \wedge x_2$	0	$0 \vee 0 \vee \overline{x}_2$	1	1	1	1	0
0 1 0	1	1	$\overline{x}_0 \wedge x_1 \wedge \overline{x}_2$	1	$x_0 \vee \overline{x}_1 \vee x_2$	0	$1 \wedge x_1 \wedge 1$	1	$0 \vee \overline{x}_1 \vee 0$	0	0	0	0	1
0 1 1	0	0	$\overline{x}_0 \wedge x_1 \wedge x_2$	0	$x_0 \vee \overline{x}_1 \vee \overline{x}_2$	0	$1 \wedge x_1 \wedge x_2$	1	$0 \vee \overline{x}_1 \vee \overline{x}_2$	1	1	1	0	1
1 0 0	1	1	$x_0 \wedge \overline{x}_1 \wedge \overline{x}_2$	1	$\overline{x}_0 \vee x_1 \vee x_2$	0	$x_0 \wedge 1 \wedge 1$	1	$\overline{x}_0 \vee 0 \vee 0$	0	0	0	0	1
1 0 1	0	0	$x_0 \wedge \overline{x}_1 \wedge x_2$	0	$\overline{x}_0 \vee x_1 \vee \overline{x}_2$	0	$x_0 \wedge 1 \wedge x_2$	1	$\overline{x}_0 \vee 0 \vee \overline{x}_2$	1	1	1	0	1
1 1 0	0	0	$x_0 \wedge x_1 \wedge \overline{x}_2$	0	$\overline{x}_0 \vee \overline{x}_1 \vee x_2$	1	$x_0 \wedge x_1 \wedge 1$	0	$\overline{x}_0 \vee \overline{x}_1 \vee 0$	1	1	1	1	0
1 1 1	0	0	$x_0 \wedge x_1 \wedge x_2$	0	$\overline{x}_0 \vee \overline{x}_1 \vee \overline{x}_2$	1	$x_0 \wedge x_1 \wedge x_2$	0	$\overline{x}_0 \vee \overline{x}_1 \vee \overline{x}_2$	1	1	1	1	0

$$f(x) = (\overline{x}_0 \vee \overline{x}_1) \wedge \overline{x}_2 = \begin{cases} (\overline{x}_0 \wedge \overline{x}_1 \wedge \overline{x}_2) \vee (0) \vee (\overline{x}_0 \wedge x_1 \wedge \overline{x}_2) \vee (0) \vee (x_0 \wedge \overline{x}_1 \wedge \overline{x}_2) \vee (0) \vee (0) \vee (0) \text{ (Disjunctive)} \\ (1) \wedge (x_0 \vee x_1 \vee \overline{x}_2) \wedge (1) \wedge (x_0 \vee \overline{x}_1 \vee \overline{x}_2) \wedge (1) \wedge (\overline{x}_0 \vee x_1 \vee \overline{x}_2) \wedge (\overline{x}_0 \vee \overline{x}_1 \vee x_2) \wedge (\overline{x}_0 \vee \overline{x}_1 \vee \overline{x}_2) \text{ (Conjunctive)} \\ [(1) \neq (x_2) \neq (0) \neq (0) \neq (0) \neq (0) \neq (x_0 \wedge x_1) \neq (x_0 \wedge x_1 \wedge x_2)] \text{ (Exclusive disjunctive)} \\ [(1) = (\overline{x}_2) = (1) = (1) = (1) = (1) = (\overline{x}_0 \vee \overline{x}_1) = (\overline{x}_0 \vee \overline{x}_1 \vee \overline{x}_2)] \text{ (Equivalence)} \end{cases}$$

Table 7.2 Intrinsic, characteristic, and specific vectors

The forms are defined formally by the following expressions.*

$$f(\boldsymbol{x}) = \begin{cases} \boldsymbol{\gamma}(f, \vee) \overset{\vee}{\underset{\wedge}{}} (\bar{\boldsymbol{T}} \overset{\wedge}{\underset{\neq}{}} \boldsymbol{x}) & \text{(Disjunctive)} \quad (7.11a) \\ \boldsymbol{\gamma}(f, \wedge) \overset{\wedge}{\underset{\vee}{}} (\boldsymbol{T} \overset{\vee}{\underset{=}{}} \bar{\boldsymbol{x}}) & \text{(Conjunctive)} \quad (7.11b) \\ \boldsymbol{\gamma}(f, \neq) \overset{\neq}{\underset{\wedge}{}} (\bar{\boldsymbol{T}} \overset{\wedge}{\underset{\vee}{}} \boldsymbol{x}) & \text{(Exclusive disjunctive)} \quad (7.11c) \\ \boldsymbol{\gamma}(f, =) \overset{=}{\underset{\vee}{}} (\boldsymbol{T} \overset{\vee}{\underset{\wedge}{}} \bar{\boldsymbol{x}}) & \text{(Equivalence)} \quad (7.11d) \end{cases}$$

Table 7.2 shows the intrinsic vector of the function f of Table 7.1 together with corresponding pairs of characteristic and specific vectors. These may be substituted in equations 7.11 (a–d) to verify that they do represent the function f.

Since $\boldsymbol{x} = \boldsymbol{T}^k = \tilde{\boldsymbol{T}}_k$ for some k, equation 7.11a may be written as

$$\boldsymbol{i}_k(f) = f(\boldsymbol{T}^k) = \boldsymbol{\gamma}(f, \vee) \overset{\vee}{\underset{\wedge}{}} (\bar{\boldsymbol{T}} \overset{\wedge}{\underset{\neq}{}} \tilde{\boldsymbol{T}}_k).$$

Consequently,

$$\boldsymbol{i}(f) = \begin{cases} \boldsymbol{\gamma}(f, \vee) \overset{\vee}{\underset{\wedge}{}} (\bar{\boldsymbol{T}} \overset{\wedge}{\underset{\neq}{}} \tilde{\boldsymbol{T}}) = \boldsymbol{\gamma}(f, \vee) \overset{\vee}{\underset{\wedge}{}} \boldsymbol{S}(\vee) & (7.12a) \\ \boldsymbol{\gamma}(f, \wedge) \overset{\wedge}{\underset{\vee}{}} (\boldsymbol{T} \overset{\vee}{\underset{=}{}} \tilde{\tilde{\boldsymbol{T}}}) = \boldsymbol{\gamma}(f, \wedge) \overset{\wedge}{\underset{\vee}{}} \boldsymbol{S}(\wedge) & (7.12b) \\ \boldsymbol{\gamma}(f, \neq) \overset{\neq}{\underset{\wedge}{}} (\bar{\boldsymbol{T}} \overset{\wedge}{\underset{\vee}{}} \tilde{\boldsymbol{T}}) = \boldsymbol{\gamma}(f, \neq) \overset{\neq}{\underset{\wedge}{}} \boldsymbol{S}(\neq) & (7.12c) \\ \boldsymbol{\gamma}(f, =) \overset{=}{\underset{\vee}{}} (\boldsymbol{T} \overset{\vee}{\underset{\wedge}{}} \tilde{\tilde{\boldsymbol{T}}}) = \boldsymbol{\gamma}(f, =) \overset{=}{\underset{\vee}{}} \boldsymbol{S}(=) & (7.12d) \end{cases}$$

Each of the matrices $S(\odot)$ appearing in the right limbs of equations 7.12(a–d) is a fixed function of $\boldsymbol{T}$ and is called the $\odot$-*specific* (e.g., disjunctive specific) *matrix*. Since $\boldsymbol{i}(f)$ is a function of $\boldsymbol{\gamma}(f, \odot)$ and $\boldsymbol{S}(\odot)$, the relation between the intrinsic vector and each characteristic vector is determined by the corresponding specific matrix.

Since $\boldsymbol{S}(\vee) = (\bar{\boldsymbol{T}} \overset{\wedge}{\underset{\neq}{}} \tilde{\boldsymbol{T}}) = (\boldsymbol{T} \overset{\wedge}{\underset{=}{}} \tilde{\boldsymbol{T}})$, it is clear that $\boldsymbol{S}(\vee) = \boldsymbol{I}$. Consequently, $\boldsymbol{\gamma}(f, \vee) \overset{\vee}{\underset{\wedge}{}} \boldsymbol{S}(\vee) = \boldsymbol{\gamma}(f, \vee)$, and therefore,

$$\boldsymbol{\gamma}(f, \vee) = \boldsymbol{i}(f). \qquad (7.13)$$

Similarly, $\boldsymbol{S}(\wedge) = \bar{\boldsymbol{I}}$, and $\boldsymbol{\gamma}(f, \wedge) \overset{\wedge}{\underset{\vee}{}} \boldsymbol{S}(\wedge) = \boldsymbol{\gamma}(f, \wedge)$, and again

$$\boldsymbol{\gamma}(f, \wedge) = \boldsymbol{i}(f). \qquad (7.14)$$

An explicit expression for $\boldsymbol{S}(\neq)$ may be obtained by induction on the dimension of the corresponding argument, and, to facilitate this, the notation $\boldsymbol{T}(n)$ and $\boldsymbol{S}(\neq, n)$ will be used for the matrices appropriate to an argument $\boldsymbol{x}$ of dimension n. $\boldsymbol{T}(n + 1)$ may be written in partitioned form as

$$\boldsymbol{T}(n + 1) = \left[\begin{array}{c|c} \bar{\boldsymbol{\epsilon}} & \boldsymbol{T}(n) \\ \hline \boldsymbol{\epsilon} & \boldsymbol{T}(n) \end{array}\right],$$

* The expression $\bar{\boldsymbol{T}} \overset{\wedge}{\underset{\neq}{}} \boldsymbol{x}$ used here for the specific vector in the disjunctive form is equivalent to the expression $\boldsymbol{T} \overset{\wedge}{\underset{=}{}} \boldsymbol{x}$ used earlier. Its use increases the uniformity of the expressions for the canonical forms.

where $\bar{\boldsymbol{\epsilon}}$ and $\boldsymbol{\epsilon}$ are both column vectors. Hence

$$S(\neq, n+1) = \left[\begin{array}{c|c} \boldsymbol{\epsilon} & \overline{T}(n) \\ \hline \bar{\boldsymbol{\epsilon}} & \overline{T}(n) \end{array}\right] \overset{\wedge}{\vee} \left[\begin{array}{c|c} \bar{\boldsymbol{\epsilon}} & \boldsymbol{\epsilon} \\ \hline \widetilde{T}(n) & \widetilde{T}(n) \end{array}\right]$$

$$= \left[\begin{array}{c|c} \mathbf{E} \wedge S(\neq, n) & \mathbf{E} \wedge S(\neq, n) \\ \hline \overline{\mathbf{E}} \wedge S(\neq, n) & \mathbf{E} \wedge S(\neq, n) \end{array}\right],$$

since $\boldsymbol{\epsilon} \overset{\circ}{\vee} \bar{\boldsymbol{\epsilon}} = \boldsymbol{\epsilon} \overset{\circ}{\vee} \boldsymbol{\epsilon} = \mathbf{E}$, and $\bar{\boldsymbol{\epsilon}} \overset{\circ}{\vee} \bar{\boldsymbol{\epsilon}} = \overline{\mathbf{E}}$. Finally,

$$S(\neq, n+1) = \left[\begin{array}{c|c} S(\neq, n) & S(\neq, n) \\ \hline \overline{\mathbf{E}} & S(\neq, n) \end{array}\right] \tag{7.15}$$

Since $S(\neq, 1) = \begin{bmatrix} 1 & 1 \\ 0 & 1 \end{bmatrix}$ it is clear that

$$S(\neq, 2) = \left[\begin{array}{cc|cc} 1 & 1 & 1 & 1 \\ 0 & 1 & 0 & 1 \\ \hline 0 & 0 & 1 & 1 \\ 0 & 0 & 0 & 1 \end{array}\right], \quad S(\neq, 3) = \begin{bmatrix} 1 & 1 & 1 & 1 & 1 & 1 & 1 & 1 \\ 0 & 1 & 0 & 1 & 0 & 1 & 0 & 1 \\ 0 & 0 & 1 & 1 & 0 & 0 & 1 & 1 \\ 0 & 0 & 0 & 1 & 0 & 0 & 0 & 1 \\ 0 & 0 & 0 & 0 & 1 & 1 & 1 & 1 \\ 0 & 0 & 0 & 0 & 0 & 1 & 0 & 1 \\ 0 & 0 & 0 & 0 & 0 & 0 & 1 & 1 \\ 0 & 0 & 0 & 0 & 0 & 0 & 0 & 1 \end{bmatrix}$$

and so forth.*

The following useful properties of $S(\neq)$ are easily verified for the foregoing examples and may be established generally by formal induction. The matrix is self-inverse with respect to the operations $(\overset{\neq}{\wedge})$, that is,

$$S(\neq) \overset{\neq}{\wedge} S(\neq) = \boldsymbol{I}. \tag{7.16}$$

Moreover, since every row of the transpose $\widetilde{S}(\neq)$ save the zeroth has an even number of ones,

$$(2\boldsymbol{\epsilon}) \,|+/\widetilde{S}(\neq) = \boldsymbol{\epsilon}^0.$$

Hence by equation 7.5,

$$\neq/\widetilde{S}(\neq) = \boldsymbol{\epsilon}^0. \tag{7.17}$$

Since (by equation 7.4) $S(=) = \bar{S}(\neq)$ and since $S(\neq)$ is of even dimension, the same result holds for $\widetilde{S}(=)$.

* This result was first obtained by Muller (1954), who employed the matrix $\boldsymbol{C}$ of binomial coefficients and showed that $\widetilde{S}(\neq) = (2\mathbf{E})|_0\boldsymbol{C}$. Also see Calingaert (1960).

Equation 7.12c gives $\boldsymbol{i}(f)$ as a function of $\boldsymbol{\gamma}(f, \neq)$ and $\boldsymbol{S}(\neq)$. This relation is more commonly written in transposed form and with $\boldsymbol{i}(f)$ replaced by the equivalent $\boldsymbol{\gamma}(f, \vee)$ as follows:

$$\boldsymbol{\gamma}(f, \vee) = \widetilde{\boldsymbol{S}}(\neq) \overset{\neq}{\wedge} \boldsymbol{\gamma}(f, \neq). \tag{7.18}$$

Since $\widetilde{\boldsymbol{S}}(\neq)$ is self-inverse (equation 7.16), premultiplication of equation 7.18 by $\widetilde{\boldsymbol{S}}(\neq) \overset{\neq}{\wedge}$ yields an identical expression for $\boldsymbol{\gamma}(f, \neq)$ as a function of $\boldsymbol{\gamma}(f, \vee)$, namely

$$\boldsymbol{\gamma}(f, \neq) = \widetilde{\boldsymbol{S}}(\neq) \overset{\neq}{\wedge} \boldsymbol{\gamma}(f, \vee). \tag{7.19}$$

The characteristic vectors of the identity function 1 and of the zero function 0 may now be derived. Clearly $\boldsymbol{i}(1) = \boldsymbol{\epsilon}$ and $\boldsymbol{i}(0) = \bar{\boldsymbol{\epsilon}}$. Hence by equations 7.13 and 7.14,

$$\boldsymbol{\gamma}(1, \vee) = \boldsymbol{\gamma}(1, \wedge) = \boldsymbol{\epsilon},$$

and

$$\boldsymbol{\gamma}(0, \vee) = \boldsymbol{\gamma}(0, \wedge) = \bar{\boldsymbol{\epsilon}}.$$

Moreover,

$$\begin{aligned} \boldsymbol{\gamma}(1, \neq) &= \widetilde{\boldsymbol{S}}(\neq) \overset{\neq}{\wedge} \boldsymbol{\epsilon} \\ &= \neq / \widetilde{\boldsymbol{S}}(\neq). \end{aligned}$$

Hence, by equation 7.17,

$$\boldsymbol{\gamma}(1, \neq) = \boldsymbol{\epsilon}^0. \tag{7.20}$$

Similarly, $\boldsymbol{\gamma}(0, \neq) = \bar{\boldsymbol{\epsilon}}$.

The relations between the characteristic vectors of a function f and of its inverse $\bar{f}$ may now be obtained. Since

$$\boldsymbol{i}(\bar{f}) = \bar{\boldsymbol{i}}(f), \tag{7.21}$$

then, by equations 7.13 and 7.14,

$$\boldsymbol{\gamma}(\bar{f}, \vee) = \bar{\boldsymbol{\gamma}}(f, \vee),$$

and $\boldsymbol{\gamma}(\bar{f}, \wedge) = \bar{\boldsymbol{\gamma}}(f, \wedge)$.

Moreover, $\boldsymbol{\gamma}(\bar{f}, \neq) = \widetilde{\boldsymbol{S}}(\neq) \overset{\neq}{\wedge} \boldsymbol{i}(\bar{f}) = \widetilde{\boldsymbol{S}}(\neq) \overset{\neq}{\wedge} \bar{\boldsymbol{i}}(f)$,

by equations 7.13, 7.19, and 7.21. Hence

$$\boldsymbol{\gamma}(\bar{f}, \neq) = (\boldsymbol{\gamma}(f, \neq) \neq \boldsymbol{\epsilon}^0) \tag{7.22}$$

by equations 7.7, 7.17, 7.19, and 7.13. Characteristic vectors of a function and of its inverse are displayed in Table 7.2.

The relation between $\boldsymbol{\gamma}(f, \neq)$ and $\boldsymbol{\gamma}(f, =)$ may now be obtained by applying equation 7.22 to equation 7.12c to yield

$$\bar{\boldsymbol{i}}(f) = \boldsymbol{i}(\bar{f}) = (\boldsymbol{\gamma}(f, \neq) \neq \boldsymbol{\epsilon}^0) \overset{\neq}{\wedge} \boldsymbol{S}(\neq).$$

	$\mathbf{i}(f)$	$\gamma(f, \neq)$	$\gamma(f, =)$	$\mathbf{i}(\bar f)$	$\gamma(\bar f, \neq)$	$\gamma(\bar f, =)$
$\mathbf{i}(f)$	$\mathbf{i}(f)$	$\tilde S(\neq) \overset{\neq}{\wedge} \gamma(f, \neq)$	$\tilde S(=) \overset{=}{\vee} \gamma(f, =)$	$\bar{\mathbf{i}}(\bar f)$	$\tilde S(=) \overset{=}{\vee} \bar\gamma(\bar f, \neq)$	$\tilde S(\neq) \overset{\neq}{\wedge} \bar\gamma(\bar f, =)$
$\gamma(f, \neq)$	$\tilde S(\neq) \overset{\neq}{\wedge} \mathbf{i}(f)$	$\gamma(f, \neq)$	$(\gamma(f, =) = \boldsymbol{\epsilon}^0)$	$\tilde S(\neq) \overset{\neq}{\wedge} \bar{\mathbf{i}}(\bar f)$	$(\gamma(\bar f, \neq) \neq \boldsymbol{\epsilon}^0)$	$\bar\gamma(\bar f, =)$
$\gamma(f, =)$	$\tilde S(=) \overset{=}{\vee} \mathbf{i}(f)$	$(\gamma(f, \neq) = \boldsymbol{\epsilon}^0)$	$\gamma(f, =)$	$\tilde S(=) \overset{=}{\vee} \bar{\mathbf{i}}(\bar f)$	$\bar\gamma(\bar f, \neq)$	$(\gamma(\bar f, =) \neq \boldsymbol{\epsilon}^0)$
$\mathbf{i}(\bar f)$	$\bar{\mathbf{i}}(f)$	$\tilde S(=) \overset{=}{\vee} \bar\gamma(f, \neq)$	$\tilde S(\neq) \overset{\neq}{\wedge} \bar\gamma(f, =)$	$\mathbf{i}(\bar f)$	$\tilde S(\neq) \overset{\neq}{\wedge} \gamma(\bar f, \neq)$	$\tilde S(=) \overset{=}{\vee} \gamma(\bar f, =)$
$\gamma(\bar f, \neq)$	$\tilde S(\neq) \overset{\neq}{\wedge} \bar{\mathbf{i}}(f)$	$(\gamma(f, \neq) \neq \boldsymbol{\epsilon}^0)$	$\bar\gamma(f, =)$	$\tilde S(\neq) \overset{\neq}{\wedge} \mathbf{i}(\bar f)$	$\gamma(\bar f, \neq)$	$(\gamma(\bar f, =) = \boldsymbol{\epsilon}^0)$
$\gamma(\bar f, =)$	$\tilde S(=) \overset{=}{\vee} \bar{\mathbf{i}}(f)$	$\bar\gamma(f, \neq)$	$(\gamma(f, =) \neq \boldsymbol{\epsilon}^0)$	$\tilde S(=) \overset{=}{\vee} \mathbf{i}(\bar f)$	$(\gamma(\bar f, =) \neq \boldsymbol{\epsilon}^0)$	$\gamma(\bar f, =)$

(1) $\gamma(f, \vee) = \gamma(f, \wedge) = \mathbf{i}(f)$

(2) $\tilde S(\neq, n) = (\tilde{\tilde{\boldsymbol{T}}}(n) \between \boldsymbol{T}(n))$

$$= \left(\begin{array}{c:c} \tilde S(\neq, n-1) & \bar{\boldsymbol{E}} \\ \hdashline \tilde S(\neq, n-1) & \tilde S(\neq, n-1) \end{array}\right)$$

(3) $\tilde S(\neq, 1) = \begin{pmatrix} 1 & 0 \\ 1 & 1 \end{pmatrix}$

(4) $\tilde S(=) = \tilde{\tilde S}(\neq)$

	0	1
$\mathbf{i}(f)$	$\bar{\boldsymbol{\epsilon}}$	$\boldsymbol{\epsilon}$
$\gamma(f, \vee)$	$\bar{\boldsymbol{\epsilon}}$	$\boldsymbol{\epsilon}$
$\gamma(f, \wedge)$	$\bar{\boldsymbol{\epsilon}}$	$\boldsymbol{\epsilon}$
$\gamma(f, \neq)$	$\bar{\boldsymbol{\epsilon}}$	$\boldsymbol{\epsilon}^0$
$\gamma(f, =)$	$\bar{\boldsymbol{\epsilon}}^0$	$\boldsymbol{\epsilon}$

Zero and identity functions

Table 7.3 Relations among characteristic vectors

Application of De Morgan's law and of the fact that $S(=) = \bar{S}(\neq)$ yields

$$\boldsymbol{i}(f) = \overline{(\boldsymbol{\gamma}(f, \neq) \neq \boldsymbol{\epsilon}^0)} \mathbin{\bar{\bar{\vee}}} S(=).$$

Comparison with equation 7.12d shows that

$$\begin{aligned} \boldsymbol{\gamma}(f, =) &= \overline{(\boldsymbol{\gamma}(f, \neq) \neq \boldsymbol{\epsilon}^0)} \\ &= (\boldsymbol{\gamma}(f, \neq) = \boldsymbol{\epsilon}^0). \end{aligned}$$

The relations among the various characteristic vectors are summarized in Table 7.3.

7.3 DECOMPOSITION

A logical function $f(\boldsymbol{x})$ is said to be *decomposable on* $\boldsymbol{u}$ if it can be written in the form

$$f(\boldsymbol{x}) = g(h(\bar{\boldsymbol{u}}/\boldsymbol{x}), \boldsymbol{u}/\boldsymbol{x}),$$

where g and h are logical functions. Since f, g, and h are functions of $\nu(\boldsymbol{u})$, $(1 + +/\boldsymbol{u})$, and $+/\bar{\boldsymbol{u}}$ variables, respectively, then if $+/\bar{\boldsymbol{u}} > 1$, both g and h are functions of fewer variables than f. Decomposition on $\boldsymbol{u}$ such that $+/\bar{\boldsymbol{u}} > 1$ thus permits f to be expressed in terms of simpler functions g and h and provides an important basis for simplification techniques.

Every function is decomposable on $\boldsymbol{u} = \boldsymbol{\epsilon}$. Moreover, if $+/\bar{\boldsymbol{u}} = 1$, then $\boldsymbol{u} = \bar{\boldsymbol{\epsilon}}^i$ for some i, and

$$f(\boldsymbol{x}) = [\bar{x}_i \wedge f(\boldsymbol{x} \wedge \bar{\boldsymbol{\epsilon}}^i)] \vee [x_i \wedge f(\boldsymbol{x} \vee \boldsymbol{\epsilon}^i)].$$

Since both $f(\boldsymbol{x} \wedge \bar{\boldsymbol{\epsilon}}^i)$ and $f(\boldsymbol{x} \vee \boldsymbol{\epsilon}^i)$ are expressible as functions of $\bar{\boldsymbol{\epsilon}}^i/\boldsymbol{x}$, then the foregoing expression is of the required form with $h(\boldsymbol{u}/\boldsymbol{x}) = x_i$. Consequently, all functions are trivially decomposable for $+/\bar{\boldsymbol{u}} = 0$ or $+/\bar{\boldsymbol{u}} = 1$.

Disjunctive canonical form

Ashenhurst (1957) determines nontrivial decompositions of $f(\boldsymbol{x})$ by arraying the intrinsic vector $\boldsymbol{i}(f)$ in a $2^{+/\bar{\boldsymbol{u}}} \times 2^{+/\boldsymbol{u}}$ matrix $\boldsymbol{F}$ defined as follows:

$$F_j^i = \boldsymbol{i}_k(f),$$

where

$$\begin{aligned} k &= (2\boldsymbol{\epsilon}) \perp \boldsymbol{k} \\ i &= (2\boldsymbol{\epsilon}) \perp (\bar{\boldsymbol{u}}/\boldsymbol{k}) \end{aligned}$$

and

$$j = (2\boldsymbol{\epsilon}) \perp (\boldsymbol{u}/\boldsymbol{k}).$$

If, for example, $\boldsymbol{u} = (1, 0, 1, 1, 0)$, then the index k of each component $\boldsymbol{i}_k(f)$ appearing in $\boldsymbol{F}$ is given by the matrix* $\boldsymbol{C}$ of Table 7.4. The table also shows

* Ashenhurst (1957) calls the matrix $\boldsymbol{C}$ a *decomposition chart* and represents $\boldsymbol{F}$ by circling each element of $\boldsymbol{C}$ which corresponds to a nonzero component of $\boldsymbol{i}(f)$.

	T	$i(f)$	h	$b \overset{\vee}{\wedge} r$	$c \overset{\vee}{\wedge} r$	$d \overset{\vee}{\wedge} r$	$m \overset{\vee}{\wedge} r$	$n \overset{\vee}{\wedge} r$
0	0 0 0 0 0	1	1	0	1	0	1	0
1	0 0 0 0 1	0	0	0	1	0	1	0
2	0 0 0 1 0	0	1	0	0	0	0	0
3	0 0 0 1 1	0	0	0	0	0	0	0
4	0 0 1 0 0	1	1	0	1	0	1	0
5	0 0 1 0 1	0	0	0	1	0	1	0
6	0 0 1 1 0	0	1	1	0	0	0	1
7	0 0 1 1 1	1	0	1	0	0	0	1
8	0 1 0 0 0	0	0	0	1	0	1	0
9	0 1 0 0 1	1	1	0	1	0	1	0
10	0 1 0 1 0	0	0	0	0	0	0	0
11	0 1 0 1 1	0	1	0	0	0	0	0
12	0 1 1 0 0	0	0	0	1	0	1	0
13	0 1 1 0 1	1	1	0	1	0	1	0
14	0 1 1 1 0	1	0	1	0	0	0	1
15	0 1 1 1 1	0	1	1	0	0	0	1
16	1 0 0 0 0	1	1	0	0	1	1	1
17	1 0 0 0 1	1	0	0	0	1	1	1
18	1 0 0 1 0	0	1	0	0	0	0	0
19	1 0 0 1 1	0	0	0	0	0	0	0
20	1 0 1 0 0	0	1	1	0	0	0	1
21	1 0 1 0 1	1	0	1	0	0	0	1
22	1 0 1 1 0	1	1	0	1	0	1	0
23	1 0 1 1 1	0	0	0	1	0	1	0
24	1 1 0 0 0	1	0	0	0	1	1	1
25	1 1 0 0 1	1	1	0	0	1	1	1
26	1 1 0 1 0	0	0	0	0	0	0	0
27	1 1 0 1 1	0	1	0	0	0	0	0
28	1 1 1 0 0	1	0	1	0	0	0	1
29	1 1 1 0 1	0	1	1	0	0	0	1
30	1 1 1 1 0	0	0	0	1	0	1	0
31	1 1 1 1 1	1	1	0	1	0	1	0

$u = (1 \quad 0 \quad 1 \quad 1 \quad 0)$

$$C = \begin{pmatrix} 0 & 2 & 4 & 6 & 16 & 18 & 20 & 22 \\ 1 & 3 & 5 & 7 & 17 & 19 & 21 & 23 \\ 8 & 10 & 12 & 14 & 24 & 26 & 28 & 30 \\ 9 & 11 & 13 & 15 & 25 & 27 & 29 & 31 \end{pmatrix}$$

$$F = \begin{pmatrix} 1 & 0 & 1 & 0 & 1 & 0 & 0 & 1 \\ 0 & 0 & 0 & 1 & 1 & 0 & 1 & 0 \\ 0 & 0 & 0 & 1 & 1 & 0 & 1 & 0 \\ 1 & 0 & 1 & 0 & 1 & 0 & 0 & 1 \end{pmatrix} \qquad \overset{a}{\begin{pmatrix} 1 \\ 0 \\ 0 \\ 1 \end{pmatrix}}$$

$b = (0 \quad 0 \quad 0 \quad 1 \quad 0 \quad 0 \quad 1 \quad 0)$

$c = (1 \quad 0 \quad 1 \quad 0 \quad 0 \quad 0 \quad 0 \quad 1)$

$d = (0 \quad 0 \quad 0 \quad 0 \quad 1 \quad 0 \quad 0 \quad 0)$

$m = (0 \quad 0 \quad 0 \quad 1 \quad 1 \quad 0 \quad 1 \quad 0)$

$n = (1 \quad 0 \quad 1 \quad 0 \quad 1 \quad 0 \quad 0 \quad 1)$

Table 7.4 Decomposition of the function $f(x)$ on u

corresponding values of $\boldsymbol{i}(f)$ and $\boldsymbol{F}$.

Let
$$\boldsymbol{p} = \overline{\boldsymbol{T}} \overset{\wedge}{\neq} \boldsymbol{x},$$
$$\boldsymbol{q} = \overline{\boldsymbol{T}} \overset{\wedge}{\neq} (\overline{\boldsymbol{u}}/\boldsymbol{x}),$$
and
$$\boldsymbol{r} = \overline{\boldsymbol{T}} \overset{\wedge}{\neq} (\boldsymbol{u}/\boldsymbol{x})$$
be the minterm vectors of $\boldsymbol{x}$, $\overline{\boldsymbol{u}}/\boldsymbol{x}$, and $\boldsymbol{u}/\boldsymbol{x}$, respectively.* Then the matrix
$$\boldsymbol{P} = \boldsymbol{q} \overset{\circ}{\wedge} \boldsymbol{r}$$
contains the components of $\boldsymbol{p}$ arrayed in the same order as the components of $\boldsymbol{i}(f)$ in the matrix $\boldsymbol{F}$. Consequently,†
$$f(\boldsymbol{x}) = \boldsymbol{i}(f) \overset{\vee}{\wedge} \boldsymbol{p} = \vee/\vee//(\boldsymbol{F} \wedge \boldsymbol{P}).$$

Decomposability depends on the structure of the matrix $\boldsymbol{F}$. If each column of $\boldsymbol{F}$ is either zero or equal to the vector $\boldsymbol{a}$, there exists a vector $\boldsymbol{c}$ such that
$$\boldsymbol{F} = \boldsymbol{a} \overset{\circ}{\wedge} \boldsymbol{c}. \tag{7.23}$$
Hence,
$$f(\boldsymbol{x}) = \vee/\vee//\boldsymbol{M},$$
where
$$\boldsymbol{M} = (\boldsymbol{a} \overset{\circ}{\wedge} \boldsymbol{c}) \wedge (\boldsymbol{q} \overset{\circ}{\wedge} \boldsymbol{r}). \tag{7.24}$$
But by equation 7.8,
$$\boldsymbol{M} = (\boldsymbol{a} \wedge \boldsymbol{q}) \overset{\circ}{\wedge} (\boldsymbol{c} \wedge \boldsymbol{r}), \tag{7.25}$$
and hence by equation 7.9,
$$\begin{aligned} f(\boldsymbol{x}) = \vee/\vee//\boldsymbol{M} &= (\vee/(\boldsymbol{a} \wedge \boldsymbol{q})) \wedge (\vee/(\boldsymbol{c} \wedge \boldsymbol{r})) \\ &= (\boldsymbol{a} \overset{\vee}{\wedge} \boldsymbol{q}) \wedge (\boldsymbol{c} \overset{\vee}{\wedge} \boldsymbol{r}). \end{aligned} \tag{7.26}$$

Since the first and last terms on the right of equation 7.26 are, respectively, functions of $\overline{\boldsymbol{u}}/\boldsymbol{x}$ and of $\boldsymbol{u}/\boldsymbol{x}$ only, the function $f(\boldsymbol{x})$ is decomposable. The required functions are simply
$$\left.\begin{aligned} h = h(\overline{\boldsymbol{u}}/\boldsymbol{x}) &= \boldsymbol{a} \overset{\vee}{\wedge} \boldsymbol{q} = \boldsymbol{a} \overset{\vee}{\wedge} [\overline{\boldsymbol{T}} \overset{\wedge}{\neq} (\overline{\boldsymbol{u}}/\boldsymbol{x})] \\ f(\boldsymbol{x}) &= g(h, \boldsymbol{u}/\boldsymbol{x}) = h \wedge [\boldsymbol{c} \overset{\vee}{\wedge} \boldsymbol{r}] \\ \boldsymbol{r} &= \overline{\boldsymbol{T}} \overset{\wedge}{\neq} (\boldsymbol{u}/\boldsymbol{x}) \end{aligned}\right\} \tag{7.27}$$

Since equation 7.27 does not represent the most general possible function of h and $\boldsymbol{u}/\boldsymbol{x}$, it appears that the characteristic matrix $\boldsymbol{F} = \boldsymbol{a} \overset{\circ}{\wedge} \boldsymbol{c}$ does not

* Although denoted by the same symbol, the matrices $\boldsymbol{T}$ are of differing dimensions as required by compatibility.

† Since $\boldsymbol{i}(f)$ is equal to $\gamma(f, \vee)$, it may be substituted for it in the disjunctive canonical form.

represent the most general function decomposable on $\boldsymbol{u}$. Ashenhurst (1957) has shown that the most general type of function decomposable on $\boldsymbol{u}$ is represented by a characteristic matrix of the form*

$$\boldsymbol{F} = (\overline{\boldsymbol{a}} \stackrel{\circ}{\wedge} \boldsymbol{b}) \vee (\boldsymbol{a} \stackrel{\circ}{\wedge} \boldsymbol{c}) \vee (\boldsymbol{\epsilon} \stackrel{\circ}{\wedge} \boldsymbol{d}) \vee (\overline{\boldsymbol{\epsilon}} \stackrel{\circ}{\wedge} \boldsymbol{e}), \tag{7.28}$$

where $\boldsymbol{b}$, $\boldsymbol{c}$, $\boldsymbol{d}$, and $\boldsymbol{e}$ are mutually disjoint and collectively exhaustive, that is,

$$\boldsymbol{b} + \boldsymbol{c} + \boldsymbol{d} + \boldsymbol{e} = \boldsymbol{\epsilon}.$$

The fourth term of equation 7.28 is identically zero and is included only for formal completeness; hence

$$\boldsymbol{F} = (\overline{\boldsymbol{a}} \stackrel{\circ}{\wedge} \boldsymbol{b}) \vee (\boldsymbol{a} \stackrel{\circ}{\wedge} \boldsymbol{c}) \vee (\boldsymbol{\epsilon} \stackrel{\circ}{\wedge} \boldsymbol{d}). \tag{7.23$'$}$$

Equation 7.24 now becomes

$$\boldsymbol{M} = ((\overline{\boldsymbol{a}} \stackrel{\circ}{\wedge} \boldsymbol{b}) \vee (\boldsymbol{a} \stackrel{\circ}{\wedge} \boldsymbol{c}) \vee (\boldsymbol{\epsilon} \stackrel{\circ}{\wedge} \boldsymbol{d})) \wedge (\boldsymbol{q} \stackrel{\circ}{\wedge} \boldsymbol{r}), \tag{7.24$'$}$$

and since conjunction is distributive over disjunction, equation 7.8 may again be applied to yield

$$\boldsymbol{M} = ((\overline{\boldsymbol{a}} \wedge \boldsymbol{q}) \stackrel{\circ}{\wedge} (\boldsymbol{b} \wedge \boldsymbol{r})) \vee ((\boldsymbol{a} \wedge \boldsymbol{q}) \stackrel{\circ}{\wedge} (\boldsymbol{c} \wedge \boldsymbol{r})) \vee ((\boldsymbol{\epsilon} \wedge \boldsymbol{q}) \stackrel{\circ}{\wedge} (\boldsymbol{d} \wedge \boldsymbol{r})). \tag{7.25$'$}$$

Moreover, since $\vee/\vee//(\boldsymbol{X} \vee \boldsymbol{Y}) = (\vee/\vee//\boldsymbol{X}) \vee (\vee/\vee//\boldsymbol{Y})$, equation 7.9 may again be applied to yield

$$f(\boldsymbol{x}) = \vee/\vee//\boldsymbol{M}$$

$$= ((\overline{\boldsymbol{a}} \stackrel{\vee}{\wedge} \boldsymbol{q}) \wedge (\boldsymbol{b} \stackrel{\vee}{\wedge} \boldsymbol{r})) \vee ((\boldsymbol{a} \stackrel{\vee}{\wedge} \boldsymbol{q}) \wedge (\boldsymbol{c} \stackrel{\vee}{\wedge} \boldsymbol{r})) \vee (\boldsymbol{\epsilon} \stackrel{\vee}{\wedge} \boldsymbol{q}) \wedge (\boldsymbol{d} \stackrel{\vee}{\wedge} \boldsymbol{r})). \tag{7.26$'$}$$

Since $\boldsymbol{q}$ is a specific vector of the disjunctive canonical form (i.e., a minterm vector), it is some column of the specific matrix $\boldsymbol{S}(\vee)$. Since $\boldsymbol{S}(\vee) = \boldsymbol{I}$, $\boldsymbol{q}$ therefore contains exactly one nonzero component, and consequently $(\overline{\boldsymbol{a}} \stackrel{\vee}{\wedge} \boldsymbol{q}) = \overline{(\boldsymbol{a} \stackrel{\vee}{\wedge} \boldsymbol{q})}$, and $\boldsymbol{\epsilon} \stackrel{\vee}{\wedge} \boldsymbol{q} = 1$. Equation 7.26 can thus be rewritten in decomposed form as

$$\left.\begin{aligned} h &= h(\overline{\boldsymbol{u}}/\boldsymbol{x}) = \boldsymbol{a} \stackrel{\vee}{\wedge} \boldsymbol{q} = \boldsymbol{a} \stackrel{\vee}{\wedge} (\overline{\boldsymbol{T}} \stackrel{\wedge}{\neq} (\overline{\boldsymbol{u}}/\boldsymbol{x})) \\ f(\boldsymbol{x}) &= g(h, \boldsymbol{u}/\boldsymbol{x}) = (\overline{h} \wedge (\boldsymbol{b} \stackrel{\vee}{\wedge} \boldsymbol{r})) \vee (h \wedge (\boldsymbol{c} \stackrel{\vee}{\wedge} \boldsymbol{r})) \vee (\boldsymbol{d} \stackrel{\vee}{\wedge} \boldsymbol{r}) \\ \boldsymbol{r} &= \overline{\boldsymbol{T}} \stackrel{\wedge}{\neq} (\boldsymbol{u}/\boldsymbol{x}) \end{aligned}\right\} \tag{7.27$'$}$$

It is interesting to note that no use has been made of the fact that $\boldsymbol{b}$, $\boldsymbol{c}$, and $\boldsymbol{d}$ are disjoint. Relaxation of this restriction does not, however, increase the generality of the matrix $\boldsymbol{F}$, since $\boldsymbol{a} \vee \boldsymbol{\epsilon} = \boldsymbol{\epsilon}$, $\boldsymbol{a} \vee \overline{\boldsymbol{\epsilon}} = \boldsymbol{a}$, and $\boldsymbol{a} \vee \overline{\boldsymbol{a}} = \boldsymbol{\epsilon}$. It does suggest, however, that the matrix $\boldsymbol{F}$ may be expressed more compactly as

$$\boldsymbol{F} = (\boldsymbol{a} \stackrel{\circ}{\wedge} \boldsymbol{m}) \vee (\overline{\boldsymbol{a}} \stackrel{\circ}{\wedge} \boldsymbol{n}),$$

* In Ashenhurst's terminology, the matrix $\boldsymbol{F}$ must be of the following form: each column is either all zeros, all ones, the vector $\boldsymbol{a}$, or the vector $\overline{\boldsymbol{a}}$.

where $\boldsymbol{m} = \boldsymbol{b} \vee \boldsymbol{d}$ and $\boldsymbol{n} = \boldsymbol{c} \vee \boldsymbol{d}$. The second line of equation 7.27′ then becomes

$$f(\boldsymbol{x}) = (\bar{h} \wedge (\boldsymbol{m} \overset{\vee}{\wedge} \boldsymbol{r})) \vee (h \wedge (\boldsymbol{n} \overset{\vee}{\wedge} \boldsymbol{r})), \qquad (7.28)$$

a reflection of the obvious fact that the third term $(\boldsymbol{d} \overset{\vee}{\wedge} \boldsymbol{r})$ of equation 7.27′ can be incorporated in the preceding terms.

Table 7.4 shows a complete example of the decomposition process for $\boldsymbol{u} = (1, 0, 1, 1, 0)$. The characteristic matrix $\boldsymbol{F}$ is obtained by applying the matrix $\boldsymbol{C}$ to $\boldsymbol{i}(f)$. Clearly

$$\begin{aligned} \boldsymbol{F} &= (\bar{\boldsymbol{a}} \overset{\circ}{\wedge} \boldsymbol{b}) \vee (\boldsymbol{a} \overset{\circ}{\wedge} \boldsymbol{c}) \vee (\boldsymbol{\epsilon} \overset{\circ}{\wedge} \boldsymbol{c}) \\ &= (\bar{\boldsymbol{a}} \overset{\circ}{\wedge} \boldsymbol{m}) \vee (\boldsymbol{a} \overset{\circ}{\wedge} \boldsymbol{n}). \end{aligned}$$

Consequently,

$$f(\boldsymbol{x}) = (\bar{h} \wedge (\boldsymbol{b} \overset{\vee}{\wedge} \boldsymbol{r})) \vee (h \wedge (\boldsymbol{c} \overset{\vee}{\wedge} \boldsymbol{r})) \vee (\boldsymbol{d} \overset{\vee}{\wedge} \boldsymbol{r}),$$

where $\quad h = \boldsymbol{a} \overset{\vee}{\wedge} \boldsymbol{q}, \quad \boldsymbol{q} = \overline{\boldsymbol{T}} \overset{\wedge}{\neq} (\bar{\boldsymbol{u}}/\boldsymbol{x}), \quad \text{and } \boldsymbol{r} = \overline{\boldsymbol{T}} \overset{\wedge}{\neq} (\boldsymbol{u}/\boldsymbol{x}).$

Since $\quad \boldsymbol{q} = (\bar{x}_1 \wedge \bar{x}_4, \bar{x}_1 \wedge x_4, x_1 \wedge \bar{x}_4, x_1 \wedge x_4),$

and $\quad \boldsymbol{a} = (1, 0, 0, 1),$

then $\quad h = (\bar{x}_1 \wedge \bar{x}_4) \vee (x_1 \wedge x_4) = (x_1 = x_4).$

Similarly,

$$\begin{aligned} \boldsymbol{b} \overset{\vee}{\wedge} \boldsymbol{r} &= (\bar{x}_0 \wedge x_2 \wedge x_3) \vee (x_0 \wedge x_2 \wedge \bar{x}_3) \\ &= x_2 \wedge (x_0 \neq x_3), \\ \boldsymbol{c} \overset{\vee}{\wedge} \boldsymbol{r} &= (\bar{x}_0 \wedge \bar{x}_3) \vee (x_0 \wedge x_2 \wedge x_3), \end{aligned}$$

and

$$\boldsymbol{d} \overset{\vee}{\wedge} \boldsymbol{r} = x_0 \wedge \bar{x}_2 \wedge \bar{x}_3.$$

Alternatively, the use of the vectors $\boldsymbol{m}$ and $\boldsymbol{n}$ yields the solution

$$\begin{aligned} f(\boldsymbol{x}) = \{\bar{h} \wedge [(\bar{x}_0 \wedge x_2 \wedge x_3) \vee (x_0 \wedge \bar{x}_3)]\} \vee \{h \wedge [(\bar{x}_0 \wedge \bar{x}_3) \\ \vee (x_0 \wedge (x_2 = x_3))]\}. \end{aligned}$$

The entire decomposition process is described by Program 7.5. Steps 1–7 determine the characteristic matrix $\boldsymbol{F}$ appropriate to the decomposition $\boldsymbol{u}$. The loop 2–7 is repeated for each value of k from zero to $2^{\nu(\boldsymbol{u})} - 1$. Step 2 determines $\boldsymbol{k}$ as the vector (of dimension $\nu(\boldsymbol{u})$) whose base two value is k. Steps 3 and 4 then specify the indices i and j appropriate to k, and step 5 specifies element $\boldsymbol{F}_j^{\,i}$.

Step 11 determines $\boldsymbol{d}$ as the vector which specifies all full column vectors of $\boldsymbol{F}$, that is, $\boldsymbol{d}_j = 1$ if and only if $\boldsymbol{F}_j = \boldsymbol{\epsilon}$. Step 12 determines $\boldsymbol{e}$ as the corresponding vector specifying the zero columns.

If $\boldsymbol{d}$ and $\boldsymbol{e}$ together exhaust the columns (that is, $\boldsymbol{d} \vee \boldsymbol{e} = \boldsymbol{\epsilon}$), then $\boldsymbol{b}$ and $\boldsymbol{c}$ (and $\boldsymbol{a}$ arbitrarily) must be set to zero. Since this is done by steps 8–10, the exit branch on equality at step 13 terminates the process correctly. If $(\boldsymbol{d} \vee \boldsymbol{e}) \neq \boldsymbol{\epsilon}$, then any column of the matrix $\overline{(\boldsymbol{d} \vee \boldsymbol{e})} / \boldsymbol{F}$ can be used to specify $\boldsymbol{a}$; step 14 uses the first column. Step 15 determines $\boldsymbol{b}$ as the vector

Step	Statement	Branch
1	$k \leftarrow 0$	(entry)
2	$(2\boldsymbol{\epsilon}(\nu(\boldsymbol{u})))\perp \boldsymbol{k} \leftarrow k$	
3	$i \leftarrow (2\boldsymbol{\epsilon})\perp(\overline{\boldsymbol{u}}/\boldsymbol{k})$	
4	$j \leftarrow (2\boldsymbol{\epsilon})\perp(\boldsymbol{u}/\boldsymbol{k})$	
5	$F_j^i \leftarrow \boldsymbol{i}_k(f)$	
6	$k \leftarrow k + 1$	
7	$k : 2^{\nu(\boldsymbol{u})}$	$<$ → 2
8	$\boldsymbol{a} \leftarrow \overline{\boldsymbol{\epsilon}}(+/\overline{\boldsymbol{u}})$	
9	$\boldsymbol{b} \leftarrow \overline{\boldsymbol{\epsilon}}(+/\boldsymbol{u})$	
10	$\boldsymbol{c} \leftarrow \overline{\boldsymbol{\epsilon}}(+/\boldsymbol{u})$	
11	$\boldsymbol{d} \leftarrow \boldsymbol{\epsilon} \overset{\wedge}{=} \boldsymbol{F}$	
12	$\boldsymbol{e} \leftarrow \overline{\boldsymbol{\epsilon}} \overset{\wedge}{=} \boldsymbol{F}$	
13	$\boldsymbol{\epsilon} : (\boldsymbol{d} \vee \boldsymbol{e})$	$=$ → exit
14	$\boldsymbol{a} \leftarrow ((\overline{\boldsymbol{d} \vee \boldsymbol{e}})/\boldsymbol{F})_0$	
15	$\boldsymbol{b} \leftarrow \overline{\boldsymbol{a}} \overset{\wedge}{=} \boldsymbol{F}$	
16	$\boldsymbol{c} \leftarrow \boldsymbol{a} \overset{\wedge}{=} \boldsymbol{F}$	
17	$\boldsymbol{\epsilon} : (\boldsymbol{b} \vee \boldsymbol{c} \vee \boldsymbol{d} \vee \boldsymbol{e})$	$\neq$ ← exit (left); $=$ → exit (right)

0-origin indexing	
f	Logical function of $\nu(\boldsymbol{u})$ variables.
$\boldsymbol{u}$	Logical vector specifying the decomposition $f(\boldsymbol{x}) = g(h(\overline{\boldsymbol{u}}/\boldsymbol{x}), \boldsymbol{u}/\boldsymbol{x})$.
$\boldsymbol{F}$	Characteristic matrix for the decomposition $\boldsymbol{u}$: $\mu(\boldsymbol{F}) = 2^{+/\overline{\boldsymbol{u}}}$; $\nu(\boldsymbol{F}) = 2^{+/\boldsymbol{u}}$.
i	Row index for $\boldsymbol{F}$.
j	Column index for $\boldsymbol{F}$.
k	Scan index for $\boldsymbol{i}(f)$.
$\boldsymbol{k}$	Base 2 representation of k.
$\boldsymbol{a}$	Nontrivial column of $\boldsymbol{F}$.
$\boldsymbol{b}$	$(\boldsymbol{b}/\boldsymbol{F})_j = \overline{\boldsymbol{a}}$.
$\boldsymbol{c}$	$(\boldsymbol{c}/\boldsymbol{F})_j = \boldsymbol{a}$.
$\boldsymbol{d}$	$(\boldsymbol{d}/\boldsymbol{F})_j = \boldsymbol{\epsilon}$.
$\boldsymbol{e}$	$(\boldsymbol{e}/\boldsymbol{F})_j = \overline{\boldsymbol{\epsilon}}$.

Legend

Program 7.5 Decomposition of f on $\boldsymbol{u}$

specifying the columns of $\boldsymbol{F}$ which are equal to $\boldsymbol{a}$, and step 16 determines $\boldsymbol{c}$ correspondingly for the vector $\boldsymbol{a}$.

The function f is decomposable on $\boldsymbol{u}$ if and only if $\boldsymbol{b}$, $\boldsymbol{c}$, $\boldsymbol{d}$, and $\boldsymbol{e}$ together exhaust all columns of $\boldsymbol{F}$. The left-pointing exit on step 17 therefore indicates nondecomposability on $\boldsymbol{u}$.

The algorithm can be extended to test all possible values of $\boldsymbol{u}$ successively and so determine all possible decompositions. Use can be made of the obvious fact that the matrix $\boldsymbol{F}$ appropriate to decomposition on $\overline{\boldsymbol{u}}$ is the transpose of the matrix $\boldsymbol{F}$ appropriate to $\boldsymbol{u}$.

Other canonical forms

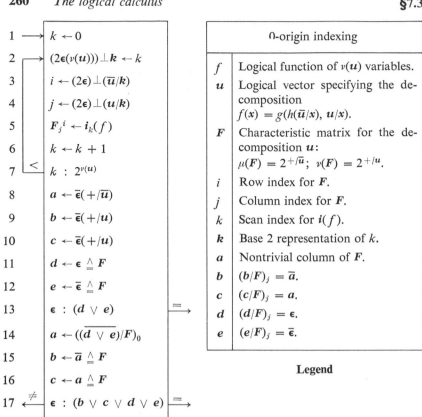

Ashenhurst (1957) remarks that decomposability is an *intrinsic* property of a logical function f and is independent of the form of its representation. It can also be shown that the particular algorithm of Program 7.5 is intrinsic in that it applies (in a slightly generalized form) to the characteristic vectors of all four canonical forms.

Since $\boldsymbol{i}(f) = \boldsymbol{\gamma}(f, \wedge) = \boldsymbol{\gamma}(f, \vee)$, it is clear that the decomposition algorithm applies directly to the disjunctive and conjunctive characteristic vectors. The case for the remaining forms will be developed for the exclusive disjunctive form only.

Let $\boldsymbol{F}$ be defined as in Program 7.5 but with $\boldsymbol{i}(f)$ replaced by $\boldsymbol{\gamma}(f, \neq)$. Moreover, let

$$\boldsymbol{p} = \overline{\boldsymbol{T}} \overset{\wedge}{\underset{\vee}{}} \boldsymbol{x}$$

$$\boldsymbol{q} = \overline{\boldsymbol{T}} \overset{\wedge}{\underset{\vee}{}} (\overline{\boldsymbol{u}}/\boldsymbol{x})$$

$$\boldsymbol{r} = \overline{\boldsymbol{T}} \overset{\wedge}{\underset{\vee}{}} (\boldsymbol{u}/\boldsymbol{x}),$$

and

$$\boldsymbol{P} = \boldsymbol{q} \overset{\circ}{\wedge} \boldsymbol{r}.$$

Then, clearly $f(\boldsymbol{x}) = \neq/\neq//(\boldsymbol{F} \wedge \boldsymbol{P})$.

As in the case of the intrinsic vector, the structure of $\boldsymbol{F}$ must be expressed in terms of the characteristic vectors of a given function h, of its inverse $\bar{h}$, and of the identity and zero functions. In the exclusive disjunctive form, $\boldsymbol{\gamma}(1, \neq) = \boldsymbol{\epsilon}^0$, $\boldsymbol{\gamma}(0, \neq) = \bar{\boldsymbol{\epsilon}}$, and if $\boldsymbol{\gamma}(h, \neq) = \boldsymbol{a}$, then $\boldsymbol{\gamma}(\bar{h}, \neq) = (\boldsymbol{a} \neq \boldsymbol{\epsilon}^0)$. The term in $\bar{\boldsymbol{\epsilon}}$ may again be disregarded and the form required of $\boldsymbol{F}$ for decomposability may (following equation 7.23′) be written as

$$\boldsymbol{F} = [(\boldsymbol{a} \neq \boldsymbol{\epsilon}^0) \overset{\circ}{\wedge} \boldsymbol{b}] \vee (\boldsymbol{a} \overset{\circ}{\wedge} \boldsymbol{c}) \vee (\boldsymbol{\epsilon}^0 \overset{\circ}{\wedge} \boldsymbol{d}), \qquad (7.23'')$$

where $\boldsymbol{b}$, $\boldsymbol{c}$, and $\boldsymbol{d}$ are mutually disjoint.

The matrix $\boldsymbol{M}$ such that $f(\boldsymbol{x}) = \neq/\neq//\boldsymbol{M}$ may now (as in the analogous case of equation 7.25′) be obtained by applying equation 7.8:

$$\boldsymbol{M} = \big(((\boldsymbol{a} \neq \boldsymbol{\epsilon}^0) \wedge \boldsymbol{q}) \overset{\circ}{\wedge} (\boldsymbol{b} \wedge \boldsymbol{r})\big) \vee \big((\boldsymbol{a} \wedge \boldsymbol{q}) \overset{\circ}{\wedge} (\boldsymbol{c} \wedge \boldsymbol{r})\big) \vee \big((\boldsymbol{\epsilon}^0 \wedge \boldsymbol{q}) \overset{\circ}{\wedge} (\boldsymbol{d} \wedge \boldsymbol{r})\big), \qquad (7.25'')$$

Equation 7.25″ will also be written as

$$\boldsymbol{M} = \boldsymbol{U} \vee \boldsymbol{V} \vee \boldsymbol{W},$$

where $\boldsymbol{U}$, $\boldsymbol{V}$, and $\boldsymbol{W}$ denote the successive matrices of the right limb.

Since $\boldsymbol{b}$, $\boldsymbol{c}$, and $\boldsymbol{d}$ are disjoint, so also are the matrices $\boldsymbol{U}$, $\boldsymbol{V}$, and $\boldsymbol{W}$. For any pair of disjoint matrices $\boldsymbol{X}$ and $\boldsymbol{Y}$, it is easily shown that

$$\neq/\neq//(\boldsymbol{X} \vee \boldsymbol{Y}) = ((\neq/\neq//\boldsymbol{X}) \neq (\neq/\neq//\boldsymbol{Y})).$$

Hence

$$f(\boldsymbol{x}) = \neq/\neq//\boldsymbol{M} = \{[(\neq/\neq//\boldsymbol{U}) \neq (\neq/\neq//\boldsymbol{V})] \neq (\neq/\neq/\boldsymbol{W})\}.$$

The application of equation 7.10 to each of the matrices $\boldsymbol{U}$, $\boldsymbol{V}$, and $\boldsymbol{W}$ now yields

$$f(\boldsymbol{x}) = \{[(((\boldsymbol{a} \neq \boldsymbol{\epsilon}^0) \overset{\neq}{\wedge} \boldsymbol{q}) \wedge (\boldsymbol{b} \overset{\neq}{\wedge} \boldsymbol{r})) \neq ((\boldsymbol{a} \overset{\neq}{\wedge} \boldsymbol{q}) \wedge (\boldsymbol{c} \overset{\neq}{\wedge} \boldsymbol{r}))] \neq ((\boldsymbol{\epsilon}^0 \overset{\neq}{\wedge} \boldsymbol{q}) \wedge (\boldsymbol{d} \overset{\neq}{\wedge} \boldsymbol{r}))\}. \qquad (7.26'')$$

Since $\boldsymbol{a}$, $(\boldsymbol{a} \neq \boldsymbol{\epsilon}^0)$, and $\boldsymbol{\epsilon}^0$ are the characteristic vectors of the functions h, $\bar{h}$, and 1, respectively, equation 7.26″ may be written in the decomposed form

$$\left.\begin{aligned} h(\overline{\boldsymbol{u}}/\boldsymbol{x}) &= \boldsymbol{a} \overset{\neq}{\underset{\wedge}{}} (\overline{\boldsymbol{T}} \overset{\wedge}{\underset{\vee}{}} (\overline{\boldsymbol{u}}/\boldsymbol{x})) \\ f(\boldsymbol{x}) &= (((\bar{h} \wedge (\boldsymbol{b} \overset{\neq}{\underset{\wedge}{}} \boldsymbol{r})) \neq (h \wedge (\boldsymbol{c} \overset{\neq}{\underset{\wedge}{}} \boldsymbol{r}))) \neq (\boldsymbol{d} \overset{\neq}{\underset{\wedge}{}} \boldsymbol{r})) \\ \boldsymbol{r} &= \overline{\boldsymbol{T}} \overset{\wedge}{\underset{\vee}{}} (\boldsymbol{u}/\boldsymbol{x}) \end{aligned}\right\} \quad (7.27'')$$

For the example of Table 7.4,

$$\boldsymbol{\gamma}(f, \neq) = (1, 1, 1, 1, 0, 0, 0, 1, 1, 0, 1, 0, 0, 0, 1, 0, 0, 1, 0, 1, 1, 1, 0, 1, 1, 0, 1, 0, 1, 0, 1, 0).$$

Table 7.6 show its decomposition in the exclusive disjunctive form.

$$\boldsymbol{F} = \begin{pmatrix} 1 & 1 & 0 & 0 & 0 & 0 & 1 & 0 \\ 1 & 1 & 0 & 1 & 1 & 1 & 1 & 1 \\ 1 & 1 & 0 & 1 & 1 & 1 & 1 & 1 \\ 0 & 0 & 0 & 0 & 0 & 0 & 0 & 0 \end{pmatrix} \quad \overset{\boldsymbol{a}}{\begin{pmatrix} 1 \\ 1 \\ 1 \\ 0 \end{pmatrix}} \quad \overset{(\boldsymbol{a} \neq \boldsymbol{\epsilon}^0)}{\begin{pmatrix} 0 \\ 1 \\ 1 \\ 0 \end{pmatrix}}$$

$$\boldsymbol{b} = (0 \; 0 \; 0 \; 1 \; 1 \; 1 \; 0 \; 1)$$

$$\boldsymbol{c} = (1 \; 1 \; 0 \; 0 \; 0 \; 0 \; 1 \; 0)$$

$$\boldsymbol{d} = (0 \; 0 \; 0 \; 0 \; 0 \; 0 \; 0 \; 0)$$

Table 7.6 Decomposition in exclusive disjunctive form

The only change required in Program 7.5 is in the specification of the vectors $\boldsymbol{d}$ and $\boldsymbol{b}$ on steps 11 and 15. These may be replaced by the following steps:

$$11 \quad \boldsymbol{d} \leftarrow \boldsymbol{\epsilon}^0 \overset{\wedge}{\underset{=}{}} \boldsymbol{F}$$

$$15 \quad \boldsymbol{b} \leftarrow (\boldsymbol{a} \neq \boldsymbol{\epsilon}^0) \overset{\wedge}{\underset{=}{}} \boldsymbol{F}.$$

The program may be made completely general (i.e., for $\boldsymbol{\gamma}(f, \odot)$) by simply replacing $\boldsymbol{\epsilon}^0$ with $\boldsymbol{\gamma}(1, \odot)$ in the foregoing steps, and replacing $\bar{\boldsymbol{\epsilon}}$ with $\boldsymbol{\gamma}(0, \odot)$ in steps 8, 9, 10, and 12.

REFERENCES

Ashenhurst, R. L., (1957), "The Decomposition of Switching Functions," *Proc. of an International Symposium on the Theory of Switching*, Harvard University, pp. 74–116.

Calingaert, P., (1960), "Switching Function Canonical Forms Based on Commutative and Associative Binary Operations," presented at the October meeting of the American Institute of Electrical Engineers.

Muller, D. E., (1954), "Application of Boolean Algebra to Switching Circuit Design and to Error Detection," *Trans. Institute of Radio Engineers*, New York, vol. *EC*-3, pp. 6–12.

EXERCISES

7.1 Use De Morgan's laws (equations 7.2 and 7.3) to establish

(a) the identity $\boldsymbol{U} \underset{\vee}{\overset{\wedge}{\cdot}} \boldsymbol{V} = \overline{\overline{\boldsymbol{U}} \underset{\wedge}{\overset{\vee}{\cdot}} \overline{\boldsymbol{V}}}$.

(b) the identity $\boldsymbol{U} \underset{\wedge}{\overset{\neq}{\cdot}} \boldsymbol{V} = \overline{\overline{\boldsymbol{U}} \underset{\vee}{\overset{=}{\cdot}} \overline{\boldsymbol{V}}}$.

(c) equation 7.4.

7.2 Show that the expressions $x = (y \neq z)$ and $y = (x \neq z)$ are equivalent.

7.3 For the function $f(\boldsymbol{x}_0, \boldsymbol{x}_1, \boldsymbol{x}_2) = (\boldsymbol{x}_0 \wedge (\boldsymbol{x}_1 \neq \boldsymbol{x}_2)) \vee (\overline{\boldsymbol{x}}_0 \wedge \overline{\boldsymbol{x}}_2)$, derive

(a) the intrinsic vector $\boldsymbol{i}(f)$.

(b) the four characteristic vectors of f.

(c) the intrinsic vector of $\bar{f}$.

(d) the four characteristic vectors of $\bar{f}$.

7.4 Use the matrix $\odot$ of equation 7.1 to summarize the canonical form expressions (equations 7.11 (a–d)) in a single equation.

7.5 Show that $\gamma(\bar{f}, \wedge) = \overline{\gamma}(f, \wedge)$.

7.6 Use De Morgan's laws and the result of Exercise 7.5 to derive equation 7.11b from 7.11a.

7.7 Show that if $\boldsymbol{y} \wedge \boldsymbol{z} = 0$, then

$$\boldsymbol{X} \underset{\wedge}{\overset{\neq}{\cdot}} (\boldsymbol{y} \vee \boldsymbol{z}) = ((\boldsymbol{X} \underset{\wedge}{\overset{\neq}{\cdot}} \boldsymbol{y}) \neq (\boldsymbol{X} \underset{\wedge}{\overset{\neq}{\cdot}} \boldsymbol{z})).$$

7.8 Let f and g be two disjoint functions (i.e., $f(\boldsymbol{x}) \wedge g(\boldsymbol{x}) = 0$ for all $\boldsymbol{x}$), and let $h = f \vee g$. Derive expressions for the four characteristic vectors of h in terms of the four characteristic vectors of f and g.

7.9 Each of the sixteen logical functions of two variables may be characterized by its intrinsic vector $\boldsymbol{i}(f)$ and be denoted by

$$f(x, y) = \beta(x, \boldsymbol{i}(f), y).$$

For example, $(x \neq y) = \beta(x, (0, 1, 1, 0), y)$. (The function $\beta(x, \boldsymbol{i}(f), y)$ is sometimes called the kth *Boolean function* and denoted by $\beta_k(x, y)$, where $k = \perp \boldsymbol{i}(f)$.) This notation can be extended to vectors $\boldsymbol{x}$ and $\boldsymbol{y}$ so as to permit different functions to be specified for each component. Thus

$$\boldsymbol{z} \leftarrow \beta(\boldsymbol{x}, \boldsymbol{F}, \boldsymbol{y}) \Leftrightarrow \boldsymbol{z}_i = \beta(\boldsymbol{x}_i, \boldsymbol{F}_i, \boldsymbol{y}_i),$$

where $\nu(\boldsymbol{F}) = \nu(\boldsymbol{x})$ and $\mu(\boldsymbol{F}) = 4$. Show that

(a) if $\boldsymbol{x} = (0, 0, 0, 0, 0, 0, 1, 1)$, $\boldsymbol{y} = (0, 1, 0, 1, 0, 1, 0, 1)$, and $\perp\!\!\perp \boldsymbol{F} = (0, 0, 0, 0, 6, 6, 6, 6)$, then $\beta(\boldsymbol{x}, \boldsymbol{F}, \boldsymbol{y})$ $= (0, 0, 0, 0, 0, 1, 1, 0)$.

(b) $\beta(\boldsymbol{x}, \boldsymbol{F}, \boldsymbol{y}) = \overline{\beta(\boldsymbol{x}, \bar{\boldsymbol{F}}, \boldsymbol{y})}$
(c) $\beta(\boldsymbol{x}, \boldsymbol{F} \vee \boldsymbol{G}, \boldsymbol{y}) = \beta(\boldsymbol{x}, \boldsymbol{F}, \boldsymbol{y}) \vee \beta(\boldsymbol{x}, \boldsymbol{G}, \boldsymbol{y})$
(d) $\beta(\boldsymbol{x}, \boldsymbol{F} \wedge \boldsymbol{G}, \boldsymbol{y}) = \beta(\boldsymbol{x}, \boldsymbol{F}, \boldsymbol{y}) \wedge \beta(\boldsymbol{x}, \boldsymbol{G}, \boldsymbol{y})$.

7.10 The functions $\beta(\boldsymbol{x}, \boldsymbol{F}, \boldsymbol{y})$ defined in Exercise 7.9 can alternatively be expressed as $\beta(\boldsymbol{x}, \boldsymbol{f}, \boldsymbol{y})$, where $\boldsymbol{f} = \perp\!\!\perp \boldsymbol{F}$. Develop relations on $\boldsymbol{f}$ corresponding to those of Exercises 7.9 (b–d).

SUMMARY OF NOTATION

S.1 CONVENTIONS

Basic conventions

(a) 1-origin indexing assumed in this summary.
(b) Controlling variables appear to the left, e.g., $\boldsymbol{u}/\boldsymbol{x}$, $\boldsymbol{b} \perp \boldsymbol{y}$, $k \uparrow \boldsymbol{x}$, and $\boldsymbol{u} \lceil \boldsymbol{x}$.
(c) Dimension n may be elided (if determined by compatibility) from $\boldsymbol{\epsilon}(n)$, $\boldsymbol{\epsilon}^k(n)$, $\boldsymbol{\alpha}^k(n)$, $\boldsymbol{\omega}^k(n)$, and $\boldsymbol{\iota}^j(n)$.
(d) The parameter j may be elided from operators $|_j$, θ_j, $\int_j$, and ι_j, and from the vector $\boldsymbol{\iota}^j$ if j is the index origin in use.
(e) The parameter k may be elided from $k \uparrow \boldsymbol{x}$ if $k = 1$.

Branching conventions

(a)

$$\left| x : y \right| \xrightarrow{\mathscr{R}}$$

The statement to which the arrow leads is executed next if $(x \mathscr{R} y) = 1$; otherwise the listed successor is executed next. An unlabeled arrow is always followed.

(b)

$$x : y, \quad \boldsymbol{r} \rightarrow \boldsymbol{s}$$

The statement numbered $\boldsymbol{s}_i$ is executed next if $(x \boldsymbol{r}_i y) = 1$. The null symbol $\circ$ occurring as a component of $\boldsymbol{r}$ denotes the relation which complements the disjunction of the remaining relations in $\boldsymbol{r}$.

(c)

$$\rightarrow \text{Program } a, b$$

Program a branches to its statement b. The symbol a may be elided if the statement occurs in Program a itself.

Operand conventions used in summary

	Scalar	Vector	Matrix	Tree
Logical	u, v, w	$\boldsymbol{u}, \boldsymbol{v}, \boldsymbol{w}$	$\boldsymbol{U}, \boldsymbol{V}, \boldsymbol{W}$	$\mathbf{U}, \mathbf{V}, \mathbf{W}$
Integral	h, i, j, k	$\boldsymbol{h}, \boldsymbol{i}, \boldsymbol{j}, \boldsymbol{k}$	$\boldsymbol{H}, \boldsymbol{I}, \boldsymbol{J}, \boldsymbol{K}$	$\mathbf{H}, \mathbf{I}, \mathbf{J}, \mathbf{K}$
Numerical	x, y, z	$\boldsymbol{x}, \boldsymbol{y}, \boldsymbol{z}$	$\boldsymbol{X}, \boldsymbol{Y}, \boldsymbol{Z}$	$\mathbf{X}, \mathbf{Y}, \mathbf{Z}$
Arbitrary	a, b, c	$\boldsymbol{a}, \boldsymbol{b}, \boldsymbol{c}$	$\boldsymbol{A}, \boldsymbol{B}, \boldsymbol{C}$	$\mathbf{A}, \mathbf{B}, \mathbf{C}$

S.2 STRUCTURAL PARAMETERS, NULL

Dimension	$\nu(\boldsymbol{a})$	Number of components in vector $\boldsymbol{a}$	§1.5
Row dimension	$\nu(\boldsymbol{A})$	Number of components in each row vector $\boldsymbol{A}^i$	
Column dimension	$\mu(\boldsymbol{A})$	Number of components in each column vector $\boldsymbol{A}_j$	
Height	$\nu(\mathbf{A})$	Length of longest path in $\mathbf{A}$	§1.23
Moment	$\mu(\mathbf{A})$	Number of nodes in $\mathbf{A}$	
Dispersion vector	$\boldsymbol{\nu}(\mathbf{A})$	$\boldsymbol{\nu}_1(\mathbf{A})$ = number of roots of $\mathbf{A}$; $\boldsymbol{\nu}_j(\mathbf{A})$ = maximum degree of nodes on level $j-1$; $\nu(\boldsymbol{\nu}(\mathbf{A})) = \nu(\mathbf{A})$	
Moment vector	$\boldsymbol{\mu}(\mathbf{A})$	$\boldsymbol{\mu}_j(\mathbf{A})$ = number of nodes on level j of $\mathbf{A}$; $\nu(\boldsymbol{\mu}(\mathbf{A})) = \nu(\mathbf{A})$	
Degree of node $\boldsymbol{i}$	$\delta(\boldsymbol{i}, \mathbf{A})$	Degree of node $\boldsymbol{i}$ of tree $\mathbf{A}$	
Degree	$\delta(\mathbf{A})$	$\delta(\mathbf{A}) = \max\limits_{\boldsymbol{i}} \delta(\boldsymbol{i}, \mathbf{A})$	
Leaf count	$\lambda(\mathbf{A})$	$\lambda(\mathbf{A})$ is the number of leaves in $\mathbf{A}$	
Row dimension of file	$\nu(\Phi)$	Number of files in each row of a file array	§1.22
Column dimension of file	$\mu(\Phi)$	Number of files in each column of a file array	
Null character	$\circ$	Null character of a set (e.g., space in the alphabet) or null reduction operator	§1.3

S.3 RELATIONS

Equality	$a = b$	a and b are identical	§1.15
Membership	$a \in \boldsymbol{b}$	$a = \boldsymbol{b}_i$ for some i	
Inclusion	$\boldsymbol{b} \supseteq \boldsymbol{a}$ $\boldsymbol{a} \subseteq \boldsymbol{b}$	$\boldsymbol{a}_j \in \boldsymbol{b}$ for all j	
Strict inclusion	$\boldsymbol{b} \supset \boldsymbol{a}$ $\boldsymbol{a} \subset \boldsymbol{b}$	$\boldsymbol{b} \supseteq \boldsymbol{a}$ and $\boldsymbol{a} \not\supseteq \boldsymbol{b}$	
Similarity	$\boldsymbol{b} \equiv \boldsymbol{a}$	$\boldsymbol{b} \supseteq \boldsymbol{a}$ and $\boldsymbol{a} \supseteq \boldsymbol{b}$	
Complementary relations	$\not\mathscr{R}$	The relation which holds if and only if $\mathscr{R}$ does not. Examples of complementary pairs: $\in, \notin$; $\supset, \not\supset$; $>, \not>$.	
Combined (*or*ed) relations		A list of relations between two variables is construed as the *or* of the relations. Thus $\boldsymbol{x} \subset \supset \boldsymbol{y}$ is equivalent to $\boldsymbol{x} \not\equiv \boldsymbol{y}$. When equality occurs as one of the *or*ed relations, it is indicated by a single inferior line, e.g., $\leq$ and $\subseteq$.	

S.4 ELEMENTARY OPERATIONS

Negation	$w \leftarrow \bar{u}$	$w = 1 \Leftrightarrow u = 0$	§1.4
And	$w \leftarrow u \wedge v$	$w = 1 \Leftrightarrow u = 1$ and $v = 1$	
Or	$w \leftarrow u \vee v$	$w = 1 \Leftrightarrow u = 1$ or $v = 1$	
Relational statement	$w \leftarrow (a \mathscr{R} b)$	$w = 1 \Leftrightarrow$ the relation $a \mathscr{R} b$ holds	
Sum	$z \leftarrow x + y$	z is the algebraic sum of x and y	
Difference	$z \leftarrow x - y$	z is the algebraic difference of x and y	
Product	$z \leftarrow x \times y$ $z \leftarrow xy$ $c \leftarrow a \times u$ $c \leftarrow au$	z is the algebraic product of numbers x and y, and c is the arbitrary character a or zero according to whether the logical variable u is one or zero.	
Quotient	$z \leftarrow x \div y$	z is the quotient of x and y	
Absolute value	$z \leftarrow \lvert x \rvert$	$z = x \times [(x > 0) - (x < 0)]$	
Floor	$k \leftarrow \lfloor x \rfloor$	$k \leq x < k + 1$	
Ceiling	$k \leftarrow \lceil x \rceil$	$k \geq x > k - 1$	
j-Residue mod h	$k \leftarrow h \mid_j i$	$i = hq + k$; $j \leq k < j + h$; and q is integral.	

S.5 VECTOR OPERATIONS

Component-by-component extension of basic operation	$\boldsymbol{c} \leftarrow \boldsymbol{a} \odot \boldsymbol{b}$	$\boldsymbol{c}_i = \boldsymbol{a}_i \odot \boldsymbol{b}_i$. Examples: $\boldsymbol{x} \times \boldsymbol{y}$, $(\boldsymbol{a} \neq \boldsymbol{b})$, $\boldsymbol{h} \mid_j \boldsymbol{i}$, $\boldsymbol{u} \wedge \overline{\boldsymbol{v}}$, $\lceil \boldsymbol{x} \rceil$.	§1.5
Scalar multiple	$\boldsymbol{z} \leftarrow x \times \boldsymbol{y}$ $\boldsymbol{z} \leftarrow x\boldsymbol{y}$ $\boldsymbol{c} \leftarrow a \times \boldsymbol{u}$ $\boldsymbol{c} \leftarrow a\boldsymbol{u}$	$\boldsymbol{z}_i = x \times \boldsymbol{y}_i$, and $\boldsymbol{c}_i = a \times \boldsymbol{u}_i$	
Reduction	$\leftarrow \odot/\boldsymbol{a}$	$c = (\cdots((\boldsymbol{a}_1 \odot \boldsymbol{a}_2) \odot \boldsymbol{a}_3)\cdots) \odot \boldsymbol{a}_\nu)$, where $\odot$ is a binary operator or relation with a suitable domain. Examples: $+/\boldsymbol{x}$, $\times/\boldsymbol{x}$, $\neq/\boldsymbol{u}$. Reduction of the null vector $\boldsymbol{\epsilon}(0)$ is defined as the identity element of the operator $\odot$. Examples: $+/\boldsymbol{\epsilon}(0) = 0$; $\times/\boldsymbol{\epsilon}(0) = 1$, $\vee/\boldsymbol{\epsilon}(0) = 0$, $\wedge/\boldsymbol{\epsilon}(0) = 1$.	§1.8
Ranking			§1.16
j-origin ***b***-index of *a*	$c \leftarrow \boldsymbol{b} \iota_j a$	$c = \circ$ if $a \notin \boldsymbol{b}$; otherwise c is the *j*-origin index of the first occurrence of a in $\boldsymbol{b}$.	
j-origin ***b***-index of ***a***	$\boldsymbol{c} \leftarrow \boldsymbol{b} \iota_j \boldsymbol{a}$	$\boldsymbol{c}_i = \boldsymbol{b} \iota_j \boldsymbol{a}_i$	
Left rotation	$\boldsymbol{c} \leftarrow k \uparrow \boldsymbol{a}$	$\boldsymbol{c}_i = \boldsymbol{a}_j$, where $j = \nu(\boldsymbol{a}) \mid_1 (i + k)$	§1.6
Right rotation	$\boldsymbol{c} \leftarrow k \downarrow \boldsymbol{a}$	$\boldsymbol{c}_i = \boldsymbol{a}_j$, where $j = \nu(\boldsymbol{a}) \mid_1 (i - k)$	
Base ***y*** value of ***x***	$z \leftarrow \boldsymbol{y} \perp \boldsymbol{x}$	$z = +/(\boldsymbol{p} \times \boldsymbol{x})$, where $\boldsymbol{p}_\nu = 1$, and $\boldsymbol{p}_{i-1} = \boldsymbol{p}_i \times \boldsymbol{y}_i$	§1.14
Compression	$\boldsymbol{c} \leftarrow \boldsymbol{u}/\boldsymbol{b}$	$\boldsymbol{c}$ is obtained from $\boldsymbol{a}$ by suppressing each $\boldsymbol{b}_i$ for which $\boldsymbol{u}_i = 0$	§1.9
Expansion	$\boldsymbol{c} \leftarrow \boldsymbol{u} \backslash \boldsymbol{b}$	$\overline{\boldsymbol{u}}/\boldsymbol{c} = 0$, $\boldsymbol{u}/\boldsymbol{c} = \boldsymbol{b}$	
Mask	$\boldsymbol{c} \leftarrow /\boldsymbol{a}, \boldsymbol{u}, \boldsymbol{b}/$	$\overline{\boldsymbol{u}}/\boldsymbol{c} = \overline{\boldsymbol{u}}/\boldsymbol{a}$, $\boldsymbol{u}/\boldsymbol{c} = \boldsymbol{u}/\boldsymbol{b}$	
Mesh	$\boldsymbol{c} \leftarrow \backslash \boldsymbol{a}, \boldsymbol{u}, \boldsymbol{b} \backslash$	$\overline{\boldsymbol{u}}/\boldsymbol{c} = \boldsymbol{a}$, $\boldsymbol{u}/\boldsymbol{c} = \boldsymbol{b}$	
Catenation	$\boldsymbol{c} \leftarrow \boldsymbol{a} \oplus \boldsymbol{b}$	$\boldsymbol{c} = (\boldsymbol{a}_1, \boldsymbol{a}_2, \ldots \boldsymbol{a}_{\nu(\boldsymbol{a})}, \boldsymbol{b}_1, \ldots \boldsymbol{b}_{\nu(\boldsymbol{b})}) = \backslash \boldsymbol{a}, \boldsymbol{\omega}^{\nu(\boldsymbol{b})}, \boldsymbol{b} \backslash$	

S.5 VECTOR OPERATIONS (continued)

Characteristic of $\boldsymbol{x}$ on $\boldsymbol{y}$	$\boldsymbol{w} \leftarrow \boldsymbol{\epsilon}_{\boldsymbol{y}}{}^{\boldsymbol{x}}$	$\boldsymbol{w}_i = (\boldsymbol{y}_i \epsilon \boldsymbol{x})$; $\nu(\boldsymbol{w}) = \nu(\boldsymbol{y})$	§1.15
jth unit vector	$\boldsymbol{w} \leftarrow \boldsymbol{\epsilon}^j(h)$	$\boldsymbol{w}_i = (i = j)$	§1.7
Full vector	$\boldsymbol{w} \leftarrow \boldsymbol{\epsilon}(h)$	$\boldsymbol{w}_i = 1$	
Zero vector	$\boldsymbol{w} \leftarrow \bar{\boldsymbol{\epsilon}}(h)$ $\boldsymbol{w} \leftarrow 0$	$\boldsymbol{w}_i = 0$	
Prefix of weight j	$\boldsymbol{w} \leftarrow \boldsymbol{\alpha}^j(h)$	First k of $\boldsymbol{w}_i$ are unity where $k = \min(j, h)$.	
Suffix of weight j	$\boldsymbol{w} \leftarrow \boldsymbol{\omega}^j(h)$	Last k of $\boldsymbol{w}_i$ are unity where $k = \min(j, h)$. (for all entries from jth unit vector to suffix of weight j: $\nu(\boldsymbol{w}) = h$)	
Maximum prefix	$\boldsymbol{w} \leftarrow \alpha/\boldsymbol{u}$	$\boldsymbol{w}$ is the max length prefix in $\boldsymbol{u}$. Example: $\alpha/(1, 1, 0, 1, 0, 1) = (1, 1, 0, 0, 0, 0)$.	§1.10
Maximum suffix	$\boldsymbol{w} \leftarrow \omega/\boldsymbol{u}$	$\boldsymbol{w}$ is the max length suffix in $\boldsymbol{u}$. Example: $\omega/(1, 1, 0, 1, 0, 1) = (0, 0, 0, 0, 0, 1)$.	
Forward set selector	$\boldsymbol{w} \leftarrow \sigma/\boldsymbol{a}$	$\boldsymbol{w}_i = 1$ if $\boldsymbol{a}_j \neq \boldsymbol{a}_i$ for all $j < i$	
Backward set selector	$\boldsymbol{w} \leftarrow \tau/\boldsymbol{a}$	$\boldsymbol{w}_i = 1$ if $\boldsymbol{a}_j \neq \boldsymbol{a}_i$ for all $j > i$	
Maxima selector	$\boldsymbol{w} \leftarrow \boldsymbol{u}\lceil\boldsymbol{x}$	$\boldsymbol{w}_i = \boldsymbol{u}_i \wedge (\boldsymbol{x}_i = m)$ where $m = \max_j (\boldsymbol{u}/\boldsymbol{x})_j$	§1.18
Minima selector	$\boldsymbol{w} \leftarrow \boldsymbol{u}\lfloor\boldsymbol{x}$	$\boldsymbol{w}_i = \boldsymbol{u}_i \wedge (\boldsymbol{x}_i = m)$ where $m = \min_j (\boldsymbol{u}/\boldsymbol{x})_j$	
Interval or j-origin identity permutation vector	$\boldsymbol{k} \leftarrow \boldsymbol{\iota}^j(h)$	$\boldsymbol{k} = (j, j+1, \ldots, j+h-1)$	§1.7
j-origin permutation vector	$\boldsymbol{k}$	$\boldsymbol{k} \equiv \boldsymbol{\iota}^j(\nu(\boldsymbol{k}))$	§1.17
j-origin mapping	$\boldsymbol{c} \leftarrow \boldsymbol{a}_{\boldsymbol{b}}$ $\boldsymbol{c} \leftarrow \boldsymbol{b}\int_j\boldsymbol{a}$	$\boldsymbol{c}_i = \circ$ if $\boldsymbol{b}_i \notin \boldsymbol{\iota}^j(\nu(\boldsymbol{a}))$; otherwise $\boldsymbol{c}_i = \boldsymbol{a}_{\boldsymbol{b}_i}$ in a j-origin system for $\boldsymbol{a}$. In the first form (that is, $\boldsymbol{c} \leftarrow \boldsymbol{a}_{\boldsymbol{b}}$), the origin cannot be specified directly.	
j-origin ordering	$\boldsymbol{k} \leftarrow \theta_j/\boldsymbol{x}$	$\boldsymbol{y} = \boldsymbol{k}\int_j\boldsymbol{x}$ is in ascending order and original relative ordering is maintained among equal components, that is, either $\boldsymbol{y}_i < \boldsymbol{y}_{i+1}$ or $\boldsymbol{y}_i = \boldsymbol{y}_{i+1}$ and $\boldsymbol{k}_i < \boldsymbol{k}_{i+1}$.	

S.6a ROW GENERALIZATIONS OF VECTOR OPERATIONS

$Z \leftarrow X \odot Y$	$Z_j^i = X_j^i \odot Y_j^i$	§1.5
$z \leftarrow \odot/X$	$z_i = \odot/X^i$	§1.8
$C \leftarrow \otimes/A$	$C = A_1 \otimes A_2 \otimes \cdots \cdots \otimes A_\nu$	§1.15
$M \leftarrow B \iota_h A$	$M^i = B^i \iota_h A^i$	§1.16
$C \leftarrow k \uparrow A$	$C^i = k_i \uparrow A^i$	§1.6
$C \leftarrow k \downarrow A$	$C^i = k_i \downarrow A^i$	
$z \leftarrow Y \perp X$	$z_i = Y^i \perp X^i$	§1.14
$C \leftarrow A_b$	$C_j = A_{b_j}$	§1.17
$C \leftarrow B \int_h A$	$C^i = B^i \int_h A^i$	
$K \leftarrow \theta_h/X$	$K^i = \theta_h/X^i$	
$C \leftarrow A \oplus B$	$C^i = A^i \oplus B^i$	§1.9
$C \leftarrow u/B$	$C^i = u/B^i$	
$c \leftarrow U/B$	$c = U^1/B^1 \oplus \cdots \cdots \oplus U^\mu/B^\mu$	
$C \leftarrow u\backslash B$	$\overline{u}/C = 0,\ u/C = B$	
$C \leftarrow U\backslash b$	$\overline{U}/C = 0,\ U/C = b$	
$C \leftarrow \backslash A, u, B\backslash$	$\overline{u}/C = A,\ u/C = B$	
$C \leftarrow \backslash a, U, b\backslash$	$\overline{U}/C = a,\ U/C = b$	
$C \leftarrow /A, u, B/$	$\overline{u}/C = \overline{u}/A,\ u/C = u/B$	
$C \leftarrow /A, U, B/$	$\overline{U}/C = \overline{U}/A,\ U/C = U/B$	
$C \leftarrow /a, U, b/$	$C = /\mathsf{E}\backslash a, U, \mathsf{E}\backslash b/$	
$W \leftarrow \alpha/U$	$W^i = \alpha/U^i$	§1.10
$W \leftarrow \omega/U$	$W^i = \omega/U^i$	
$W \leftarrow \sigma/U$	$W^i = \sigma/U^i$	
$W \leftarrow \tau/U$	$W^i = \tau/U^i$	
$W \leftarrow U\lceil X$	$W^i = U^i\lceil X^i$	§1.18
$W \leftarrow U\lfloor X$	$W^i = U^i\lfloor X^i$	

S.6b COLUMN GENERALIZATIONS OF VECTOR OPERATIONS

$\boldsymbol{Z} \leftarrow \boldsymbol{X} \odot \boldsymbol{Y}$	$\boldsymbol{Z}_j^i = \boldsymbol{X}_j^i \odot \boldsymbol{Y}_j^i$	§1.5
$\boldsymbol{z} \leftarrow \odot//\boldsymbol{X}$	$\boldsymbol{z}_j = \odot/\boldsymbol{X}_j$	§1.8
$\boldsymbol{C} \leftarrow \otimes//\boldsymbol{A}$	$\boldsymbol{C} = \boldsymbol{A}^1 \otimes \boldsymbol{A}^2 \otimes \cdots \cdots \otimes \boldsymbol{A}^{\mu}$	§1.15
$\boldsymbol{M} \leftarrow \boldsymbol{B}\ \iota_h\ \boldsymbol{A}$	$\boldsymbol{M}_j = \boldsymbol{B}_j\ \iota_h\ \boldsymbol{A}_j$	§1.16
$\boldsymbol{C} \leftarrow \boldsymbol{k} \Uparrow \boldsymbol{A}$	$\boldsymbol{C}_j = \boldsymbol{k}_j \uparrow \boldsymbol{A}_j$	§1.6
$\boldsymbol{C} \leftarrow \boldsymbol{k} \Downarrow \boldsymbol{A}$	$\boldsymbol{C}_j = \boldsymbol{k}_j \downarrow \boldsymbol{A}_j$	
$\boldsymbol{z} \leftarrow \boldsymbol{Y} \perp\!\!\perp \boldsymbol{X}$	$\boldsymbol{z}_j = \boldsymbol{Y}_j \perp \boldsymbol{X}_j$	§1.14
$\boldsymbol{C} \leftarrow \boldsymbol{A}^{\boldsymbol{b}}$	$\boldsymbol{C}^i = \boldsymbol{A}^{\boldsymbol{b}_i}$	§1.17
$\boldsymbol{C} \leftarrow \boldsymbol{B} \int\!\!\int_h \boldsymbol{A}$	$\boldsymbol{C}_j = \boldsymbol{B}_j \int_h \boldsymbol{A}_j$	
$\boldsymbol{K} \leftarrow \theta_h//\boldsymbol{X}$	$\boldsymbol{K}_j = \theta_h/\boldsymbol{X}_j$	
$\boldsymbol{C} \leftarrow \boldsymbol{A} \oplus\!\oplus \boldsymbol{B}$	$\boldsymbol{C}_j = \boldsymbol{A}_j \oplus \boldsymbol{B}_j$	§1.9
$\boldsymbol{C} \leftarrow \boldsymbol{u}//\boldsymbol{B}$	$\boldsymbol{C}_j = \boldsymbol{u}/\boldsymbol{B}_j$	
$\boldsymbol{c} \leftarrow \boldsymbol{U}//\boldsymbol{B}$	$\boldsymbol{c} = \boldsymbol{U}_1/\boldsymbol{B}_1 \oplus \cdots \cdots \oplus \boldsymbol{U}_\nu/\boldsymbol{B}_\nu$	
$\boldsymbol{C} \leftarrow \boldsymbol{u}\backslash\backslash\boldsymbol{B}$	$\bar{\boldsymbol{u}}//\boldsymbol{C} = 0,\ \boldsymbol{u}//\boldsymbol{C} = \boldsymbol{B}$	
$\boldsymbol{C} \leftarrow \boldsymbol{U}\backslash\backslash\boldsymbol{b}$	$\bar{\boldsymbol{U}}//\boldsymbol{C} = 0,\ \boldsymbol{U}//\boldsymbol{C} = \boldsymbol{b}$	
$\boldsymbol{C} \leftarrow \backslash\backslash\boldsymbol{A}, \boldsymbol{u}, \boldsymbol{B}\backslash\backslash$	$\bar{\boldsymbol{u}}//\boldsymbol{C} = \boldsymbol{A},\ \boldsymbol{u}//\boldsymbol{C} = \boldsymbol{B}$	
$\boldsymbol{C} \leftarrow \backslash\backslash\boldsymbol{a}, \boldsymbol{U}, \boldsymbol{b}\backslash\backslash$	$\bar{\boldsymbol{U}}//\boldsymbol{C} = \boldsymbol{a},\ \boldsymbol{U}//\boldsymbol{C} = \boldsymbol{b}$	
$\boldsymbol{C} \leftarrow //\boldsymbol{A}, \boldsymbol{u}, \boldsymbol{B}//$	$\bar{\boldsymbol{u}}//\boldsymbol{C} = \bar{\boldsymbol{u}}//\boldsymbol{A},\ \boldsymbol{u}//\boldsymbol{C} = \boldsymbol{u}//\boldsymbol{B}$	
$\boldsymbol{C} \leftarrow //\boldsymbol{A}, \boldsymbol{U}, \boldsymbol{B}//$	$\bar{\boldsymbol{U}}//\boldsymbol{C} = \bar{\boldsymbol{U}}//\boldsymbol{A},\ \boldsymbol{U}//\boldsymbol{C} = \boldsymbol{U}//\boldsymbol{B}$	
$\boldsymbol{C} \leftarrow //\boldsymbol{a}, \boldsymbol{U}, \boldsymbol{b}//$	$\boldsymbol{C} = /\mathsf{E}\backslash\backslash\boldsymbol{a}, \boldsymbol{U}, \mathsf{E}\backslash\backslash\boldsymbol{b}/$	
$\boldsymbol{W} \leftarrow \alpha//\boldsymbol{U}$	$\boldsymbol{W}_j = \alpha/\boldsymbol{U}_j$	§1.10
$\boldsymbol{W} \leftarrow \omega//\boldsymbol{U}$	$\boldsymbol{W}_j = \omega/\boldsymbol{U}_j$	
$\boldsymbol{W} \leftarrow \sigma//\boldsymbol{U}$	$\boldsymbol{W}_j = \sigma/\boldsymbol{U}_j$	
$\boldsymbol{W} \leftarrow \tau//\boldsymbol{U}$	$\boldsymbol{W}_j = \tau/\boldsymbol{U}_j$	
$\boldsymbol{W} \leftarrow \boldsymbol{U}\lceil\lceil\boldsymbol{X}$	$\boldsymbol{W}_j = \boldsymbol{U}_j\lceil\boldsymbol{X}_j$	§1.18
$\boldsymbol{W} \leftarrow \boldsymbol{U}\lfloor\lfloor\boldsymbol{X}$	$\boldsymbol{W}_j = \boldsymbol{U}_j\lfloor\boldsymbol{X}_j$	

S.7 SPECIAL MATRICES

Full matrix	$W \leftarrow \mathbf{E}(p, q)$	$W_j{}^i = 1$	$\mu(W) = p$, $\nu(W) = q$, for p and q integers. Elision of p and q if dimensions determined by compatibility.	§1.13
Zero matrix	$W \leftarrow \overline{\mathbf{E}}(p, q)$ $W \leftarrow 0$	$W_j{}^i = 0$		
Superdiagonal	$W \leftarrow {}^k\mathbf{I}(p, q)$	$W_j{}^i = (i + k = j)$		
Identity	$W \leftarrow \mathbf{I}(p, q)$	$W = \mathbf{I}^0(p, q)$		
Upper left (triangle)	$W \leftarrow$ ◰(p, q)	$W_j{}^i$		
Upper right	$W \leftarrow$ ◳(p, q)	$W^i_{\nu+1-j}$ $= (i + j \leq m)$, $m = \min(p, q)$		
Lower left	$W \leftarrow$ ◱(p, q)	$W^{\mu+1-i}_j$		
Lower right	$W \leftarrow$ ◲(p, q)	$W^{\mu+1-i}_{\nu+1-j}$		

S.8 TRANSPOSITION

Diagonal	$C \leftarrow \tilde{B}$ $C \leftarrow \overset{\nwarrow}{B}$	$C_i{}^j =$	$B_j{}^i$	§1.12
Counter diagonal	$C \leftarrow \overset{\nearrow}{B}$	$C^{\nu(B)+1-j}_{\mu(B)+1-i} =$		
Horizontal	$C \leftarrow \vec{B}$	$C^{\mu(B)+1-i}_j =$		
Vertical	$C \leftarrow \overset{\uparrow}{B}$	$C^i_{\nu(B)+1-j} =$		
Vector	$y \leftarrow \vec{x}$ $y \leftarrow \overset{\uparrow}{x}$	$y_i = x_{\nu+1-i}$		

S.9 SET OPERATIONS

Intersection	$c \leftarrow b \cap a$	$c = \epsilon_b{}^a / b$	§1.15
Difference	$c \leftarrow b \triangle a$	$c = \bar{\epsilon}_b{}^a / b$	
Union	$c \leftarrow b \cup a$	$c = b \oplus (a \triangle b)$	
Cartesian product	$C \leftarrow b^1 \otimes \cdots \otimes b^n$	$C^{1+d \perp (k-\epsilon)} = (b_{k_1}{}^1, b_{k_2}^2, \ldots b_{k_n}^n)$; $d_j = \nu(b^j)$; $1 \leq k_j \leq d_j$ Clearly, $\nu(C) = n$, and $\mu(C) = \times/d$	

S.10 GENERALIZED MATRIX PRODUCT

$C \leftarrow A \overset{\odot_1}{\odot_2} B$	$C_j^i = \odot_1/(A^i \odot_2 B_j)$, where $\odot_2$ produces a vector (i.e., is not the operator $\perp$), and $\odot_1$ is a reduction operator (and hence C_j^i is a scalar).	§1.11
$C \leftarrow A \overset{\circ}{\odot} b$	$C^i = (A^i \odot b)$, where $\odot$ is any operator which produces a vector of dimension $\nu(b)$.	
$C \leftarrow a \overset{\circ}{\odot} B$	$C_j = (a \odot B_j)$, where $\odot$ is any operator which produces a vector of dimension $\nu(a)$.	
$C \leftarrow a \overset{\circ}{\odot} b$	$C_j^i = (a_i \odot b_j)$.	

S.11 FILES

File	Φ_j^i	A representation of a of the form $(p_1, a_1, p_2, a_2, \ldots, a_{\nu(a)}, p_{\nu(a)+1}, \circ, p_{\nu(a)+2}, \ldots, p_{\nu(p)})$, where p_h is the partition at position h, $p_1 = p_{\nu(p)} = \lambda$, and $(\alpha^1 \wedge \omega^1)/p \subseteq \boldsymbol{\lambda}$.	§1.22
Position file	$\pi(\Phi_j^i) \leftarrow h$	Set file to position h. Called *rewind* if $h = 1$, and *wind* if $h = \nu(p)$.	
Record (from position h)			
Forward	${}_0\Phi_j^i \leftarrow a, \boldsymbol{\lambda}_k$	$a_h \leftarrow a, p_{h+1} \leftarrow \boldsymbol{\lambda}_k$; stop at position $h+1$. Zero prescript may be elided and $\boldsymbol{\lambda}_1$ may be elided.	
Backward	${}_1\Phi_j^i \leftarrow a, \boldsymbol{\lambda}_k$	$a_{h-1} \leftarrow a$; $p_{h-1} \leftarrow \boldsymbol{\lambda}_k$; stop at position $h-1$. $\boldsymbol{\lambda}_1$ may be elided.	
Read (from position h)			
Forward	$a, b \leftarrow {}_0\Phi_j^i$	$a \leftarrow a_h$; $b \leftarrow p_{h+1}$; stop at position $h+1$. Associated branch is controlled by p_{h+1}, and b may be elided. Zero prescript may be elided.	
Backward	$a, b \leftarrow {}_1\Phi_j^i$	$a \leftarrow a_{h-1}$; $b \leftarrow p_{h-1}$; stop at position $h-1$. Associated branch is controlled by p_{h-1} and b may be elided.	
File array			
Full	Φ	Array of files Φ_j^i, for $i \in \iota^1(\mu(\Phi))$, $j \in \iota^1(\nu(\Phi))$.	
Row	Φ^i	Row of files Φ_j^i, for $j \in \iota^1(\nu(\Phi))$.	
Column	Φ_j	Column of files Φ_j^i, for $i \in \iota^1(\mu(\Phi))$.	
Compression			
Row	u/Φ	Selection as in corresponding operations on matrices.	
Column	$u//\Phi$		

S.12 TREES

Path $\boldsymbol{i}$	$\boldsymbol{c} \leftarrow \mathbf{A}^{\boldsymbol{i}}$	$\boldsymbol{c}_1$ is the $\boldsymbol{i}_1$th root of $\mathbf{A}$; $\boldsymbol{c}_j$ is the $\boldsymbol{i}_j$th node of the nodes on level j reachable from node $\boldsymbol{c}_{j-1}$.	§1.23
Node $\boldsymbol{i}$	$\boldsymbol{c} \leftarrow (\mathbf{A}^{\boldsymbol{i}})_{\nu(\boldsymbol{i})}$	The final node of path $\mathbf{A}^{\boldsymbol{i}}$.	
Subtree $\boldsymbol{i}$	$\mathbf{C} \leftarrow \mathbf{A}_{\boldsymbol{i}}$	$\mathbf{C}$ is the subtree of $\mathbf{A}$ rooted in node $\boldsymbol{i}$.	
Component-by-component	$\mathbf{C} \leftarrow \mathbf{A} \odot \mathbf{B}$	$(\mathbf{C}^{\boldsymbol{i}})_{\nu(\boldsymbol{i})} = (\mathbf{A}^{\boldsymbol{i}})_{\nu(\boldsymbol{i})} \odot (\mathbf{B}^{\boldsymbol{i}})_{\nu(\boldsymbol{i})}$.	
Path reduction	$\mathbf{C} \leftarrow \odot/\mathbf{A}$	Reduction by operator or relation $\odot$ on nodes in left list order.	
Level reduction	$\mathbf{C} \leftarrow \odot//\mathbf{A}$	Reduction by operator or relation $\odot$ on nodes in right list order.	
j-origin $\boldsymbol{b}$-index	$\mathbf{B} \leftarrow \boldsymbol{b}\ \iota_j\ \mathbf{A}$	$(\mathbf{B}^{\boldsymbol{i}})_{\mu(\boldsymbol{i})} = \boldsymbol{b}\ \iota_j\ ((\mathbf{A}^{\boldsymbol{i}})_{\nu(\boldsymbol{i})})$	
j-origin mapping	$\mathbf{C} \leftarrow \boldsymbol{b} \int_j \mathbf{A}$	Rooted subtree $\mathbf{C}_i$ is a single null character node if $\boldsymbol{b}_i \notin \boldsymbol{\iota}^j(\mu_1(\mathbf{A}))$; otherwise $\mathbf{C}_i = \mathbf{A}_{\boldsymbol{b}_i}$, where $\mathbf{A}$ is treated in a j-origin system.	
Full right list matrix	$C \leftarrow]\mathbf{A}$	The rows of the index matrix $\overline{\alpha}^2/C$ are the right (left) justified index vectors (with null fill to the common dimension $\nu(\mathbf{A})$) arranged in increasing order; C_1 and C_2 are the corresponding degree and node vectors of $\mathbf{A}$.	
Full left list matrix	$C \leftarrow [\mathbf{A}$		
Right list matrix	$C \leftarrow \alpha^2/]\mathbf{A}$	The degree and node vector columns of the full right (left) list.	
Left list matrix	$C \leftarrow \alpha^2/[\mathbf{A}$		
Tree compression	$\mathbf{C} \leftarrow \mathbf{U}/\mathbf{A}$	$\mathbf{C}$ is obtained from $\mathbf{A}$ by suppressing node $\boldsymbol{i}$ if node $\boldsymbol{i}$ of $\mathbf{U}$ is zero and reconnecting so that for each remaining pair of nodes, the one lies in the subtree rooted at the second if and only if it did so in $\mathbf{A}$.	
Path compression	$\mathbf{C} \leftarrow \boldsymbol{u}/\mathbf{A}$	$\mathbf{C}$ is obtained from $\mathbf{A}$ by suppressing all nodes on level j if $\boldsymbol{u}_j = 0$, and reconnecting as in the compression $\mathbf{U}/\mathbf{A}$.	
Level compression	$\mathbf{C} \leftarrow \boldsymbol{u}//\mathbf{A}$	$\mathbf{C}$ is obtained from $\mathbf{A}$ by suppressing rooted subtree $\mathbf{A}_j$ if $\boldsymbol{u}_j = 0$.	
Level mesh	$\mathbf{C} \leftarrow \backslash\backslash\mathbf{A}, \boldsymbol{u}, \mathbf{B}\backslash\backslash$	$\overline{\boldsymbol{u}}//\mathbf{C} = \mathbf{A}$; $\boldsymbol{u}//\mathbf{C} = \mathbf{B}$	
Level mask	$\mathbf{C} \leftarrow //\mathbf{A}, \boldsymbol{u}, \mathbf{B}//$	$\overline{\boldsymbol{u}}//\mathbf{C} = \overline{\boldsymbol{u}}//\mathbf{A}$; $\boldsymbol{u}//\mathbf{C} = \boldsymbol{u}//\mathbf{B}$.	
Path catenation	$\mathbf{C} \leftarrow \mathbf{A} \oplus \mathbf{B}$	$\mathbf{C}$ is obtained by connecting roots of $\mathbf{B}$ to leaves of $\mathbf{A}$, allotting successive groups of at most $\lceil \mu_1(\mathbf{B}) \div \lambda(\mathbf{A}) \rceil$ roots of $\mathbf{B}$ to each successive leaf of $\mathbf{A}$.	

S.12 TREES (continued)

Full tree	$\mathbf{W} \leftarrow \mathbf{E}$	Each node of **W** is unity and the structure of **W** is determined by compatibility.	§1.23
	$\mathbf{W} \leftarrow \mathbf{E}(k)$	Each node of **W** is unity; **W** is homogeneous (i.e., all nodes on any level have a common degree) and $\nu(\mathbf{W}) = k$.	
Zero tree	$\mathbf{W} \leftarrow \overline{\mathbf{E}}$ $\mathbf{W} \leftarrow 0$	Each node of **W** is zero and the structure of **W** is determined by compatibility.	
	$\mathbf{W} \leftarrow \overline{\mathbf{E}}(k)$	Each node of **W** is zero; **W** is homogeneous and $\nu(\mathbf{W}) = k$.	
Path tree	$\mathbf{W} \leftarrow {}^{u}\mathbf{E}$	$\overline{u}/\mathbf{W} = 0$; $u/\mathbf{W} = \mathbf{E}$; structure of **W** determined by compatibility.	
	$\mathbf{W} \leftarrow {}^{u}\mathbf{E}(k)$	$\overline{u}/\mathbf{W} = 0$; $u/\mathbf{W} = \mathbf{E}$; **W** is homogeneous and $\nu(\mathbf{W}) = k$.	
Level tree	$\mathbf{W} \leftarrow {}_{u}\mathbf{E}$	$\overline{u}//\mathbf{W} = 0$, $u//\mathbf{W} = \mathbf{E}$; structure of **W** determined by compatibility.	
	$\mathbf{W} \leftarrow {}_{u}\mathbf{E}(k)$	$\overline{u}//\mathbf{W} = 0$; $u//\mathbf{W} = \mathbf{E}$; **W** is homogeneous and $\nu(\mathbf{W}) = k$.	
Maximization Minimization	$\mathbf{W} \leftarrow \mathbf{U} \lceil \mathbf{A}$ $\mathbf{W} \leftarrow \mathbf{U} \lfloor \mathbf{A}$	$\mathbf{W} = \mathbf{U} \wedge (\mathbf{A} = m\mathbf{E})$, where m is the maximum (minimum) over all nodes of $\mathbf{U}/\mathbf{A}$.	
Maximum path prefix	$\mathbf{W} \leftarrow \alpha/\mathbf{U}$	**W** is obtained from **U** by zeroing all nodes of every subtree rooted in a zero node.	
Maximum path suffix	$\mathbf{W} \leftarrow \omega/\mathbf{U}$	**W** is obtained from **U** by zeroing every node which contains a zero node in its subtree.	
Forward path set selector	$\mathbf{W} \leftarrow \sigma/\mathbf{A}$	$(\mathbf{W}^{i})_{\nu(i)} = 1$ if $(\mathbf{A}^{i})_{\nu(i)}$ differs from all preceding nodes of path $\mathbf{A}^{i}$.	
Backward path set selector	$\mathbf{W} \leftarrow \tau/\mathbf{A}$	$(\mathbf{W}^{i})_{\nu(i)} = 1$ if $(\mathbf{A}^{i})_{\nu(i)}$ differs from all other nodes of its subtree.	
Maximum level prefix	$\mathbf{W} \leftarrow \alpha//\mathbf{U}$	$\epsilon^{j}/\mathbf{W} = \alpha/\epsilon^{j}/\mathbf{U}$	
Maximum level suffix	$\mathbf{W} \leftarrow \omega//\mathbf{U}$	$\epsilon^{j}/\mathbf{W} = \omega/\epsilon^{j}/\mathbf{U}$	
Forward level set selector	$\mathbf{W} \leftarrow \sigma//\mathbf{A}$	$\epsilon^{j}/\mathbf{W} = \sigma/\epsilon^{j}/\mathbf{A}$	
Backward level set selector	$\mathbf{W} \leftarrow \tau//\mathbf{A}$	$\epsilon^{j}/\mathbf{W} = \tau/\epsilon^{j}/\mathbf{A}$	

Index